Assets, Crimes, and the State

Organised crime, corruption, and terrorism are considered to pose significant and unrelenting threats to the integrity, security, and stability of contemporary societies. Alongside traditional criminal enforcement responses, strategies focused on following the money trail of such crimes have become increasingly prevalent. These strategies include anti-money laundering measures to prevent 'dirty money' from infiltrating the legitimate economy, proceeds of crime powers to target the accumulated assets derived from crime, and counter-terrorist financing measures to prevent 'clean' money from being used for terrorist purposes.

This collection brings together 17 emerging researchers in the fields of anti-money laundering, proceeds of crime, counter-terrorist financing and corruption to offer critical analyses of contemporary anti-assets strategies and state responses to a range of financial crimes. The chapters focus on innovative anti-financial crime measures and assemblages of governance that have become a feature of late modernity and on the ways in which individual nation states have responded to anti-money laundering and counter-terrorist financing requirements in light of their specific social, political, and economic contexts. This collection draws on perspectives from law, criminology, sociology, politics, and other disciplines. It adopts a much-needed international approach, focusing not only on expected jurisdictions, such as the United States and United Kingdom, but also on analysis from countries such as Qatar, Kuwait, Iran, and Nigeria. The authors stand out for their fresh and original research, which places them at the cutting edge of the subject.

This book provides a comprehensive, insightful, and original study of an important and developing field for academics, students, practitioners, and policymakers in multiple jurisdictions.

Katie Benson is Lecturer in criminology at Lancaster University where she teaches and researches in the areas of money laundering and organised, white-collar, and financial crimes.

Colin King is Reader in Law at the Institute of Advanced Legal Studies, University of London.

Clive Walker is Professor Emeritus of Criminal Justice Studies at the School of Law, University of Leeds, where he has served as the Director of the Centre for Criminal Justice Studies and as Head of School.

Transcional Criminal Justice

Series Editor: Saskia Hufnagel
Queen Mary University of London, UK

The concept of 'transnational criminal justice' has frequently been interpreted in the academic literature as 'international criminal justice' or 'global criminal justice'. Many publications that use the term 'transnational' therefore discuss international criminal justice and international legal frameworks. Another form of studies that has developed under the umbrella of transnationality in the field of criminal law is comparative. There has hence been a move from the terminology of 'international', 'global' and 'comparative' criminal justice towards 'transnational' criminal justice.

This series considers these developments, but focuses primarily on publications that adhere to a more literal interpretation of the term 'transnational'. The aim of the series is to provide a forum for discussion of bilateral and multilateral relationships between nations in the field of criminal justice. International law influences these relationships, but is not the focus here. Equally, to explain transnational relationships, comparative analyses are required. While incorporating comparative studies in this series, their aim is the explanation of challenges to criminal justice cooperation in bilateral or multilateral relationships.

Titles in this series

Criminal Networks and Law Enforcement
Global Perspectives On Illegal Enterprise
Saskia Hufnagel and Anton Moiseienko

Terrorism, Criminal Law and Politics
The Decline of the Political Offence Exception to Extradition
Julia Jansson

Assets, Crimes, and the State
Innovations in 21st Century Legal Responses
Edited by Katie Benson, Colin King and Clive Walker

For more information about this series, please visit: www.routledge.com/Transnational-Criminal-Justice/book-series/TRANSCJ

Assets, Crimes, and the State

Innovations in 21st Century Legal Responses

Edited by Katie Benson, Colin King, and Clive Walker

Routledge
Taylor & Francis Group
LONDON AND NEW YORK

First published 2020 by Routledge

2 Park Square, Milton Park, Abingdon, Oxon OX14 4RN
605 Third Avenue, New York, NY 10017

Routledge is an imprint of the Taylor & Francis Group, an informa business

First issued in paperback 2021

British Library Cataloguing-in-Publication Data
A catalogue record for this book is available from the British Library

Library of Congress Cataloging-in-Publication Data
Names: Benson, Katie, editor. | King, Colin, editor. | Walker, Clive, editor.
Title: Assets, crimes, and the state : innovations in 21st century legal responses / [edited by] Katie Benson, Colin King, Clive Walker.
Description: New York : Routledge, 2020. | Series: Transnational criminal justice | Includes bibliographical references and index.
Identifiers: LCCN 2019044887 (print) | LCCN 2019044888 (ebook) | ISBN 9780367025922 (hardback) | ISBN 9780429398834 (ebook)
Subjects: LCSH: Money laundering—Law and legislation. | Organized crime—Law and legislation. | Corruption—Law and legislation. | Terrorism—Finance—Law and legislation. | Money laundering—Prevention. | Terrorism—Finance—Prevention. | Money laundering—Prevention—International cooperation.
Classification: LCC K1089 .A98 2020 (print) | LCC K1089 (ebook) | DDC 364.16/8–dc23
LC record available at https://lccn.loc.gov/2019044887
LC ebook record available at https://lccn.loc.gov/2019044888

ISBN: 978-0-367-02592-2 (hbk)
ISBN: 978-1-03-217434-1 (pbk)
DOI: 10.4324/9780429398834

Typeset in Galliard
by Apex CoVantage, LLC

Contents

Acknowledgements

The first stage of our endeavours in the production of this book involved a grant of funding from the Arts and Humanities Research Council (ref: AH/P00640X/1) which is gratefully acknowledged.

In the second stage, a two-day conference was held at the Queen Mary University of London (QMUL) Criminal Justice Centre in May 2018. Thanks to the directors of that centre for their support and hosting.

The keynote address at the conference was delivered by Professor Susan Rose-Ackerman of Yale University.

Janine Meier, a PhD candidate in law at QMUL, provided excellent editorial and reference checking support.

Contributors

Ahmed Almutawa is a Bahraini employed as a police officer within the Royal Academy of Police Department of Bahrain's Ministry of Interior. He holds a bachelor's degree in law and police science and a master's degree in criminology and police science. He is currently a PhD candidate at the University of Leeds where he is completing a thesis entitled 'The Legitimacy of Counter-Terrorism Financing Measures in Bahrain' with reference to the United Kingdom.

Noura T. A. Al-Oumi is Assistant Professor in the Criminal Law Department, Faculty of Law at Kuwait University. She received her PhD in 2013 from the University of Leeds. She has an LLM from the University of Kent and an LLB from Kuwait University.

Khaled S. Al-Rashidi is Lecturer at the School of Law, Kuwait University. Khaled has an LLB degree from Kuwait University and holds an LLM degree in criminal law and criminal justice from the University of Leeds. Currently, he is a PhD candidate at the School of Law, University of Leeds, where he is preparing his thesis on the phenomenon of corruption in Kuwait. Khaled is interested in criminological and criminal law issues in general and counter-corruption laws more specifically. Before 2015, Khaled worked as a state lawyer for four years, defending the state in the administrative courts.

Katie Benson is Lecturer in Criminology at Lancaster University where she teaches and researches in the areas of money laundering and organised, white-collar, and financial crimes. Her primary research focus is the involvement of legal professionals in the facilitation of money laundering and the criminal justice and regulatory responses to this. Previously, Katie was Knowledge Manager at the Scottish Crime and Drug Enforcement Agency and worked with, or provided advisory/consultancy services to, various government bodies, law enforcement organisations, research institutions and investigations.

Sam Bourton is Lecturer in Law at the University of the West of England, Bristol. She teaches on the LLB and LLM programmes, with modules including Foundations for Law, the Law of Financial Crime and Regulation, and International Financial Crime. Sam is also a PhD candidate whose thesis aims to provide a comparative analysis of tax evasion law and enforcement in the United Kingdom and United States of America. Her research primarily focuses on the law of financial crime, particularly the law pertaining to tax evasion and money laundering.

Craig Fletcher is Associate Lecturer at Manchester Metropolitan University and currently writing up his PhD, which is looking into the impact of post-conviction confiscation measures on the defendant and their families. Prior to entering academia, Craig was employed as a probation service officer in Manchester and for many years delivered youth crime intervention programmes in the North West of England. His teaching and research interests centre on the philosophies and theories of punishment, the Proceeds of Crime Act 2002, and the politics of imprisonment.

Doron Goldbarsht is Lecturer in the School of Law at Macquarie University in Sydney, Australia, and a member of the Optus Macquarie University Cyber Security Hub. Goldbarsht hold a bachelor's degree and a master's degree in law, specialising in commercial law, from the Hebrew University of Jerusalem, and a PhD from the University of New South Wales. His master's thesis investigates how democracies combat the financing of terrorism via charitable organisations, whilst his doctoral thesis discusses the development and compliance of non-binding norms in the field of counter-terrorist financing. His current research focuses on managing the relationship between financial inclusion and anti-money laundering and counter-terrorist financing objectives and state compliance with soft law.

Samuel Andrew Hardy is Post-Doctoral Research Fellow in Cultural Heritage and Conflicts at the Norwegian Institute in Rome for the Heritage Experience Initiative of the University of Oslo. He is exploring the functioning of trafficking of cultural goods during conflicts in the Mediterranean and Middle East and its interaction with destruction of cultural property, propaganda about cultural heritage, and other problems, such as displacement and forced migration. His research and analysis are available at https://conflictantiquities.wordpress.com/.

Colin King is Reader in Law at the Institute of Advanced Legal Studies, University of London. He was an Academic Fellow at the Honourable Society of the Inner Temple from 2014 to 2017. In March 2016, Colin gave oral evidence at the Home Affairs Select Committee Inquiry into the Proceeds of Crime Act. Recent publications include *Negotiated Justice and Corporate Crime: The Legitimacy of Civil Recovery and Deferred Prosecution Agreements* (King and Lord, Palgrave, 2018), *The Palgrave Handbook of Criminal and Terrorism Financing Law* (King, Walker and Gurulé, eds, Palgrave, 2018), and *Counter-Terrorism, Constitutionalism, and Miscarriages of Justice: A Festschrift for Professor Clive Walker* (Lennon, King and McCartney, eds, Hart, 2019).

Zeynab Malakoutikhah is a Postgraduate Researcher at the School of Law, University of Leeds, and is also affiliated with the Centre for Criminal Justice

Studies. Her doctoral thesis examines 'the counter-terrorism financing regime in domestic and international law: a case study of Iran with special references to the United Kingdom.' She obtained an LLM in International Human Rights Law at the University of Reading. Her master's thesis investigated 'the jurisdiction of the International Criminal Court (ICC) over the Islamic State of Iraq and al-Sham (ISIS).'

Nicholas Mills is ESRC funded Doctoral Researcher in law studying at the University of Reading. With a specific interest in the fields of corporate and white-collar crime, his PhD thesis seeks to explore the efficacy of the UK approach towards corporate criminal activity and its regulation. The research intends to specifically examine the self-regulatory nature of anti-bribery and corruption provisions contained within the Bribery Act 2010 and whether this approach can be developed to increase ethical business practice.

Steven Montagu-Cairns is a specialist in regulation and financial crime within multinational financial groups. He holds the post of Lecturer in finance and corporate law at the University of Leeds. Having undertaken his PhD research at the University of Liverpool, Montagu-Cairns now publishes widely in the areas of financial regulation, financial crime, and corporate governance. His research interests focus on the elements of control and responsibility within international financial institutions, more specifically, the roles and liabilities of formal regulators, the board of directors, and the corporation. He is the co-convenor of the banking and finance stream of the Socio-Legal Studies Association and a member of the Society of Legal Scholars.

Foivi Mouzakiti is a PhD candidate at the School of Law of Queen Mary, University of London and a Lecturer in Law at Royal Holloway (University of London). Her thesis is entitled 'Financial Surveillance in the Fight against Money Laundering and Terrorist Financing in the EU: The Case of the Financial Intelligence Units.' Her research interests include financial crime, privacy, and data protection law.

Olufemi Olaoye graduated with a degree in law from the University of Ibadan. He is currently conducting LLM research on money laundering and terrorist financing at the University of Manitoba, Canada. He was previously Counsel at the Dispute Resolution Practice of Olaniwun Ajayi LP (Nigeria).

Gauri Sinha holds a PhD specialising in anti-money laundering (AML) compliance and currently works as Senior Lecturer in Law at Kingston University, London. Her research interests include financial crime, financial regulation, and corporate accountability. Gauri also consults on AML compliance, a recent project involved advising the Government of Jamaica on financial sanctions and asset freezing laws. Her recommendations are currently being drafted as potential amendments to the law. Prior to joining Kingston, Gauri worked at PricewaterhouseCoopers as a senior associate in the Forensic Department where she consulted several global banks and commercial organisations on

AML issues. In addition, she consulted with the World Bank as a financial crime specialist and worked with KPMG as an AML Analyst.

Nathanael Tilahun is Assistant Professor of public international law at Erasmus University Rotterdam and a member of the Association of Certified Anti-Money Laundering Specialists. He has previously held visiting faculty and researcher positions at the University of Cambridge, Queen Mary University of London, Hofstra University New York, and University of California, Berkeley.

Clive Walker is Professor Emeritus of Criminal Justice Studies at the School of Law, University of Leeds, where he has served as Director of the Centre for Criminal Justice Studies and Head of School. He was awarded a PhD in 1982 and an LLD in 2015 by the University of Manchester. He became Queen's Counsel (Hon) in 2016. He has written extensively on constitutional, terrorism, and Internet issues. His books on terrorism and emergencies are recognised and cited widely and include *The Civil Contingencies Act 2004: Risk, Resilience and the Law in the United Kingdom* (Oxford University Press, 2006), *Terrorism and the Law* (Oxford University Press, 2011), *The Anti-Terrorism Legislation* (3rd ed., Oxford University Press, 2014), and the *Routledge Handbook of Law and Terrorism* (Routledge, 2015). He was appointed in 2010 by the Home Office as Senior Adviser to the independent reviewer of terrorism legislation. His research on the financing of terrorism is reflected in his works with Colin King and Jimmy Gurulé: *Dirty Assets: Emerging Issues in the Regulation of Criminal and Terrorist Assets* (Ashgate, Farnham, 2014) and *The Palgrave Handbook of Criminal and Terrorism Financing Law* (Palgrave MacMillan, London, 2018).

Sirajo Yakubu is a Senior Lecturer in law at the Faculty of Law, Nile University of Nigeria, Abuja, and is the Principal Partner at Resolute Consultants, Nigeria, a firm that provides training on AML compliance. He is also a Writer/ Contributor at KYC360, the London-based online AML knowledge portal. He obtained his PhD in law from the University of London with the thesis titled 'A Critical Appraisal of the Law and Practice Relating to Money Laundering in USA and UK.' He has been organising workshops and serving as a panellist at the Cambridge International Symposium on Economic Crime since 2016. He was formerly Senior Personal Assistant to the vice-president/ president of the Federal Republic of Nigeria during the vice-presidency and presidency of President Goodluck E. Jonathan.

Ilaria Zavoli is Lecturer in law at the School of Law of the University of Leeds and a qualified lawyer in Italy. Ilaria's research interests lie in the areas of international criminal law, international law, and criminal law. In particular, her recent focus has been on money laundering issues in the real estate market. Ilaria holds a law degree *cum laude* and a postgraduate specialisation diploma in law *cum laude* from the University of Bologna (Italy). She also holds an advanced master's in public international law with a specialisation in international criminal law from Leiden University (the Netherlands). Ilaria completed a PhD in international criminal law at the University of Leeds (United Kingdom), and her research project focused on *in absentia* proceedings in international criminal justice. Between 2017 and 2018, Ilaria worked as Research Fellow for the project 'Corruption, Dirty Capital and the London Property Market' at the University of Sussex.

1 Dirty money and the new responses of the 21st century

Katie Benson, Colin King, and Clive Walker

In 1989, the Financial Action Task Force (FATF) was established by the G7, primarily in response to assets arising from illegal drug production and trafficking. According to the G7 Economic Declaration in July 1989,

> Its mandate is to assess the results of cooperation already undertaken in order to prevent the utilization of the banking system and financial institutions for the purpose of money laundering, and to consider additional preventive efforts in this field, including the adaptation of the legal and regulatory systems so as to enhance multilateral judicial assistance.[1]

Their progeny subsequently produced what would become the FATF 40 Recommendations, which were endorsed by the G7 in 1990.[2] As is evident from its mandate, there was no emphasis on terrorist financing at that time. It took until almost a decade later for international law making to emerge on terrorism financing, not from the aloof FATF but from the United Nations (UN) as delivered in two tranches. First came the UN Security Council Resolution (UNSCR) 1267, dealing with 'the situation in Afghanistan', which necessitated the imposition of sanctions against named individuals in the Taliban 'faction',[3] an idea quickly extended to their allies in Al-Qaida in 1999.[4] Second, the International Convention for the Suppression of the Financing of Terrorism was agreed in 1999.[5] Implementation of both aspects was low key before 9/11, with just four ratifications of the convention[6] and the listing of around a quarter of the totals which would be reached after

1 G7, Economic Declaration, Paris Summit (July 16, 1989) para. 53 (<http://www.g8.utoronto.ca/summit/1989paris/communique/index.html>).
2 The history is recounted in Sutton, G.W., 'The new FATF standards' (2012–2013) 4 *George Mason Journal of International and Comparative Law* 68; Nance, M.T., 'The regime that FATF built: An introduction to the Financial Action Task Force' (2018) 69 *Crime, Law and Social Change* 109.
3 UNSCR 1267 of 15 October 1999, art.4(b).
4 UNSCR 1333 of 19 December 2000, art.8.
5 UNGA Resolution 54/109 of 9 December 1999.
6 See Bantekas, I., 'The international law of terrorist financing' (2003) 97 *American Journal of International Law* 315.

9/11.[7] Following 9/11, a wave of international edicts, including Special Recommendations from the FATF in October 2001, and national legislation rolled out everywhere, firmly placing the focus on terrorist finances front and centre. Whilst there are notable differences between the anti-money laundering (AML) and counter-terrorist financing (CTF) approaches, so too are there significant overlaps and convergence.[8] Indeed, the current global standards promulgated by the FATF have by now largely fused AML and CTF so that national legislation likewise starts with the same premises and contains broadly the same features across the board. Convergence is ongoing, with the ideas of pre-emption so hallowed in counter-terrorism, now increasingly applied to criminal assets through devices such as unexplained wealth orders (UWOs) and civil recovery.[9]

Initially established with a one-year mandate,[10] the FATF has subsequently developed into the primary driver behind the global AML/CTF regime both in terms of normative production and administrative enforcement. It generally outperforms potential rivals, such as the Egmont Group, the Organisation for Economic Co-operation and Development (OECD), the UN Office on Drugs and Crime (UNODC), and the World Bank, though their collaborative efforts are also duly noted in this book. Its stated objectives are now

> to set standards and promote effective implementation of legal, regulatory and operational measures for combating money laundering, terrorist financing and other related threats to the integrity of the international financial system. The FATF is therefore a 'policy-making body' which works to generate the necessary political will to bring about national legislative and regulatory reforms in these areas.[11]

The emphasis on following the money with a view to both suppression and investigation is now firmly established as part of the state response to organised crime, corruption, and terrorism. As Nance notes, 'Regardless of whether FATF's net impact is positive or negative, it is indisputable that the fight against illicit money has bled into nearly every corner of government activity'.[12] Even so, fundamental aspects of the regime remain controversial. These aspects represent in many ways an agenda for action and debate in the 21st century for AML and CTF and,

7 For initial listings under UNSCR, see SC/6844 of 13 April 2000 (<http://www.un.org/press/en/2000/20000413.sc6844.doc.html>); SC/6988 of 25 January 2001 (<http://www.un.org/press/en/2001/afg124.doc.htm>).

8 King, C. and Walker, C., 'Counter terrorism financing: A redundant fragmentation?' (2015) 6(3) *New Journal of European Criminal Law* 372.

9 See the UK Criminal Finances Act 2017.

10 In April 2019, it was announced that the FATF was given a permanent mandate: FATF, *Mandate* (FATF, 2019).

11 FATF, 'Who We Are' (<http://www.fatf-gafi.org/about/whoweare/>). For a critical assessment, see van Duyne, P. et al., *The Critical Handbook of Money Laundering: Policy, Analysis and Myths* (Palgrave, 2018) Ch. 5.

12 Nance, M.T., 'The regime that FATF built: An introduction to the Financial Action Task Force' (2018) 69 *Crime, Law & Social Change* 109, 110.

therefore, form key subjects for this book. In brief, they revolve around four controversies: purpose, legitimacy, ambit, and effectiveness.

As for purpose, the FATF in its early guise assumed the form of financial, accounting, policing, and legal technocrats. Organised crime and money laundering were important scourges, especially for countries such as Italy and the USA.[13] But the risk was by no means predominant, even as a crime problem, for most other countries. However, after a decade had passed, change was afoot.

For the CTF field, according to former vice-president Dick Cheney,

> in a sense, 9/11 changed everything for us. 9/11 forced us to think in new ways about threats to the United States, about our vulnerabilities, about who our enemies were, about what kind of military strategy we needed in order to defend ourselves.[14]

So, after 9/11, it became accepted wisdom that the hitherto hesitant steps taken in the application of sanctions and international convention were inadequate and that finance was to become a key battleground in CTF. The crucial change in outlook involved, of course, the acceptance that national security is now under threat. Consequently, a much wider range of conceivable options to deal with national security threats were placed on the table and were seen as priorities in a way that the threats from crime, even organised crime, had failed to engender.

A more gradual evolution has occurred with criminal financing, but the position has eventually been adopted, step-by-step, that the subversion of financial processes for criminal processes also triggers national security responses. In the United Kingdom, an early indicator of change was the decision in 1996 to task the Security Service with 'support of the activities of police forces and other law enforcement agencies in the prevention and detection of serious crimes'.[15] By 2019, one can be sure that the transformation is complete, so UK strategic statements now confirm that organised crime and money laundering awake strong national security responses[16] alongside any policing reactions.[17] In short, 'money held in the UK by those linked to organised crime and/or corruption also has the potential to represent a threat to the UK's national security'.[18]

13 These jurisdictions were early adopters of specialist legislation: See (Italy) Codice delle leggi antimafia e delle misure di prevenzione, L. 646/1982 within L. 575/1965 (now d.lgs.159/2011); (USA) Racketeer Influenced and Corrupt Organizations Act 1970, 18 USC s.1961.

14 Quoted in Dunmire, P.L., '"9/11 changed everything": An intertextual analysis of the Bush Doctrine' (2009) 20 *Discourse & Society* 195.

15 Security Service Act 1996, s.1.

16 HM Government, *National Security Strategy and Strategic Defence and Security Review 2015: Third Annual Report* (2019) paras. 1.16, 2.63–86.

17 The lead policing response is taken by the National Crime Agency: http://www.nationalcrimeagency.gov.uk/.

18 HM Government, *Economic Crime Plan 2019–22* (2019) para. 8.4. A more circumspect view is offered by the House of Commons Treasury Committee, *Economic Crime: Anti-Money Laundering Supervision and Sanctions Implementation* (2017–19 HC 2010).

It follows that AML and CTF serve two purposes. One is the integrity of the financial sectors and assuring money flows are sound, the protection of which serves the interests of the financial institutions and their customers. In this purpose, the state should act as a facilitator but should not add burdens or fundamentally compromise the ethos of the relationships of trust which are essential both to the financial objectives of customers and the financial profits of the institutions. Clearly, those ideals are no longer predominant, with added costs for all and even summary ejections by sanctions or de-banking now imposed. The second purpose is the upholding of national security, and here the intervention of intelligence agencies will be associated with state dominance and secretive processes. These purposes and methods can easily be antithetical to the stated private-dominated purposes. How these purposes are to coexist is one of the key new problems of the 21st century.

The second controversy relates to legitimacy. The role of the FATF has been emphasised up to this point, as if there is no question about this international instrument of choice. But by what authority has the FATF assumed this position of power? The answer lies in the power of its backers – the top table is filled by 37 member state jurisdictions plus two regional bodies (the European Commission and the Gulf Cooperation Council) which comprise predominantly western powers and their allies (though China and Russia cannot be disregarded).[19] This private club of the rich seems to care little for international dialogue or even international law values, as evidenced by the admission of Saudi Arabia as a full member[20] just two days after the eviscerating report of the special rapporteur on extrajudicial, summary, or arbitrary executions about the killing of Jamal Khashoggi placed responsibility on that regime.[21] In response, the position of the UN appears meek. Rather than raising objections about more legitimate modes of international discourse and law making being circumvented,[22] it has instead adopted the surprising stance of treating the FATF as if it were commissioned as a branch of the UN. Thus, by UNSCR 2462, the Security Council

> [stresses] the essential role of the Financial Action Task Force (FATF) in setting global standards for preventing and combatting money laundering, terrorist financing and proliferation financing and its Global Network of FATF-style regional bodies (FSRBs) and *taking note* with appreciation of

19 See further http://www.fatf-gafi.org/about/membersandobservers/.

20 FATF, Outcomes FATF Plenary, 16–21 June 2019 (<http://www.fatf-gafi.org/publications/fatfgeneral/documents/outcomes-plenary-june-2019.html#Four>, 21 June 2019).

21 Special rapporteur on extrajudicial, summary, or arbitrary executions, *Investigation into the Unlawful Death of Mr. Jamal Khashoggi* (A/HRC/41/CRP.1, 19 June 2019).

22 See Ní Aoláin, F., 'The massive perils of the latest U.N. resolution on terrorism' *Just Security* (<http://www.justsecurity.org/64840/the-massive-perils-of-the-latest-u-n-resolution-on-terrorism>, 8 July 2019); Morse, J.C., 'Blacklists, market enforcement, and the global regime to combat terrorist financing' (2019) 73 *International Organization* 511.

> the 'FATF Consolidated Strategy on Combating Terrorist Financing' and its operational plan [and] . . .
>
> *strongly urges* all States to implement the comprehensive international standards embodied in the revised Forty FATF Recommendations on Combating Money Laundering, and the Financing of Terrorism and Proliferation and its interpretive notes.[23]

In summary, the chosen instruments of AML and CTF entail problems for legitimacy because they lack transparency, democracy, integrity, and accountability. The problem has been described in the context of the FATF, but other mechanisms can also be challenged on these grounds.

The third controversy concerns ambit; as befits the late modern environment, a multitude of actors and devices are involved which straddle the public and private sectors.[24] One might suppose that the effect is to dilute national sovereignty of powerful countries, but, more likely, it gives them more options and choices. A further important feature is the prime involvement of private actors, especially from financial institutions. However, the private sector is being increasingly expanded, including by the European Union's (EU) Money Laundering Directives, the fifth edition of which extends the regime to letting agents and art dealers.[25] Notwithstanding its expansion, 'coherence and uniformity are still lacking gravely'.[26] Moreover, there remains a lack of consensus as to the role of private actors in AML,[27] with corresponding objections from the likes of charities that have been deputed to stand in the front line of CTF. The ensuing shift from a rules-based approach to one based on risk has proved problematic,[28] with many private actors still adhering to a formalistic rules-based approach as a form of self-protection.[29]

23 Recital 11 and art.4. The FATF merits eight other mentions, compared to four in total for the UNODC.

24 See de Goede, M., 'Counter-terrorism financing assemblages after 9/11' in King, C., Walker, C., and Gurulé, J. (eds.), *The Palgrave Handbook of Criminal and Terrorism Financing Law* (Palgrave MacMillan, 2018).

25 Directive (EU) 2018/843 of the European Parliament and of the Council of 30 May 2018 amending Directive (EU) 2015/849 on the prevention of the use of the financial system for the purposes of money laundering or terrorist financing and amending Directives 2009/138/EC and 2013/36/EU.

26 Verhage, A., 'Global governance = global compliance? The uneven playing field in anti-money laundering' in van Erp, J., Huisman, W., and Vande Walle, G. (eds.), *The Routledge Handbook of White-Collar and Corporate Crime in Europe* (Routledge, 2015) 471.

27 For an economic discussion, see Sandulescu, M., 'Reconciling the anti-money laundering compliance duties and the commercial objectives of the bank' in van Duyne, P. et al. (eds.), *Corruption, Greed and Crime Money: Sleaze and Shady Economy in Europe and Beyond* (Wolf Legal Publishers, 2014).

28 Pellegrina, L.D. and Masciandaro, D., 'The risk-based approach in the new European anti-money laundering legislation: a law and economics view' (2009) 5(2) *Review of Law & Economics* 931.

29 Bello, A.U., *Improving Anti-Money Laundering Compliance: Self-Protecting Theory and Money Laundering Reporting Officers* (Palgrave, 2016).

This expanded responsibilisation of private actors within AML/CTF[30] comes at a cost. The British Bankers Association has claimed, for example, that its members spend at least £5 billion on compliance every year.[31] In its consultation on the transposition of the Fifth Money Laundering Directive, the UK government emphasised the need for a proportionate balance between managing the burden on business and actively discouraging money laundering and terrorist financing.[32] Inevitably though, AML/CTF obligations will impact upon businesses. The question is, at what point do such obligations become disproportionate? For instance, one counterproductive (and unintended) consequence of the global AML/CTF regime has been de-risking (and de-banking) of customers by financial institutions, which have particularly impacted customers in low- and lower-middle income countries.[33]

Impact, whether intended or unintended, takes us to the fourth controversy – namely, effectiveness, costs, and benefits. In truth, it is impossible to gauge with any accuracy the global extent of money laundering (ML), and even the FATF is hesitant to make claims:

> Estimates should be treated with caution. They are intended to give an estimate of the magnitude of money laundering. Due to the illegal nature of the transactions, precise statistics are not available and it is therefore impossible to produce a definitive estimate of the amount of money that is globally laundered every year. The FATF therefore does not publish any figures in this regard.[34]

It is almost as difficult to produce accurate estimates as to the costs of doing AML. Even if the (monetary) costs are confined to those directly associated with ongoing policymaking, sanctions, financial intelligence units (FIUs), AML supervision, law and judicial enforcement, and the duties of the private sector, it is impossible to provide accurate or precise figures.[35] Therefore, a definitive cost/benefit analysis is beyond reach. Thus around three decades after the establishment of the FATF and the EU's First Money Laundering Directive,[36] it is impossible

30 See, Bergstrom, M., Svedberg Helgesson, K., and Morth, U., 'A new role for for-profit actors? The case of anti-money laundering and risk management' (2011) 49(5) *Journal of Common Market Studies* 1043.

31 *Response to Cutting Red Tape Review: The Effectiveness of the UK's AML Regime* (2015).

32 HM Treasury, *Transposition of the Fifth Money Laundering Directive: Consultation* (2019) 4.

33 Ramachandran, V., Collin, M., and Juden, M., 'De-risking: An unintended negative consequence of AML/CFT regulation' in King, C., Walker, C., and Gurulé, J. (eds.), *The Palgrave Handbook of Criminal and Terrorism Financing Law* (Palgrave, 2018).

34 FATF, 'How Much Money Is Laundered Per Year?' (<http://www.fatf-gafi.org/faq/moneylaundering/>).

35 Such costs are considered in Ferwerda, J., 'The effectiveness of anti-money laundering policy: A cost-benefit perspective' in King, C., Walker, C., and Gurulé, J. (eds.), *The Palgrave Handbook of Criminal and Terrorism Financing Law* (Palgrave, 2018).

36 Council Directive 91/308/EEC of 10 June 1991 on prevention of the use of the financial system for the purpose of money laundering.

to say whether it works or not. As Vettori points out, 'Although the international community began to focus its attention on money laundering a rather long time ago, there is still very little scientific knowledge about the effectiveness and efficiency of the countermeasures adopted to combat the phenomenon.'[37]

Likewise, in the CTF field, a recent study which was commissioned by the Egmont Group illustrates the obstacles which face any possibility of effectiveness.[38] In the highly fluid formations of late modernity, terrorism can consist of single actors (though rarely are they truly 'loners')[39] or very small groups. Their visibility is consequently diminished compared to the more hierarchical organisations that preceded them – the likes of ETA, Hizballah, the IRA, and the LTTE. The ephemeral and small-scale formation inevitably results in curtailed abilities and, therefore, much cheaper running costs. Thus, the research study found that small amounts of cash were involved in CTF and that 40% involved cash transactions. The prospect thereby arises that all the scrutiny and intelligence in the world from the formal financial sector (or even others scooped into the enterprise, including casinos, lawyers, and charities) will not detect this level or format of terrorism financing unless the terrorism financiers are foolish enough to use highly monitored routes to reach highly suspect recipients.[40] Nevertheless, the national and international authorities remain insistent on expending every effort.[41]

Alongside direct monetary costs of AML and CTF, an account must be taken of indirect non-monetary costs.[42] As (more and more) private actors are required to gather, weigh, and report yet more information,[43] it is important to recognise the importance of rights, such as privacy. This is particularly important as FIUs are bestowed with ever-increasing powers to gather and share information.[44]

37 Vettori, B., 'Evaluating anti-money laundering policies: Where are we?' in Unger, B., and van der Linde, D. (eds.), *Research Handbook on Money Laundering* (Edward Elgar, 2013) 474.

38 *Information Exchange Working Group, Counter Terrorist Financing Project: Lone actors and Small Cells* (Egmont Group, 2019).

39 See Hamm, M. and Spaaj, R., *Lone Wolf Terrorism in America* (NCJRS, 2015); Johnson, N.F. et al., 'New online ecology of adversarial aggregates: ISIS and beyond' (2016) 352 *Science* 1459; Barnea, A., 'Challenging the "lone wolf" phenomenon in an era of information overload' (2018) 31 *International Journal of Intelligence and Counter Intelligence* 217; Schuurman, B. et al., 'End of the Lone Wolf: The typology that should not have been' (2018) 42 *Studies in Conflict & Terrorism* 771.

40 Thus it was possible to detect the transfer of a sum as small as £233 where the good offices of Western Union in Syria were involved: *R v Sally Lane and John Letts* [2018] UKSC 36; http://www.cps.gov.uk/cps/news/sally-lane-and-john-letts-sentenced-sending-money-daesh-supporting-son.

41 See the resistance to increasing the thresholds for SARs: Law Commission, *Anti Money Laundering: The SARs regime* (Law Com 384, 2017–19 HC 2098).

42 Ferwerda, J., 'The effectiveness of anti-money laundering policy: A cost-benefit perspective' in King, C., Walker, C., and Gurulé, J. (eds.), *The Palgrave Handbook of Criminal and Terrorism Financing Law* (Palgrave, 2018).

43 Amicelle, A., 'Towards a "new" political anatomy of financial surveillance' (2011) 42(2) *Security Dialogue* 161.

44 See Mühl, B., 'Access by law enforcement agencies to financial data' in Unger, B. and van der Linde, D. (eds.), *Research Handbook on Money Laundering* (Edward Elgar, 2013).

How can we strike a balance between privacy, on the one hand, and the need for state authorities to have access to information in tackling money laundering (ML)/terrorist financing (TF), on the other?

Despite these worries, one fears that the temptation for one future round of money laundering recommendations as to ambit will be to extend AML/CTF duties to general retail outlets. The logical conclusion seems to be down the path towards a universal legal duty to inform the authorities of mere suspicions,[45] with not only financial transactions but also workplace exchanges[46] and even family intimacies[47] all becoming the sites for enforced mutual surveillance. The manifold problems arising from this expansion include whether the authorities can cope with the potentially vast flow of notices [the experience of Suspicious Activity Reports (SARs) does not augur well] and whether the notification will be based on more than misunderstandings, misinterpretations, or, worse still, prejudice or spite.

Having traversed the major 21st-century controversies in AML/CTF – namely, purpose, legitimacy, ambit, and effectiveness, the approach of this book should now be explored. A number of guiding objectives should be emphasised. The overall theme for the book is a critical approach to contemporary strategies/state responses, especially those that could be said to be innovative in design or application, to different crimes of finance or controls over assets based on, or backed by, crimes. We, therefore, insisted on a focus on 'new state responses of the 21st century' and emphasised that our contributors must take a critical approach to their selected responses/strategies. The subject matter involves three aspects which are adopted as titles for the three parts of the book. First is 'Innovative Techniques and New Perspectives on Existing Techniques,' which covers the development of anti-financial crime measures, including beneficial owner registers and increased transparency, UWOs, and confiscation. The second aspect is 'Innovative Assemblages of Government,' which reflects upon increased cooperation and information sharing and the involvement of private actors within a late modern globalised financial network, including as gatekeepers or responsibilised professionals. The third aspect is 'Country-Specific Insights or Rebellion,' the latter arising when international standards are felt to be incompatible or unpalatable. In this way,

45 A duty of this kind already exists in regard to terrorism information under the Terrorism Act 2000, s.38B. See Walker, C., 'Conscripting the public in terrorism policing: towards safer communities or a police state?' [2010] *Criminal Law Review* 441.

46 This idea was suggested in the context of counter-terrorism prevention when Chief Superintendent Nik Adams argued that the number of prevention referrals coming from the private sector should increase: Counter Terrorism Policing, 'Businesses to help spot signs of radicalisation' 6 March 2019 (<http://www.counterterrorism.police.uk/businesses-to-help-spot-signs-of-radicalisation>).

47 In the London Bridge Inquest, the determination in relation to the victims of Khuram Butt pointedly noted, 'Multiple warning signs about the extremist views and conduct of one attacker were known to a number of his close family members in the months and years before the attack. In the main these were not reported to the authorities' (<https://londonbridgeinquests.independent.gov.uk/determinations-sheets>, 2019).

this collection deliberately adopts a much-needed international and comparative approach which, alongside chapters on expected jurisdictions, such as the United States and United Kingdom, places an emphasis on findings from the Middle East and elsewhere. In order to address these three themes, we have sought to commission emerging scholars who are not solely repeating or reworking their existing published narratives but are adding original and important research from law, criminology, sociology, and political science perspectives. A brief summary of the chapter contents will now be given.

Within Part I, 'Innovative Techniques and New Perspectives on Existing Techniques,' Sam Bourton explores the financial intelligence provisions of both the AML framework and the OECD's Common Reporting Standard and considers the effectiveness and proportionality of both. She is concerned primarily with tax offences, which are now explicitly provided for in both the FATF Standards and the EU Fourth Money Laundering Directive. Yet, as Bourton points out, 'conceptual difficulties arise in criminalising the laundering of criminal proceeds derived from tax evasion'. In the UK, Her Majesty's Revenue and Customs (HMRC) is now the largest recipient of SARs data,[48] though there have been questions as to whether HMRC is best suited to doing AML.[49] Bourton opines that the inclusion of tax evasion as a predicate offence, and consequently the application of the SARs regime to that offence, 'has been successful to a limited extent'; however, she then questions the impact that this has had on individual privacy and costs to financial institutions. It is important, then, that some effort 'is made to weigh the quantifiable costs and benefits of the inclusion of tax evasion as a predicate offence to laundering.' This leads Bourton to consider other potential mechanisms for obtaining financial intelligence in relation to tax, such as the Common Reporting Standard (CRS), which requires the collection of vast amounts of information. Furthermore, in many jurisdictions (including the UK), automatic exchange of information is now operationalised: of course, this is likely to have an impact on tax evasion, but 'at what expense is this success likely to be achieved?'

The focus on financial intelligence (and associated concerns for privacy, for example) continues in the next chapter by Foivi Sofia Mouzakiti. A key development over the past three decades has been the emphasis on financial intelligence. In their early years, FIUs were intended to receive, analyse, and disseminate financial information.[50] As with other aspects of the AML regime, FIUs themselves

48 HMIC, *An Inspection of Her Majesty's Revenue and Customs Performance in Addressing the Recovery of the Proceeds of Crime from Tax and Duty Evasion and Benefit Fraud: Revisit 2013* (HMIC, 2014) 31.

49 Indeed, in June 2018, the CEO of HMRC (Jon Thompson) floated the idea that HMRC might not be best suited to fulfilling the AML supervisory role that it currently undertakes: House of Commons Treasury Committee, *Economic Crime: Anti-Money Laundering Supervision and Sanctions Implementation* (2017–19 HC 2010) para. 104.

50 International Monetary Fund, *Financial Intelligence Units: An Overview* (World Bank, 2004). As the number of FIUs increased, it was deemed necessary to establish an informal association of FIUs in 2004 – the Egmont Group.

have evolved and expanded. No longer are they regarded merely as responsible for policing ML, they now have extensive powers that enable them to further gather, and share, information. Whilst there have been efforts to categorise FIUs using different labels (whether administrative, policing, judicial, or the ever popular 'hybrid'),[51] such categorisations can often hide operational difficulties.[52] Against this backdrop, Mouzakiti explores what she describes as 'a fragmented and difficult to navigate framework' under EU law. She traces plans for further expansion of FIU powers and interconnectedness and expresses concerns that that will negatively impact on privacy rights and data protection. It is axiomatic, then, that some restraint on FIU powers is desirable. These issues are particularly important, not least given ongoing efforts to expand the list of offences that fall within the remit of FIUs – most notably tax crimes.[53] With further change to be implemented in national law in accordance with the Fifth Money Laundering Directive, it is clear that we can expect yet more developments in this area. At the same time, though, as Mouzakiti emphasises, 'the fundamental human rights dimension . . . must not be overlooked.'

Another significant development during the lifespan of the FATF has been the shift from a rules-based approach towards the risk-based approach. According to the FATF's 2007 Guidance,

> By adopting a risk-based approach, competent authorities and financial institutions are able to ensure that measures to prevent or mitigate money laundering and terrorist financing are commensurate to the risks identified. This will allow resources to be allocated in the most efficient ways. The principle is that resources should be directed in accordance with priorities so that the greatest risks receive the highest attention.[54]

The risk-based approach is now central to the FATF regime, and it continues to develop. For example, as this collection was being finalised, the FATF concluded a public consultation on (further) guidance for legal professionals, accountants, and trust and company service providers, which was subsequently adopted at its June 2019 plenary.[55] The shift to the risk-based approach is intuitively appealing

51 International Monetary Fund, *Financial Intelligence Units: An Overview* (World Bank, 2004) 9–17.

52 Amicelle, A. and Chaudieu, K., 'In search of transnational financial intelligence: Questioning cooperation between Financial Intelligence Units' in King, C., Walker, C., and Gurulé, J. (eds.), *The Palgrave Handbook of Criminal and Terrorism Financing Law* (Palgrave, 2018).

53 Alldridge, P., *Criminal Justice and Taxation* (Oxford University Press, 2017).

54 FATF, *Guidance on the Risk-Based Approach to Combatting Money Laundering and Terrorist Financing: High Level Principles and Procedures* (2007) 2 (<https://www.fatf-gafi.org/publications/fatfrecommendations/documents/fatfguidanceontherisk-basedapproachtocombatingmoneylaunderingandterroristfinancing-highlevelprinciplesandprocedures.html>).

55 FATF, *Public Consultation on the Draft Risk-Based Approach Guidance for Legal Professionals, Accountants and Trust and Company Service Providers* (25 February 2019), (<http://www.fatf-gafi.org/publications/fatfgeneral/documents/public-consultation-guidance-tcsp.html>).

in that it ought to result in a move away from a 'tick-box' culture. Yet the reality is rather different, and many private actors harbour a 'desire for a totally automatic detection system that would obviate the need for individual decision making'.[56] In her chapter, Gauri Sinha offers a critique of the risk-based approach, suggesting that it 'brought similar problems as the rule based approach.' She contends that there are contradictions within the risk-based approach, not least the concept of 'risk' itself. Furthermore, there is ambiguity surrounding what is (or is not) 'suspicious' – a central aspect of the AML regime. Unsurprisingly, then, there are practical repercussions, and Sinha explores how 'ambiguities and complexities' impact upon the Financial Conduct Authority in its AML supervision role.

In the next chapter, Sirajo Yakubu argues that, notwithstanding the positive 2018 FATF evaluation of the United Kingdom,[57] it is important to keep the law under review and to improve efficiency. Therefore, he focuses on the recent adoption of UWO, a tool that enables enforcement agencies to acquire crucial information. Given their infancy, UWOs are still uncertain instruments of law and policy; however, they have already withstood some legal challenge.[58] Notwithstanding this judicial imprimatur, doubts persist – for example, in relation to financial privacy, self-incrimination, reputational damage, and the reversed burden of proof. Yakubu argues, however, that such concerns do not stand up to scrutiny. A further question might be asked about the effectiveness of this new tool. Of course, it is too early to judge their impact in the United Kingdom, though experiences elsewhere do lend weight to the idea that UWOs might not significantly tackle dirty assets. As Smith and Smith have stated in the Australian context,

> Australia's unexplained wealth regime has not been greatly successful to date, but has great potential if it can be better integrated and coordinated. Governments must be realistic about what these laws can achieve and should appreciate the importance of a well-coordinated and efficient use of state and Commonwealth agency resources.[59]

Whilst the foregoing chapters in Part I of the book have taken a somewhat systems-based and institutional perspective towards the new techniques of AML, a more human perspective is added in the chapter by Craig Fletcher. Here at last the impacts are plain to see when considering confiscation orders. Much has already been written about post-conviction confiscation orders, but this literature

56 Favarel-Garrigues, G., Godefroy, T. and Lascoumes, P., 'Sentinels in the banking industry: Private actors and the fight against money laundering in France' (2008) 48 *British Journal of Criminology* 1, 11.

57 FATF, *United Kingdom: Mutual Evaluation Report* (December 2018) (<https://www.fatf-gafi.org/publications/mutualevaluations/documents/mer-united-kingdom-2018.html>).

58 *National Crime Agency v Hajiyeva* [2018] EWHC 2534 (Admin).

59 Smith, M. and Smith, R., *Procedural Impediments to Effective Unexplained Wealth Legislation in Australia*. (Trends and Issues in Crime and Criminal Justice No. 153, Australian Institute of Criminology, 2016) 7.

has focused primarily on doctrinal legal analysis[60] or policy analysis of how confiscation orders have been applied in practice.[61] Here, Fletcher offers an entirely new insight into the operation of confiscation orders by drawing upon the personal accounts of those subject to confiscation orders. This chapter explores the potential adverse effects of such orders – the human consequences of the policy that crime should not pay.[62] His research demonstrates how confiscation orders impact upon family members as much as the subject of the order, as well as undermine rehabilitation efforts through their collateral effect on family and social life. Though offenders accept the risk of ill-gotten gains being confiscated, the way that such orders operate has resulted in resistance to the confiscation order for a variety of reasons. Against ongoing review of confiscation orders in the United Kingdom,[63] this focus on the 'lived reality' is particularly timely.

The first two chapters of Part II, 'Innovative Assemblages of Government,' consider the role of legal professionals as 'gatekeepers' within the AML/CTF regime and as potential 'professional enablers' of money laundering. The responsibilisation of non-state actors in the financial sector and, later, non-financial businesses and professions[64] has become a key feature of AML/CTF policy in the last three decades. The incorporation of legal professionals into this regime has been particularly controversial, with concerns raised about the implications for the principle of lawyer-client confidentiality, conflicts between duty to a client and the duty to report suspicious activity, and the potential risk to lawyers who come into contact with 'dirty' money.[65] Nathaneal Tilahun analyses the actions and discourse of legal professional associations and their members following their designation as AML/CTF gatekeepers. He argues that the official narrative offered by legal professional associations that 'depicts lawyers' resistance to gatekeeping as a fight for the preservation of liberal democratic values' masks the 'underlying

60 Alldridge, P., 'Proceeds of crime law since 2003: Two key areas' [2014] *Criminal Law Review* 171.

61 Bullock, K. and Lister, S., 'Post-conviction confiscation of assets in England and Wales: Rhetoric and reality' in King, C. and Walker, C. (eds.), *Dirty Assets: Emerging Issues in the Regulation of Criminal and Terrorist Assets* (Ashgate, 2014).

62 See Performance and Innovation Unit, *Recovering the Proceeds of Crime* (Cabinet Office, 2000).

63 Law Commission, 'Confiscation regime review to ensure crime doesn't pay' (7 November 2018) (<http://www.lawcom.gov.uk/confiscation-regime-review-to-ensure-crime-doesnt-pay/>).

64 Designated non-financial businesses and professions in the FATF Recommendations are casinos; real estate agents; dealers in precious metals or stones; lawyers, notaries and other independent legal professionals; accountants; trust and company service providers. FATF, *International Standards on Combating Money Laundering and the Financing of Terrorism and Proliferation* (2012–2019) Recommendation 22.

65 See Xanthaki, H., 'Lawyers' duties under the draft EU Money Laundering Directive: Is confidentiality a thing of the past?' (2001) 5 *Journal of Money Laundering Control* 103; Shepherd, K.L., 'Guardians at the gate: The Gatekeeper Initiative and the risk-based approach for transactional lawyers' (2009) 43 *Real Property, Trust & Estate Law Journal* 607; Mitsilegas, V. and Vavoula, N., 'The evolving EU anti-money laundering regime: Challenges for fundamental rights and rule of law' (2016) 23 *Maastricht Journal of European and Comparative Law* 261.

drivers' of this resistance. Tilahun suggests that there is an 'unarticulated institutional consciousness' within the legal profession that sees the gatekeeping role as a threat to (i) the position or reputation of legal professionals as public-interest actors and (ii) the independence or self-governance of the profession. Resistance to AML/CTF obligations represents a need to position the profession as 'neither in alliance with the state nor identifying with the subjects of state discipline'. This feature is contrasted with the way the banking sector perceives its gatekeeping role as an 'entrustment of public power or deputation into a governmental role', and so the chapter concludes with a call for governing bodies and standard setters, such as the FATF, to ensure that regulatory initiatives take account of the institutional cultures of different sectors or professions.

In the following chapter, Katie Benson considers the institutional characteristics of the legal profession from an alternative perspective, exploring how features of the profession can provide opportunities for lawyers to facilitate money laundering on behalf of their clients. Based on the analysis of cases of solicitors convicted of money laundering offences in the United Kingdom, the chapter highlights how transactions that serve to launder criminal proceeds (such as the purchase or sale of property or the movement of funds through a law firm's client account) can be hidden amongst lawyers' routine activities and are 'parasitical' on the 'legitimate transactions they carry out as a function of their regular occupational role'. Furthermore, principles of confidentiality and legal professional privilege, which are fundamental to the lawyer-client relationship, may shield illicit transactions from scrutiny and make investigations into suspected misconduct more difficult. Benson also considers whether the organisational characteristics of legal practices (or types of practice) could create opportunities for the facilitation of money laundering. She suggests, for example, that 'high levels of autonomy and a lack of effective oversight' within a law firm could 'allow lawyers to conduct transactions involving illicit funds with relative impunity' and raises concerns about the changing nature of the legal services market, which has seen the introduction of new forms of providers as the goal of a greater competition market is pursued. This pursuit may lead to increased workloads and financial pressures and reduced oversight within firms, creating greater risk of misconduct or regulatory non-compliance.

Moving from assemblages in terms of people such as legal professionals, the remaining chapters in Part II consider new assemblages in terms of systems. The first in the series by Doron Goldbarsht is titled 'New Payment Systems' and considers their potential counter-terrorist financing risks and the legal response in the United Kingdom. The rapid development, increased functionality, and growing use of new payment systems (NPSs), underlined by the recent announcement by Facebook to commence a Libra payment device,[66] has created global challenges for national and international regulators and for private-

66 See 'Libra: Facebook's digital currency' *Financial Times* (<http://www.ft.com/content/0c5c4012-9100-11e9-b7ea-60e35ef678d2>, 1 August 2019).

sector institutions. How can they ensure that these systems are not misused for ML/TF purposes? Consequently, the AML/CTF authorities are seeking to develop and implement new regulations for NPSs but without blocking innovation. This chapter explains that the basic need for terrorist organisations to raise, move, and use funds has remained constant; however, their methods of raising and managing funds have evolved over time. The possible resort to emerging innovative payment systems seems apposite since they involve attributes such as transnationality and small scale, but the chapter assesses the CTF risks as low and regulatory efforts as strong. Indeed, the danger is perhaps more directed towards the hindrance of the development of NPS ecosystems and the inclusiveness of financial frameworks.

Ilaria Zavoli's chapter focuses on the use of cryptocurrencies in the UK real estate market and the potential money laundering risks that this poses. Like legal professionals, real estate agents are designated as 'gatekeepers' in the AML/CTF framework and are expected to fulfil the customer due diligence (CDD) and suspicious activity reporting requirements of the UK Money Laundering Regulations.[67] In this chapter, Zavoli suggests that the increasing use of cryptocurrencies in property transactions creates significant challenges for estate agents. Confirming the source and legitimacy of funds in property purchases using cryptocurrencies is particularly problematic for a number of reasons, including the anonymity and issues of traceability of cryptocurrency transactions; the lack of traditional financial intermediaries (such as banks) in property transactions using cryptocurrencies, with payments being made directly from sender to receiver; and limitations to information sharing because of this lack of intermediaries. The chapter, which draws on interviews with UK estate agents and compliance officers, also highlights estate agents' lack of understanding of cryptocurrencies and how they operate and their concerns about being able to fulfil their AML obligations, 'especially the CDD checks that require the identification of the parties involved in real estate transactions and the assessment of the nature and purpose of the transactions'. Zavoli concludes that future policy in this area must address the problem of anonymity and lack of traditional intermediaries in property transactions using cryptocurrencies and include tailored training on cryptocurrencies for real estate agents.

To conclude Part II, an activity that has attracted significant attention recently, with implications for both how it is countered and who is tasked to counter it, is the use of the arts and antiquities market to launder proceeds of crime. In the United States, for example, the Illicit Art and Antiquities Trafficking Prevention Bill was brought before the 115th Congress in May 2018.[68] The Bill amends the

67 Money Laundering, Terrorist Financing and Transfer of Funds (Information on the Payer) Regulations 2017, SI 2017/692.

68 HR 5886–115th Congress (2017–2018), introduced by Rep. Luke Messer (Indiana). The bill subsequently lapsed but is expected to be brought back before the current Congress: Carrigan, M, US anti-money laundering bill could reappear early next year. *The Art Newspaper*, 11 December 2018.

Bank Secrecy Act 1970[69] to require art and antiquities dealers to comply with reporting, record keeping, and other requirements under that Act. Likewise, at the EU level, the Fifth Money Laundering Directive extends the AML regime to actors in the art market.[70] In the United Kingdom, the government has recognised the vulnerabilities of these markets to laundering.[71] Furthermore, because of the devastating activities of the Islamic State in Iraq and Syria, the trafficking of cultural property has provided a source of income for terrorist groups which must be countered.[72] Notwithstanding these policy developments, there is a notable lack of data. In his chapter, Samuel Andrew Hardy instead draws upon open-source material to document how art and antiquities can be used for laundering criminal money. As an archaeologist, Hardy has first-hand experience of the environment. He acknowledges practical difficulties in bringing art dealers within the AML and CTF regimes (specifically concerning the application of the law) and argues that to 'make a significant impact, state and civil society need to move from the law's refinement to its enforcement'.

Finally, Part III of the book seeks to apply the four themes outlined earlier in the context of 'country-specific insights or rebellion'. The first instalment deals with an important aspect of 'following the money' research and practice – namely, the emphasis on proceeds of corruption. Primarily, scholarly literature has tended to focus on grand corruption.[73] Yet it is important to also consider proceeds of corruption by otherwise legitimate corporations,[74] which was made painfully evident in the United Kingdom in recent years by action taken by the Serious Fraud Office (SFO) against influential corporations such as Rolls-Royce and Tesco; these corporations were required to pay substantial monetary penalties, yet were able to avoid criminal prosecution.[75] In his chapter, Nicholas Mills questions how corporate corruption might best be addressed, asking whether the current self-regulatory approaches are effective or appropriate. He argues that deficiencies of self-regulation have led to an overly reactive approach by the state in the context of corporate crime and that 'a proactive and imaginative outlook' is needed. Given the financial rewards of corruption, it is evident that even tougher

69 See 31 USC s.5312(a)(2).

70 Directive 2018/843 of the European Parliament and of the Council of 30 May 2018.

71 HM Treasury, *Transposition of the Fifth Money Laundering Directive: Consultation* (April 2019) 23–24.

72 UN Security Council Resolution 2199 of 12 February 2015, para. 16. For discussion in the context of ISIS, see Vlasic, M. and DeSousa, J.P., 'The illicit antiquities trade and terrorism financing: From the Khmer Rouge to Daesh' in King, C., Walker, C., and Gurulé, J. (eds.), *The Palgrave Handbook of Criminal and Terrorism Financing Law* (Palgrave, 2018).

73 Notable examples include Sharman, J., *The Despot's Guide to Wealth Management: On the International Campaign against Grand Corruption* (Cornell University Press, 2017). See also FATF, *Laundering the Proceeds of Corruption* (2011).

74 Lord, N. and Levi, M., 'Organizing the finances for and the finances from transnational corporate bribery' (2017) 14(3) *European Journal of Criminology* 365.

75 For further discussion, see King, C. and Lord, N., *Negotiated Justice and Corporate Crime: The Legitimacy of Civil Recovery Orders and Deferred Prosecution Agreements* (Palgrave, 2018).

responses are required. As Mills contends, 'An increased focus on proactive regulation and enforcement is necessary to monitor the arguably disjointed nature towards economic crimes'.

The corruption theme continues in the next chapter, where Steven Montagu-Cairns considers the possibility of enacting a failure to prevent money laundering offence as a response to corporate criminality. Given practical difficulties in successfully prosecuting corporate crime under UK law, most notably as a result of the identification principle, UK legislators have enacted alternative approaches, such as failure to prevent offences and deferred prosecution agreements. Indeed, in some instances, these have been combined by prosecutors. For example, the Deferred Prosecution Agreement between the SFO and Rolls-Royce was negotiated based on allegations of bribery that would fall within section 7 of the Bribery Act 2010 (in other words, a failure to prevent bribery). Montagu-Cairns argues, 'The implementation of a failure to prevent money laundering offence would offer significant advantages in combating economic crime and align with the UK government's anti-corruption strategy.' He is critical of the 'missed opportunity' to include an omissions-based offence in the Sanctions and Anti-Money Laundering Act 2018.

Looking beyond the United Kingdom, it is vital to consider innovative developments in other jurisdictions. For example, whilst the United Kingdom has adopted unexplained wealth orders as an investigative tool against corruption and serious crime,[76] other countries have adopted criminal law offences, particularly illicit enrichment offences. Such an offence is provided for in the UN Convention Against Corruption (UNCAC).[77] This offence operates on the basis that 'the enrichment of the corrupt official becomes the most visible manifestation of corruption.'[78] Indeed, it has been suggested that the United Kingdom should adopt such an offence to tackle corruption.[79] In her chapter, Noura T. A. Al-Oumi considers experiences from Kuwait where an illicit enrichment offence was enacted in 2016. Drawing upon examples, she illustrates difficulties in traditional methods to target corruption and recover stolen funds. She rejects arguments that the illicit enrichment offence undermines procedural safeguards, such as the burden of proof, the presumption of innocence, and the privilege against

76 Sproat, P., 'Unexplained wealth orders: An explanation, assessment and set of predictions' (2018) 82(3) *Journal of Criminal Law* 232.

77 UNCAC, art.20 provides the following: 'Subject to its constitution and the fundamental principles of its legal system, each State Party shall consider adopting such legislative and other measures as may be necessary to establish as a criminal offence, when committed intentionally, illicit enrichment, that is, a significant increase in the assets of a public official that he or she cannot reasonably explain in relation to his or her lawful income.'

78 Muzila, L., Morales, M., Mathias, M., and Berger, T., *On the Take: Criminalizing Illicit Enrichment to Fight Corruption* (World Bank, 2012) 5.

79 Maton, J. and Humphreys, J., 'Illicit enrichment offence: An overdue new law with potential for wide-reaching benefits,' All-Party Parliamentary Group on Anti-Corruption blog (<http://www.anticorruptionappg.org/what-should-the-next-government-prioritise-in-the-fight-against-corruption-part-two/>, 6 January 2015).

self-incrimination. Nonetheless, she recognises that there are practical difficulties so that further innovative approaches are recommended to tackle corruption.

In the next chapter, Khaled S. Al-Rashidi also considers corresponding developments in the Kuwaiti context. Specifically, he focuses on three corruption-related offences – namely, public money offences, illicit enrichment offences, and money laundering. Notwithstanding significant legal developments in Kuwait law, Al-Rashidi suggests that these offences are insufficient to effectively tackle corruption (which very much takes the grand corruption format) in Kuwait. He argues that further powers are needed, such as civil forfeiture and UWOs. He contends that such innovative approaches are an important, and necessary, aspect of focusing on corrupt finances, going to the heart of the counter-corruption strategy. Ultimately, however, in the absence of any external factors to galvanise action, Al-Rashidi is resigned to the pessimistic reality that 'Kuwaiti policymakers will not spontaneously opt for innovative approaches to combat corruption effectively'.

Another country that appears to have a strong AML/CTF regime on paper, yet suffers profound difficulties in practice, is Nigeria. In his chapter, Olufemi Olaoye outlines the 'elaborate' legal framework within that country. Notwithstanding this legal matrix, corruption-related difficulties remain endemic. A notable illustration of the deficiencies in the Nigerian framework was the suspension of Nigeria from the Egmont Group of FIUs in 2017. This suspension came about

> following repeated failures on the part of the FIU to address concerns regarding the protection of confidential information, specifically related to the status of suspicious transaction report (STR) details and information derived from international exchanges, as well as concerns on the legal basis and clarity of the NFIU's independence from the Economic and Financial Crimes Commission (EFCC).[80]

To address these concerns, Nigeria introduced further legislation, and the Egmont Group lifted its suspension in October 2018.[81] Olaoye states that the lifting of this suspension will certainly aid efforts to combat ML/TF but that 'the episode illustrates once again that Nigeria tends to be reactive and reluctant in the fight against ML/TF, with reform usually implemented on the pain of sanction or threat of it from the global community.' He goes on to question whether international standards can be implemented in national legislation 'without proper appreciation of the fitness of these standards to local circumstances and prevailing realities.'

80 Egmont Group, *Co-Chairs' Statement: 24th Plenary of the Egmont Group of Financial Intelligence Units* (7 July 2017) (<https://egmontgroup.org/en/content/co-chairs%E2%80%99-statement-24th-plenary-egmont-group-financial-intelligence-units>).

81 Egmont Group, *Co-Chairs' Statement: 25th Plenary of the Egmont Group of Financial Intelligence Units* (5 October 2018) (<https://egmontgroup.org/en/filedepot_download/1659/58>).

The book concludes with two chapters which deal with outliers in the CTF field. One might argue that both arise from fundamental disputes about legitimacy and ambit – who 'owns' the CTF narrative and how is it defined? As for ownership, this introduction pointed the finger towards the FATF and its ilk. However, in the chapter by Ahmed Almutawa, 'The Qatar Crisis, Legitimacy, and the Use of Sanctions against Terrorist Financing', the directive role is taken by a coalition of Arab states headed by Saudi Arabia. On June 5, 2017, Saudi Arabia, the United Arab Emirates, Bahrain, and Egypt accused Qatar of breaches of CTF international laws by providing a safe haven for extremists and terrorist financiers. To coerce compliance, the coalition initiated economic and political sanctions against Qatar. This chapter analyses the legitimacy of this use of unilateral sanctions as a response to Qatar's alleged shortcomings. Assuming the factual evidence for the actions can be substantiated, it is first argued that the sanctions may be characterised as lawful countermeasures to Qatar's failures to meet its international obligations to counter-terrorism. However, it is then argued that the legitimacy of the sanctions is weakened by both the lack of collective authority for imposition and their impact on individual human rights. Then it is suggested that the coalition could reinforce the legitimacy of sanctions by establishing an independent mechanism to mitigate the impact of the sanctions on individual human rights by dealing with issues and complaints, authorising special dispensation, and awarding compensation. Whatever the rights or wrongs, the treatment of Qatar is a cautionary tale for some Western states, which face the uncomfortable truth that the precedents they have set may be applied in unexpected and uncontrolled ways in the future.

The final chapter in the collection illustrates in an even more extreme way the deep disputes about the ambit of the CTF regime, in this case arising from the contours of the meaning of 'terrorism'. Ironically, the definition of 'terrorism' is more explicit in the context of CTF than in most other areas of international counter-terrorism law. Article 2(1) of the International Convention for the Suppression of the Financing of Terrorism 1999 states that an offence of terrorism financing is committed by

(a) An act which constitutes an offence within the scope of and as defined in one of the treaties listed in the annex; or
(b) Any other act intended to cause death or serious bodily injury to a civilian, or to any other person not taking an active part in the hostilities in a situation of armed conflict, when the purpose of such act, by its nature or context, is to intimidate a population, or to compel a government or an international organization to do or to abstain from doing any act.

Whilst this definition has both its critics and supporters,[82] it represents a fundamentally flawed conception to a number of non-Western states, most prominently

82 Nine treaties were then listed. For analysis of the definition, see Lavalle, R., 'The International Convention for the Suppression of the Financing of Terrorism' (2000) 60 *Heidelberg Journal of International Law* 491; Bianchi, A., *Enforcing International Norms against Terrorism* (Hart, 2004) chs 8, 15, 16; Schott, P.A., *Reference Guide to Anti-Money Laundering and Countering the Financing of Terrorism* (2nd supp. ed., World Bank Publications, 2006).

Iran, because of its failure to carve out an exception for the self-determination of peoples and, above all, the Palestinian people. The ensuing battle of wills between Iran, the FATF, and its Western backers is the subject of the chapter by Zeynab Malakoutikhah, 'Iran Responds: International Counter-Terrorism Financing Framework'. The author describes how Iran has been recognised as both a victim and state sponsor of terrorism. Following the 9/11 attacks, Iran declared its commitment to implement UNSCR 1373, but the adjustment of its domestic regulations to align with the international CTF framework has proven unattainable. As a non-Western state, acting under very different normative beliefs and structures, it cannot conscionably comply with international expectations because Iranian regulations adopt a different definition of terrorism which exempts favoured national liberation movements, such as Hizballah. Consequently, Iran is not a party to the International Convention for the Suppression of the Financing of Terrorism, and it is depicted as a high-risk and non-cooperative jurisdiction by the FATF. This chapter explains Iran's responses to the international CTF framework from 2001 to 2019 and why it is committed to rebellion for the sake of its allied national liberation movements.

As described in the Acknowledgements, the production of this book has involved the complications of a research grant and a conference in 2018, as well as the subsequent production of texts. As a result of the passage of time, we have taken the opportunity to update and have checked the viability of all cited websites up to 1 October 2019.

Part I

Innovative techniques and new perspectives on existing techniques

2 Too much information? Evaluating the financial intelligence gathering provisions of the Fourth European Union Anti-Money Laundering Directive and the Common Reporting Standard in combatting tax evasion

Sam Bourton

Introduction

The term 'tax evasion' refers to an 'illegal activity, where registered individuals or businesses deliberately omit, conceal, or misrepresent information in order to reduce their tax liabilities.'[1] Tax evasion causes significant harm to national revenues and, accordingly, harm to public infrastructure or services or an increased burden upon the majority of compliant taxpayers. Although these harms are difficult to quantify, it is clear that tax evasion presents a high cost to worldwide revenues, with losses in the United Kingdom alone estimated at £5.3 billion.[2] The financial crisis of 2008 instigated a global impetus to combat this financial crime with the aim of recouping the resultant high public deficits suffered in many jurisdictions.[3] Further action proliferated following revelations concerning tax evasion, such as the Panama Papers,[4] which exemplified how offshore jurisdictions could be used by individuals to evade their national tax liabilities.

The effects of globalisation, advances in technology, and increasing mobility of capital have enabled individuals to hide income or profits offshore. From the tax evader's perspective, concealing wealth offshore results in a lower probability of detection, as, in contrast to domestically held income, tax-related information

1 HM Revenue & Customs, 'Measuring Tax Gaps 2018 Edition: Tax Gap Estimates for 2016–17' (2018) 20.

2 *Ibid.*, 5.

3 Hardouin, P., 'The aftermath of the financial crisis' (2011) 18(2) *Journal of Financial Crime* 148, 149.

4 Hamilton, M.M., 'Panamanian law firm is gatekeeper to vast flow of murky offshore secrets' (International Consortium for Investigative Journalists, 3rd April 2016) (<https://panamapapers.icij.org/20160403-mossack-fonseca-offshore-secrets.html>).

is not automatically accessible to the tax authority.[5] Consequently, at the international level, innovative techniques have recently been developed to facilitate the exchange of information and assistance in tax matters between states, with the aim of providing much-needed information to combat this financial crime. A notable development is the OECD Common Reporting Standard (CRS), which requires states automatically to exchange information obtained from financial institutions on a periodic basis with one another.[6] Further, tax evasion is now included as a predicate offence for money laundering purposes in both the Financial Action Task Force (FATF) Recommendations[7] and the concomitant Fourth European Union Anti-Money Laundering Directive,[8] triggering the application of the suspicious activity reporting regime to tax offences.

The aim of this chapter is to evaluate the effectiveness of both the financial intelligence provisions of the anti-money laundering (AML) framework and the Organisation for Economic Co-operation and Development's (OECD) CRS in combatting tax crimes, alongside an analysis of the effectiveness and proportionality of retaining both information-obtaining mechanisms. In examining effectiveness, the chapter aims to determine whether the relevant legal provisions achieve their stated aims of facilitating the prevention, detection, and punishment of tax offences, alongside the recovery of the proceeds of fiscal crime. It is acknowledged that there are significant obstacles to comprehensively measuring the effectiveness of AML instruments in light of their objectives, particularly through a cost-benefit analysis, as many potential benefits are impossible to measure.[9] Moreover, quantifiable benefits, such as the volume of criminal proceeds recovered in connection with the AML framework, are not the best indicators of its effectiveness, as its primary aim is to disrupt and prevent crime rather than collect funds for law enforcement agencies.[10] However, in contrast, one of the primary indicators, if not *the* primary indicator, of the effectiveness of tax evasion law and its enforcement is its ability to facilitate the collection of revenue and

5 Johannesen, N. and Zucman, G., 'The end of bank secrecy? An evaluation of the G20 tax haven crackdown' (2014) 6 *American Economic Journal* 65, 68.

6 OECD, *Standard for Automatic Exchange of Financial Account Information in Tax Matters* (2nd ed., CRS, 2017).

7 Financial Action Task Force, *International Standards on Combating Money Laundering and the Financing of Terrorism & Proliferation: The FATF Recommendations* (2012, updated October 2018).

8 Council Directive 2015/849 of 20 May 2015 On the Prevention of the Use of the Financial System for the Purposes of Money Laundering or Terrorist Financing [2015] OJ L141/73.

9 See Levi, M., Reuter, P. and Halliday, T., 'Can the AML system be evaluated without better data?' (2018) 69 *Crime, Law and Social Change* 307; Ferwerda, J., 'The effectiveness of anti-money laundering policy: A cost-benefit perspective' in King, C., Walker, C., and Gurulé, J. (eds.), *The Palgrave Handbook of Criminal and Terrorism Financing Law* (Palgrave MacMillan, 2018) 317.

10 Goldby, M., 'Anti-money laundering reporting requirements imposed by English law: Measuring effectiveness and gauging the need for reform' (2013) 4 *Journal of Business Law* 367, 383.

recover revenue lost through tax offences.[11] Accordingly, this chapter asserts that it is possible to provide some insight as to the effectiveness of these measures in combatting tax evasion by examining the quantifiable costs and benefits of the AML framework's application to tax offences and the CRS, which have been reported thus far.

In furtherance of this aim, the first section examines the evolution of AML legislation, followed by an outline of AML financial intelligence gathering mechanisms and an evaluation of their success in combatting tax offences. The second section examines the evolution of the OECD's attempts to promote assistance between states in relation to tax matters, focusing on attempts to promote the exchange of information between states in the form of the CRS. This section will examine the effectiveness of the CRS in preventing and detecting tax crimes, whilst highlighting the risks that the CRS poses to privacy and data protection. The final section then examines the effectiveness and proportionality of retaining the financial intelligence gathering provisions in both the CRS and AML framework. Ultimately, this chapter argues that, whilst increased cooperative action between states is essential in combatting tax crimes, these initiatives have developed in parallel to one another, with little consideration paid to the proportionality of retaining overlapping systems of obtaining information.

The evolution of the AML framework

The term 'money laundering' refers to the 'process whereby criminals attempt to hide and disguise the true origin and ownership of the proceeds of their criminal activities.'[12] Since the late 1980s, money laundering has been the subject of extensive international efforts at eradicating this practice,[13] with the idea that an effective preventive framework will make it harder for criminals to launder the proceeds of their crimes and thereby enjoy their profits, removing the motivation for committing the predicate offence.[14] These international initiatives include several United Nations (UN) conventions,[15] the recommendations proffered by the FATF[16] and several European Union (EU) directives.[17]

11 The collection of tax has long been prioritised by HMRC, see HM Revenue & Customs, 'HMRC's Criminal Investigation Policy' (Guidance, 4 September 2018) (<http://www.gov.uk/government/publications/criminal-investigation/hmrc-criminal-investigation-policy>).

12 Ryder, N., 'The financial services authority and money laundering: A game of cat and mouse' (2008) 67 *Cambridge Law Journal* 635.

13 UN Convention Against Illicit Traffic in Narcotic Drugs and Psychotropic Substances 1988 (1582 UNTS 95) (Vienna Convention).

14 Harvey, J., 'An evaluation of money laundering policies' (2005) 8 *Journal of Money Laundering Control* 339.

15 Vienna Convention (fn 13); UN Convention against Transnational Organized Crime 2000 (2225 UNTS 209) (Palermo Convention).

16 FATF (fn 7).

17 See especially Council Directive 2015/849 on the prevention of the use of the financial system for the purposes of money laundering or terrorist financing (Fourth AML Directive).

At the inception of the international AML framework, AML initiatives were aimed solely at countering the laundering of proceeds derived from drug trafficking offences, and it was not envisaged that such a framework would apply to tax evasion.[18] Gradually, the AML framework expanded to cover the laundering of the proceeds of serious or organised crime[19] and, controversially, the financing of terrorism.[20] One of the first signs of the expansion towards fiscal offences occurred in 1998 as part of a G7 Initiative on Harmful Tax Competition, whereby the G7 agreed to take action against tax offences by utilising and sharing information generated by the AML regime.[21] Soon after, the FATF called on states to ensure that suspicious transactions were reported, regardless of whether they also concerned tax offences.[22] However, the FATF Recommendations did not explicitly require tax evasion to be a predicate offence for AML purposes until the 2012 revision of the recommendations. Following this inclusion, the Fourth EU AML Directive mandated that tax offences were to be included as predicate offences to laundering.[23]

In the United Kingdom, tax offences were included as predicate offences to money laundering long before that obligation was imposed at an international level. This development was secured by the Criminal Justice Act 1993, which extended the money laundering offence to the proceeds of any offence in England and Wales or conduct which would otherwise be an offence if it had occurred there.[24] Although there was initial ambiguity over whether the AML framework applied to tax offences, and institutional reluctance to use the framework for such cases,[25] it soon became clear that tax offences were included as predicate offences for the purposes of the United Kingdom's AML framework.[26]

The relationship between money laundering and tax evasion

At first glance, it may seem appropriate to include tax evasion as a predicate offence for money laundering purposes; if tax evasion is a crime like any other,

18 Vienna Convention (fn 13).
19 Palermo Convention (fn 15).
20 See for instance, Roberge, I., 'Misguided policies in the war on terror? The case for disentangling terrorist financing from money laundering' (2007) 27 *Politics* 196; King, C. and Walker, C., 'Counter terrorism financing: A redundant fragmentation?' (2015) 6 *New Journal of European Criminal Law* 372; Compin, F., 'Terrorism financing and money laundering: Two sides of the same coin?' (2018) 25 *Journal of Financial Crime* 962.
21 G7 Initiative on Harmful Tax Competition (Birmingham Summit 15–17 May 1998); text available from the University of Toronto's G8 Information Centre (<http://www.g8.utoronto.ca/summit/1998birmingham/harmfultax.html>).
22 Interpretive Note to Recommendation 13 of the FATF Recommendations (2003 version).
23 Dir. 2015/849, art.3(4)(f).
24 Criminal Justice Act 1988, s.93A(7) (as amended by Criminal Justice Act 1993, ss.29–31).
25 A UK treasury official and the British Banker's Association initially gave assurances that the framework did not encompass tax offences. Bridges, M., 'Tax evasion: A crime in itself: The relationship with money laundering' (1996) 4 *Journal of Financial Crime* 161, 164.
26 *Ibid.*

why should legislatures not criminalise the laundering of the proceeds of this particular offence? In this respect, affording tax evasion parity of treatment in AML legislation simply confirms and reinforces the serious nature of this offence. Nevertheless, conceptual difficulties arise in criminalising the laundering of criminal proceeds derived from tax evasion. First, tax evasion is a distinct crime in that, whereas money laundering refers to the process of concealing the origin of illegally obtained income, tax evasion concerns the illegal concealment of legally obtained income.[27] In this respect, the 'laundering' of the funds is a core element of the offence itself,[28] so it may be regarded as inappropriate to use the same legal framework as a form of 'uncritical over-criminalization.'[29] Thus, what was considered tax evasion only may now be regarded as tax evasion and money laundering with consequences as to the priority tax evasion receives in terms of law enforcement.[30] Second, the inclusion of tax evasion potentially incurs serious consequences in terms of the labelling function of the criminal law;[31] as profits derived from criminal activities are taxable,[32] it may be easier for prosecutors to charge criminals with laundering the proceeds of tax evasion, as opposed to the 'true' predicate offence.[33]

These conceptual difficulties also lead to practical difficulties in applying national AML legislation to the laundering of the proceeds of this offence. In the United Kingdom, money laundering offences criminalise undertaking certain actions in respect of criminal property.[34] However, in cases concerning tax evasion, it is often difficult to identify whether an offence has been committed, and if it has, the property that is the subject of the offence. This is because the non-payment of tax does not typically equate to a criminal offence unless the owner of the funds possesses the requisite *mens rea* of the tax offence.[35] Consequently, it may be difficult to determine the intention of the individual concerned and, thus, the nature of the funds involved.[36] In addition, although it may be straightforward to identify criminal property where the individual has obtained a tax rebate through fraud,[37] the crime of tax evasion often fails to produce any identifiable proceeds

27 Oliver, K.E., 'International taxation: Tax evasion as a predicate offense to money laundering' (2002) 27 *International Legal Practitioner* 55, 60.
28 Levi, M. and Reuter, P., 'Money laundering' (2006) 34 *Crime and Justice* 289, 292.
29 Mitsilegas, V. and Vavoula, N., 'The evolving EU anti-money laundering regime: Challenges for fundamental rights and rule of law' (2016) 23 *Maastricht Journal of European and Comparative Law* 261, 267.
30 Alldridge, P., *Criminal Justice and Taxation* (Oxford University Press, 2017) 173.
31 Alldridge, P. and Mumford, A., 'Tax evasion and the Proceeds of Crime Act 2002' (2005) 25 *Legal Studies* 353, 373.
32 For a review of the case law, see Curtis, R., 'It's a Fair Cop' (2005) 155 *Taxation* 1.
33 Oliver (fn 27).
34 See, for instance, Proceeds of Crime Act 2002, ss.327–329.
35 With the exception of the strict liability offence contained in Taxes Management Act 1970, s.106B-D.
36 Bridges, M.J. and Green, P., 'Tax evasion and money laundering: An open and shut case?' (1999) 3 *Journal of Money Laundering Control* 51, 56.
37 Fisher, J., 'The anti-money laundering disclosure regime and the collection of revenue in the United Kingdom' (2010) 3 *British Tax Review* 235, 243–244.

but rather the 'deferral of a debt'[38] or 'cost savings.'[39] In such cases, it is difficult to distinguish the criminal property involved from other legitimate funds. In light of such complications, it may be asked why AML legislation needs to encompass tax offences.[40] The answer to this question seems, at least in part, to lie in the financial intelligence provisions of the AML regulatory framework and their potential utility in detecting and preventing tax crimes. The international AML framework requires jurisdictions to put in place measures requiring financial institutions to, amongst other things, conduct due diligence on their customers;[41] keep records of identification documents and account information, including transactions;[42] and submit suspicious activity reports (SARs) where they suspect, or have reasonable grounds to suspect, that the funds concerned consist of the proceeds of criminal activity.[43] In addition, national jurisdictions must set up Financial Intelligence Units (FIUs) to receive SARs.[44] These measures have the potential to enable national authorities to detect tax crimes by investigating any suspicions reported by financial institutions.

Evaluating the use of SARs in detecting and combatting tax crimes

As noted earlier, although it has long been recognised that a comprehensive evaluation of the effectiveness of the AML framework is near impossible to undertake,[45] some insight as to the benefit provided by the financial intelligence provisions in tax cases may be gleaned from the enforcement actions that have arisen from this data. The United Kingdom's revenue collection authority, Her Majesty's Revenue and Customs (HMRC), was unable to access data emanating from SARs until 1998.[46] Since then, HMRC has received regular reports from the FIU and is now the largest recipient of SAR data.[47] Whilst HMRC was initially criticised for making little use of SARs,[48] those SARs that were investigated led to the recovery of small-scale sums; from 2004 to 2007, HMRC recovered £27 million from 7,150 investigations.[49] HMRC's use of SARs improved with the move to feed SAR data into the Connect database, which enables the matching

38 Alldridge and Mumford (fn 31).
39 Alexander, R.C., '"Cost savings" as proceeds of crime: A comparative study of the United States and the United Kingdom' (2011) 45 *International Lawyer* 749.
40 Alldridge, P., *What Went Wrong with Money Laundering Law?* (Palgrave MacMillan, 2016) 27.
41 FATF Recommendations (fn 7), Recommendation 10.
42 *Ibid.*, Recommendation 11.
43 *Ibid.*, Recommendation 20.
44 *Ibid.*, Recommendation 29.
45 Levi *et al.* (fn 9).
46 G7 Initiative (fn 21).
47 Her Majesty's Inspectorate of Constabulary, *An Inspection of Her Majesty's Revenue and Customs Performance in Addressing the Recovery of the Proceeds of Crime from Tax and Duty Evasion and Benefit Fraud (Revisit 2013)* (2014) 30.
48 *Ibid.*
49 National Audit Office, *Tackling the Hidden Economy* (2007–08 HC 341-I) 22.

of SAR data with other data held by HMRC.[50] In 2016–2017, this intelligence supported the collection of £22.1 million in taxes and penalties,[51] and in 2017–2018, SAR data assisted HMRC in recovering over £47 million through civil enquiries.[52] Nevertheless, despite the vast number of SARs received by HMRC, it appears that SARs currently have a marginal, yet growing, role in the United Kingdom in the detection of tax evasion and the recovery of unpaid tax and penalties. This is highlighted by comparing the sums recovered to the total sum of £30.3 billion collected by HMRC through compliance activities in 2017–2018.[53] Indeed, the Fraud Investigation Service of HMRC alone recovered £5.47 billion through civil and criminal investigations into tax fraud and evasion during the same period.[54] Unfortunately, it is unclear how useful SAR data was in obtaining convictions for tax evasion or the laundering of the proceeds thereof.[55] Nevertheless, it appears that the utility of SAR data in combatting tax evasion has been utilised more fully by other revenue collection authorities. For instance, Australia reported that from 2008 to 2013, between $131 million and $572 million was recovered each year following tax authority access to FIU data, and in 2012, Austria secured 61 criminal tax prosecutions using this information.[56]

Accordingly, it appears as though the inclusion of tax evasion as a predicate offence, and in turn the application of the reporting regime to suspicions of tax offences, has been successful to a limited extent in preventing and addressing tax crimes. However, it is unclear to what extent this success has been achieved at the expense of individual privacy and costs to financial institutions. At a fundamental level, although it is now commonly accepted that financial privacy must be overridden by obligations contained in the AML framework to prevent the laundering of funds derived from serious criminal activity,[57] it is unclear whether such acceptance must extend to measures aimed at preventing tax evasion or the laundering of the proceeds of tax crimes. One drawback is that including tax evasion as a predicate offence for AML purposes dramatically increases the amount of personal information that is disclosed to national authorities. In many

50 Monger, T., 'Pointless POCA?' (2014) 174 *Taxation* 8.

51 National Crime Agency, *Suspicious Activity Reports (SARs): Annual Report 2017*, 35.

52 National Crime Agency, *Suspicious Activity Reports (SARs): Annual Report 2018*, 10.

53 HM Revenue & Customs, *Annual Report and Accounts 2017–18* (2017–18 HC 1222) 21.

54 Freedom of Information request submitted by Pinsent Masons, 'HMRC's Elite Fraud Team collects £5.47 billion in extra tax – up 7% in just the last year' (20 September 2018) (<https://www.pinsentmasons.com/about-us/announcements/hmrcs-elite-fraud-team-collects-547-billion-in-extra-tax--up-7-in-just-the-last-year>).

55 Law Commission, *Anti-Money Laundering: The SARs Regime* (Law Com No 236, 2018) 60.

56 OECD, *Improving Co-operation between Tax and Anti-Money Laundering Authorities: Access by Tax Administrations to Information Held by Financial Intelligence Units for Criminal and Civil Purposes* (2015) 14.

57 Nguyen, C.L., 'Preventing the use of financial institutions for money laundering and the implications for financial privacy' (2018) 21 *Journal of Money Laundering Control* 47; Sharman, J.C., 'Privacy as Roguery: Personal financial information in an age of transparency' (2009) 87 *Public Administration* 717; Ping, H., 'Banking secrecy and money laundering' (2004) 7 *Journal of Money Laundering Control* 376.

jurisdictions, tax evasion is highly prevalent amongst the national population leading to an onerous reporting obligation for financial institutions.[58]

In addition, the foregoing difficulties are repeated in the application of the SAR regime to tax evasion offences. Here, the difficulty in identifying whether a tax offence has been committed due to the uncertainty surrounding the taxpayer's intention is likely to (further) encourage defensive reporting by financial institutions under the Proceeds of Crime Act 2002, section 330.[59] The similarity of the methods used to evade and avoid tax is also likely to lead to widespread reporting of arrangements concerning tax avoidance, a lawful activity.[60] Further, the difficulties in identifying the criminal property arising from tax offences is likely to encourage a financial institution to report every transaction entered into by the suspected tax evader, whereas, for other crimes, reports only need to be made in respect to dealings with the particular proceeds of the offence.[61] Alldridge notes the potential infringement of Article 8 of the European Convention on Human Rights.[62] Moreover, the collection and dissemination of financial intelligence under the AML framework will continue to increase with the adoption of the Fourth EU AML Directive,[63] which requires Member States to ensure that their FIUs can 'rapidly, constructively and effectively ensure the widest range of international cooperation with third countries' FIUs.'[64]

The current costs of the AML framework, largely borne by financial institutions, are substantial. For instance, in 2016, the British Bankers' Association claimed that its members spend £5 billion annually on compliance with financial crime prevention measures.[65] Considering the volume of individuals and transactions that fail to be reported in respect to tax offences, it is highly likely that the addition of this predicate has increased the costs of the reporting regime. Despite the problems inherent in evaluating AML policy outlined earlier,[66] it is imperative that some attempt is made to weigh the quantifiable costs and benefits of the inclusion of tax evasion as a predicate offence to laundering to determine the appropriateness of this course of action. This analysis must include an assessment of the utility of other potential mechanisms for obtaining financial intelligence in relation to tax matters, such as the CRS.

58 Stessens, G., *Money Laundering: A New International Law Enforcement Model* (Cambridge University Press, 2004) 168.

59 Rhodes, J., 'Legislative comment: The Proceeds of Crime Act 2002 and tax evasion' (2004) 1 *Private Client Business* 51, 57.

60 Fisher (fn 37).

61 Alldridge, P., 'Are tax evasion offences predicate offences for money-laundering offences?' (2001) 4 *Journal of Money Laundering Control* 350, 354.

62 *Ibid.*

63 Dir. 2015/849 (fn 17).

64 *Ibid.*, Recital 58; The Money Laundering, Terrorist Financing and Transfer of Funds (Information on the Payer) Regulations 2017, SI 2017/692, Reg. 50.

65 British Bankers' Association, *Response to Cutting Red Tape Review: The Effectiveness of the UK's AML Regime* (2015).

66 Levi *et al.* (fn 9).

The OECD and international cooperation in tax matters

In 1963, the OECD drafted a Model Double Taxation Convention (DTC) – namely, the Model Taxation Convention on Income and on Capital.[67] The convention was primarily aimed at preventing double taxation, yet Article 26 of the convention, which provided for the exchange of information in tax matters between states, eventually became one of the primary legal bases for the exchange of information to prevent tax evasion.[68] In 1979, the OECD, in conjunction with the Council of Europe (CoE), issued the Multilateral Convention on Mutual Administrative Assistance in Tax Matters, which provided for the exchange of information on a multilateral basis.[69] Both conventions provided for several forms of information exchange, yet, initially, the most prevalent was the provision of information on request. These instruments had the potential to act as powerful tools in detecting tax avoidance and evasion by allowing states to request access to previously inaccessible information.[70] However, the effectiveness of the Conventions was hampered by the way in which states, particularly tax havens, implemented and interpreted their obligations.

At first, many states restricted the exchange of information provisions of the DTC to information concerning the implementation of the DTC itself and not the wider enforcement of taxes generally.[71] In addition, many states refused to exchange information protected by bank secrecy laws, considering this situation to fall within one of the recognised grounds for refusal.[72] Further, requests constituting 'fishing expeditions' or 'speculative requests that have no apparent nexus to an open inquiry or investigation' were prohibited.[73] This hampered attempts to combat tax evasion, as authorities had to identify a potential tax evader before making a request for information, yet often needed the desired information to identify potential tax evaders.[74] Moreover, many states did not sign up to either convention; the Multilateral Convention was initially open to CoE/OECD members only, and there was little incentive for states that imposed no or minimal taxation to enter into DTCs.[75]

67 OECD, *Model Tax Convention on Income and on Capital 2014 (Full Version)* (2015) (DTC).

68 Oberson, X., *International Exchange of Information in Tax Matters: Towards Global Transparency* (Edward Elgar, 2015).

69 OECD, Council of Europe, *The Multilateral Convention on Mutual Administrative Assistance in Tax Matters: Amended by the 2010 Protocol* (2011).

70 Kerzner, D.S. and Chodikoff, D.W., *International Tax Evasion in the Global Information Age* (Palgrave Macmillan, 2016) 67.

71 Picciotto, S., *International Business Taxation: A Study in the Internationalization of Business Regulation* (Picciotto, 2013) 274–275.

72 Such as art.26(3) of the OECD DTC; amended by art.26(5).

73 *Ibid.*, at C(26)-4.

74 McIntyre, J., 'How to end the charade of information exchange' (2009) *Tax Notes International* 255.

75 Dean, S.A., 'The incomplete global market for tax information' (2008) 49 *Boston College Law Review* 605, 650–651.

Over several decades, the OECD attempted to rectify these issues. In 2000, the Global Forum on Transparency and Exchange of Information for Tax Purposes was created to expand the range of countries involved in information exchange.[76] Soon after, Tax Information Exchange Agreements (TIEAs) were developed to provide a more appropriate legal basis for tax haven jurisdictions to exchange information,[77] and bank secrecy was removed as a ground for refusal.[78] In 2012, group requests were permitted, so long as the group of taxpayers could be identified with specificity.[79] However, before the effect of these changes could be fully appreciated, there were several attempts to move towards the automatic exchange of information. In 2004, the EU adopted the Savings Directive, which required the automatic exchange of information relating to savings interest paid within the EU,[80] and in 2010, the United States enacted the Foreign Account Tax Compliance Act (FATCA), which requires foreign financial institutions to identify and report information regarding their US account holders on a periodic basis or else face a withholding tax of 30% on US source income.[81] In 2013, the United Kingdom, along with France, Germany, Italy, and Spain, announced an agreement to automatically exchange tax information with one another based on the model of the US FATCA agreements.[82] Soon after, the G20 recognised automatic exchange of information as the new international standard and the OECD published and began to promote the CRS.[83]

The CRS

One aim of the CRS is to increase cooperation between tax authorities to increase transparency and thereby facilitate the detection and prevention of tax evasion.[84] In furtherance of this aim, the CRS 'calls on jurisdictions to obtain information from their financial institutions and automatically exchange that

76 OECD, 'Global Forum on Transparency and Exchange of Information for Tax Purposes' (<http://www.oecd.org/tax/transparency/>).

77 OECD, 'Agreement on Exchange of Information on Tax Matters' (<http://www.oecd.org/tax/exchange-of-tax-information/2082215.pdf>, 2016).

78 *Ibid.*, see Article 5(4) and commentary; the DTC and Multilateral Convention were also amended.

79 For the background to this development see, Noseda, F., 'Article 26 of the OECD Model Tax Convention – group requests – the birth of a new international standard? Recent developments in Switzerland and potential ramifications for other jurisdictions' (2014) 1 *British Tax Review* 1.

80 Council Directive 2003/48/EC of June 3, 2003, on taxation of savings income in the form of interest payments [2003] OJ L 157/38.

81 Introduced by Foreign Account Tax Compliance Act of 2009 (H.R. 3933) and subsequently enacted in Hiring Incentives to Restore Employment Act of 2010, Public Law 111–147 (the HIRE Act), which added Chapter 4 of Subtitle A ss.1471–1474 to the US IRC.

82 Treasury, H.M., 'New UK multilateral action to combat tax evasion' (Press Release, 9 April 2013).

83 OECD, *Standard for Automatic Exchange of Financial Account Information in Tax Matters* (2nd ed., CRS, 2017).

84 *Ibid.*

information with other jurisdictions on an annual basis.'[85] The CRS requires financial institutions to collect vast amounts of information in respect to reportable accounts, defined as any individual or entity account held by tax residents of a jurisdiction participating in the CRS or a passive non-financial entity with controlling persons in such a jurisdiction.[86] The information to be exchanged includes the individual's name, address, tax identification number, date and place of birth, account number, account balance or value, and certain sums paid into the account.[87] This information is sent by the financial institution to the appropriate national authority and exchanged with the country of residence of the individual concerned.[88]

Although many states initially only committed to exchanging information on request, the aforementioned legal instruments from the OECD provided for several types of information exchange, including automatic exchange of information. Therefore, bilateral treaties based on the DTC, the OECD/CoE Multilateral Convention, TIEAs, and EU Directives implementing the CRS[89] may all be used as the legal basis for the automatic exchange of information. Once signed, states must enter into a Competent Authority Agreement that 'operationalises' the automatic exchange of information between them.[90] Additionally, the CRS must be implemented in national law.[91] As of June 2018, 49 jurisdictions, including the United Kingdom, had committed to undertake the first automatic exchanges in 2017, 53 jurisdictions committed to undertake first exchanges in 2018, and four jurisdictions have set a date of 2019/2020.[92]

Evaluating the CRS in detecting and preventing tax crimes

If the CRS is implemented and enforced correctly in each jurisdiction,[93] it is likely to bring in significant revenue for national governments that will be able to use this new data to detect and address tax non-compliance. For example, although to date the true benefits of the CRS are unknown,[94] in the United Kingdom, the

85 OECD, 'Automatic exchange portal: What is the CRS?' (<http://www.oecd.org/tax/automatic-exchange/common-reporting-standard/>).

86 OECD CRS, s.8(D).

87 *Ibid.*, s.1(A)(1).

88 *Ibid.*, see s.2(1) of the Competent Authority Agreement.

89 Council Directive 2011/16/EU of 15 February 2011 on administrative cooperation in the field of taxation and repealing Directive 77/799/EEC [2011] OJ L 64/I (as amended).

90 OECD CRS, 13.

91 In the United Kingdom, see the International Tax Compliance Regulations 2015, SI 2015/878.

92 OECD, 'AEOI: Status of Commitments' (June 2018) (<http://www.oecd.org/tax/transparency/AEOI-commitments.pdf>).

93 This will require the closure of existing loopholes. See, for instance, OECD, *Public Input Received on Misuse of Residence by Investment Schemes to Circumvent the Common Reporting Standard* (Compilation of Comments, 2018).

94 European Commission, 'Report from the Commission to the European Parliament and the Council on the application of Council Directive 2011/16 EU on administrative cooperation in the field of direct taxation' COM (2017) 781 Final, 4.

CRS was predicted to increase tax revenues by £75 million to £270 million annually.[95] The deterrent effect of the CRS is also likely to be substantial. Some appreciation of its magnitude may be gleaned from the fact that in 2015, transparency initiatives led to a 3% decline in offshore wealth held by individuals in North America and Western Europe.[96] Accordingly, notwithstanding the lack of reliable empirical estimates, it is clear that the CRS is highly likely to be successful in detecting and preventing tax evasion. However, at what expense is this success likely to be achieved?

The CRS's adoption of a 'generalized basis of information exchange' whereby reporting is automatic and not based on indications of tax non-compliance, let alone tax evasion, has been considered to pose a grave risk to privacy and data protection.[97] This is because the CRS requires the periodic exchange of vast amounts of personal information, regardless of whether this information is required for tax purposes.[98] In this respect, the EU Article 29 Data Protection Working Party has consistently highlighted its concerns over the CRS's compatibility with data protection law,[99] and the first legal challenge has been initiated.[100] Several commentators have also expressed concerns over the safety of individuals who are the subject of reports, as information will be exchanged with governments who are considered corrupt[101] and who may use information for inappropriate purposes.[102]

In this latter respect, the CRS contains several safeguards, including that information may only be provided to persons or authorities who are concerned with the administration or enforcement of the tax system or its supervision without prior agreement, and any information exchanged must be treated as secret and protected by domestic data protection safeguards.[103] In addition, information should not be exchanged with countries that do not observe common privacy

95 HM Revenue & Customs, 'Tax Administration: Regulations to Implement the UK's Automatic Exchange of Information Agreements' (Impact Assessment, March 2015).

96 Beardsley, B. et al., 'Global Wealth 2016: Navigating the New Client Landscape' (Boston Consulting Group, 15 June 2016) (<http://www.bcg.com/publications/2016/financial-institutions-consumer-insight-global-wealth-2016.aspx>).

97 Noseda, F., 'Common reporting standard and EU beneficial ownership registers: Inadequate protection of privacy and data protection' (2017) 23 *Trusts & Trustees* 404.

98 *Ibid.* at 407; see also Case C-362/14 *Maximillian Schrems v Data Protection Commissioner* [2015] OJ C 398.

99 Article 29 Data Protection Working Party, 'Statement of the WP29 on Automatic Inter-State Exchanges of Personal Data for Tax Purposes' (4 February 2015) (<https://iapp.org/media/pdf/resource_center/wp230_interstate-tax-data-exchange_02-2015.pdf>).

100 Miscon de Reya (law firm), 'Legal Challenge to Common Reporting Standard (CRS) and Beneficial Ownership (BO) Registers' (1 August 2018) (<http://www.mishcon.com/news/firm_news/legal-challenge-to-common-reporting-standard-crs-and-beneficial-ownership-bo-registers>).

101 Commentators often point to CRS jurisdictions' status on Transparency International, *Corruption Perceptions Index 2017* (Transparency International, 2018).

102 As feared by some Venezuelans and Argentinians; see Lotmore, K.W., 'The decline of financial privacy and its costs to society' (2017) 23 *Trusts & Trustees* 944, 952.

103 OECD CRS, 81–82.

and data protection guidelines.[104] Nevertheless, the provision of vast amounts of personal information under the CRS renders it questionable whether these safeguards are sufficient in practice. Many revenue collection authorities have illustrated their inability to prevent data leaks. For example, in 2014/2015 alone, HMRC recorded over 6,000 data breaches.[105] Further, the wealth of data generated is likely to provide significant temptation to cyber criminals.[106]

A related development concerns the Fourth AML Directive, which requires Member States to establish central registers containing information regarding the beneficial owners of companies[107] and trusts,[108] enabling the verification of information provided under the CRS. These registers are likely to facilitate the detection and prevention of several financial crimes, including tax evasion, by allowing investigators to discover the true owners of these entities and structures.[109] However, the same objections regarding privacy and data protection may be raised here; if anything, these concerns are exacerbated when considering the revisions to this directive, which require the central registers pertaining to companies to be available to any member of the public[110] and the central register concerning trusts to be available to anyone who can demonstrate a legitimate interest.[111] These registers have the potential to become 'a register of who-owns-everything,' at least in regard to high net-worth individuals,[112] exposing identified persons to the risk of identity theft,[113] kidnapping, blackmail, violence, or intimidation.[114] This is recognised in the Directive, which, alongside data protection safeguards,[115] provides that access to the registers should be restricted when there is such a risk to

104 *Ibid.*; see also OECD, *Keeping It Safe: The OECD Guide on the Protection of Confidentiality of Information Exchanged for Tax Purposes* (2012) 7.

105 National Audit Office, *Protecting Information across Government* (2016–17 HC 625-I) 22.

106 McGill, R.K., Haye, C.A. and Lipo, S., *G.A.T.C.A.: A Practical Guide to Global Anti-Tax Evasion Frameworks* (Palgrave Macmillan, 2017) 225–234.

107 Dir. 2015/849 (fn 17), art.30.

108 *Ibid.*, art.31.

109 *Ibid.*, Recital 14.

110 Directive 2018/843 of the European Parliament and of the Council of 30 May 2018 amending Directive (EU) 2015/849 on the prevention of the use of the financial system for the purposes of money laundering or terrorist financing [2018] OJ L 156/43, Article 1(15)(c).

111 *Ibid.*, Article 1(16)(d).

112 Forstater, M., 'Beneficial openness? Weighing the costs and benefits of financial transparency' (CMI Working Paper, 2017) (<http://www.cmi.no/publications/6201-beneficial-openness> 19.

113 Information Commissioner's Office, 'Response to HM Treasury's Consultation on Money Laundering Regulations 2017' (12 April 2017) (<https://ico.org.uk/media/about-the-ico/consultation-responses/2017/2013938/ico-response-hmt-money-laundering-regulations-20170412.pdf>).

114 Vail, N., 'Cracking Shells: The Panama Papers & Looking to the European Union's Anti-Money Laundering Directive as a Framework for Implementing a Multilateral Agreement to Combat the Harmful Effects of Shell Companies' (2017) 5 *Texas A&M Law Review* 133, 148.

115 Dir. 2015/849 (fn 17), Art.30(5).

the beneficial owner.[116] However, it is difficult to envisage how Member States will be able to make this determination in advance.

Moreover, aside from the human cost, the financial costs of implementing the CRS are likely to be astronomical. HMRC has estimated the total costs faced by businesses in complying with the CRS at between £80 million and £227 million.[117] The benefits of the CRS to HMRC are likely to exceed these costs if revenue recovered as a result of the CRS meets or surpasses anticipated figures.[118] Nevertheless, the cost of other measures providing for the automatic exchange of information in tax matters must also be considered. For instance, in the United Kingdom, compliance with FATCA was estimated to cost businesses between £1,100 million and £2,000 million.[119] These costs dwarf anticipated benefits of between £25 million and £55 million per year in increased tax revenue.[120]

Too much information?

Considering the significant financial costs of both the CRS and financial intelligence provisions of the AML framework, alongside their implications for privacy and data protection, is there a need to retain both mechanisms of obtaining information for the purposes of combatting tax evasion? In answering this question, a cost-benefit analysis of these mechanisms must be attempted. This is particularly important in a tax context, where enforcement decisions are intertwined with economic considerations. In addition, both national governments and international organisations should determine the relative harm considered to be posed by tax crimes. Only then can it be determined whether the costs of these measures, including the potential risks to individuals, are proportionate to the risk and harm posed by tax evasion and the ability of such infringements to combat it.

If tax evasion is considered to be a serious crime worthy of extensive international cooperation, and the CRS is deemed effective in detecting and preventing tax crimes, then the potential harm and costs posed by the CRS may be accepted in furtherance of this aim. However, in this respect, if every jurisdiction signs up to, implements, and enforces the CRS correctly, there should, in theory, be little need for tax evasion to be a predicate offence to laundering,[121] at least for the purposes of the reporting obligation. The primary advantage in retaining both financial intelligence frameworks is that SARs concerning tax evasion will facilitate enforcement by showing authorities where to look in the mass of data generated by the CRS. Similarly, if the CRS is considered too costly in human and financial terms, it may need to be abolished. Here, if all jurisdictions prescribed tax evasion

116 *Ibid.* Art.30(9).
117 HMRC (fn 95).
118 *Ibid.*
119 HM Revenue & Customs, 'The International Tax Compliance (United States of America) Regulations 2013' (Impact Note, August 2013).
120 *Ibid.*
121 Alldridge, P., *What Went Wrong with Money Laundering Law?* (fn 40) 71.

as a predicate offence to laundering, SARs would be made whenever tax offences are suspected, providing valuable intelligence to national authorities. Although this arrangement would not catch as many instances of tax evasion as the CRS, infringements of privacy and data protection are more likely to be proportionate when there is at least a suspicion that an offence has been committed.[122] However, this arrangement would necessitate a return to the former international tax standard, the exchange of information on request, so that authorities may follow up SARs by obtaining further information. This could potentially be coupled with a more restricted form of automatic exchange, as in the past.

Conclusion

Both the CRS and the financial intelligence provisions of the AML framework are innovative techniques that are likely to be successful in preventing and detecting tax crimes. However, both measures have the potential to affect the rights of individuals by infringing on privacy and data protection norms. In addition, both measures have and will continue to generate significant costs for financial institutions. The FATF and OECD initiatives have developed in parallel to one another, in response to external events, without consideration of the proportionality of retaining both systems of obtaining information in tax cases. Careful consideration needs to be paid to the costs and benefits of retaining both financial intelligence mechanisms, both at a national and international level. A balance must be sought between the public interest in fighting serious crimes, such as tax evasion and personal interests.

122 Here, the limitation on the right to privacy and data protection is more likely to be 'limited to what is strictly necessary' Case C-362/14, para. 93.

3 Cooperation between financial intelligence units in the EU

Challenges for the rights to privacy and data protection

Foivi Mouzakiti

Introduction

> Alan, a European resident, helped his brother by exchanging various currencies in differing amounts at a financial institution. His brother managed a company in a neighbouring country, which operated both a photocopying business and a foreign exchange office. . . . However, the scale of the currency transactions and the fact that the funds were being brought across the border unnecessarily raised the suspicions of the bank clerk. He reported his concerns to his senior management who decided to disclose to the national FIU. After the FIU had received the disclosure from the financial institution, inquiries against the national intelligence database seemed to show that, for both Alan and his brother, no negative intelligence was registered. Nevertheless, by exchanging intelligence with foreign FIUs the national FIU determined that the two brothers were the targets of an investigation for illegal drug trafficking in other European countries.[1]

Long story short, Alan (a courier for a criminal organisation) was convicted for money laundering. This passage, for all its simplicity, illustrates how – and why – Financial Intelligence Units (FIUs) cooperate with each other.

The emergence of FIUs was triggered by the establishment of the anti-money laundering regime in the European Union (EU), a regime that called for some institutional machinery[2] that would administer the surveillance of money movements at the national level.[3] Partly because of the preventive nature of this regime and partly because of the lack of EU competence in criminal matters at

1 Egmont Group of Financial Intelligence Units, 'FIUs in Action: 100 Cases from the Egmont Group' (<http://www.jfiu.gov.hk/info/doc/21-100casesgb.pdf>, 2000).

2 Bowling, B. and Sheptycki, J., *Global Policing* (Sage, 2012) 69–70.

3 Amicelle, A. and Favarel-Garrigues, G., 'Financial surveillance: Who cares?' (2012) 5(1) *Journal of Cultural Economy*, 105; Halliday, T., Levi, M. and Reuter, P. 'Global surveillance of dirty money: Assessing assessments of regimes to control money-laundering and combat the financing of terrorism' (Center on Law and Globalization <http://orca.cf.ac.uk/88168/1/Report_Global%20Surveillance%20of%20Dirty%20Money%201.30.2014.pdf>, 30 January 2014).

the time,[4] this task was not assigned to the 'traditional' policing sector.[5] Instead, special agencies (housed under the umbrella of larger organisations) were set up and tailored to the task.[6] These 'new policing' institutions spread rapidly throughout the EU after the adoption of the First Anti-Money Laundering Directive and became known as FIUs.[7] In partnership with the reporting entities, which provided them with information on potentially suspicious transactions,[8] FIUs became the intelligence hubs nestled between the reporting and law enforcement sectors.[9] They are responsible for receiving, analysing, and possibly disseminating this information to their counterparts in the EU and beyond – and to a wide range of law enforcement authorities for further action.[10] In support of these tasks, they enjoy the right to access a series of financial, administrative, and law enforcement databases.[11]

FIUs have come a long way since the First Anti-Money Laundering Directive. Beginning their journey as 'authorities responsible for combating money laundering,'[12] they emerged from anti-money laundering legislation more akin to intelligence agencies, furnished with extensive information-gathering (and information-sharing) powers. This development, however, did not happen in one fell swoop. For the most part, the EU legislator was reluctant to put forward detailed provisions on FIUs, leaving it to the Member States to structure them as they saw fit – both in substantive and institutional terms. As a result, FIUs in the EU come in different shapes and sizes; a blend of administrative, police, judicial

4 European Commission, *First Report on the Implementation of the Money Laundering Directive (91/308/EEC) to be Submitted to the European Parliament and to the Council* (COM (95) 54 final) 13–14, 16–17.

5 Levi, M. and Maguire, M., 'Something old, something new; something not entirely blue: Uneven and shifting modes of crime control' in Newburn, T. and Peay, J. (eds.), *Policing: Politics, Culture and Control* (Hart Publishing, 2012), 195.

6 Vervaele, J.A.E., 'Surveillance and criminal investigation: Blurring of thresholds and boundaries in the criminal justice system?' in Gutwirth, S., Leenes, R., and De Hert, P. (eds.), *Reloading Data Protection* (Springer, 2013).

7 Mitsilegas, V., 'New forms of transnational policing: The emergence of financial intelligence units in the European Union and the challenges for human rights: Part 1' (1999) 3(2) *Journal of Money Laundering Control* 147.

8 Favarel-Garrigues, G., Godefroy, T. and Lascoumes, P., 'Reluctant partners?: Banks in the fight against money laundering and terrorism financing in France' (2011) 42(2) *Security Dialogue* 179.

9 De Goede, M., 'The chain of security' (2017) 44(1) *Review of International Studies* 24.

10 Article 32(3) of Directive (EU) 2015/849 of the European Parliament and of the Council of May 20, 2015, on the prevention of the use of the financial system for the purposes of money laundering or terrorist financing, amending Regulation (EU) No 648/2012 of the European Parliament and of the Council, and repealing Directive 2005/60/EC of the European Parliament and of the Council and Commission Directive 2006/70/EC OJ L 141/73 – hereafter, 'Fourth AML Directive.'

11 Fourth AML Directive, art.32(4).

12 Council Directive 91/308/EEC of June 10, 1991, on Prevention of the Use of the Financial System for the Purpose of Money Laundering, art.6.

and even 'hybrid' authorities, networked under a common mandate, make up the EU's FIU structure.[13]

This chapter deals with FIU cooperation within the EU. As we shall see, the EU legal framework on FIU cooperation has developed spasmodically, propelled by international money laundering standards or (more recently) by counter-terrorism policies. The result is a fragmented and difficult to navigate framework but most importantly – and this forms the key argument of this chapter – one that raises significant challenges for the rights to privacy and data protection. FIUs feature prominently in the security agendas of the EU,[14] and plans to further enhance their interconnectedness and powers are underway.[15] The impact of their information processing powers on the rights to privacy and data protection is worrisome, not least because, as the following sections demonstrate, there is a prevailing uncertainty over the data protection safeguards applicable to their activities.

FIU cooperation – unravelling the EU legal framework

In today's global economy, traces of financial transactions are scattered across multiple jurisdictions. Therefore, in order to 'follow the money,' information must cross borders. To use Alan's example, had the national FIU not been able to obtain information from another Member State's FIU, it would probably have concluded that Alan is a law abiding citizen. During the early years of the

13 For an extensive overview of the different FIU models in the EU, see EU FIUs Platform, 'Mapping Exercise and Gap Analysis on FIUs' Powers and Obstacles for Obtaining and Exchanging Information' (<https://ec.europa.eu/transparency/regexpert/index.cfm?do=groupDetail.groupDetailDoc&id=33583&no=2>, 15 December 2016) 5–7 (hereafter referred to as 'Mapping Exercise'). However, the fact that FIUs belong in the same model does not mean that they don't have significant operational differences. For a criticism of this categorization, see Amicelle, A. and Chaudieu, K., 'In search of transnational financial intelligence: Questioning cooperation between financial intelligence units' in King, C., Walker, C., and Gurulé, J. (eds.), *The Palgrave Handbook of Criminal and Terrorism Financing Law* (Palgrave MacMillan, 2018) 649.

14 European Commission, *Communication From the Commission to the European Parliament, the Council, the European Economic and Social Committee and the Committee of the Regions – The European Agenda on Security* (COM/2015/ 185 final) 10, 13–14 and 17; European Commission, *Communication from the Commission to the European Parliament and the Council on an Action Plan for Strengthening the Fight against Terrorist Financing* (COM/2016/50 final) 7, 9.

15 Directive (EU) 2019/1153 of the European Parliament and of the Council of June 20, 2019, laying down rules facilitating the use of financial and other information for the prevention, detection, investigation, or prosecution of certain criminal offences and repealing Council Decision 2000/642/JHA PE/64/2019/REV/1. For legislative history, see European Commission, *On Improving Cooperation between EU Financial Intelligence Units* (SWD (2017) 275 final); European Commission, *Fourteenth Progress Report towards an Effective and Genuine Security Union* (COM/2018/ 211 final) 3; European Commission, Proposal for a Directive of the European Parliament and of the Council laying down rules facilitating the use of financial and other information for the prevention, detection, investigation or prosecution of certain criminal offences and repealing Council Decision 2000/642/JHA (COM/2018/213 final).

anti-money laundering regime, however, FIU cooperation was far from effortless. The establishment of different FIU models throughout the EU complicated information exchange between them; for instance, police FIUs could not exchange information with administrative FIUs and vice versa.[16] Yet, the first two anti-money laundering Directives did not address FIU cooperation.

Whilst the EU legislator was silent, international standard setters, such as the Financial Action Task Force (FATF) and the Egmont Group (the transgovernmental network of 159 FIUs), were not. Under the influence of these bodies, cooperation between EU FIUs was dealt with in 2000 through a third pillar council decision,[17] which largely reflected the Egmont Group's principles of information exchange[18] and called for FIU cooperation regardless of the differences in their institutional model.[19] This provided the impetus[20] for the creation of the FIU.net, a decentralised computer network that facilitates the exchange of information between FIUs in the EU to this day.[21] In the words of Udo Kroon, chief information officer of FIU.net,

> It shapes a virtual information cloud between the FIUs and their (over 550) distributed government, commercial and public information sources and it enables real time analysis of distributed dynamic information and knowledge otherwise legally, organisationally, technically, and/or financially impossible to achieve.[22]

16 European Commission, *Second Commission Report to the European Parliament and the Council on the Implementation of the Anti-Money Laundering Directive* (COM /1998/ 401 final) 14–15.

17 Council decision of October 17, 2000, concerning arrangements for cooperation between financial intelligence units of the Member States in respect of exchanging information (2000/642/JHA) OJ L 271/4.

18 European Commission, On the Implementation of the Council Decision of October 17, 2000, concerning arrangements for cooperation between Financial Intelligence Units of the Member States in respect of exchanging information (2000/642/JHA) COM (2007) 827 final at 1. See also Financial Action Task Force (FATF) *The Forty Recommendations*' (FATF, 1996) Recommendation 32. For the latest version of the principles, see Egmont Group, Principles of Information Exchange between FIUs (<https://egmontgroup.org/en/filedepot_download/1658/37>, 2013).

19 See European Council, 'Tampere European Council 15 and 16 October 1999–Presidency Conclusions' (<http://www.europarl.europa.eu/summits/tam_en.htm>) para. 54.

20 Council of the EU, Document 12831/01 (Presse 364, 16.10.2001) para. 14. See also Council of the EU, 'Information on the FIU.NET Project' Document 9459/02 (31 May 2002); Article 7 of Council Decision 2000/642/JHA.

21 The FIU.net was created following an initiative of the Dutch FIU, alongside the FIUs of France, Italy, Luxembourg, and the United Kingdom. In 2003, the European Commission decided to finance the Netherlands Justice Ministry for the further development of the FIU.net. See European Commission, *On the Prevention of and Fight against Organised Crime in the Financial Sector* (COM (2004) 262 final) para. 2.5. For more information on the FIU.net, see Europol, 'Financial Intelligence Units – FIU.net' (<http://www.europol.europa.eu/about-europol/financial-intelligence-units-fiu-net>).

22 Kroon, U., 'Ma 3 Tch: Privacy and Knowledge: "Dynamic Networked Collective Intelligence"' in Hu, X. et al. (eds.), *2013 IEEE International Conference on Big Data – Workshop 3: Workshop on Big Data and Society* (IEEE, 2013), 23, 24.

The aforementioned Council Decision, however, (which is still in force) only partially covers EU FIUs cooperation. It was adopted before the anti-money laundering framework was reformed to include counter-terrorist financing[23] and therefore does not cover information exchanges for those purposes. Although the Commission acknowledged this gap and the 'need to consider whether to bring provisions of the Decision up-to-date covering the area of counter-terrorism financing,'[24] it did not take any steps to that effect.

The Third Anti-Money Laundering Directive (the first to cover terrorist financing) strongly encouraged,[25] but did not regulate, FIU cooperation. The only relevant provision was Article 38, which merely called upon the Commission to facilitate the coordination efforts of FIUs.[26] This generic approach was similar to the FATF's then-Recommendation 31, which simply called on countries to ensure that their FIUs have effective mechanisms of cooperation in place.[27] In the decade that followed, however, it became apparent that this approach prevented FIUs from effectively exchanging information.[28] So, in response to repeated calls at the EU level[29] and propelled by the FATF's revised Recommendations of 2012, which expanded the FIU-related provisions significantly,[30] the

23 Zagaris, B., 'The merging of the anti-money laundering and counter-terrorism financial enforcement regimes after September 11, 2001' (2004) 22(1) *Berkeley Journal of International Law* 123.

24 European Commission, *On the Implementation of the Council Decision of 17 October 2000 Concerning Arrangements for Cooperation between Financial Intelligence Units of the Member States in Respect of Exchanging Information (2000/642/JHA)* (COM/2007/827 final) 9.

25 Recital 40 of Directive 2005/60/EC of the European Parliament and of the Council on the Prevention of the Use of the Financial System for the Purpose of Money Laundering and Terrorist Financing – hereafter 'the Third AML Directive.'

26 Third AML Directive, art.38.

27 See Financial Action Task Force, *The Forty Recommendations* (FATF, 2003) Recommendation 31.

28 European Commission, *Report from the Commission to the European Parliament and the Council on the Application of Directive 2005/60/EC on the Prevention of the Use of the Financial System for the Purpose of Money Laundering and Terrorist Financing* (COM/2012/168 final) 11. The advocate general's remarks in the *Jyske Bank Gibraltar* case are particularly relevant in that regard: Case C-212/11, *Jyske Bank Gibraltar Ltd* v. *Administración del Estado*, Judgment of the Court of Justice (Third Chamber) [2013] ECLI:EU:C:2013:270, Opinion of AG Bot, paras 63–70. See further, Incalza, T., 'National anti-money laundering legislation in a unified Europe: Jyske' (2014) 51(6) *Common Market Law Review* 1829.

29 *Ibid.*, 11. See also European Council, *The Stockholm Programme: An Open and Secure Europe Serving and Protecting Citizens* (2010/ C 115/01) 23; European Parliament, *Report on Organised Crime, Corruption and Money Laundering: Recommendations on Action and Initiatives to be Taken (Final Report)* (2013/2107(INI)) paras 99–100; Commission, Staff Working Document, *Impact Assessment Accompanying the Document Proposal for a Directive of the European Parliament and of the Council on the Prevention of the Use of the Financial System for the Purpose of Money Laundering, Including Terrorist Financing and Proposal for a Regulation of the European Parliament and of the Council on Information Accompanying Transfers of Funds* (SWD/2013/ 021 final) 101–102.

30 See FATF, *Interpretive Note to Recommendation 29 (Financial Intelligence Units* (FATF, 2013).

Fourth Anti-Money Laundering Directive broke the long-standing silence over FIU cooperation.

Similarly to the 2000 Council Decision, the Fourth AML Directive mandates FIU cooperation 'to the greatest extent possible' – institutional model aside.[31] More specifically, it calls on Member States to ensure that their FIUs exchange any information relevant to money laundering or terrorist financing 'spontaneously or upon request . . . even if the type of predicate offences that may be involved is not identified at the time of the exchange.'[32] Given that tax crimes are now explicitly included in the list of predicate offences, the Directive stipulates that the existence of different national definitions of tax crimes should not hinder the exchange of information between FIUs.[33] When responding to requests from foreign counterparts, FIUs are now empowered to employ all the domestic powers available to them for obtaining and analysing information.[34] In the United Kingdom, for instance, the Criminal Finances Act 2017, sections 12 and 37, created a new information-gathering power for the FIU: the 'further information order.' This power enables the UK FIU to apply to the court for an order that will require the regulated sector to provide information relating to a suspicious activity report.[35] Further, in the spirit of supporting FIU cooperation, it may do the same on behalf of a foreign FIU.[36] Another novelty of the Directive is the requirement to forward suspicious transaction reports (STRs) that concern another Member State to the FIU of that Member State.[37] It is too early to tell to what extent FIUs will apply this (rather open-ended) provision in practice, but it is certain that the network of EU FIUs is becoming more and more interconnected.

This observation is further supported by the fact that the Fourth AML Directive formally recognised the EU FIUs Platform,[38] an informal network of EU FIUs that works to promote FIU cooperation.[39] It is also the first Directive to

31 Fourth AML Directive, art.52.

32 Fourth AML Directive, art.53(1). See also Böszörmenyi, J. and Schweighofer, E., 'A review of tools to comply with the fourth EU anti-money laundering directive' (2015) 29(1) *International Review of Law, Computers & Technology* 63, 69–71.

33 Fourth AML Directive, art.57. See also the study conducted for the PANA Committee of the European Parliament: Scherrer, A., Amicelle, A., Berg, J., and Chaudieu, K., *Fighting Tax Crimes: Cooperation between Financial Intelligence Units* (Ex-Post Impact Assessment Unit, 2017).

34 Fourth AML Directive, art.53(2).

35 POCA 2002, s. 339ZH and Terrorism Act 2000, s. 22B as amended by the Criminal Finances Act 2017. See also Home Office, *Criminal Finances Act: Further Information Orders* (Circular 010/2018).

36 *Ibid.*

37 Fourth AML Directive, art.53(1). See also EU FIUs Platform, 'Mapping Exercise' (fn 13) 171–175.

38 Fourth AML Directive, Recital 55.

39 Fourth AML Directive, art.51. See also European Commission, 'Register of Commission Expert Groups and Other Similar Entities-EU FIUs Platform' (<http://ec.europa.eu/transparency/regexpert/index.cfm?do=groupDetail.groupDetail&groupID=3251>, 28 October 2014).

refer to the FIU.net[40] by calling on Member States to ensure that their FIUs cooperate in the application of technologies that allow them to 'match their data with that of other FIUs in an anonymous way.'[41] This provision is tailored to reflect the (privacy by design) 'Ma3tch'[42] technology that was adopted by the FIU.net in 2012 and enables FIUs to anonymously cross-check and exchange information online.[43]

These forms of FIU cooperation are not totally unrestrained. First of all, information between EU FIUs must be shared only for the purposes of processing or analysis by the FIU, a rule that ensures compliance with the data protection principle of purpose limitation.[44] Pursuant to that principle, personal data may only be collected for specified, explicit, and legitimate purposes and not further processed in a manner which is incompatible with those purposes.[45] Second, an FIU may refuse to exchange information with an EU counterpart but only in exceptional circumstances – that is, when the exchange could be contrary to fundamental principles of its national law.[46] Third, the transmitting FIU may impose restrictions and conditions for the use of the information it provides.[47] Finally, if an EU FIU wishes to share the information it received from another EU FIU with, say, a law enforcement authority, it has to obtain the prior consent of the

40 In January of 2016, the FIU.net was embedded in Europol. See Europol, 'Financial Intelligence Units – FIU.net – Coordinated Crimes Need a Coordinated Response' (<http://www.europol.europa.eu/about-europol/financial-intelligence-units-fiu-net>).

41 Fourth AML Directive, arts.53(1) and 56(2).

42 The 'a^3' in 'Ma^{3}tch' stand for 'autonomous anonymous analysis.' The FIU.net 'enables the completely confidential cross-checking of personal data so as to identify patterns that can be further examined by means of detailed information exchanges. If requests are made involving specific names, the 'Case Match' function can identify matches in the files of all participating FIUs. The 'Cross-Match' function can compare entire databases and find common names. The data made available for matching are encrypted using hashing mechanisms that guarantee absolute irreversibility and hence complete confidentiality. Matching is anonymous and only later is it traced to the underlying name. The instrument is said to be vital for finding foreign connections with regard to persons whose foreign activities were not previously known. See Banca d' Italia, 'Financial Intelligence Unit for Italy,' *Annual Report for 2014* (<https://www.bancaditalia.it/pubblicazioni/relazione-annuale/2014/index.html>, 2015) 86.

43 Balboni, P., Kroon, U., and Macenaite, M., 'Data protection and data security by design applied to financial intelligence' in Reimer, H., Pohlmann, N., and Schneider, W. (eds.), *ISSE 2013 Securing Electronic Business Processes* (Springer, 2013) 73.

44 Fourth AML Directive, arts.53, 54, 55. Article 5(1)(b) of Regulation (EU) 2016/679 of the European Parliament and of the Council of 27 April 2016 on the protection of natural persons with regard to the processing of personal data and on the free movement of such data, and repealing Directive 95/46/EC (GDPR), art.8(2) of the Charter of Fundamental Rights. See also Egmont Group of Financial Intelligence Units, 'Principles for Information Exchange between Financial Intelligence Units' (<https://egmontgroup.org/en/filedepot_download/1658/37>, 28 October 2013).

45 Article 29 Working Party, *Opinion 03/2013 on Purpose Limitation* (00569/13/EN WP 203, 2 April 2013).

46 Fourth AML Directive, art.53(3).

47 Fourth AML Directive, art.54.

transmitting FIU.[48] Consent, however, may be refused in limited circumstances. A refusal is only justified if the dissemination would a) fall beyond the scope of application of its anti-money laundering and counter-terrorist financing provisions, b) could lead to impairment of a criminal investigation, c) would be clearly disproportionate to the legitimate interests of a natural or legal person or the Member State of the requested FIU, or d) would otherwise not be in accordance with fundamental principles of national law of that Member State.[49]

Reflecting on the foregoing developments, it becomes clear that the EU legislator envisages a model of FIU cooperation underpinned by maximum information exchange.[50] As discussed in the following section, however, a passing reference to the 'joint analysis' of transnational cases suggests a model that goes well beyond mere information exchange.[51]

Just a few months after the adoption of the Fourth AML Directive in 2015, a wave of renewed calls for greater FIU powers and cooperation emerged. They were triggered by serious terrorist attacks mainly in France and Germany, which brought terrorist financing to the forefront of the EU's security agenda. As a result, the council called on the commission to present proposals to 'strengthen, harmonise and improve the powers of, and the cooperation between Financial Intelligence Units (FIU's), notably through the proper embedment of the FIU. net network for information exchange in Europol.'[52] FIUs also featured prominently in the commission's subsequent Action Plan against terrorist financing,[53] so it should not come as a surprise that the commission tabled a proposal to amend the Fourth AML Directive in 2016.[54] Cooperation between FIUs was identified as one of the key areas for improvement.[55] But what was it that needed improvement?

As the preceding analysis demonstrated, little seems to stand in the way of information exchange between FIUs, but, according to FIU officials, this is not the case. In fact, they have repeatedly suggested that the differences in the

48 Fourth AML Directive, art.55(1).

49 Fourth AML Directive, art.55(2).

50 Mitsilegas, V. and Vavoula, N., 'The evolving EU anti-money laundering regime: Challenges for fundamental rights and the rule of law' (2016) 23(2) *Maastricht Journal of European and Comparative Law* 261.

51 Fourth AML Directive, art.51.

52 Council of the EU, *Outcome of the Council Meeting, 3432nd Council Meeting, Justice and Home Affairs* (Document 14382/15, Brussels, 20 November 2015) 6.

53 European Commission (COM/2016/50 final) (fn 14).

54 *Ibid.* at 7; European Commission, *Proposal for a Directive of the European Parliament and of the Council amending Directive (EU) 2015/849 on the Prevention of the Use of the Financial System for the Purposes of Money Laundering or Terrorist Financing and Amending Directive 2009/101/EC* (COM/2016/ 450 final).

55 European Commission – Staff Working Document, *Impact Assessment Accompanying the Document Proposal for a Directive of the European Parliament and the Council amending Directive (EU) 2015/849 on the Prevention of the Use of the Financial System for the Purposes of Money Laundering or Terrorist Financing and Amending Directive 2009/101/EC* (SWD (2016) 223 final) 8.

national definitions of predicate offences impede their cooperation.[56] In order to rectify this situation, the 2018 Fifth Anti-Money Laundering Directive[57] clarifies that such differences should not hinder the exchange (and use) of information between FIUs or its distribution to law enforcement.[58]

But the story of FIU cooperation does not end here. Whilst these developments were unfolding, the EU FIUs Platform was conducting a study of the obstacles to FIUs' access to, and exchange of, information.[59] In response, in April 2018, the Commission published yet another proposal which aims to repeal the (redundant) 2000 Council Decision and to facilitate (amongst other things) FIU cooperation.[60] This proposal was adopted under Article 87(2) of the Treaty on the Functioning of the European Union, which enables the EU to put forward measures regarding the collection, storage, and exchange of information and common investigative techniques in relation to the detection of serious forms of organised crime, with the aim of establishing police cooperation between the Member States' competent authorities in relation to the prevention, detection, and investigation of criminal offences. The Commission considers this legal basis to be appropriate, despite the fact that not all Member States have given police status to their FIUs.[61] As far as content is concerned, the proposal has a strong focus on efficiency and aims to complement the existing provisions on FIU cooperation; to that end, it sets time limits for the exchange of information between FIUs.[62] It also unfolds a series of data protection provisions, especially in relation to sensitive information, the maintenance of records of information exchanges, and the restriction of data subjects' access rights.[63]

Whilst it remains to be seen how EU FIUs will apply these new and far-reaching cooperation tools, a pattern starts to emerge whereby the EU legislator has equipped FIUs with a toolkit that enables them to 'integrate' their core functions. They may be individual agencies, but the plan is to extend their connectivity so as to be able, with the support of the latest technology (FIU.net and 'Ma^{3}tch'), to operate as a single virtual entity.

Is this objective desirable? The response to this question depends, at least partially, on whether the rights to privacy and data protection, as guaranteed by Articles 7

56 European Commission (SWD (2017) 275 final) (fn 15) 10.

57 Directive (EU) 2018/843 of the European Parliament and of the Council of May 30, 2018, amending Directive (EU) 2015/849 on the prevention of the use of the financial system for the purposes of money laundering or terrorist financing and amending Directives 2009/138/EC and 2013/36/EU – hereafter, the 'Fifth AML Directive.'

58 Fifth AML Directive, Recital 18, art.1(33), (35) and (36).

59 EU FIUs Platform, 'Mapping exercise' (fn 13).

60 European Commission (COM/2018/213 final) (fn 15).

61 European Commission – Staff Working Document, *Impact Assessment Accompanying the Proposal for a for a Directive of the European Parliament and of the Council Laying Down Rules Facilitating the Use of Financial and Other Information for the Prevention, Detection, Investigation or Prosecution of Certain Criminal Offences and Repealing Council Decision 2000/642/JHA* (SWD (2018) 115 final) 24.

62 *Ibid.*, art.9(2).

63 *Ibid.*, Chapter V.

and 8 of the Charter of Fundamental Rights of the EU (and the data protection framework), are fully safeguarded. As we shall see in the following section, so long as FIUs continue to operate outside a clear legal framework and data protection safeguards, their increasing interconnectedness will pose risks for those rights.

FIU cooperation – at what cost for the rights to privacy and data protection?

It is not, of course, possible to carry out here an exhaustive assessment of the privacy and data protection challenges that emerge out of the cooperation between EU FIUs. Instead, this section highlights the areas that are cause for concern.

The first point of concern arises from the fact that FIUs in the EU reflect different institutional models. In the case of administrative (and sometimes hybrid) FIUs, the agency that receives STRs is kept separate from the agency that investigates on the basis of these reports (hence their comparison to a 'buffer').[64] This separation sends the message that the suspicious transactions reporting system is not directly linked to criminal investigations and proceedings.[65] This institutional setting is particularly beneficial for individuals, as it better safeguards the rights to privacy and data protection.[66] This is because the information included in a STRs is governed by different sets of data protection safeguards during the analysis (by the FIU) and investigation (by, say, law enforcement) stages, respectively;[67] after all, the purpose of the analytical stage is to determine if a transaction merits further investigation. If the reported transaction is declared suspect by the FIU, the information is from then on governed by a separate data protection regime, which allows the FIU to share it with a series of national authorities in the sphere of law enforcement and beyond.[68] By contrast, some police FIUs[69]

64 However, the FIU of Cyprus, for instance (which is located in the Attorney General's Office but classifies itself as a hybrid FIU), does not adhere to this logic. Though an investigation is generally only initiated after the conclusion of the analysis stage, the practices of the Cypriot FIU reveals that such separation does not always exist; in certain instances, the two functions may be undertaken simultaneously, or investigatory tools may be employed during the analysis stage. See Council of Europe, Moneyval, *Anti – Money Laundering and Combatting the Financing of Terrorism, Report on Fourth Assessment Visit of Cyprus* (2011) 52.

65 Mitsilegas and Vavoula (fn 50).

66 *Ibid.*

67 De Goede (fn 9) 12–13.

68 The Dutch FIU, for instance, receives 'unusual transaction reports' (UTR), which are stored in the UTR database. It then proceeds to analyse them, and only those who are declared 'suspicious transaction reports' are included in the STR database, which is accessible to law enforcement. The data included in the UTR database are classified as 'personal data,' whereas those in the STR database are classified as 'police data' and are governed by a different legal framework. See FATF, *Anti-Money Laundering and Counter-Terrorist Financing Measures: Mutual Evaluation Report of the Netherlands* (25 February 2011) 91–95.

69 Similar observations apply to some judicial FIUs: EU FIUs Platform, 'Mapping Exercise' (fn 13) 123; FATF, *Anti-Money Laundering and Counter-Terrorist Financing Measures: Mutual Evaluation Report of Luxembourg, Executive Summary* (19 February 2010) 7.

do not maintain a strict separation between the analysis of STRs and criminal investigations.[70] In Austria, for instance, STRs are not pre-sorted (to determine whether the suspicion is, indeed, substantiated), but the full range of investigative powers available to law enforcement authorities may be employed in response to each and every report.[71] The merging of the two activities not only is in contrast to the Fourth AML Directive (investigation is not amongst the FIU functions)[72] but also against the data protection principle of purpose limitation.[73] Thus, a strong argument can be made that, by calling upon FIUs to 'cooperate with each other to the greatest extent possible, regardless of their organisational status,'[74] the EU legislator undermines the privacy and data protection safeguards guaranteed by the establishment of an administrative FIU since the latter is called upon to routinely share personal data that is kept outside the criminal justice system with EU FIUs that do not maintain the same strict separation.

The further use and dissemination of the transmitted information is also problematic.[75] In the previous section, it was revealed that if the receiving EU FIU wishes to share information received from another FIU with, say, a local police authority, it needs to obtain the prior consent of the providing FIU.[76] Yet, in a recent meeting of the EU FIUs Platform, 'two FIUs indicated a challenge within their national legislation that the prosecutors are not bound by the FIU prior consent rules.'[77] Therefore, a contradiction arises between the EU provisions on FIU cooperation and some national laws, a contradiction that may give rise to the use of information for purposes other than those authorised by the providing FIU (such as evidentiary purposes). In these circumstances, the data protection principle of purpose limitation is, once again, at stake. This observation leads to another interesting point – the potential loss of control of the exchanged information. How can an FIU that disseminates information to its EU counterpart be realistically expected to ensure that the information's subsequent uses take place within the parameters of its authorisation? The EU legislator has not touched upon this issue, but it raises a real practical problem given the large amounts of data exchanged between FIUs.[78]

70 EU FIUs Platform, 'Mapping Exercise' (fn 13) 8, 116.

71 FATF, *Anti-Money Laundering and Counter-Terrorist Financing Measures: Mutual Evaluation Report of Austria* (26 June 2009) 73.

72 Fourth AML Directive, art.32(3).

73 General Data Protection Regulation, art.5(1)(b); art.8(2) of the Charter of Fundamental Rights.

74 Fourth AML Directive, art.52.

75 Article 29 Working Party, *Opinion 14/2011 on Data Protection Issues Related to Money Laundering and Terrorist Financing* (01008/2011/EN WP186, 13 June 2011), Annex at 17.

76 Fourth AML Directive, art.55(1). Refusal of prior consent is possible under art.55(2).

77 EU FIUs Platform, '35th Meeting of the EU FIUs Platform' (<https://ec.europa.eu/transparency/regexpert/index.cfm?do=groupDetail.groupMeetingDoc&docid=14661>, 2018) para. 9.

78 This problem has been acknowledged by the Commission: European Commission (SWD (2017) 275 final) (fn 15) 6. See also Joined Cases C-293/12 and C-594/12 *Digital Rights Ireland Ltd v. Ireland* (08.04.2014) para. 60–62.

Moving on, and as noted earlier, Article 53(1) of the Fourth Directive requires EU FIUs to promptly forward a STR that concerns another Member State to the FIU of that Member State. This provision was introduced to address the conundrum whereby certain companies, established in one Member State but operating under the freedom to provide services, had to file a report on suspicious transactions to the FIU of the Member State of their establishment, even when the suspicious transaction took place in a different Member State. For instance, Amazon is registered in Luxembourg but operates throughout the EU. If Amazon becomes aware of a suspicious transaction, say, in Germany, it still has to file the STR with Luxembourg's FIU.[79] But Luxembourg's FIU cannot effectively investigate suspicious transactions taking place in Germany.[80] Article 53(1) found a way around this, by requiring the FIU of Luxembourg to share the STR with the German FIU. This provision applies irrespective of whether the STR involves (in the FIU's opinion) substantiated suspicion or not; the mere fact that there is a link to another Member State is enough to trigger the obligation to share it. Clearly, this requirement is underpinned by a 'data sharing by default' attitude which begs the question whether the routine transfer of information that involves unsubstantiated suspicion to another EU FIU constitutes a necessary and proportionate interference with the rights to privacy and data protection.[81]

The possibility for 'joint analysis' amongst EU FIUs presents further challenges. The Fifth AML Directive cursorily mentions 'joint analysis,'[82] but its far-reaching potential has been nonetheless noticed by FIUs. In fact, they have been working intensely, under the umbrella of the EU FIUs Platform, to develop 'new ways for FIUs to work together to have a common output at the end – with actionable outcome.'[83] Thus, the platform has been coordinating pilot projects on joint analysis as a kind of a trial run, aiming to uncover legal and operational obstacles to joint analysis and to search for solutions. The first such project, led by the FIU-the Netherlands, focused on the joint analysis of financial

79 EU FIUs Platform, '26th Meeting of the EU FIUs Platform' (<https://ec.europa.eu/transparency/regexpert/index.cfm?do=groupDetail.groupDetailDoc&id=22161&no=1>, 2015) para. 3.

80 EU FIUs Platform, 'Mapping Exercise' (fn 13) 172 and '27th Meeting of the EU FIUs Platform' (<https://ec.europa.eu/transparency/regexpert/index.cfm?do=groupDetail.groupDetailDoc&id=24950&no=2>, January 2016) para. 5.

81 According to art.52(1) of the Charter of Fundamental Rights, any limitation on the exercise of the rights and freedoms laid down by the Charter must be provided for by law, respect their essence and, subject to the principle of proportionality, limitations may be made to those rights and freedoms only if they are necessary and genuinely meet objectives of general interest recognised by the Union or the need to protect the rights and freedoms of others. See also Joined Cases C-293/12 and C-594/12 *Digital Rights Ireland Ltd v. Ireland* (08.04.2014) para. 52.

82 Fourth AML Directive, art.51.

83 EU FIUs Platform, '29th Meeting of the EU FIUs Platform' (<https://ec.europa.eu/transparency/regexpert/index.cfm?do=groupDetail.groupDetailDoc&id=27186&no=1>, June 2016) para. 3.

flows related to EU-wide migration crimes.[84] The idea was to identify 'red flag indicators' of financial transactions relating to these crimes, which would serve as a basis for reporting suspicious activities to the competent authorities. The FIU.net comes into play here; the participating FIUs created 'Ma3tch' filters, which contained 2,000 subjects. The results of the project revealed several legal, IT, and operational obstacles. Leaving the practical issues aside, the participating FIUs notably observed that some national legal frameworks did not allow FIUs to create 'Ma3tch' filters by using law enforcement and tax data (alongside FIU data).[85] But, according to the platform, cross-matching solely between FIU data is not enough for joint analysis to be effective.[86] But whilst FIUs are looking to 'open up databases as much as possible,'[87] the Fifth AML Directive provides no guidance as to what constitutes joint analysis, what type of data can be shared for those purposes, and under what data protection safeguards. These are important questions for the EU legislator, not least because a lack of legal clarity is breeding ground for disproportionate data processing by FIUs that remain free to determine the answer to those questions themselves.

A final problem is that information exchanges between FIUs do not take place under a clear legal environment – and the same applies to the applicable data protection framework too. On the one hand, FIU cooperation is governed (simultaneously) by the Fifth AML Directive and by the 2000 Council Decision (terrorist financing excluded). On the other hand, the data protection framework applicable to EU FIUs remains uncertain.[88] Under the reformed EU data protection framework, the General Data Protection Regulation (GDPR) governs general data processing, but a different instrument, which replaced the Council Framework Decision 2008/977/JHA, governs law enforcement processing – the Data Protection Law Enforcement Directive ('the Directive').[89] So, which of the two instruments applies to the processing of data by FIUs? In short, the Member States can decide, in accordance with their legal framework. In the Commission's view, FIUs, as a public administration, are subject to the GDPR.[90] Still, in a recent meeting of the EU FIUs Platform, 'concerns were raised with regards to the applicability of the GDPR versus the Directive in general and more specifically

84 *Ibid.* at para. 2.
85 *Ibid.*, para. 3.
86 *Ibid.*
87 *Ibid.*
88 For an overview of the European Data Protection Supervisor's (EDPS) opinion on this issue, see Buttarelli, G., 'EDPS opinion on the proposal for the fourth anti-money laundering Directive,' (<https://edps.europa.eu/sites/edp/files/publication/13-07-04_money_laundering_en.pdf>, 4 July 2013).
89 Directive (EU) 2016/680 of the European Parliament and of the Council of April 27, 2016, on the protection of natural persons with regard to the processing of personal data by competent authorities for the purposes of the prevention, investigation, detection, or prosecution of criminal offences or the execution of criminal penalties, and on the free movement of such data, and repealing Council Framework Decision 2008/977/JHA OJ L 119/89.
90 EU FIUs Platform, '35th Meeting' (fn 77) para. 8.

to administrative FIUs.'[91] In fact, FIUs in the EU continue to be subject to different data protection frameworks, which in turn translates into uneven data protection safeguards. For instance, the UK FIU applies the GDPR, whereas the Luxembourg FIU applies the Directive.[92] This divergence will give rise to challenges for FIU cooperation, since the information exchanged between them will be protected in different ways. The question also arises whether it is lawful, from a privacy and data protection perspective, to require an EU FIU that maintains stricter data protection safeguards (for instance, short data retention periods) to provide STR information to an EU counterpart with lower safeguards in place.

Concluding remarks

This chapter has followed the evolution of the EU's legal framework on FIU cooperation. For the most part, the EU legislator refrained from introducing detailed provisions on FIUs, even more so when it came to the exchange of information between them. Eventually, however, the pressure for more effective and widespread sharing of financial information altered this laconic stance. The series of sporadic legislative interventions that followed aimed to facilitate FIU cooperation and, indeed, they did so. However, the existing patchwork of loosely defined transnational FIU functions raises several challenges for the rights to privacy and data protection.

Policymakers tend to treat information sharing amongst EU FIUs as an operational issue, but there is also a fundamental rights dimension to it which must not be overlooked. Highlighting this dimension is even more important at a time when FIUs are seeking to increase their engagement with IT tools, such as the FIU.net and the accompanying 'Ma3tch' tools, which automate part of their information-sharing functions, extend their capabilities,[93] and give them the opportunity 'to act as one, without the necessity to become one.'[94]

91 *Ibid.*, para. 8.

92 Interview with UK FIU (August 2018); Interview with Luxembourg FIU (January 2019).

93 Schweighofer, E., Heussler, V. and Kieseberg, P., 'Privacy by design data exchange between CSIRTs' in Schweighofer, E., Leitold, H., Mitrakas, A., and Rannenberg, K. (eds.), *Privacy Technologies and Policy* (Springer International Publishing, 2017) 104. They note that 'Ma3tch can also generate knowledge, recognise profiles, predict behaviour patterns, and (in the future) analyse social networks.

94 European Commission – Migration and Home Affairs, 'FIU.net: Empowering the FIUs and Partners in Their Cross-Border Cooperation' (<https://ec.europa.eu/home-affairs/financing/fundings/projects/HOME_2013_ISEC_FP_C1_4000005000_en>), where the FIU.net project is described as a platform 'for FIUs, that enables them to act as one, without the necessity to become one.'

4 Risk-based approach

Is it the answer to effective anti-money laundering compliance?

Gauri Sinha

Aims and introduction

The risk-based approach (RBA) is fundamental to anti-money laundering (AML) compliance in the United Kingdom and requires all parties in the fight against money laundering (including law enforcement, government departments, regulators, and industry) to focus on outputs. Such a focus should mean that AML resources are applied where they have the biggest impact and where the risk is the greatest.[1] Whilst the EU Fourth Money Laundering Directive[2] and the UK Money Laundering Regulations[3] place an increased emphasis on the RBA, this chapter argues that it is crucial to take a step back and assess the effectiveness of the approach. The objective of this chapter is to consider whether the RBA as currently implemented in the AML regime leads to more effective AML compliance. The chapter further argues that the RBA is both undefined and unguided. The arguments follow a dual path: first, the concept of 'risk' in the AML context is questioned. Second, the contradiction between how the legal requirements define the RBA and how the Financial Conduct Authority (FCA) seeks to implement it is analysed. Effectiveness in the context of applying the RBA would entail minimum wasted effort or expense on the part of regulated entities and maximum utilisation of suspicious activity reports on the part of law enforcement. This would also translate into a more proportionate AML regime.

Banks and financial institutions as primary AML compliance partners are the key focus of this chapter. The rationale for this focus is based on the numbers – between April 2017 and March 2018, banks accounted for over 80% of the 463,938

1 Financial Conduct Authority, 'Money Laundering and Terrorist Financing' (<http://www.fca.org.uk/firms/financial-crime/money-laundering-terrorist-financing>, 3 August 2015).

2 Council Directive 2015/849 on the prevention of the use of the financial system for the purposes of money laundering or terrorist financing, amending Regulation 648/2012 and repealing Directive 2005/60 and Commission Directive 2006/70 [2015] OJ L141/73 (4MLD). The 4MLD is transposed into national law by way of the 2017 Money Laundering Regulations.

3 Money Laundering, Terrorist Financing and Transfer of Funds (Information on the Payer) Regulations 2017, SI 2017/692.

suspicious activity reports (SARs) submitted to the National Crime Agency (NCA).[4] Adding together the percentages of SARs from all other types of credit or financial institutions brings this figure to 96.45%.[5] Overwhelmingly, the financial sector clearly bears the greatest burden of compliance. The NCA as the Financial Intelligence Unit and the FCA as the UK Financial Regulator are key players in the compliance regime and hence their relationship with banks and financial institutions will also be discussed.

The RBA: origin and definition

There is now a global AML regime that Member States have enacted following the recommendations of Financial Action Task Force (FATF),[6] as well as standards set out by the European Union (EU).[7] Prior to the RBA, there was a focus on complying with the rule-based approach. The rule-based approach set out clear criteria on what constituted a suspicious transaction – for example, a list of prohibited activities or specific transactions that required customer due diligence.[8]

The rule-based approach was quick to falter due to reasons that may now seem obvious. Rules were considered too prescriptive, which meant that there was no freedom left for regulated entities[9] to use their own initiative.[10] It also failed in the very objective of combatting the crime, as the money launderer was often one step ahead and devised new strategies to circumvent the rules. One such example is depositing sums of money just below the threshold that would require the reporting of that transaction, therefore avoiding the trigger to generate a suspicious transaction report.[11]

From the regulated entity's point of view, the rule-based approach encouraged a 'tick-box' exercise,[12] whereby if the rules had been applied, which was required equally in all instances, not much else needed to be done.[13] The rule-based AML

4 NCA, *Suspicious Activity Reports (SARs) Annual Report 2018* (2018).

5 *Ibid.*

6 FATF, *International Standards on Combatting Money Laundering and the Financing of Terrorism and Proliferation* (FATF/OECD, 2012). For further discussion of the global AML regime, see Bergstrom, M., 'The global AML regime and the EU AML directives: Prevention and control' in King, C., Walker, C., and Gurulé, J. (eds.), *The Palgrave Handbook of Criminal and Terrorism Financing Law* (Palgrave MacMillan, 2018).

7 Directive 2015/849 (fn 2).

8 FATF, *The Forty Recommendations of the Financial Action Task Force on Money Laundering* (1990).

9 In this chapter, regulated entities or regulated organisations refer to those with obligations to disclose suspicions of criminal property or money laundering.

10 Ai, L., Broome, J. and Yan, H., 'Carrying out a risk-based approach to AML in China: Partial or full implementation?' (2010) 13(4) *Journal of Money Laundering Control* 394.

11 Takats, E., 'A theory of "Crying Wolf": The economics of money laundering enforcement' (2011) 27(1) *Journal of Law, Economics & Organization* 32.

12 Harvey, J. and Lau, S., 'Crime-money, reputation and reporting' (2009) 52 *Crime Law and Social Change* 57.

13 Ross, S. and Hannan, M., 'Money laundering and risk-based decision-making' (2007) 10 *Journal of Money Laundering Control* 106.

regulatory system resulted in an 'information overload' by way of over-reporting of suspicious transactions and thereby reducing the investigative capacity of law enforcement agencies.[14] As a result, the large number of SARs generated under this system became a recognised problem.[15] The regulated entities were clearly not proving to be discerning partners in the fight against money laundering, and law enforcement was failing as well.

In this stifling environment, the introduction of the RBA was seen as a breath of fresh air. This new approach was intended to result in SARs that would lead to a 'productive regulatory or law-enforcement response,'[16] with regulated entities recognising 'existence of the risk(s), undertaking an assessment of the risk(s) and developing strategies to manage and mitigate the identified risks.'[17] However, it, nonetheless, brought similar problems as the rule-based approach.[18]

The RBA does not have a set definition, as the very essence of the approach is to provide flexibility to the regulated entities. In following the RBA, entities are expected to group customers into high-, standard-, and low-risk categories. This decision is based on variables such as country or geographic risk, customer risk, and product or service risk,[19] all of which may increase or decrease the perceived risk posed by a particular customer or transaction. Thus a reporting officer is required to group a customer into one of the three categories depending on the information provided by the customer and the documents received. However, these categories are not well defined and the decision where to place the customer is a complex one. A 'one-size-fits-all' approach will not apply as the risk assessment for each bank should be based on a holistic view of the information obtained in the context of their application of customer due diligence (CDD) measures through the RBA, thereby preparing a customer risk profile. This will determine the level and type of ongoing monitoring and support the bank's decision whether to enter into, continue, or terminate the business relationship.[20] Whilst recognising that banks are at a high risk of money laundering, the Home Office and HM Treasury have also placed the RBA at the heart of AML compliance, necessitating the requirement for relevant persons subject to Money Laundering Regulations 2017 ('ML Regs') to identify, assess, manage, and mitigate risk for the purposes of preventing and detecting money laundering and terrorist financing.[21]

14 Levi, M. and Reuter, P., 'Money laundering' (2006) 34(1) *Crime and Justice* 289.
15 KPMG (Professional Services Network), *Review of the Regime for Handling Suspicious Activity Reports* (2003).
16 Harvey and Lau (fn 12).
17 FATF, *Guidance on the Risk-Based Approach to Combating Money Laundering and Terrorist Financing: High Level Principles and Procedures* (2007).
18 Challenges posed by the risk-based approach are discussed in section 3 of this chapter.
19 FATF, *Specific Risk Factors in Laundering the Proceeds of Corruption* (2012).
20 FATF, *Risk-Based Approach Guidance for the Banking Sector* (2014).
21 Home Office & HM Treasury, *National Risk Assessment of Money Laundering and Terrorist Financing 2017* (2017).

Challenges posed by the RBA

Contradictions in the RBA

The RBA begs a fundamental question – what is 'risk' in the AML context? Assuming that risk is measurable, it would mean that a reporting officer in a regulated entity would (almost) accurately be able to calculate the money laundering risks associated with a customer or transaction. However, whilst on the one hand the RBA allows a reporting officer to exercise flexibility in carrying out such a calculation, the law on the other hand significantly constrains this flexibility, as discussed in this section.

In the United Kingdom, the ML Regs 2017 were introduced to strengthen the RBA as laid out by the Fourth Money Laundering Directive. The ML Regs create a system of regulatory obligations for businesses under the supervision of the FCA and the relevant professional and regulatory bodies recognised within the regulations.[22] One prominent change brought about by these regulations is the requirement, *inter alia*, to conduct enhanced checks on politically exposed persons (PEPs), whether domestic or foreign.[23] This would mean that the spouse or relative of a person holding public office would automatically be considered high risk, irrespective of their customer profile, thus giving rise to the risk that the distinction between suspicious and non-suspicious will become a bureaucratic decision instead of a risk-based one.

A further example of rigidity in the RBA is that the 2017 Regulations necessitate the application of enhanced due diligence measures in any business relationship or transaction with a person established in a 'high-risk' third country.[24] Following the same reasoning, simplified due diligence is considered sufficient in cases where the customer is resident or established in a European Economic Area (EEA) state and where the geographic risk of money laundering is low.[25] In reality, this means that any person originating from a sanctioned country (for example, Iran) would automatically be categorised as high risk, and any person originating from a low-risk country (such as the United Kingdom) would automatically be low risk, assuming there are no other red flags. This categorisation begs the question, what is the rationale for accepting someone from the United Kingdom and rejecting someone from Iran when vast amounts of money are estimated to be laundered through the United Kingdom and a tiny portion relates to Iranians?[26]

22 Law Commission, *Anti-Money Laundering: The SARs Regime Consultation Paper* (Law Com No. 236, 2018) para 1.8.

23 ML Regs, Reg.35. The term PEP means an individual who is entrusted with prominent public functions, other than as a middle ranking or more junior official, family member of such a person, or 'known close associate' of such a person.

24 ML Regs, Reg.33.

25 ML Regs, Reg.37(c).

26 *The Independent*, 'Counting the cost of money laundering,' (<http://www.independent.co.uk/news/business/news/counting-the-cost-of-money-laundering-a8122916.html>,

Whilst high-risk activities may typically include cash intensive businesses,[27] such as restaurants and retail shops, there is nothing inherent in them that would force these entire areas to be considered high-risk *per se*. A major concern with the AML regime's attempt to delineate activities into high risk and low risk is that it cannot compartmentalise an entire category (for instance, customers based in a country subject to political sanctions) because not all customers in these areas will have the same risk profile. This approach tends to leave banks confused and 'nervous whether their own perception of risk will match regulatory expectations' leading to possible non-compliance or 'excessive' compliance, such as defensive reporting or automatically filing reports of, say, all PEPs, even if there is nothing inherently suspicious about a particular transaction.[28]

Therefore, the concept of risk with respect to AML has not been given the meaning that the RBA demands and is often subject to the categories that are already laid out by the law. This is contradictory to the very essence of the RBA, which purports to allow room for flexibility and exercise of judgement. The result is an ill-defined RBA resulting in defensive reporting, which is discussed in the next section.

The concept of suspicion

Considering this point further, the contribution of the concept of 'suspicion' to the inefficiencies of the RBA cannot be underestimated. SARs, which form the cornerstone of money laundering reporting in the United Kingdom, hang on the loose scales of 'suspicion.' Broadly speaking, a SAR alerts law enforcement to 'suspicious' client or customer activity that may indicate money laundering or terrorist financing. Whether to submit a SAR or not is a decision made by the reporting officer, depending on the perceived risk posed by the customer/transaction. The SARs regime is closely linked to the RBA, evidenced in the increased effort to tie the two together. It is envisaged by the Home Office and HM Treasury that the RBA will be applied to inform the SAR regime so that efforts can be focused towards those individuals and organisations that pose the highest money laundering and terrorism financing risks.[29]

Under the Proceeds of Crime Act 2002 ('POCA'), a person commits an offence if he fails to make the required disclosure of suspicion stated earlier if he (i) knows or (ii) suspects or (iii) has reasonable grounds for knowing or

---

5 February 2018). For a discussion on the proportionality of the AML regime, see van Duyne, P.C., Harvey, J. and Gelemerova, L., 'A "risky" risk approach: Proportionality in ML/TF regulation' in King, C., Walker, C., and Gurulé, J. (eds.), *The Palgrave Handbook of Criminal and Terrorism Financing Law* (Palgrave MacMillan, 2018).

27 HM Treasury and Home Office (fn 21).

28 Demetis, D. and Angell, I., 'The risk-based approach to AML: Representation, paradox, and the 3rd directive' (2007) 10(4) *Journal of Money Laundering Control* 412.

29 HM Treasury and Home Office, *Action Plan for Anti-Money Laundering and Counter-Terrorist Finance* (2016).

suspecting that another person is engaged in money laundering.[30] The third category here is the problematic one. As money laundering legislation shifted from criminal penalties for 'failing' to report crimes one did actually suspect to those for failing to report crimes that one 'objectively' ought to have suspected, the tension about reasonable expectations (on what to report) became progressively greater.[31] In an attempt to address the undefined nature of suspicion, Longmore LJ in *R v. Da Silva* stated,

> It seems to us that the essential element in the word 'suspect' and its affiliates, in this context, is that the defendant must think that there is a possibility, which is more than fanciful, that the relevant facts exist. A vague feeling of unease would not suffice. But the statute does not require the suspicion to be 'clear' or 'firmly' grounded and based on 'reasonable grounds.'[32]

However, it can be argued that what is more than fanciful is a mere feeling and is likely to differ from one reporting officer to another.

The problem presented in this trend in case law is that the boundary between a real but 'vague feeling of unease' and the thought that there is 'a more than fanciful possibility' that a transaction might involve money laundering is easy to articulate but almost impossible to identify in practice.[33] The subjective nature of suspicion also gives rise to the possibility of confusion with unusual transactions, thus adding another layer of complexity to the decision process. For example, a transaction which appears unusual is not necessarily suspicious. Even customers with a stable and predictable transactions profile will have periodic transactions that are unusual for them, which may or may not translate into suspicion.[34]

The Law Commission makes two primary observations on the lack of statutory definition or guidance on the concept of suspicion. First, the low threshold of suspicion, whilst providing simplicity, inadvertently catches activity that is unusual or not commonplace, thus affecting the quality of the reports submitted. Second, without a clear definition, guidance, or a requirement for reasonable grounds, suspicion can be inconsistently applied by those who have to decide whether to report their concerns.[35] As a consequence of this low threshold of suspicion, the NCA is facing an overwhelmingly high number of SARs,[36] possibly indicating a defensive reporting culture or box-ticking exercise on the part

30 POCA, s.330.

31 Levi, M. and Gilmore, W., 'Terrorist finance, money laundering and the rise and rise of mutual evaluation: A new paradigm for crime control?' (2002) 4 *European Journal of Law Reform* 337.

32 *R v. Da Silva* [2006] EWCA Crim 1654[16].

33 Marshall, P., 'Does Shah v. HSBC Private Bank Ltd make the anti-money laundering consent regime unworkable?' (2010) 5 *Journal of International Banking and Financial Law* 287.

34 Joint Money Laundering Steering Group (JMSLG), *Suspicious Activities, Reporting and Data Protection* (2017).

35 Law Commission (fn 22) para 2.64.

36 NCA (fn 4). The NCA received 463,938 SARs between April 2017 and March 2018.

of regulated organisations.[37] It has been argued that the objective test applied to disclosure offences for the regulated sector means that risk-averse professionals and employees prefer to report rather than risk prosecution for a failure to do so.[38] The compliance costs faced by the regulated sector are also increasing. The British Bankers' Association (now UK Finance) estimated that its members are spending at least £5 billion annually on core financial crime compliance, including enhanced systems and controls and recruitment of staff.[39]

Although it is easy to assume that SARs communicate all and only suspicious cases, the large number of 'false positives' demonstrate the fallacy of such a view.[40] Significantly, the SAR regime was repeatedly criticised in the United Kingdom's first national risk assessment in 2015.[41] The following year, the government's Action Plan acknowledged that radical changes to the regime were required.[42] Due to the need to protect those who make disclosures, it is not routinely recorded when an SAR leads to investigation or prosecution by the Crown Prosecution Service, making it difficult to provide exact statistics on the effectiveness of the SAR regime. However, the Law Commission has published data on consent SARs for this purpose, as refusal of consent would indicate that further action by law enforcement agencies was anticipated or in process. Of the 27,471 consent SARs during that period, consent was refused in only 1,558 cases (5.67%).[43] The ineffectiveness of the AML regime has been recognised in another study, questioning the high rating that the United Kingdom received in the Mutual Evaluation Report published by FATF.[44] It has been noted that viewing the 'value' of the AML regime in these arbitrary 'league table' terms is too simplistic, given the scale of money laundering assessed to be occurring in practice through the United Kingdom's economy.[45]

37 Sinha, G., 'To suspect or not to suspect: Analysing the pressure on banks to be "policemen"' (2014) 15 *Journal of Banking Regulation* 75.

38 Goldby, M., 'Anti-money laundering reporting requirements imposed by English law: Measuring effectiveness and gauging the need for reform' (2013) *Journal of Business Law* 367.

39 British Bankers' Association, 'Response to Cutting Red Tape Review- The Effectiveness of UK's AML Regime' (<https://www.bba.org.uk/policy/bba-consultation-responses/bba-response-to-cutting-red-tape-review-effectiveness-of-the-uks-aml-regime/>, 2015).

40 Demetis and Angell (fn 28).

41 HM Treasury and Home Office, *UK National Risk Assessment of Money Laundering and Terrorist Financing* (2017).

42 Home Office and HM Treasury (fn 29).

43 Law Commission (fn 22) para 2.22. Consent SARs are now referred to as a 'Defence against Money Laundering' ('DAML'). The aim of Consent SARs is to provide law enforcement with an appropriate amount of time to undertake investigations without funds being dissipated particularly in complex transactions. See Criminal Finances Act 2017, Part 1, s.10(2), inserting POCA, s.335(6A).

44 FATF, *Anti-Money Laundering and Counter Terrorist Financing Measures, United Kingdom Mutual Evaluation Report* (FATF, 2018). The report found that UK's AML system is effective in many respects.

45 Keatinge, T., Moiseienko, A., Keen, F., Artingstall, D., and Wood, H., *No Rest for the Wicked: Driving Change in the UK's Post-FATF Evaluation AML Regime* (RUSI, 2019).

The background context is that the United Kingdom follows an 'all crimes' approach towards AML, which essentially means that no matter how trivial the criminal activity, if there is a suspicion that it involves property which might be laundered, then there is an obligation to report it.[46] However, the 'all crimes' approach actually seems to be contradictory to the RBA. The adoption of this 'leave no stone unturned' approach has the consequence that front-line reporters, such as bank staff, are not required to make any assessment as to the seriousness or otherwise of any underlying offence. It has also been observed that an 'all crimes' approach discredits and weakens the AML regime in a much broader sense, with participants questioning the intelligence value of technical SARs. A focus on technical SARs diverts resources away from areas of real money laundering risk.[47] Labelling transactions as 'suspicious' on a 'just in case' basis would also mean that more customers are being placed in the 'enhanced' risk category than is actually required, thereby defeating the purpose of the RBA, which calls for AML checks to be placed on a risk-sensitive basis.

As a possible way forward, the Law Commission has proposed amending the reporting threshold in POCA[48] from suspicion to 'reasonable grounds to suspect.'[49] The commission proposes this to be a cumulative test that would require subjective suspicion on the part of a reporter, supported by objective grounds for that suspicion, a test frequently deployed in investigative contexts. It is suggested by the commission that this revised threshold will foster a decline in defensive SARs of minimal intelligence value. Although the commission acknowledges that it may be 'a layer of unnecessary complexity' for reporters required to delineate reasonable grounds, it adds that these operational challenges could be mitigated with appropriate AML training and guidance.[50] Whilst raising the threshold may be appealing, it has been argued that it is likely to result in operational challenges. The Fourth Money Laundering Directive requires SARs to be made where an obliged entity 'knows, suspects, or has reasonable grounds to suspect' money laundering or terrorist financing. Thus raising the threshold would be non-compliant with the directive.[51]

Contradiction between how the law defines the RBA and how the FCA seeks to implement it

So far, this chapter has discussed challenges in the application of the RBA. In order to maintain a balanced discussion, it is crucial to understand the expectations of

46 House of Lords European Union Committee, Money Laundering and the Financing of Terrorism (2008–09 HL 132).

47 Kebbell, S., '"Everyone's looking at nothing": The legal profession and the disproportionate burden of the Proceeds of Crime Act 2002' (2017) *Criminal Law Review* 741.

48 POCA, s.330.

49 Law Commission 2018 (fn 22) para 8.26.

50 Law Commission 2018 (fn 22) para 9.30.

51 Kebbell, S., 'The law commission: Anti-money laundering and counter-terrorism financing-reform of the suspicious activity reporting regimes' (2018) 11 *Criminal Law Review* 880.

the FCA and how they collide or merge with the aims of banks and financial institutions. This is because attitudes towards AML compliance are largely shaped by the demands of the FCA. Against this background, this chapter now tests the relationship dynamics between the FCA as the regulator and the banks and financial institutions as compliance partners. Focus will be on the ambiguities and complexities surrounding the RBA as advocated by the FCA and the reliance on financial penalties as an effective deterrent.

Tension between the FCA and banks/financial institutions

The FCA describes the RBA as a means that focuses on outputs, stressing that although there is a need to have procedures with regard to CDD and monitoring, the law does not prescribe details.[52] This mode of approach places private actors at the heart of AML prevention, hence transferring responsibility from public agencies to private agents.[53] The FCA requires firms to establish and maintain effective systems and controls to counter the risk that they might be used to further financial crime.[54] However, the key point is that what constitutes effective systems and controls has not been defined by the FCA.

Whilst testing their relationship dynamics, it is important to remember that collaboration between the public and private sector does not always flow naturally. Whilst the private sector may not welcome being co-opted by the government, law enforcement agencies are also 'reluctant to take private businesses into its confidence out of fear of jeopardising its case, either prior to or during the prosecutorial stage.'[55] The reasons bring to the forefront the tension between state sovereignty and 'neo-liberal governmentality.'[56] The state, being the sovereign power, 'imposes' AML laws and regulations on the private sector; as a result, the private sector functions as a 'neoliberal' government carrying out a series of surveillance practices.[57] However, this public-private collaboration, although in the nature of policing, remains 'non-voluntary.'[58] On an everyday basis, therefore, the public-private collaboration in the fight against money laundering and terrorist financing is not based on a relationship of trust or parity.

In fact, the regulatory approach has been considered the top AML concern in a 2014 report published by KPMG. Sixty-three percent of respondents said that

52 See FCA, 'Money Laundering and Terrorist Financing' (<https://www.fca.org.uk/firms/financial-crime/money-laundering-terrorist-financing>, 2018).

53 Ross and Hannan (fn 13).

54 FCA, *Financial Crime Guide: A Firm's Guide to Countering Financial Crime Risks* (2019).

55 Reuter, P. and Truman, E., *Chasing Dirty Money: The Fight against Money Laundering* (Institute of International Economics, 2004) 176.

56 Amoore, L. and Goede, M., 'Governing by Risk in the War on Terror' in Amoore, L. and Goede, M. (eds.), *Risk and the War on Terror?* (Routledge, 2008) 5.

57 Favarel-Garrigues, G., Godefroy, T., and Lascoumes, P., 'Reluctant partners? Banks in the fight against money laundering and terrorism financing in France' (2011) 42(2) *Security Dialogue* 179.

58 Bowling, B. and Sheptycki, J., *Global Policing* (Sage Publications, 2011) 199.

regulators should provide additional guidance, and 43% of respondents indicated that a stronger relationship with regulators would be a welcomed change in approach.[59] It appears that the FCA recognises the need for a public-private partnership in the implementation of the AML regime. The latest annual report states that the FCA is working with the Joint Money Laundering Intelligence Taskforce, set up in partnership with the financial sector to combat money laundering.[60] The FCA is also involved in the design of the National Economic Crime Centre, a public-/private-sector partnership on economic crime.[61]

Whether these initiatives are successful is yet to be evaluated. However, ample scope remains for collaboration, as evidenced in the FCA's 2017–2018 AML annual report[62] that continues to find deficiencies in the application of the RBA. Amongst the most common deficiencies are the ineffective application of enhanced due diligence, which in turn led to poor identification and monitoring of customers who were PEPs or who were high risk. The FCA further states that transactions that are unusual, lack an obvious economic or lawful purpose, are complex, large, or lend themselves to anonymity should be placed in the high risk or enhanced due diligence category.[63] On this basis, then, and reflecting the box-ticking behaviour that the law presently encourages around the law of suspicion, a transaction made from, say, the United Kingdom to Saudi Arabia that is not part of a customer's usual transaction patterns automatically gets categorised as high risk. This outcome may be avoided with better communication between banks and the FCA in an effort to jointly understand money laundering typologies instead of focusing on tick-box compliance.

Although financial institutions may be failing to grasp the essence of the RBA as espoused by the FCA, the cause relates to the inability to implement RBA as espoused by the law, which results in this disharmony of expectations, as discussed at length earlier in this chapter, along with the need to take a step back and re-evaluate the use of 'suspicion' to inform risk categories. Whilst the regulated sector is more inclined towards compliance, the FCA is primarily concerned with the outcome of that compliance. These inherently divergent objectives increase the need to clarify the law in order to minimise the chances of differing interpretations of the factors that inform AML risk categories.

Thus the consequences of the weaknesses in applying an RBA model result in a vicious circle. Banks are identified as possessing inefficient controls, the FCA imposes increasing penalties on banks, and the banks react by seeming to comply instead of actual effective compliance. In this scenario, the question that needs to be asked is whether the 'comply or explain' approach leading to increased fines is really working. This deterrent approach of the regulator is discussed in the next section.

59 KPMG, 'Global Anti-Money Laundering Survey' (<https://assets.kpmg/content/dam/kpmg/pdf/2014/02/global-anti-money-laundering-survey-v5.pdf>, 2014).

60 FCA, *Anti-Money Laundering Annual Report 2017–18* (2018).

61 *Ibid.*

62 *Ibid.*

63 FCA, *Financial Crime Guide* (fn 54).

Increasing financial penalties is not the key to an effective RBA

The most recent annual AML report published by the FCA makes it clear that the FCA expects firms to take appropriate but proportionate measures in meeting their financial crime obligations, applying a risk-sensitive approach to identifying PEPs and then applying enhanced due diligence measures, as the ML Regs 2017 require.[64] It follows that a majority of penalties levied by the FCA focuses on the lack of effective application of the RBA. In 2012, the Financial Services Authority (FSA) fined Coutts & Company (Coutts) £8.75 million for failing to take reasonable care to establish and maintain effective AML systems and controls relating to high-risk customers, including PEPs.[65] In 2014, Standard Bank was fined £7.6 million for failure to have adequate risk systems to manage high-risk customers.[66] The most recent penalty imposed on Deutsche Bank for £163 million was due to a failure to obtain sufficient information about its customers to inform the risk-assessment process and to provide a basis for transaction monitoring.[67]

Observing the trend of penalties earlier, it would seem that the FCA considers rising penalties as one of the key motivators towards an effective RBA. However, in the context of AML, whether the increasing penalties have actually contributed towards this change is questionable. In the wake of these heavy corporate fines, individual prosecutions are almost non-existent.[68]

Despite the increasing penalties, the deluge of SARs and resultant inefficiencies, as discussed earlier, indicate that the increasing penalties make banks more defensive than compliant. This point was also observed by the FSA in its thematic review, wherein it noted examples of banks attempting to 'clean up their act' just before the visit. In one instance, a bank changed the status of numerous high-risk clients to low risk, and in another example, three banks added relevant information to their customer due-diligence files for the first time, very shortly before the FSA visit.[69]

Apart from defensive compliance, another factor that dilutes the reliance on fines is their depiction as a cost of doing business, with compliance all too often

64 FCA, *Anti-Money Laundering Annual Report 2017–18* (fn 60).

65 Financial Services Authority (FSA), 'Final Notice to Coutts & Company' (<https://www.fca.org.uk/publication/final-notices/coutts-mar12.pdf>, 23 March 2012).

66 FCA, 'Standard Bank PLC Fined £7.6m for Failures in Its Anti-Money Laundering Controls' (<https://www.fca.org.uk/news/press-releases/standard-bank-plc-fined-%C2%A376m-failures-its-anti-money-laundering-controls>, 23 January 2014).

67 FCA, 'FCA Fines Deutsche Bank £163 Million for Serious Anti-Money Laundering Controls Failings' (<https://www.fca.org.uk/news/press-releases/fca-fines-deutsche-bank-163-million-anti-money-laundering-controls-failure>, 31 January 2017).

68 The lack of prosecutions of perpetrators is also crucial; however, it is outside the scope of this chapter.

69 FSA, *Banks Management of High Money-Laundering Risk Situations: How Banks Deal with High-Risk Customers (Including Politically Exposed Persons), Correspondent Banking Relationships and Wire Transfers* (<https://www.fca.org.uk/publication/corporate/fsa-aml-final-report.pdf>, 2011).

seen as 'unlikely to have any impact on individuals, who have little or no loyalty to the firm and are primarily motivated by short-term revenue generation.'[70] The 'downside' for banks is potentially small: seemingly large fines are, in fact, only a small fraction of profits, and there is very limited personal responsibility of individual bankers. For instance, HSBC admitted to a series of money laundering charges and was fined $1.9 billion by the US authorities, the largest ever fine imposed for failings in AML compliance up to that date.[71] However, the seemingly high fine represents only four weeks' earning for HSBC.[72] As for damage to the reputation of the bank, the profits for HSBC have been steady since 2012.[73]

Large fines levied by the FCA include the £72 million penalty imposed on Barclays Bank plc in November 2015 for failing to minimise the risk that it may be used to facilitate financial crime.[74] Yet the total profit made by Barclays in the same year (£2.1 billion)[75] means that the fine is a mere 0.2% of this total. This amount seems too low to have a deterrent effect on a private organisation that may not have law enforcement objectives at the forefront in the first place.

The penalty on Deutsche Bank, the biggest imposed by the FCA so far in the United Kingdom,[76] totalled £163 million, though still less than half that imposed by the New York Department of Financial Services, which fined Deutsche Bank $425 million.[77] This difference is despite the fact that both fines were for the same reason – failing to prevent around $10 billion in suspicious trades being laundered out of Russia. One may wonder if such an enormous amount created a significant dent in profits. Speaking on the profits of the third quarter of 2018, Christian Sewing, chief executive officer of Deutsche Bank, said in a statement,

70 House of Lords and House of Commons Parliamentary Commission on Banking Standards, *Changing Banking for Good* (2013–14 HL 27/HC 175) para. 202.

71 BBC News, 'HSBC to pay $1.9bn in US money laundering penalties' (<http://www.bbc.co.uk/news/business-20673466>, 11 December 2012).

72 Pratley, N., 'HSBC fine: What does it take for a bank to be prosecuted?' (<https://www.theguardian.com/business/nils-pratley-on-finance/2012/dec/11/hsbc-money-laundering-fine>, 11 December 2012).

73 Szmigiera, M., 'Profits of HSBC from 2007 to 2018' (<https://www.statista.com/statistics/224577/hsbcs-profit/>, 5 August 2019).

74 FCA, 'FCA fines Barclays £72 million for poor handling of financial crime risks' (<https://www.fca.org.uk/news/press-releases/fca-fines-barclays-%C2%A372-million-poor-handling-financial-crime-risks>, 26 November 2015).

75 Barclays Bank Plc, 'Results Announcement' (<https://www.home.barclays/content/dam/barclayspublic/docs/InvestorRelations/ResultAnnouncements/2015FYResults/20160301_FY15_Results_Announcement.pdf>, 31 December 2015).

76 FCA, 'FCA fines Deutsche Bank £163 million for serious anti-money laundering controls failings'(<https://www.fca.org.uk/news/press-releases/fca-fines-deutsche-bank-163-million-anti-money-laundering-controls-failure>, 31 January 2017).

77 Freifeld, K. and Schuetze, A. 'Deutsche [Bank] fined $630 million for failures over Russian money laundering' (<https://www.reuters.com/article/us-deutsche-mirrortrade-probe/deutsche-fined-630-million-for-failures-over-russian-money-laundering-idUSKBN15E2SP>, 30 January 2017).

'We are on track to be profitable in 2018, for the first time since 2014.'[78] This attitude reflects that fines are not capable of having a deterrent effect on large global organisations and, therefore, will not lead to a more effective application of the RBA.

In summary, it is contended that more stringent fines change the focus of compliance to a 'tick-box exercise' and the objective of reducing crime through AML regulations recedes in the background. What is required is an understanding of how the law may be applied to discourage the tick-box approach, not encourage it. If 'escaping' penalties becomes the primary motivator for compliance, the RBA, and as a result the role of the FCA, loses its real meaning.

Conclusion

In analysing the weaknesses of the RBA towards AML compliance, this chapter has taken a step back to the former rule-based system, which gave precise rules to regulated organisations, thus encouraging formalistic over-reporting. The current RBA was introduced with a view to overcoming this drawback and affording organisations more flexibility. However, this chapter contends that this approach has again created similar problems that existed within the rule-based approach. Although some might say that compliance has become more flexible, it has become more complicated to define what exactly organisations need to do in order to ensure that they are compliant to meet regulatory expectations. A major hurdle stems from the conceptualisation of risk. The definition of 'risk' in an AML context remains vague and difficult to grasp. Vague estimations result in ill-defined high and low-risk categories.

'Suspicion' as the cornerstone of AML reporting also significantly contributes to an inefficient RBA. The low threshold of suspicion leads to a 'box-ticking' exercise on the part of reporters who find it 'easier' to red flag a transaction as suspicious than to face the risk of personal liability under the Proceeds of Crime Act. This means that the 'enhanced risk' category that is meant to include only high-risk customers so that maximum checks can be placed on them, gets diluted with 'just in case' customers, thus defeating the purpose of the RBA.

In order to attain a holistic picture, it is important to look at the RBA from the other side, which is from the lens of the FCA. It is often overlooked that the objectives of the private and the public sector are not naturally aligned, which makes it harder to achieve the law enforcement objective that is thrust on the private sector. Therefore, collaboration, not collision, is the key. Since the introduction of the credible deterrence strategy, the FCA has imposed increasing fines on banks and financial institutions that have not effectively implemented the RBA. Whilst the amount of these penalties is increasing, the analysis finds that they

78 Amaro, S., 'Deutsche Bank shares slide 5% as third quarter profits slump' *CNBC* (<https://www.cnbc.com/2018/10/24/deutsche-bank-q3-2018-earnings.html>, 24 October 2018).

do not sustain a deterrent effect and instead often become digested as a routine cost of doing business. In theory, the RBA is a better approach to combat money laundering. There remains, however, much difficulty in its implementation. Through this chapter, it is hoped that some of these challenges have been spotlighted.

5 Unexplained wealth orders

An evolving approach to enhancing the effectiveness of the anti-money laundering regime in the United Kingdom

Sirajo Yakubu

Introduction

In its 2018 Mutual Evaluation Report (MER) on the United Kingdom's anti-money laundering and countering the financing of terrorism (AML/CFT) measures, the Financial Action Task Force (FATF) analysed the level of UK compliance with the FATF Recommendations and the effectiveness of the United Kingdom's AML/CFT regime.[1] According to the MER, the United Kingdom has in place an effective AML/CFT regime and sanctions imposed for money laundering (ML) are broadly effective, proportionate, and dissuasive.[2] Notwithstanding the highly positive FATF evaluation report, however, research demonstrates that the AML regime in the United Kingdom does not sufficiently disrupt ML and terrorist financing (TF).[3] Indeed, the MER did acknowledge that major improvements are still needed to strengthen supervision and implementation of preventive measures and to ensure that financial intelligence is fully exploited.[4]

The stance adopted in this chapter is that a continuous review of AML law is needed to close loopholes and to improve efficiency. As AML law evolves, gaps are inevitable, and criminals can exploit such gaps to launder proceeds of crime. Thus, the law is regularly amended to confront new threats and to remedy defects in the law. For example, the law had expanded to cover regulated persons that, hitherto, either were not covered or were partially covered. This need for action was evident following the 9/11 attacks when the Money Laundering Regulations

1 Financial Action Task Force, 'Anti-money laundering and counter-terrorist financing measures – United Kingdom: Mutual Evaluation Report' (<http://www.fatf-gafi.org/media/fatf/documents/reports/mer4/MER-United-Kingdom-2018.pdf>, December 2018).

2 *Ibid.*, 67.

3 Yakubu, S., *PhD Thesis: A Critical Appraisal of the Law and Practice Relating to Money Laundering in the UK and USA* (University of London, 2017); Home Office and Her Majesty's Treasury, UK Action Plan on Anti-Money Laundering and Counter-Terrorist Financing 2016 (Action Plan 2016) 7, 8–9; Harvey, J., 'An evaluation of money laundering policies' (2005) 8(4) *Journal of Money Laundering Control* 339, 341.

4 Financial Action Task Force (fn 1) 5; Keatinge, T. et al., 'No rest for the wicked: Driving change in the UK's post-FATF evaluation AML regime' (<https://rusi.org/sites/default/files/20190219_fatf_uk_evaluation_web.pdf>, Whitehall Report 1–19, Royal United for Services Institute, 2019).

2001 were issued to bring bureau de change and money services businesses within the scope of the AML regime.[5] Despite such legislative efforts, there is no sign that the spate of money laundering is reducing.[6] Indeed, in 2017, new Money Laundering Regulations[7] were introduced in the United Kingdom in response to the European Union (EU) Fourth Money Laundering Directive,[8] whilst in 2018, the EU Fifth Money Laundering Directive[9] was passed, which will entail further changes to the AML regime, such as the extension to art dealers.

Against this context of an expanding and deepening AML regime, it is important to also consider effectiveness.[10] Taking its ordinary dictionary meaning, the term 'effective' means 'successful in producing a desired or intended result.'[11] Although assessing the effectiveness of the AML regime using quantitative methods is difficult due to the lack of data on the actual volume of money laundering,[12] it is not impossible to assess the effectiveness of the regime using qualitative methods. Effectiveness of an item of legislation is largely determined by (a) the purpose of the legislation (which sets the benchmark for what the legislation aims to achieve), (b) the substantive content and legislative expression (which determine how the law will achieve the desired results and how this aspiration is communicated to its subjects), (c) the overarching structure (determines how the new provisions interact with the legal system), and (d) the real-life results of legislation (indicates what has been achieved).[13]

Effectiveness reflects the relationship between the purpose and the effects of legislation and expresses the extent to which it is capable of influencing the behaviour of the target population towards the desired direction.[14] The effectiveness of AML law can be determined by critically examining the extent to which the law in practical terms performs the functions it is designed for, as well as examining the burden the AML regime places on regulated persons.[15] In this

5 Money Laundering Regulations 2001, SI 2001/3641. See Alexander, R., 'The money laundering regulations' (2004) 8 *Journal of Money Laundering Control* 75.
6 Harris, M., 'Unexplained wealth orders: The new anti-money laundering weapon' (2018) 7(6) *Compliance and Risk Journal* 6.
7 Money Laundering, Terrorist Financing and Transfer of Funds (Information on the Payer) Regulations 2017, SI 2017/692.
8 Directive 2015/849 of the European Parliament and of the Council of 20 May 2015.
9 Directive 2018/843 of the European Parliament and of the Council of 30 May 2018.
10 See Unger, B. et al., *The Economic and Legal Effectiveness of the European Union's Anti-Money Laundering Policy* (Edward Elgar, 2014).
11 Oxford Dictionary online (<https://en.oxforddictionaries.com/definition/effective>).
12 Reuter, P. and Truman, E., *Chasing Dirty Money: The Fight against Money Laundering* (Institute for International Economics, 2004) 192.
13 Mousmouti, M., 'The "effectiveness test" as a tool for law reform' (2014) 2(1) *IALS Student Law Review* 5.
14 *Ibid.*, 4 (citing Xanthaki, H., 'On transferability of legislative solutions: The functionality test' in Stefanou, C. and Xantaki, H. (eds.), *Drafting Legislation: A Modern Approach* (Ashgate, 2008) 17).
15 Her Majesty's Treasury, *Anti-Money Laundering and Counter Terrorist Finance Supervision Report 2014–15* (2016) 11 (describing an effective AML/CFT regime as one that focuses resources proportionately on the risks and reduces unnecessary burdens on business that do not effectively prevent ML and TF).

context, effective AML law and practice would disrupt the illicit flow of proceeds of crime. According to the UK government's Action Plan 2016:

> A successful anti-money laundering and counterterrorist finance regime will result in the relentless disruption of money laundering and terrorist finance activities, the prosecution of those responsible and the recovery of the proceeds of crime. A successful regime will dissuade those seeking to undertake money laundering and terrorist finance activities from doing so.[16]

Alongside consideration of 'effectiveness,' it is also useful to consider the term – 'disruption' – which appears in this quote: 'Disruption' means 'an interruption in the usual way that a system, process, or event works.'[17] According to the National Crime Agency (NCA), 'disruption' is a measurement of impact against serious organised crime.[18] So, what impact has the UK AML law had against ML and TF? According to the MER, the United Kingdom has in place an effective AML/CFT regime and sanctions imposed for ML are broadly effective, proportionate, and dissuasive.[19] The United Kingdom also uses alternative methods to disrupt money laundering:

> Where a conviction for ML cannot be obtained, UK authorities are able to utilise various tools to disrupt and sanction ML, including pursuing alternative offences, asset recovery, tax investigations, or orders to restrict activity.[20]

The 2018 MER boosts the UK government's confidence in its fight against the flow of dirty money and TF, not least given that out of the 60 countries evaluated, the United Kingdom has been adjudged to have one of the toughest AML regimes in the world – stronger than any other country assessed to date.[21] Reacting to the 2018 MER, John Glen, then Economic Secretary to the Treasury and City Minister, said,

> There is absolutely no place for dirty money or the people that launder it in our country, so I am incredibly proud that today's report confirms that the UK has one of the strongest regimes in the world for deterring these criminals . . . we will continue to improve our defences and work with our

16 Home Office and Her Majesty's Treasury, *UK Action Plan on Anti-Money Laundering and Counter-Terrorist Financing 2016* (2016) 9.

17 Cambridge Dictionary (<https://dictionary.cambridge.org/dictionary/english/disruption>).

18 National Crime Agency, *National Strategic Assessment of Serious and Organised Crime* (2016) 9.

19 Financial Action Task Force (fn 1) 67.

20 *Ibid.*, 69.

21 Her Majesty's Treasury, 'UK Takes Top Spot in Fight against Dirty Money: New Report from the Financial Action Task Force Ranks the UK World-leading in the Fight against Illicit Finance' (<http://www.gov.uk/government/news/uk-takes-top-spot-in-fight-against-dirty-money>, 7 December 2018).

international partners to find, disrupt, and prosecute anyone dealing in illicit money.[22]

Similarly, Ben Wallace, then Minister for Security and Economic Crime, said,

> The UK has taken a leading role in the global fight against illicit finance. I'm delighted with today's report which shows our efforts are being recognised, and sends a strong message to criminals that we will come for them, their assets and their money.[23]

Notwithstanding the positive soundings in the wake of the FATF MER of 2018, it is important to approach such plaudits with caution. Indeed, previous research by this author indicates that a number of factors undermine the effectiveness of AML law and practice. These factors include providing a large volume of data, shifting the responsibility for detecting money laundering from the government to the private sector, emphasising 'following the money,' collaborating with insiders, and shifting the focus from predicate crimes to money laundering.[24] Furthermore, the fact that the United Kingdom remains central to global ML schemes brings into question the relevance of this evaluation.[25]

Because of the ineffectiveness of the AML regime, certain measures need to be taken to enhance its disruptive effect. This chapter explores an important development in this regard – namely, the new unexplained wealth order (UWO) regime. This chapter argues that whilst the introduction of the UWO into the UK AML regime is a step in the right direction, there are hurdles to a successful UWO application. Further, it is likely that respondents to UWOs may initiate human rights challenges to orders made against them. This chapter thus discusses the UWO and the obstacles associated with its application. The chapter then analyses human rights issues likely to arise from UWO proceedings.

UWOs

The AML landscape in the United Kingdom received a significant boost through the enactment of the Criminal Finances Act 2017, which substantially amended the Proceeds of Crime Act ('POCA') 2002. One of the major changes that the legislation brought about is the introduction of UWOs.[26] Section 1 of the Criminal Finances Act 2017 (which inserts section 362A into POCA 2002) defines a UWO as an order requiring the respondent to provide a statement:

22 *Ibid.*

23 *Ibid.*

24 Yakubu (fn 3) 299–312.

25 Keatinge, T., 'RUSI experts react to UK's Financial Action Task Force Mutual Evaluation Report' (<https://rusi.org/rusi-news/rusi-experts-react-uk-financial-action-task-force-mutual-evaluation-report>, 2018).

26 POCA 2002 s.362A(3).

(a) setting out the nature and extent of the respondent's interest in the property in respect of which the order is made; (b) explaining how the respondent obtained the property (including how any costs incurred in obtaining it were met); (c) where the property is held by the trustees of a settlement, setting out such details of the settlement as may be specified in the order; and (d) setting out such other information regarding the property as may be so specified.

The concept of UWOs can be traced to the United Nations (UN) Convention Against Corruption (UNCAC).[27] The UNCAC urges Member States to take action against corruption in both the public and private sectors.[28] The UNCAC also urges Member States to put in place measures to combat ML in order to make corruption less attractive.[29] Wherever there is corruption, there is likely to be ML, as the ultimate aim is the enjoyment of the ill-gotten assets.[30] Unless ML is attacked, crimes that generate illicit proceeds will continue to flourish because there is a symbiotic relationship between ML and the predicate crimes.[31]

Prior to the UNCAC, a number of countries had enacted an offence of illicit enrichment;[32] however, the United Kingdom has been reluctant to do so.[33] Instead, the United Kingdom introduced the UWO, which is consistent with the spirit of the UNCAC, Article 20.[34] The offence of illicit enrichment and UWOs are somewhat similar. For example, both are concerned with 'proceeds of crime.' Furthermore, there is a presumption of guilt in the case of illicit enrichment, whilst, with UWOs, there is a presumption that assets were acquired with the proceeds of a crime unless the contrary is shown.[35] However, the two concepts are distinct legal responses. Whereas illicit enrichment is a criminal offence, the UWO does not in itself create any offence. Secondly, whilst the offence of illicit enrichment focuses on domestic officials, the focus of the UWO is on foreign Politically Exposed Persons (PEPs) or those connected to a crime.[36]

27 For analysis of the UNCAC 2003 provisions against corruption and money laundering see Carr, I. and Goldby, M., 'Recovering the proceeds of corruption: UNCAC and anti-money laundering standards' (2011) 2 *Journal of Business Law* 170.

28 See UNCAC 2003, Arts.7–13.

29 UNCAC, Arts.14, 23 and 24.

30 Carr and Goldby (fn 27) 172.

31 Chaikin, D. and Sharman, J.C., *Corruption and Money Laundering: A Symbiotic Relationship* (Springer, 2009).

32 Boles, J.R., 'Criminalizing the problem of unexplained wealth: Illicit enrichment offenses and human rights violations' (2014) 17 *New York University Journal of Legislation and Public Policy* 835, 849–852.

33 Rider, B., 'Explaining the unexplained' (2018) 39(2) *Company Lawyer* 33, 35.

34 Thomas-James, D., 'Editorial: Unexplained wealth orders in the criminal finances bill: A suitable measure to tackle unaccountable wealth in the UK?' (2017) 24(2) *Journal of Financial Crime* 178.

35 POCA 2002 s.362(c); Thomas-James, D., 'Does the UK need to create a criminal offence of illicit enrichment – or is the unexplained wealth order provision of the criminal offence bill 2016 a welcome compromise' in Fisher, J. (ed.), 'Unexplained Wealth Orders: Thoughts on Scope and Effect in the UK' (<https://brightlinelaw.co.uk/wp-content/uploads/2019/07/Unexplained_Wealth_Order_-_Briefing_Papers_Final.pdf>, January 2017) 18.

36 Thomas-James (fn 34).

Arguably, removing illicit enrichment from the hands of criminals is far more important than merely criminalising it. However, in many instances, a lack of evidence hinders enforcement authorities' efforts in recovering laundered proceeds of crime. This problem could arise, for example, where the property is in the United Kingdom, but the evidence is located abroad and cannot be obtained easily. It could include a situation where assets are successfully laundered, but their emergence into the economy gives rise to suspicion as to their origin. Thus, the UWO becomes a necessary tool to help with civil recovery to combat ML.[37]

Based on the UNCAC's Article 20 definition of illicit enrichment, the term 'unexplained wealth' can be described as a significant increase in the assets of public officials that they cannot reasonably explain in relation to their lawful income.[38] In some countries, it is commonplace to see civil servants and public officials owning properties that are beyond their known legitimate earnings[39] or to see people without legitimate employment driving expensive cars.[40] Through ML, proceeds of crime emerge in the legitimate economy as clean assets. Thus the emergence of unexplained wealth raises suspicion as to the legitimacy of the sources of such wealth.[41]

A UWO can be described as the legal mechanism through which illicit enrichment or unexplained wealth can be attacked. The process normally involves a court issuing an order to a person suspected of having accumulated assets worth more than his lawful earnings to explain the source of his wealth. The UWO procedure allows enforcement authorities[42] to apply to the High Court for an order to compel the respondent to explain the nature and extent of his interest in the property in respect of which the order is made and how he obtained the property, including how the cost was met.[43] The respondent could be the owner or someone having possession of the property.

The use of UWOs to tackle ML has started yielding positive results. Less than a year after the implementation of the UWO legislation, the NCA successfully obtained two UWOs against a foreign PEP, Zamira Hajiyeva.[44] Hajiyeva was the wife of Jahangir Hajiyev, the former chairman of the state-owned International Bank of Azerbaijan. Hajiyeva subsequently applied to the High Court to discharge a UWO in respect of a property in London, which was purchased in 2009 for £11.5 million by a company controlled by the respondent.[45]

37 See Rider (fn 33) 33.

38 UNCAC 2003, Art.20.

39 For example, James Ibori, a former Governor of Delta State in Nigeria, was convicted for laundering the proceeds of his corrupt practices: *R v Ibori (Onanafe James)* Unreported, 17 April 2012 (Southwark Crown Court), [2018] EWCA 2291 (Crim).

40 Booz Allen Hamilton (consulting firm), *Comparative Evaluation of Unexplained Wealth Orders: Prepared for the US Department of Justice* (National Institute of Justice, 2011), 133.

41 Rider, B., 'The price of probity' (1999) 7(2) *Journal of Financial Crime* 105, 112.

42 The law enforcement agencies are NCA, HMRC, FCA, DPP, and SFO (POCA 2002, s.362A(7)).

43 POCA 2002, s.362A.

44 *National Crime Agency v Hajiyeva* [2018] EWHC 2534 (Admin).

45 *Ibid.*, 12.

One important question is why a respondent should be forced by law to explain personal financial dealings to state authorities. The easy answer to this question could be that the person is responding to an investigation in a civil matter and so rules about self-incrimination are not apparently applicable.[46] One of the grounds on which Hajiyeva sought to discharge the UWO is that the UWO offends the privilege against self-incrimination and spousal privilege. Indeed, POCA 2002, as amended by CFA 2017, provides that a UWO may, in connection with requiring the respondent to provide the statement mentioned in subsection (3), also require the respondent to produce documents of a kind specified or described in the order.[47] For example, this provision could mean, where the order requires a respondent to explain how he obtained a property, the order may also require the respondent to provide documents to support any claim.

The Court held that the UWO did not offend the privilege under section 14 of the Civil Evidence Act 1968 because the evidence did not disclose a real and appreciable risk that Mrs Hajiyeva or her husband will be prosecuted for offences in the United Kingdom.[48] The section 14 privilege allows a person in civil proceedings to refuse to answer any question or produce any document or thing which might be incriminatory.[49] Section 14 states,

> The right of a person in any legal proceedings other than criminal proceedings to refuse to answer any question or produce any document or thing if to do so would tend to expose that person to proceedings for an offence or for the recovery of a penalty – (a) shall apply only as regards criminal offences under the law of any part of the United Kingdom and penalties provided for by such law; and (b) shall include a like right to refuse to answer any question or produce any document or thing if to do so would tend to expose the spouse or civil partner of that person to proceedings for any such criminal offence or for the recovery of any such penalty.

However, this right is a qualified one, as it does not apply to criminal offences outside the United Kingdom. In any case, the threshold test for privilege has to be met by pointing to the question in the order, which if answered might be incriminating as mere assertion is not sufficient.[50]

46 Civil Evidence Act 1968, s.14(1)(a). Also, see *Jefferson Ltd v Bhetcha* [1979] 1 WLR 898; *Den Norske Bank A.S.A. v Antonatos and Another* [1999] QB 271; *C Plc and Another v P (Attorney General Intervening)* [2007] EWCA Civ 493; Walker, C., 'An exploration of the "right to silence"' (1980) 9 *Anglo American Law Review* 257.

47 POCA 2002 s.362A(5).

48 *National Crime Agency v Hajiyeva* (fn 44) [108], 5909, citing *In re Westinghouse Electric Corpn. Uranium Contract Litigation MDL Docket No. 235 (Nos. 1 and 2)* [1978] A.C. 547.

49 For an analysis of Civil Evidence Act 1968 section 14, see Moules, R., 'The privilege against self-incrimination and real evidence' (2007) 66 *Cambridge Law Journal*, 528.

50 *National Crime Agency v Hajiyeva* (fn44) [108] citing also *JSC BTA Bank v Ablyazov* [2009] EWCA Civ 1125.

Considering the importance of tackling foreign corruption in particular and proceeds of crime in general, section 14 should not unduly impede the operation of the UWO legislation. Indeed, the High Court expressed the view that Parliament in creating the UWO procedure necessarily intended that the privilege be abrogated.[51] As UWOs impose a requirement to provide information and to produce documents,[52] these powers would be rendered largely nugatory if privilege applied.[53]

There is also the risk of reputational damage to those subject to a UWO: any investigation into the financial affairs of individuals may cause reputational harm and financial loss.[54] However, as Hajiyeva's case shows, that may not be the case with a UWO application. A respondent's identity may be concealed by way of anonymity order until the court determines the matter. Indeed, that happened in the Hajiyeva proceedings, where she had previously been referred to as 'A.' To limit the problems that UWO applications might cause respondents, the government put in place safeguards, such as judicial oversight and limits on the number of enforcement authorities that can apply to UWOs.[55] Whilst the CFA 2017 contains these and more safeguards,[56] other factors are relevant, such as for how long the authorities will keep the information supplied in response to a UWO and whether the information will be shared with other agencies.[57]

Before the court issues the order, the enforcement authority must prove: that there is reasonable ground for suspecting that the wealth is disproportionate to known income, that the respondent is a PEP or that he (or an associate) is involved in a serious crime, that the property is more than £50,000, and that the respondent holds the property.[58] If the order is issued, the respondent must respond within the time specified in the order; otherwise, the presumption that the property is recoverable is triggered.[59] Where the respondent cannot give a satisfactory explanation or where the respondent fails to respond, then the property is presumed to be recoverable.[60] However, before the property can be seized, a subsequent application is required as part of the civil recovery process under Part 5 of POCA 2002. Another advantage of UWO is that it has a retrospective

51 *Ibid.*, 110.

52 POCA ss.362A(3), (5), and (6).

53 *National Crime Agency v Hajiyeva* (fn44) 112.

54 *Shah and another v HSBC Private Bank (UK) Limited* [2010] EWCA Civ 31 (Shah suffered reputational and financial loses in Zimbabwe when the news broke that he was being investigated in the United Kingdom for money laundering).

55 Criminal Finances Bill Privacy Impact Assessment (2016) (<http://www.parliament.uk/documents/impact-assessments/IA16-011H.pdf>).

56 For example, CFA 2017 s.362F(1) provides that statements a respondent made while responding to a UWO may not be used against him in evidence in criminal proceedings.

57 POCA 2002, s.362G did not specify for how long enforcement authorities can retain documents/information a respondent supplied in response to a UWO.

58 POCA 2002, s.362B (property's worth was reduced from the initial proposal of £100,000.00 as a compromise for the amending legislation to pass through the Lords swiftly).

59 POCA 2002, s.362C.

60 POCA 2002, s.362C(2).

effect.[61] This means that the date on which the supposed illicit enrichment took place is irrelevant.

Importantly, the UWO is free-standing in the sense that it does not require a precursor or parallel civil or criminal proceedings before an application is made.[62] Thus the adoption of UWOs is an appropriate legal response to the problem of unexplained wealth.[63] However, there are some concerns. One is that identifying the respondent in a UWO application could have a significant impact on the respondents and their families if the names are published. However, the court may treat this concern on a case-by-case basis. In Hajiyeva's case, it was held that there was no evidence to suggest either the respondent or her husband would be at any risk or further risk of prosecution in their country of origin due to the disclosure of their identities.[64]

Another concern is that the presumption that the property amounts to unexplained wealth, unless the respondent proves otherwise,[65] appears to be a reversed burden of proof. In other words, the respondent is expected to justify his/her wealth. Of course, in criminal matters, asking a defendant to prove his case would amount to a reversal of the burden of proof and would be inconsistent with the 'golden thread' of the English criminal justice system.[66] However, the reversed burden of proof in UWO proceedings is justified on the basis that the UWO does not create a criminal offence.[67] Whilst the UWO is not a criminal indictment, a criminal offence is committed where the respondent who purported to comply knowingly gives a misleading statement.[68]

One important question is whether UWO legislation would deter laundering of the proceeds of crime into the United Kingdom. For such legislation to be seen as effective, it should not just help enforcement authorities in their civil recovery efforts but also deter foreign corrupt PEPs and others involved in criminal activities from laundering proceeds of crime into, or within, the United Kingdom. Whilst UWOs could help in investigating the source of proceeds of crime for the purpose of civil recovery, the deterrent effect has been doubted.[69] Although it is too early to determine how effective the UWO regime will be in deterring ML, what is known is that in its first year, only two UWOs were secured against the Home Office projection of 20 UWOs per year during the infancy of

61 POCA s.362B(5)(b).
62 Grimes, J. and Napley, K., 'Analysis – unexplained wealth orders: Insight and analysis' (2017) 1355 *Tax Journal* 12.
63 Thomas-James (fn 34).
64 *National Crime Agency v A* [2018] EWHC 2603 (Admin).
65 POCA 2002, s.362C.
66 *Woolmington v. DPP* [1935] AC 462. For wider discussion of reversed burdens, see Hamer, D., 'The presumption of innocence and reversed burdens: a balancing act' (2007) 66 *Cambridge Law Journal* 142.
67 Thomas-James (fn 34).
68 POCA 2002, s.362E.
69 Trainor, S., 'What are the potential deterrence effects of unexplained wealth orders? A criminological exploration' in Fisher (fn 35), 22.

the legislation.[70] Whether the UWO regime will deflect unexplained wealth away from the United Kingdom thus remains to be seen.

It is important to also consider practical obstacles to meeting the requirements for obtaining a UWO. One of the requirements is that there must be a reasonable ground for suspecting that the known sources of the respondent's lawfully obtained income would have been insufficient to enable the respondent to obtain the property. Whether a suspicion arises as to the provenance of the funds with which a foreign PEP acquired a property will depend on many factors, including the following: whether the investigator knows how much a foreign PEP earns in his country, the access that a foreign PEP has to a loan facility, whether the investigator knows what type of businesses foreign PEPs are by the law of their own countries allowed to engage in, and the time at which the property was acquired.

Knowledge of how much a PEP earns in his own country is critical to any investigation preceding a UWO application. For example, Nigerian senators receive about ₦ (Nigerian Naira) 13 million (equivalent to £27,500) per month as an allowance to cover monthly expenses in addition to a monthly salary of about £2,000.[71] Thus it is within a Nigerian senator's lawful means to own a property worth more than £500,000. The £27,500 monthly allowance alone translates to £1.32 million, assuming a tenure of office of four years, and these earnings do not include the severance package received when leaving office after four years. As the cost of living in Nigeria is low, politicians can make savings from their lawful earnings, even if they completely shun corruption. Despite this calculation, suspicion may arise where a Nigerian PEP (depending on her/his known lawful earnings) acquires a property in the United Kingdom above a certain value (say, for example, if the property is worth £200,000 or more) because it is expected that a PEP has other major responsibilities, such as family maintenance and staff costs, which require money to be spent. Furthermore, because of ingrained fraud and corruption factors in Nigeria, properties bought by a Nigerian PEP in the United Kingdom and other countries are likely to raise suspicion, even if acquired entirely with legitimate earnings. In the context of UWO applications, then, it is vital that enforcement authorities have good knowledge about the practices in countries of foreign PEPs.

A further factor to bear in mind is any external income earned by a foreign PEP. For example, in Nigeria, public servants, including politicians, are allowed to engage in agricultural business whilst serving in office. Thus, in response to a UWO, it might be easy for a PEP to provide some evidence that they obtained the property through legal means, even if the property

70 Home Office, 'Impact Assessment on Criminal Finances Bill – Unexplained Wealth Orders' (HO0282, <https://assets.publishing.service.gov.uk/government/uploads/system/uploads/attachment_data/file/621205/Impact_Assessment_-_UWOs.pdf>, 20 June 2017) 3.

71 Busari, K., 'Confirmed: Nigerian senators receive N13.5 million monthly, apart from salaries' *Premium Times* (<http://www.premiumtimesng.com/news/headlines/261085-confirmed-nigerian-senators-receive-n13-5-million-monthly-apart-from-salaries.html>, 7 March 2018).

was bought with stolen money. Evidence of inheritance can also be used in response to a UWO. For example, in Nigeria, the Wills Act 1837[72] and legislation of various States of the Federation allow a testator to dispose of property freely. Thus the possibility of a PEP adducing fake evidence that someone bequeathed properties to the suspect in a will cannot be ruled out and might thereby cover up corrupt practices.

Potential human rights issues

The possibility of tension between UWOs and human rights as provided under the European Convention of Human Rights (ECHR), such as the right to a fair trial and presumption of innocence, cannot be ignored. The presumption that the property targeted by the order amounts to unexplained wealth, unless the respondent proves otherwise,[73] raises concern over the presumption of innocence as provided under ECHR Article 6(2). The reversal of the burden of proof under the UWO legislation also appears to conflict with the principle of a fair trial under ECHR Article 6(1).

With regard to the burden of proof, ECHR Article 6(1) has two limbs: civil and criminal. Whilst the burden of proof always lies with the prosecution under the criminal limb, under the civil limb the burden can shift without contravening ECHR Article 6(1). Yet even in civil matters (like a UWO proceeding), defendants could allege a violation of the presumption of innocence where they fear that UWO proceedings could jeopardise their defence in parallel corruption prosecutions.

In *Gale and Another v Serious Crime Agency*,[74] the Supreme Court considered whether the presumption of innocence was infringed in a civil recovery proceeding in England, which came after a Portuguese court acquitted the defendant. The Supreme Court held that

> on no view does this jurisprudence support [the] submission that the appellant's acquittal in Portugal precludes the English court in proceedings under POCA from considering the evidence that formed the basis of the charges in Portugal. The link between the Portuguese criminal proceedings and the English civil proceedings, which Strasbourg would appear to consider so critical, is not there. Nor does this jurisprudence lend any support to the proposition that the criminal standard must be applied to proof of criminal conduct in proceedings under POCA.[75]

72 This Act continued to apply after Nigeria became independent in 1960. Interpretation Act (CAP 123 L.F.N.) 2004 s.45(1) provides that the Common Law of England and the Doctrines of Equity and the Statutes of General Application, which were in force in England on January 1, 1900, are applicable in Nigeria, only in so far as local jurisdiction and circumstances shall permit.

73 POCA 2002, s.362C.

74 [2011] UKSC 49.

75 *Ibid.*, 35.

At the European Court of Human Rights (ECtHR) level, in the case of *Gogitidze and Others v. Georgia*,[76] the Court also had to determine whether Article 6 of the ECHR was breached. The two issues relevant to the present discussion were whether the reversal of burden of proof is justified under the civil limb of Article 6(1) and whether bringing confiscation proceedings before the termination of criminal proceedings against the applicant violated the principle of presumption of innocence. This application emanated from a confiscation proceeding in Georgia involving the former Deputy Minister of the Interior and president of the Audit Office of the Ajarian Autonomous Republic, Republic of Georgia, his two sons and his brother. Following a change in political leadership, the Ajarian Public prosecutor initiated proceedings before the Ajarian Supreme Court to confiscate properties suspected to have been acquired with proceeds of corruption.[77] The prosecutor provided evidence which showed that, whilst the first applicant had earned €1,644 and €6,023, respectively, in official salaries when he had occupied the aforementioned two posts in the Ajarian government, the total value of the properties that he and the other applicants had acquired corresponded to some €450,000.[78] The applicants appealed to the Constitutional Court of Georgia on the basis that the burden of proof had shifted, and the presumption of innocence had been violated in the confiscation proceedings. On the shifting of the burden of proof, the Constitutional Court of Georgia held that given the 'civil' nature of the proceedings in question, it was acceptable that the burden of proof in the proceedings should be shifted onto the respondent.[79] On the presumption of innocence, the Court held that since the proceedings in question had been 'civil' and not 'criminal,' criminal law guarantees could not apply.[80]

On application to the ECtHR, the Court rejected the applicants' arguments. On the reversal of the burden of proof, the Court reiterated that

> there can be nothing arbitrary, for the purposes of the 'civil' limb of art.6(1) of the Convention, in the reversal of the burden of proof onto the respondents in the forfeiture proceedings in rem after the public prosecutor had submitted a substantiated claim.[81]

On the presumption of innocence, the Court held that

> [on the]more extensive, aspect of art.6(2) of the Convention, the role of which is to prevent the principle of presumption of innocence from being undermined after the relevant criminal proceedings have ended with an outcome other than conviction (such as acquittal, discontinuation of the

76 App. No. 36862/05, 12 May 2015.
77 *Ibid.*, 27–30.
78 *Ibid.*, 12.
79 *Ibid.*, 41.
80 *Ibid.*, 42.
81 *Ibid.*, 122.

> criminal proceedings as being statute-barred, the death of an accused, and so on), is of no relevance in the present case.[82]

Although a UWO is not a criminal proceeding, the ruling of the ECtHR in *Salabiaku v France*[83] is further relevant to analysing the issue of reversed burden of proof in a UWO application because the burden of proving how the property subject to a UWO application was acquired rests squarely on the respondent. Despite involving a criminal matter where the burden of proof lies squarely on the prosecution, the ECtHR upheld the decision of the first instant court, declaring that the Court did not apply the Customs Code in a way which conflicts with Article 6(2). The Court stated, 'Presumptions of fact or of law operate in every legal system. Clearly, the Convention does not prohibit such presumptions in principle.'[84] It continued,

> It does, however, require the Contracting States to remain within certain limits in this respect as regards criminal law. . . . Article 6(2) does not therefore regard presumptions of fact or of law provided for in the criminal law with indifference. It requires States to confine them within reasonable limits which take into account the importance of what is at stake and maintain the rights of the defence.[85]

In view of these decisions, it is unlikely that UWO procedures would contravene Article 6.

Conclusion

The introduction of the UWO regime into the POCA 2002, the primary UK AML legislation, is a significant boost in tackling ML. UWOs can potentially help enforcement authorities in their civil recovery efforts, because those authorities otherwise find it difficult to pursue proceeds of crime for lack of evidence as to the source of such proceeds. This difficulty could arise, for example, where the property is in the United Kingdom, but the evidence is located abroad and cannot be obtained easily. The UWO regime has already started yielding results with the UWOs obtained against Hajiyeva. However, the success of the regime is likely to depend on how law enforcement overcome the obstacles discussed earlier. On the strength of *Gale*, *Gogitidze*, and *Salabiaku*, as well as the initial challenges to the UWO provisions, human rights challenges to the UWO provisions will not succeed, but evidential intricacies and limited resources for law enforcement will remain as challenges.

82 *Ibid.*, 125.
83 *Salabiaku v France*, App. No. 10589/83, A141-A, 1988.
84 *Ibid.*, 28.
85 *Ibid.*

6 Social value or social harm? The impact of the Proceeds of Crime Act 2002 upon the defendant and their families

Craig Fletcher

Introduction

Asset recovery is now a well-established part of an ever-expanding criminal justice system and is considered an 'important tool in global efforts to disrupt organised crime.'[1] The development of asset recovery powers has been accompanied by several key policy documents,[2] which set out the underpinning rationales and a set of objectives which are designed to appeal to the 'authoritarian within'[3] and gain popular support. Such a strategy is adopted so as to manufacture consent and engender a sense of 'deserved retribution'[4] against individuals who are said to profit from their criminality. More recently, several official reports[5] have highlighted apparent failures in the asset recovery regime with a view to expanding confiscation powers rather than addressing its shortcomings, such as the circumvention of due process safeguards[6] or the pursuance of gross proceeds rather than net profits.[7] Academic research and literature has also critically analysed the many facets of asset recovery.[8] What is absent, however, are the accounts of those who are subject to this punishment. In failing to account for the 'view from

1 Fisher, J. and Bong-Kwan, J., 'Confiscation: Deprivatory and punitive – back to the way we were' [2018] *Criminal Law Review* 192, 193.

2 Such as Performance and Innovation Unit, *Recovering The Proceeds of Crime* (Cabinet Office, 2000).

3 Scraton, P., *Power, Conflict and Criminalisation* (Routledge, 2007) 230.

4 Hudson, B., *Understanding Justice: An Introduction to Ideas, Perspectives and Controversies in Modern Penal Theory* (2nd ed., Open University Press, 2003) 55.

5 Home Affairs Committee, *Proceeds of Crime: Fifth Report of Session 2016–17* (2016–17 HC.25); Committee of Public Accounts, *Confiscation Orders: Progress Review – Seventh Report of Session 2016–17* (2016–17 HC 124); National Audit Office, *Confiscation Orders* (2013–14 HC 738); National Audit Office, *Confiscation Orders: Progress Review* (2015–16 HC 886).

6 Hendry, J. and King, C., 'Expediency, legitimacy, and the rule of law: A systems perspective on civil/criminal procedural hybrids' (2017) 11(4) *Criminal Law and Philosophy* 733.

7 Alldridge, P., 'The limits of confiscation' [2011] 11 *Criminal Law Review* 827.

8 See Bullock, K. and Lister, S., 'Post-conviction confiscation of assets in England and Wales: Rhetoric and reality' in King, C. and Walker, C. (eds.), *Dirty Assets: Emerging Issues in the Regulation of Criminal and Terrorist Assets* (Ashgate, 2014).

below,'[9] a 'regime of truth'[10] has been constructed which has become our 'institutionalized and professionalized manifestations of knowledge'[11] and which has failed to discuss the impact of confiscation beyond its capacity to recover assets. There is a lack of research investigating the potential adverse effects of being subject to the Proceeds of Crime Act (POCA), such as stigma, loss of the family home, relationship breakdown, loss of employment, depression, and suicide. The importance of such research is heightened by an understanding that the impact of these adverse effects is likely to extend beyond the confiscation defendant and infringe upon (innocent) family members and undermine an offender's chances of 'going straight.' In response to this epistemic void, this chapter provides an original insight into the lived realities of those who are subject to post-conviction confiscation in the United Kingdom, drawing upon the experiences of 38 confiscation defendants and their wider family members.[12]

Positioning the responses of those subject to confiscation

Given that human/object relations are inherently complex, this chapter has been careful not to imply a determinate causal link between confiscation and an individual's subsequent responses to the confiscation order. Instead, this chapter sets out a range of possibilities based on the narratives of those subject to this punishment. Many of the research participants agreed with the principle of recovering ill-gotten gains, conceding that, like imprisonment, it is part and parcel of 'doing business.' However, their 'support' for asset recovery was eroded by the 'procedural injustice'[13] experienced during their confiscation ordeal. Whilst it is accepted by most people that by its very nature punishment is not supposed to be a pleasant experience, the importance of regulating punishment so as to safeguard against excess has been widely recognised.[14]

The research participants detailed a plethora of reasons as to why they felt aggrieved by the confiscation process, including (i) being presented with grossly inflated calculations of 'benefit' that bear little relation to the profits of their criminality, (ii) being unable to defend against criminal lifestyle and hidden asset assumptions, (iii) inept and incompetent legal defences, and (iv) the use of informal coercive methods that 'encourage' defendants to accept the prosecution's

9 Scraton (fn 3).

10 Foucault, M., *Power/Knowledge: Selected Interviews and Other Writings 1972–1977* (trs. Gordon, C. et al., Pantheon Books, 1980) 131.

11 Scraton, P. and Chadwick, K., 'Critical research' in McLaughlin, E. and Muncie, J. (eds.), *The Sage Dictionary of Criminology* (Sage Publications, 2013) 108.

12 Narrative methods, guided by some of the principles of Tom Wengraf's Biographic-Narrative Interpretive Method (BNIM), were utilised during this research: Wengraf, T., *Qualitative Research Interviewing* (Sage Publications, 2001).

13 See, generally, Tyler, T.R., 'Procedural justice, legitimacy, and the effective rule of law' (2003) 30 *Crime and Justice* 283.

14 See, e.g., Woolf, H. and Tumim, S., *Prison Disturbances April 1990* (Cm. 1456, 1991).

calculations of benefit through methods such as threatening to indict family members if they do not.

These procedural injustices influenced how the research participants responded to their confiscation order in the long term and go some way to explain the 'situational logic'[15] that underpins their resistance towards the confiscation regime. Therefore, it is important to try and understand their responses from the perspectives of these individuals having already been punished for the predicate offence with a punishment that is 'commensurate' to the harm caused by the offence; making decisions in response to their confiscation case often from the violent and sparse conditions of prison and so being more inclined to agree to anything to try and avoid their prison sentence being extended; being involved in a typically long, drawn-out confiscation process that impacts on their prison sentence progression and greatly impacts on their families' lives on the outside (to the point where many relationships had broken down); being faced with serving, or have previously served, an additional prison sentence in default for failing to satisfy their order in full (despite strongly contesting its calculation) and, seeing their confiscation order increasing with a statutory levy of 8% interest,[16] which means that many will be unlikely to ever pay their confiscation order off/in full and, therefore, confiscation constitutes a life sentence which greatly reduces their life prospects.

At the bedrock of the confiscation regime lies two figures relevant to the court's calculations: the 'benefit' figure, which is the amount that the financial investigator has 'calculated' to have been made through crime, and the 'available' amount, which is calculated according to the amount of realisable assets of a defendant. The available amount is the amount a defendant must pay in order to avoid the imposition of the default prison sentence, whilst the benefit amount is a figure which remains an open-ended debt that can be recovered at a later date. These figures, however, have been described as 'complete fiction.'[17]

Drawing upon empirical research with 100 financial investigators, Bullock provides insight into the problematic way in which these figures are constructed.[18] She highlights that a combination of the criminal lifestyle assumptions contained under the POCA, section 75, and the significant discretion afforded to financial investigators enables some of them to 'go wide' in their calculations, whilst others may choose to 'go narrow,' leading to 'artificially inflated' and 'widely speculative calculations.'[18]

For Bullock then, the confiscation regime figures are 'built on sand' and 'paint a deeply misleading picture of the nature of the criminal economy, the amount

15 Hedström, P., Swedberg, R., and Udéhn, L., 'Popper's situational analysis and contemporary sociology' (1998) 28(3) *Philosophy of the Social Sciences* 339.

16 POCA, s.12.

17 Home Affairs Committee, *Proceeds of Crime: Fifth Report of Session 2016–17* (2016–17 HC 25) Q45.

18 Bullock, K., 'Criminal benefit, the confiscation order and the post-conviction confiscation regime' (2014) *Crime, Law and Social Change* 45, 52.

that defendants have derived from crime and what might be recovered from them.'[19] It is this foundational inconsistency and instability that the confiscation regime rests upon and from which confiscation begins to take on the shape of a lottery. The wider impact of miscalculation might also be felt in the wider context of desistance. For Laub and Sampson,[20] desistance is more likely to occur when an individual has a strong emotional attachment to attaining and maintaining societal goals, such as employment, marriage, and parenthood. Their theory also suggests that when this bond is weakened or broken, offending is more likely to occur. Therefore, understanding the long-term impact of inaccurately calculated confiscation orders upon such desistance factors was a key objective of this current research.

Furthermore, the confiscation figures need to be considered within the context of section 22 powers. Section 22 allows the court to make a reconsideration of the available amount when new assets come to light. In theory, this allows for the confiscation of after-acquired legitimate assets up to the value of the benefit figure, taking account the uplift in inflation. As Bullock points out, this provision enables the court to recover after-acquired and legitimate assets, and so from a revenue raising perspective, it is in the interest of the state to generate inflated benefit figures.[21]

This section of the chapter has begun to explain the experiential reality of the 'space' in which confiscation defendants respond to their confiscation orders. The next section briefly outlines an alternative surveillance function of confiscation, a function that is often overlooked and which the findings of this chapter should be considered alongside.

The 'view from below'

During interviews, respondents consistently described how confiscation proceedings were different to the criminal proceedings that preceded them. They described a process in which their attendance and participation was irrelevant because the confiscation process was 'rigged' to guarantee that the defendant was financially incapacitated indefinitely rather than to determine the true extent of their financial gain. A recurring complaint from several of the research participants was that they had been advised by their legal representatives during their initial confiscation hearing not to be too concerned with the benefit figure, as it is the available figure that is important, as this carries the immediate threat of a default prison sentence. Yet the benefit figure is also of great potential significance – as some of the research participants were beginning to find out. These participants complained of a 'smash and grab' approach in which solicitors take the path of least resistance by encouraging their clients not to challenge

19 Bullock (fn 18) 63.

20 Sampson, R.J. and Laub, J.H., *Crime in the Making: Pathways and Turning Points Through Life* (Harvard University Press, 1993).

21 Bullock (fn 18) 54.

the benefit figure, enabling them to pick up their money and 'ride off into the sunset' on the pretence that they have done their job. However, by the time the benefit figure had become an issue for the research participants (which can be 10 or 20 years down the line), they were finding out that they had no right to recourse. All of the people interviewed during this research had been defended by a legal aid defence, a service which has for the past decade been severely hit by austerity cuts.[22] The resources that their legal teams were able to apply to their confiscation cases were determined by the finances made available under the legal aid regime and not by the complexity of the case; inevitably, this undermined the ability of the legal team to represent the best interests of the defendant.

The consequence of often poor advice given by their solicitors was that many of the participants agreed to inflated benefit figures which they strongly disagreed with, but they did so on the understanding that their available amount would be 'negotiated' down via an informal process between prosecution and defence that took place within the corridors of the court away from scrutiny. Although this correlates with Bullock's research,[23] the voices elicited within this research described a less consensual and more coercive process. For example, the research participants were told that they had no option but to agree to the order because 'if they pissed the judge off then he is likely to dig deeper and you'll get a bigger order' or their family's finances would be investigated if they did not agree to the figures. Whilst the use of plea-bargaining measures is justified on grounds of efficiency and to minimise the distress caused to victims, it is important to point out that this is not what is occurring here; coercion is not the same as plea bargaining. As several of the research participants explained, such underhanded methods are utilised on the understanding that the offender's family tends to be his or her 'Achilles' heel'; they are more inclined to agree to a confiscation order if the offender's family is placed under threat.

What was consistent within the research was that confiscation defendants were not told about section 22 powers at any point during their confiscation trials. Instead, this was something that became apparent to them after their confiscation order had been 'agreed' on and, therefore, it was too late. The research participants stated that they would not have agreed to the benefit figure had they known of the section 22 powers. Now faced with the prospect of having their legitimately acquired assets confiscated, several of them explained how this acted as a disincentive to gaining legitimate employment, as Ryan[24] starkly pointed out: 'What's the point of going to work if they can come along and take yeh car and yeh house of yeh?'

Whilst it could be argued that a confiscation defendant has a moral responsibility to pay an order based on what he or she has illegitimately acquired, as previously discussed, this obligation is mitigated by the realisation that confiscation

22 Garside, R. and Ford, M., *The Coalition Years: Criminal Justice in the United Kingdom–2010 to 2015* (Centre for Crime and Justice Studies, 2015).

23 Bullock (fn 18).

24 All research participants' names have been changed in the interests of anonymity.

orders tend to be grossly inflated and fail to reflect their illegitimate gains. Furthermore, the subsequent confiscation of after-acquired legitimate assets completely undermines the principal aim of asset recovery – the confiscation of 'ill-gotten gains.' In disincentivising the attainment of legitimate employment, confiscation policy also undermines rehabilitative strategies that set out to help offenders live law-abiding and useful lives. Therefore, confiscation policy is counterintuitive from a rehabilitative perspective.[25] The disincentivising impact of the confiscation process is best captured by Sophie, who stated,

> It's like a game of snakes and ladders, you take a few steps forward and then, boom, you're back to square one with nothing. You go to work, you buy a house and then you spend the next 25 years paying the mortgage for them to then come along and take it off yeh, that's wrong! . . . So of course I'm not going to slog my guts out for the next 25 years only to lose my house, no fucking way!

This exposes an important tension within confiscation policy. If the long-term pursuance of confiscation debt disincentivises legitimate employment, then the confiscation order is unlikely to be paid.

This tension is further exposed in the following extract from Gary who had realised all available assets and paid as much money as he was able to but was still forced to serve an additional prison sentence in default. Despite this, he was committed in his attempts to move forward in his life and was able to secure legitimate employment. However, Gary was then summoned back to court on his confiscation order, which had been continually accruing interest, and the judge imposed an 'attachment of earnings' order to his salary. This meant that on top of the other statutory deductions, such as tax and national insurance, he was left with very little disposable income. He went on to explain that the reduction in his disposable income imposed socio-economic disadvantage on him and his family in two ways: first, there was significantly less money to spend on family activities and, secondly, he was no longer able to afford to make pension contributions, which would provide security in later life. Ultimately, he packed his job in:

> I went to court and they wanted to put an attachment of earnings on my wages at something like 17%. So, on top of the tax and national insurance I'm already paying, I'm paying like the higher tax rate then, but I'm on the minimum wage so what I'm left with is nothing. It's like an added tax for criminals.

For several research participants, the statutory levy of 8% interest meant that the amount they could afford to pay each month by way of an 'attachment of

25 Ministry of Justice, *Transforming Rehabilitation: A Revolution in the Way We Manage Offenders* (Cm. 8517, 2013).

earnings' was less than the amount being added in interest. Therefore, despite making monthly payments from their legitimate earnings, their confiscation order was increasing in value. Some, like Karl, pointed out the demoralising effect, whilst others pointed out that their confiscation order was in effect a life sentence:

> How are they getting away with it? I make payments every month, yet me order goes up. What chance have I got of ever paying it off? Seriously, that can't be right can it? . . . It's legalised theft!

Whilst such insights begin to raise important questions about [dis]proportionality, they also expose further contradictions within the ideology of confiscation. The recovery of monies derived from accruing interest is a further step away from the idea that such processes confiscate 'ill-gotten' gains, which brings into question the legitimacy of the legislation.

Loss of the family home and the impact on the wider family

Whilst the previous section of this chapter has exposed some of the procedural injustices that characterise post-conviction confiscation, this section sets out to link those injustices to the material, emotional, and psychological impact upon the defendant and their families. Despite stable accommodation being widely considered essential to building further protective factors that help to reduce reoffending,[26] the asset deemed most at risk for those subject to a confiscation order is the family home, as this tends to be the most valuable asset that they possess. This research revealed that having to sell the family home brought about great uncertainty for the defendant and his or her family and put further strain upon those relationships. The loss of the family home was also a punishment that was considered to disproportionately bear down upon the family rather than the confiscation defendant (who was often in prison), and this had emotional, practical, and psychological ramifications for everybody involved, as Jo begins to unravel:

> Confiscating a family home, and let's get this straight this wasn't an eight-bedroomed mansion or something, it was just an ordinary terraced, family home, yeh? But it's not about the bricks and mortar, its more about the stability that signified for the kids, do you understand me like?

For this mother of five, the cumulative effect of being separated from her children through imprisonment and then having to deal with the guilt of knowing

26 Wilson, W. and Bellis, A., *Housing Support for Ex-Offenders (England and Wales)* (Briefing Paper SN02989, House of Commons, 2017).

that her children were about to lose their home because of the confiscation order was too much. The following extract, also provided by Jo, provides an insight into the level of guilt and self-loathing that she felt knowing that the impact of her choices fell most harshly upon her children:

> Yeh know, the guilt was paralysing in prison when it really hit me that my lifestyle choices had ended up damaging the people that I loved the most in the world. Genuinely. I felt suicidal at times. I couldn't breathe.

The impact of losing the family home was explained in more detail by other participants who had already lost their family home through the confiscation process. For some, it meant that their children were rehoused to a different area, resulting in them having to change schools and move away from their friends, extended family, and other support structures, some of which had helped with childcare. For some mothers, the loss of childcare meant that they were no longer able to go to work. For many families, this meant that in addition to losing one breadwinner through incarceration, they also lost their second income, which had a devastating impact. Some research participants explained that the disruption caused through moving schools impacted greatly upon their children's education and emotional welfare. For those children too young to understand what was going on, it was difficult for the parent to explain why they had to leave their friends behind and move schools. For those children old enough to understand what was occurring, they had to deal with being the 'new kid' in school alongside the stigmatising effect that characterises parental imprisonment.

Some research participants detailed the long-term marginalising effects of confiscation, effects which are ignored within the official discourse. Some research participants explained the difficulties in proving eligibility for welfare benefits because on paper they had assets, albeit placed under restraint by the courts, which meant that their 'wealth' exceeded the amount permitted under a means-tested welfare system, despite them not being able to access it. The confiscation process is neither understood nor recognised by the welfare system in the United Kingdom. Through necessity, in order to secure a roof above their children's heads, some research participants explained that they had been pushed into further debt, typically through extortionately high interest and unscrupulous doorstep loan sharks.

It was also explained that securing another home was especially difficult because they did not have the financial means to secure another mortgage, their credit history had been destroyed as a result of the confiscation process, and, as there is a social housing shortage, they struggled to meet the rental eligibility criteria, often being assessed as 'risky' tenants due to the ongoing confiscation process. Many research participants explained their desperation by this stage – a precarious position as discussed later in the chapter.

As the loss of the family home tended to occur whilst the confiscation defendant was in prison, for the person's children, who were already struggling to cope with the loss of a parent, having to move away from their family and friends had a devastating impact upon their lives, leading to attachment issues, nightmares, noticeable changes in behaviour and performance at school, bed-wetting, depression, and even self-harm. For Eddie, the impact on his teenage daughter, who was at the time on medication for depression, added to his increasing inability to cope:

> Me daughter had to have counselling because, errm, basically, because of seeing me get upset about how I was unable to pay this POCA and losing our home, err, a house that she was born in and brought up in for over seventeen and a half years with all those memories and all her friends that she has grew up with, she has had to move away from and for what? For six and a half grand. They are prepared to ruin my family's life for six and a half grand. And she watched her dad have a breakdown because of this POCA, having to live with the guilt and not being able to do anything about it. She watched me fall to bits in tears worrying about having to go back to prison and losing our home.

Whilst it is acknowledged that all types of offences, including low-level offending, generate harm, the use of draconian measures that can bring about such significant hardship for relatively small sums of money appears disproportionate and unjust, and as a result, such insights force us to reconsider the actual purpose of this punishment.

It is also important to consider these findings within an understanding that the person most impacted by the hardships derived by the confiscation process is not the offender who is in prison but the wider family. For example, as the defendant is incapacitated, it tends to be his or her partner, sibling, or parents who are left with the responsibility of selling the person's property in line with strict confiscation and anti-money laundering rules and communicate this with the confiscation solicitor, making alternative housing and schooling arrangements for their children, juggling the practical and welfare demands of single parenting, and trying to arrange regular visits to the prison so that the defendant's children can see their father or mother. It is no wonder then that many of these individuals explained that these demands impacted greatly upon their ability to focus on their own lives and their well-being, with the mounting stress taking its toll. Some discussed how they had begun self-medicating through alcohol to help them cope or were taking prescription medication for depression. From a human rights perspective, this raises obvious concerns, but even from an economic perspective, a punishment that justifies itself on the basis of recovering cash but instead increases demands on both the healthcare and welfare systems does not appear to make good business sense. Of even more concern is the potentially long-term impact of such hardship and marginalisation on the children, especially considering the existing evidence highlighting the structural disadvantage already faced by children of prisoners.[27]

27 Minson, S., 'Direct harms and social consequences: An analysis of the impact of maternal imprisonment on dependent children in England and Wales' (2018) *Criminology and Criminal Justice* 1 (<https://doi.org/10.1177/1748895818794790>).

All-or-nothing

More often than not, public understanding of confiscation derives from the media, which tend to portray the defendants as unwilling to relinquish their assets rather than them being unable to. As a result, the defendant is perceived as 'undeserving,' and the confiscation process is once again legitimised. However, the research provided several examples that challenged the perception of the uncompliant confiscation defendant. Some research participants discussed how they had sold their family home and handed the proceeds from the sale over to the court but despite this, because their 'available' amount figure was made up of other assets for which they no longer possessed or had control over, the default prison sentence was still imposed. Such assets, which were often listed as 'hidden assets' or 'tainted gifts' by the financial investigator, are 'impossible' to recover, as Daniel explains:

> **Daniel:** I couldn't pay the order because they had listed items as hidden assets that weren't hidden, I just didn't have them. Had I known that they were going to send me back to prison anyway I wouldn't have sold me house. . . . I just thought by selling me house and giving them the money that they would see sense, yeh know, that I had tried me best to pay me POCA.
>
> **Interviewer:** What do you mean when you say that you didn't have the hidden assets?
>
> **Daniel:** Well I couldn't get the wedding and engagement ring back from my ex-missus because we had split up whilst I was in prison. But, of course, I couldn't get her to come to court and admit that because we had gone through an acrimonious divorce, and we no longer spoke to each other; we hate each other's guts! To be honest, I expect she has probably pawned them in anyway cos I think she has remarried now, so there was nothing that I could do to get them back anyway, err, so I'm not sure what the court expected me to do.

This example gives credence to the suggestion that confiscation orders, and the assumptions that are contained within them, are particularly difficult to defend against even when the defendant provides the court with evidence to the contrary.[28] Other reasons that assets listed in the available amount were no longer 'available' included lost, stolen, used as a stake when gambling, cashed-in and dissipated on day-to-day living before arrest, exchanged for drugs or other illegitimate items, taxed by other criminals, gifted away, or used to pay a (drug) debt. The most frequent explanation, however, was that they never owned the assets in the first place. For items such as cars and jewellery, they stated that they

28 Lawrence, I., 'Draconian and manifestly unjust: How the confiscation regime has developed' (2008) 76 *Amicus Curiae* 22.

were often listed on their confiscation orders based on hearsay evidence or 'police intelligence,' typically from undercover operations. As Declan pointed out,

> Being seen talking to somebody in a Porsche doesn't mean that I own it. If they are saying that I own it then surely they should be able to trace it, otherwise they can just say whatever they like.

Further, the imposition of a default sentence based on assets that are suggested to be 'hidden' or have been gifted away raises serious ethical questions, especially when the defendant no longer has control over those items. As voiced by the research participants, 'How do you prove something is not "hidden" if it is not hidden, it just simply doesn't exist?' The legislature's unwavering commitment to ensure that not one penny is left in the hands of the offender has allowed for a confiscation system to be constructed with features that are difficult to defend against and are not necessarily conducive to the usual jurisprudential objectives of fairness and justice.

What Daniel's experience also indicates is that despite him making efforts to satisfy his confiscation order by selling his house, this counted for little. Whilst it reduced the amount of time he had to serve in default, he was, nonetheless, sent back to prison and forced to re-endure the debilitating effects of incarceration and the difficulties of reintegration afterwards. This all-or-nothing approach symbolises confiscation's punitive character and thus becomes more problematic when it is considered alongside a growing evidence base that suggests that confiscation figures are grossly inflated and tend to be partially made up by accrued interest.

How do they respond?

In this section, we consider how the defendants and their families responded to their confiscation predicaments. Many of them accepted the recovery of assets that were proven to be illegitimately acquired, but they did not agree with a system that inaccurately constructs confiscation figures with a view to confiscating legitimately acquired assets. In response to this injustice, it meant that the confiscation process was met with resistance by defendants because they quickly realised that it was not about recovering illegitimate gains but about financially incapacitating them indefinitely.

It is important to acknowledge the impact on the self-perception of those subject to a system that is perceived as grossly unjust. For example, in telling their accounts, it becomes apparent that the participants identify themselves as 'victims' of their confiscation experiences because of the procedural unfairness that characterises the confiscation process. As most confiscation defendants were responding to their confiscation cases straight after conviction and throughout their prison sentences, the 'victim script' or defensive position that this induced denied them their opportunity to repent on the circumstances that led to them being in that situation. Given that being able to repent has important consequences for redemption, identity, and desistance,[29] the prioritising of asset recovery over rehabilitation appears counterintuitive.

The impact upon rehabilitation was a theme that dominated the accounts of those subject to confiscation. In recognition of the prospect of having future legitimately acquired assets confiscated, several of the research participants discussed how they took evasive action to prevent this from occurring. This included working cash in hand, not putting money into their bank accounts, not registering themselves as living at a particular address so as to make it difficult for them to be traced, and not putting assets in their name. In the following example, Jo explains that she has come across many confiscation defendants who have been 'forced' to respond to their confiscation case in a non-pro-social way:

> And people do the default sentences and come out to pay the money because the default sentence doesn't wipe the debt does it? Its hanging over people's heads indefinitely. And then you go underground to try and escape the CPS finding you; you don't put yourself on an electoral register, you don't open a bank account, you don't put anything in your name so you can hide from them. I know enough people like that, they go underground. Well they don't go underground, they get forced underground. They don't go back to formal work, they do cash-in-hand work or they open up businesses under somebody else's name so that they can create a smokescreen and become invisible because they want to move on but the system wants to nail you down for your past and hold you there.

The need to take evasive action featured more consistently within the accounts of those whose partners worked legitimately, as the threat of confiscation to their jointly owned assets was deemed unfair. In circumstances where the family home had been listed as an available asset by the financial investigator despite it being legitimately acquired, or partially legitimately acquired, there was a heightened sense of injustice paralleled by a motive of defiance. The risk posed to their partner's legitimately acquired assets was viewed as particularly problematic As Kevin points out,

> That's fucking wrong in it? That's not confiscating money from crime. She's legit, her assets are legit and she wasn't even with me when I committed the offences. That's theft, not confiscation.

As a result, some research participants explained that they felt they had no choice but to 'detach' themselves from their families 'on paper.' This was heightened when they had children because it was understood that their children could be denied any inheritance from the accumulation of assets, even if the source

29 Maruna, S., *Making Good: How Ex-Convicts Reform and Rebuild Their Lives* (American Psychological Association Books, 2001).

of the inheritance could be proved to be legitimate. The longevity and punitive character of this punishment is thus emphasised.

A number of participants discussed how being subjected to an ongoing confiscation case took its toll on them and their families in various ways, including relationship breakdowns, depression, and recidivism. The following extract taken from Jo's narrative captures how the disproportionate impact of confiscation can result in a 'nothing-to-lose' mentality:

> It's like a triple punishment with the trauma of being sent to prison and being separated from my kids and then having to deal with this whole proceeds of crime ordeal which brings a whole load of stress and tension, but to then lose your family home on top all seems a little too excessive to me. Can you imagine the guilt I was carrying knowing all the trauma that I have caused my children? If you push people to the edge then they have nothing to lose, do you know what I mean? And that will mean different things to different people, yeh? For some people that might be depression, self-harm and suicide and for others it might mean reoffending, either way it encourages desperation cos you're in a nothing-to-lose situation.

Despite there being an increasing recognition of the role that the 'family' can play in supporting desistance,[30] it would appear that confiscation practice is contributing to the breakdown of family relationships. This is captured in the following example in which Ryan discusses his co-defendant's confiscation case:

> It's driving families apart. [Co-defendant] said, err, that life is difficult when you're on a POCA cos you can't be proper straight. Yeh can't put things in yeh name cos they can confiscate them off yeh. He said that it caused so many arguments that in the end he and [his wife] split up. She was sick of having to live this lie and having to put everything in her name and then be worried in case they [financial investigators] came onto her for it. So yeh have to ask, what is it really all about? Yeh? How can that be justified? It's hard enough getting by when you come out of prison as it is without all the strain caused by POCA.

The most prominent theme within the research, however, was the reality that being subject to a confiscation order that was increasing with 8% interest was driving people back into crime. Some research participants explained that this meant having to commit crime whilst in prison and in doing so generate some money that could be laundered through a business on the outside so as to be able

30 Thus, 'family and marital relationships' are included as one of nine reoffending/desistance factors by the National Offender Management Service (NOMS): *NOMS Evidence and Segmentation: Companion Document to NOMS Commissioning Intentions from 2014* (<https://assets.publishing.service.gov.uk/government/uploads/system/uploads/attachment_data/file/280924/evidence-segmentation-2014.pdf>, 17 October 2013).

to pay off their confiscation order and avoid the default sentence. For others, this meant that they were committing crime alongside their legitimate job when they were released from prison in order to compensate for the money that they were losing through the attachment of earnings order. Many research participants perceived there to be 'no [legitimate] way out':

> I can see why some lads might just think 'fuck it, it's not worth working for nothing and living in constant fear of being sent back to prison and always being debted up to them when yeh could go back to drug dealing and make some money that would enable yeh to pay the confiscation order off.' I mean what's the risk of going back to drug dealing? The worst-case scenario is that yeh get caught and go back to jail, the exact same outcome of not drug dealing isn't it because I'm being sent back to jail anyway on the proceeds of crime.
>
> (Daniel)

As the desistance literature suggests, when an individual has been punished, he or she is susceptible to either positive change or relapse[31] and, therefore, the structural barriers to desistance caused by the confiscation process act as a societal harm that increases the risk of further victimisation and the cost to the taxpayer in various ways. Several of the research participants described how because of the ongoing confiscation process, they felt trapped, 'anchored' to their criminal past, and denied the opportunity to move on in their lives and the loss of hope was evident in several of their interviews. The frustration of not being able to move on from their confiscation ordeal is best captured by Karl:

> If I'm not here then me family don't have to go through the stigma of being involved with someone that has been criminal and, and this POCA thing goes away. No [Karl], no POCA, and me family can be left alone to get on with their lives without that constant fear that they are gunna come and post another court letter through the door or something.

Conclusion

This chapter offers an alternative account of post-conviction confiscation, an account that had previously failed to materialise. At the heart of this chapter is the 'lived reality' of those subjected to confiscation, which begins to expose some of the contradictions between confiscation ideology and confiscation 'reality.' In doing so, this chapter challenges the underpinning 'confiscating ill-gotten gains' mantra that has been used to legitimise these special powers. In particular, it has shown that confiscation significantly impedes rehabilitation and impacts negatively on the wider family and children, in particular, way beyond the regular processes of criminalisation and imprisonment.

31 Maruna (fn 29).

In highlighting the psychosocial logic that underpins a confiscation defendant's responses to the impact of a confiscation order, this chapter has shown that confiscation can disincentivise the attainment of legitimate employment, encourage non-pro-social behaviours, push people back into offending, cause relationships to break down, and lead to depression, self-harm, and suicidal thoughts. As a result, this chapter strongly contests those official accounts that forcefully propagate confiscation powers on the grounds of deterrence and crime control. Instead, it argues that the confiscation system in the United Kingdom is a system of iatrogenic harm that has completely abandoned any commitment to proportionality and, as a result, represents an affront to human rights legislation and to the 'legitimacy' of state punishment. This chapter has highlighted the structural barriers that are generated because of the confiscation process and the significant constraining effect that they have for agency. Whilst it accepts that these constraints and oppressive conditions do not determine how an individual responds, this chapter explains how those responses are shaped and influenced.

Part II

Innovative assemblages of government

7 Legal professionals as dirty money gatekeepers

The institutional problem

Nathanael Tilahun

Introduction

A growing trend in global anti-money laundering and counter-terrorism financing (AML/CTF) governance is the coerced enlistment of business entities and professional groups as front-line enforcers, or 'gatekeepers,'[1] of the regime. This 'responsibilisation'[2] of businesses and professionals converts those actors into local interlocutors of a global regime, a role that manifestly falls outside of their ordinary corporate or professional functions.

The global AML/CTF regime, primarily developed by the Financial Action Task Force (FATF), requires professionals from both financial and non-financial sectors to serve as an 'army of professionals'[3] at the frontlines of rule enforcement. Financial institutions are defined as legal and natural persons that undertake, as businesses, one or multiple financial activities, such as lending, depositing, transferring money, currency exchange, trading in money instruments and securities, portfolio management, and issuing and managing means of payment.[4] Non-financial institutions are businesses and professions that do not undertake any of the earlier referenced 13 financial activities as businesses but are particularly connected to the mobility of assets. The specific non-financial actors designated by the FATF are casinos, real estate agents, dealers in precious metals, dealers in precious stones, trust and company service providers, lawyers, notaries, and other independent legal professionals and accountants.[5]

1 Shepherd, K.L., 'Guardians at the gate: The gatekeeper initiative and the risk-based approach for transactional lawyers' (2009) 43 *Real Property, Trust & Estate Law Journal* 607. On gatekeepers in general, see Kraakman, R.H., 'Gatekeepers: The anatomy of a third-party enforcement strategy' (1986) 2 *Journal of Law, Economics, & Organization* 53, 54.

2 Garland, D., 'The limits of the Sovereign state: Strategies of crime control in contemporary society' (1996) 36(4) *British Journal of Criminology* 445, 452–455; O'Malley, P. and Palmer, D., 'Post-Keynesian policing' (1996) 25(2) *Economy and Society* 137.

3 Sahl, J.P., 'Lawyer ethics and the Financial Action Task Force: A call to action' (2014) 59 *New York Law School Law Review* 457, 476.

4 For detailed definition, see Financial Action Task Force, *International Standards on Combating Money Laundering and the Financing of Terrorism & Proliferation* (2012) (<http://www.fatf-gafi.org/recommendations.html>), 117 (Glossary). (Henceforth 'FATF Recommendations'.)

5 *Ibid.*

The gatekeeping obligations of these professional actors under the FATF regime fall broadly into two types of functions: the relatively passive role of conducting due diligence and the role of active cooperation with the state.[6] These actors are required to take due diligence steps before entering into, and throughout the duration of, their engagement with a client or customer, including identifying and verifying the client/customer, identifying the beneficial (ultimate) ownership of financial transactions, understanding the nature and purpose of the business relationship with the client/customer, and continually monitoring this relationship.[7] The other type of gatekeeper role, where professionals are required to actively cooperate with the state, includes obligations of data collection, storage and transfer to the state ('record-keeping obligation'),[8] and submission of suspicious activity reports (SARs), with the accompanying no-tipping off rule ('reporting obligation').[9]

This chapter discusses how legal professionals perceive and react to their gatekeeping obligations and what consequences for the AML/CTF legal regime flow from the nature of their perceptions and reactions. The departure point of this discussion is the assertion, further substantiated in the chapter, that there has been fierce resistance to gatekeeping duties from the legal profession. This observation invites us to investigate what motivation drives the said resistance. The chapter undertakes this investigation by stepping into the discursive and institutional elements of the resistance within national and international legal professional associations. The analysis deconstructs official legal narratives offered by these associations and introduces an alternative institutional factor to explain the resistance to gatekeeping. This factor is 'institutional consciousness,' a term developed in this chapter to refer to the prevailing perception and attitude within an organised professional group concerning its role and interests. To further amplify the role of institutional consciousness in lawyers' resistance to gatekeeping, contrast will be made with another institutional context (the banking sector) where gatekeeping rules have been met with a different kind of reaction. This comparison shows how AML/CTF rules are perceived and contested differently as they come into contact with various organised professional actors who have distinctive consciousness about their profession.

The first part of the chapter maps the dominant official self-narrative within the transnational legal professional community regarding gatekeeping. It shows that lawyers' resistance to gatekeeping is framed as a legal and political struggle for the preservation of liberal democratic values. The subsequent section elaborates the concept of institutional consciousness and deploys it to probe the official narrative of professional resistance. In doing so, it reveals that the underlying drivers of lawyers' resistance to gatekeeping, particularly in North America where gatekeeping rules are still successfully staved off, are institutional concerns regarding

6 *Ibid.*, rec.22–23.
7 *Ibid.*, rec.10.
8 *Ibid.*, rec.11.
9 *Ibid.*, rec.20–21.

the *public image* and *self-governance* of the profession. The last section will then contrast legal professionals' response to gatekeeping with that of banking professionals. This section will highlight the two diverging sets of concerns and perceptions generated by a common gatekeeping regime. It shows how institutional consciousness plays a critical role in the implementation of innovative AML/CTF initiatives and how such an 'across-the-board' regulatory initiative could overlook such institutional nuances of its subjects at some cost to its effectiveness.

The findings of the chapter are drawn from qualitative textual data from organisational archives (particularly those of legal professional associations), academic publications by legal professionals, and independent quantitative surveys on institutional perceptions. The analysis has a socio-legal approach by combining discourse analysis of texts (such as policy documents and meeting records) with legal doctrinal interpretation of regulatory instruments. The discourse analysis helps uncover unarticulated (or not officially espoused) perceptions and strategic choices within legal professional associations through hermeneutical tools, such as analysis of word meanings, analogies, argumentative moves, context, and coherence between rhetoric and action.

Resistance to gatekeeping: the liberal democratic self-narrative

Legal professional associations across the world have generally resisted the implementation of the FATF gatekeeping regulations in a more ferocious manner than other financial and non-financial professional groups. The resistance has taken the form of academic and professional publications,[10] policy and advocacy activities by legal professional associations,[11] and constitutional review legal proceedings.[12] The aim was to make the FATF reconsider its policy and/or ensure that states do not (fully) implement FATF's lawyer regulation.

Legal professionals' resistance to gatekeeping is predominantly framed in legal and political terms that are built around liberal democratic premises. The legal argument is that gatekeeping obligations are incompatible with widely accepted

10 *See* Komárek, J., 'Legal professional privilege and the EU's fight against money laundering' (2008) 27 *Civil Justice Quarterly* 13; Mitsilegas, V. and Vavoula. N., 'The evolving EU anti-money laundering regime: Challenges for fundamental rights and rule of law' (2016) 23 *Maastricht Journal of European and Comparative Law* 261.

11 Shepherd, K.L., 'The gatekeeper initiative and the risk-based approach to client due diligence: The imperative for voluntary good practices guidance for U.S. lawyers' (2010) *Journal of the Professional Lawyer* 83, 87; Osborne, D.E., 'The Financial Action Task Force and the legal profession' (2015) 60 *New York Law School Law Review* 421.

12 See *Jamaican Bar Association* v. *The Attorney General and General Legal Counsel* [2014] JMSC Civ. 179; *Nigeria Bar Association* v. *Attorney General of the Federation & Central Bank of Nigeria*, reported in Ahiauzu, N., 'Applicability of anti-money laundering laws to legal practitioners in Nigeria: NBA v. FGN & CBN' (2016) 19 *Journal of Money Laundering Control* 329; *Canada (Attorney General)* v. *Federation of Law Societies of Canada* [2015] SCC 7, 1 S.C.R. 401 (hereinafter '*Federation of Law Societies* case').

legal rules related to the principle of the independence of the legal profession. Even when these concerns are not articulated into self-standing legal rules, the bigger picture of the liberal democratic values at stake should render gatekeeping obligations undesirable.

Legal professionals claim that the gatekeeping obligations threaten legal professional privilege (LPP) and, by implication, the administration of justice. Osborne argues that the 'independence of lawyers and duties owed to citizens [encapsulated in LLP], are inherent aspects of a free and democratic society.'[13] In states where LPP or the independence of the legal profession constitute a self-standing legal norm, such has been argued before courts of law. In states where that is not the case, the legal argument is crafted by resorting to other legal norms that are said to constitute building blocks or origins of LPP. The most common amongst these norms are the right to a fair trial, the rights to privacy and private and family life, and the relationship of fidelity between lawyers and clients.[14] The legal case against lawyers' gatekeeping duty is built on the premise that these norms are fundamental in systems that have any claim to freedom and democracy, and LPP is merely a purpose-built repackaging of these norms within professional practice.

Politically speaking, the independence of the legal profession from the state is asserted as a value that should not be superseded by any other policy objective, including the need to fight financial crimes. It is argued that the imposition of the gatekeeping role makes lawyers inappropriate 'insider' actors within the state's apparatus and the political system in general, whilst they should have been left 'outside' of it.[15] Consequently, gatekeeping rules are described as universal threats to the independence of the legal profession, which 'cannot and should not be sacrificed even in the face of a profound and global threat.'[16]

Linking LPP and the fundamentals of liberal democracy has been an argument commonly deployed by legal professionals before courts of law in different states with varying degrees of success. Successful legal challenges of this sort by legal professionals have in some states led to the suspension or revocation of national implementation of the FATF lawyer regulations.[17] The most publicised and consequential amongst these successful litigation approaches was launched by the

13 Osborne (fn 11), 426.

14 Mitsilegas and Vavoula (fn 10) at p. 273. *See* also, Xanthaki, H., 'Lawyers' duties under the draft EU money laundering directive: Is confidentiality a thing of the past?' (2001) 5 *Journal of Money Laundering Control* 103, 105–107.

15 Svedberg Helgesson, K. and Mörth, U., 'Involuntary public policy-making by for-profit professionals: European lawyers on anti-money laundering and terrorism financing' (2016) 54 *Journal of Common Market Studies* 1216.

16 Paton, P.D., 'Cooperation, co-option or coercion? The FATF lawyer guidance and regulation of the legal profession' (2010) *Journal of the Professional Lawyer* 165, 189.

17 For example, *Jamaican Bar Association* v. *The Attorney General and General Legal Counsel* [2014] JMSC Civ. 179; *Nigeria Bar Association* v. *Attorney General of the Federation & Central Bank of Nigeria,* reported in Ahiauzu, N., 'Applicability of anti-money laundering laws to legal practitioners in Nigeria: NBA v. FGN & CBN' (2016) 19 *Journal of Money Laundering Control* 329.

Federation of Law Societies in Canada, which culminated in 2015 in the *Federation of Law Societies* case.[18] Less successful resistance was waged in Belgium,[19] France,[20] and the United Kingdom.[21]

The key argument in most of these cases is that tampering with LPP, especially by requiring lawyers to make suspicious transaction reports about their clients, disrupts the administration of justice by making clients distrustful of their lawyers (hence denying fair trial), by violating lawyers' own rights to privacy of correspondence or generally by subtracting from lawyers' loyalty to their clients.

However, a broader look at the engagement of legal professional associations with governmental gatekeeping initiatives reveals that the core of the resistance to these initiatives, particularly in North America, is not primarily driven by *legal* and *political* concerns. Instead, *institutional* concerns are at play. These institutional concerns are not necessarily self-serving or invalid but instead intertwine with the legal and political concerns. The following section reveals this institutional dimension underneath the official narrative of legal and political concerns.

Resistance to gatekeeping: the institutional dimension

The institutional factor behind legal professionals' resistance to gatekeeping is one of attitude towards the legal regime in question. This shared awareness or perception amongst legal professionals regarding the impact of AML/CTF gatekeeping rules on the profession will be referred to henceforth as 'institutional consciousness.' This consciousness is institutional, as opposed to individual or societal, in that its concern is the impact of the law on the professional community as an organised group. The concept of institutional consciousness draws insights and analogy from the concepts of 'legal consciousness' and 'legal culture' developed extensively in the wider law and society literature.[22] The essential takeaway from these concepts is attentiveness to the study of law's interaction with social cognitive elements, such as traditions, opinions, and ways of thinking. In other words, it is studying how the law is experienced and interpreted in a particular group, understanding the law not according to the dictates of doctrinal rules of interpretation, but according to how people think and talk about it.

The institutional consciousness that animates legal professionals' resistance to gatekeeping pertains to the position and the interest of the profession vis-à-vis the disciplining state. In the AML/CTF regime, the state has a policing role over regulated entities, including the legal profession. This policing role, executed

18 *Federation of Law Societies* case (fn 12).

19 *Ordre des Barreaux Francophones et Germanophone and Others v. Conseil des Ministres,* European Court of Justice, Case C-305/05, Judgment of 26 June 2007.

20 *Michaud* v. *France*, 6 December 2012, ECtHR, App. No. 12323/11.

21 *Bowman* v. *Fels* [2005] EWCA (Civ) 226, paras. 41–42.

22 Friedman, L., 'Legal Culture and Social Development' (1969) 4 *Law & Society Review* 29; Cotterrell, R., *Living Law: Studies in Legal and Social Theory* (Oxford University Press, 1997); Ewick, P. and Silbey, S., *The Common Place of Law: Stories From Everyday Life* (University of Chicago Press, 1998).

both through punishment (including financial penalties) and engagement (such as information sharing), depicts a process of discipline, whereby the regulated entities are coerced or conditioned into obedience to the state.[23] Such a process of discipline creates a power relationship between the disciplining state and the regulated entities at the receiving end of discipline.

The unarticulated institutional consciousness that animates the resistance to gatekeeping is the legal professionals' need to extricate themselves from the prism of disciplinary power relationship between the state and regulated subjects. There arises a need to position the profession as neither in alliance with the state nor identifying with the subjects of state discipline but as an outsider watchdog to the disciplinary process. This stance may appear identical to the official narrative that lawyers are fighting for professional independence as a defence of legal and political ideals of justice and democracy, as discussed in the preceding section. The key distinction here is, however, that professional independence is sought not (merely) as a pursuit of justice or democracy but as a projection of group image and interests.

The following discussion substantiates this claim by revealing two specific manifestations of group concern underneath the resistance to gatekeeping. These are concerns for the (i) public image and (ii) self-regulation of the profession. The analysis is based on a qualitative archival study of the preparatory history of the FATF's guidance document for the legal profession on the implementation of FATF Recommendations (the *Lawyer Guidance*), and on a discourse analysis of legal professional associations' response to that document. The data is gathered from publicly available organisational publications (policy statements, newsletters, press releases), first-hand accounts of meetings by legal professionals, and legal instruments between 2007 and 2015.

Public image of the profession

Legal professionals' resistance to gatekeeping is driven by a concern for the reputational status of the profession. There is a felt need to project an image of the profession as an independent guardian of the law and not a mere subject of the law. The view emanates from a consciousness regarding the relative positioning of the profession vis-à-vis other professions or businesses and not necessarily from a normative commitment to the positioning of the profession vis-à-vis the state, as officially espoused in the liberal democratic argument. The evidence for this proposition comes from observing the nature of the issues that were key points of contention between the legal professionals and the FATF.

During the preparation of the *Lawyer Guidance*, an important point of contention was the very need for the existence of the *Lawyer Guidance*. The FATF categorised legal professionals in a group of regulated actors known as 'designated

23 See Roele, I., 'Disciplinary power and the UN security council counter terrorism committee' (2013) *Journal of Conflict and Security Law* 1; Ali, N.T., *Regulatory Counter-Terrorism: A Critical Appraisal of Dynamic Global Governance* (Routledge, 2018) chaps 6 and 7.

non-financial businesses and professions' (DNFBPs), which, in addition to lawyers and notaries, consists of casinos, real estate agents, dealers in precious metals and stones, trust and company service providers, and accountants.[24] In 2007, the FATF invited all DNFBPs to a series of meetings for the preparation of guidance documents on the implementation of FATF Recommendations. Whilst all other DNFBPs proceeded to participate, legal professionals put forward demands at first and engaged in substantive talks only in the second round of meetings.[25] The main demands were that legal professionals be treated separately from the other DNFBPs and that the FATF produce empirical evidence on the AML/CTF vulnerability of lawyers and, therefore, justify the need for regulation.[26]

Legal professionals took the very fact of being regulated for AML/CTF purposes alongside commercial actors as a shocking offence to the 'unique role of lawyers' as guardians of freedom and justice.[27] The painting of the legal profession with the same brush as casinos and banks appeared to reduce the profession to a mere business that provides services for a price and in need of watchful government eyes. They argued that lawyers 'and not casinos, serve to protect our citizens' freedoms and liberties.'[28] Representatives of the International Bar Association (IBA) and bar associations from North America, Europe, Japan, Australia, New Zealand, and Hong Kong engaged the FATF with letters and draft proposals for a lighter and more trusting treatment of lawyers due to their unique public role.[29] In response to this demand, the FATF agreed to the preparation of a separate guidance for the legal profession, the *Lawyer Guidance*.[30]

In subsequent meetings for the drafting of the *Lawyer Guidance*, the document was also criticised for having the wrong focus: that it aims to suppress bad lawyers instead of empowering good lawyers.[31] A system focused on suppressing bad lawyers presumes a significant amount of bad lawyers, a claim which lawyers disputed. Duncan Osborne, vice-president of the International Academy of Estate and Trust Law, who took part in consultative meetings between FATF and lawyers, records that during these meetings, lawyers repeatedly sought to

24 FATF Recommendations (fn 4), 116–124 (Glossary).

25 Shepherd (fn 1), 629. See same paper for detailed history of the legal profession's engagement with the FATF.

26 *Ibid.*

27 Osborne (fn 11), 425; Terrill, J.A. and Breslow, M.A., 'The role of lawyers in combating money laundering and terrorist financing: Lessons from the English approach' (2015) 60 *New York Law School Law Review* 433, 436.

28 *Ibid.* (Osborne), 427.

29 Shepherd (fn 1). *See* also American Bar Association, American College of Trust and Estate Counsel, Council of Bars and Law Societies of Europe, Japan Federation of Bar Associations, Federation of Law Societies of Canada, Conseil National des Barreaux, Federation of European Bars, Self-regulatory Organisation of Swiss Lawyers and Notaries, *Joint Statement by the International Legal Profession on the Fight against Money-Laundering* (2003) (<http://www.ccbe.org/NTCdocument/signed_statement_0301_1183723072.pdf>).

30 FATF, *Risk-Based Approach Guidance for the Legal Profession* (2008).

31 Osborne (fn 11).

establish that they do not pose an AML/CTF risk.[32] The FATF did not agree, and lawyers consequently accused the FATF of being not only 'misguided' on the facts[33] but also 'biased'[34] against the interests of the legal profession, driven by 'wilful obliviousness'[35] to fact. The fact is, according to lawyers, that there is no empirical evidence seriously or systematically implicating legal professionals in financial crimes.[36]

Although the involvement of lawyers in criminal finance is the subject of controversy and limited research,[37] the FATF has produced typologies of actual cases of lawyers' complicity, compiled from various national legal systems, as far back as 2003.[38] In addition, researchers and national and international regulatory bodies, such as the UK National Crime Agency, Europol, and the World Economic Forum, have since produced similar evidence.[39] Nevertheless, legal professionals insisted that a more extensive typology and indisputable evidence of their complicity be brought forth. They argued that if lawyers are at all implicated, it must be through unwitting vulnerabilities, and these can be tackled by adopting good practices and guidelines prepared by the professional associations themselves.[40]

Such documents were subsequently produced by legal professional associations. A key illustration is the so-called *Lawyer Guide Report* adopted by the American Bar Association (ABA), the Council of Bars and Law Societies of Europe, and the IBA.[41] The *Report* provides guidance to help lawyers avoid violating AML/CTF rules *unwittingly*, showing how to reduce 'vulnerabilities of the legal profession to misuse by criminals.'[42] Such guidance is claimed to be 'sufficient to help lawyers avoid unwitting assistance to unlawful activities.'[43] Underlying these moves

32 *Ibid.*, 428.
33 *Ibid.*
34 *Ibid.*, 423.
35 *Ibid.*, 431.
36 Zagaris, B., 'Gatekeepers initiative: Lawyers and the bar ignore it at their peril' (2008) 23 *Criminal Justice* 28, 32.
37 Benson K., 'Money laundering, anti-money laundering, and the legal profession' in King, C., Walker, C., and Gurulé, J. (eds.), *The Palgrave Handbook of Criminal and Terrorism Financing Law* (Palgrave Macmillan, 2018) 109–133.
38 FATF, *Report on Money Laundering Typologies 2003–2004* (2004) 24–27.
39 Benson (fn 37) 112–113; Schneider, S., 'Testing the limits of solicitor-client privilege' (2006) 9 *Journal of Money Laundering Control* 27; He, P., 'Lawyers, notaries, accountants and money laundering' (2006) 9 *Journal of Money Laundering Control* 62; Cummings, L.P. and Stepnowsky, P.T., 'My brother's keeper: An empirical study of attorney facilitation of money laundering through commercial transactions' (2011) *Professional Lawyer* 1; Middleton, D. and Levi, M., 'Let sleeping lawyers lie: Organized crime, lawyers and the regulation of legal services' (2015) 55 *British Journal of Criminology* 647.
40 International Bar Association, American Bar Association, and the Council of Bars and Law Societies of Europe, *A Lawyers Guide to Detecting and Preventing Money Laundering* (2014); Osborne 2015 (fn 11) 425.
41 International Bar Association et al., *ibid.*
42 *Ibid.*, 24.
43 Osborne (fn 11), p. 425.

is an assertion that because lawyers are self-driven guardians of the public interest, all that is needed is to enlighten them to the traps of dirty money, so they will not stumble into them.

Self-regulation of the profession

The resistance to gatekeeping obligations is fiercest in the United States and Canada, where legal professional associations have been able to block the countries' compliance with FATF standards. These two countries are repeatedly criticised for failing to implement customer identification, record keeping, suspicious transaction reporting, and no-tipping off obligations, as well as for failing to supervise the profession.[44] Canada has even been subjected to FATF's 'follow-up' procedure – a monitoring step triggered before severe countermeasures could be invoked for non-compliance.[45]

A survey of the policy documents and discourse of legal professional associations in these two countries reveals that the resistance to gatekeeping is also driven by a perceived threat to the self-regulation of the profession; hence, it relates not just to *what* is being required but also to *who* is requiring it. This is evidenced by the fact that these associations, whilst resisting national implementation of FATF rules, adopted more or less similar AML/CTF standards into their self-governance documents.

In Canada, the Federation of Law Societies of Canada, which, together with the Canadian Bar Association, launched the constitutionality challenge against Canada's implementation of lawyers' gatekeeping under the Proceeds of Crime Act (POCA),[46] later adopted internal rules which 'apart from mandatory secret reports on client activities, effectively replicated the substance of the FATF Recommendations.'[47] The Federation objected to the requirement under the POCA[48] of 2000 to report cash transactions of CAN$10,000 or more automatically, but it then adopted in 2004 model rules prohibiting lawyers (and Quebec notaries) from processing any cash amount above CAN$7,500.[49] The Federation further adopted in 2008 rules on client identification and verification that replicate the know-your-customer (KYC) requirements contained in

44 *See* FATF, *Anti-Money Laundering and Counter-Terrorist Financing Measures – United States Fourth Round Mutual Evaluation Report* (December 2016), *Third Round Mutual Evaluation Report* (2006), *Anti-Money Laundering and Counter-Terrorist Financing Measures – Canada Fourth Round Mutual Evaluation Report* (2016), *Third Round Mutual Evaluation Report* (2008).

45 FATF, *Mutual Evaluation of Canada–6th Follow-Up Report* (2014).

46 *Federation of Law Societies* case (fn 12).

47 Paton, P.D., 'Cooperation, co-option or coercion? The FATF lawyer guidance and regulation of the legal profession' (2010) *Journal of the Professional Lawyer* 165, 189.

48 Proceeds of Crime (Money Laundering) and Terrorist Financing Act (S.C. 2000, c. 17).

49 Federation of Law Societies of Canada, 'Model Rule on Cash Transactions,' (2004) (<https://flsc.ca/wp-content/uploads/2018/10/No-Cash-Rule.pdf>).

FATF standards.[50] The KYC requirements adopted by the Federation are actually stricter than those of the FATF.[51] As Ronald MacDonald, then vice-president of the Law Societies Federation, explained, the Federation 'supports know your client regulation in principle and recognizes it as both necessary and appropriate.'[52] But by adopting self-regulatory measures that essentially replicate the FATF requirements, legal professionals have 'eliminated the need for federal regulation of the legal profession.'[53] At the victorious conclusion of the *Federation of Law Societies'* case, MacDonald again remarked that the Federation does not have much objection to the substance of gatekeeping rules; instead, 'all we're saying is that . . . in order to protect the independence of the bar and solicitor-client privilege . . . we should be doing it.'[54]

In the United States, the ABA took steps to divert the Federal government from legislating the FATF standards into domestic law. The ABA established a task force to follow up on the FATF and US government's policy and devise pre-emptive courses of action. Following the work of the task force, the ABA adopted a Good Practices Guidance document,[55] a Formal Opinion on client due diligence,[56] and, together with international lawyers' associations, a *Lawyers Guide*.[57] The Good Practices Guidance and Formal Opinion 463 contained most of the due diligence standards adopted by the FATF;[58] some representatives of ABA further stated that such standards are in fact already practised informally by lawyers.[59] Reports documenting the preparatory history of these self-governance instruments note that the latter are conceived in response to legislative proposals being floated in the US Congress.[60] The chairperson of the task force, Kevin Shepherd, acknowledged that these documents were adopted with the hope that

50 Federation of Law Societies of Canada, 'Model Rule on Client Identification and Verification,' (2008) (<https://flsc.ca/wp-content/uploads/2018/10/Client-Identification-and-Verification-Final-rule-2Oct2018.pdf>).

51 MacDonald, R.J., 'Money laundering regulation: What can be learned from the Canadian experience' (2010) *Journal of the Professional Lawyer* 143, 146.

52 *Ibid.*, 150.

53 *Ibid.*, 149.

54 Grat, J., 'Money-laundering rules don't apply to lawyers: B.C. court' *Globe & Mail* (30 September 2011) (<http://www.theglobeandmail.com/report-on-business/industry-news/the-law-page/money-laundering-rules-dont-apply-to-lawyers-bc-court/article596286/>).

55 ABA, *Guidance for Lawyers to Detect and Combat Money Laundering and Terrorist Financing* (2013).

56 ABA, *Formal Opinion 463: Client Due Diligence, Money Laundering, and Terrorist Financing* (23 May 2013) (<http://www.americanbar.org/content/dam/aba/administrative/professional_responsibility/formal_opinion_463.authcheckdam.pdf>).

57 ABA, IBA, and CBLSE, *A Lawyer's Guide to Detecting and Preventing Money Laundering* (2014).

58 *See*, e.g., Formal Opinion 463, para. 2; Good Practices Guidance, 8.

59 Terrill, J.A., and Breslow, M.A., 'The role of lawyers in combating money laundering and terrorist financing: Lessons from the English approach' (2015) 60 *New York Law School Law Review* 433, 436, 441.

60 Healy, N.M. et al., 'U.S. and international anti-money laundering developments' (2009) 43 *International Lawyer* 795, 796.

it 'would obviate the need for Congress to enact legislation designed to impose a rules-based system on US lawyers.'[61] Furthermore, the ABA adopted a resolution explicitly urging Congress to 'refrain from enacting federal legislation that would regulate the legal profession through AML initiatives,'[62] even whilst endorsing the need for lawyers to undertake customer due diligence and other AML/CTF measures.

In the Canadian and American lawyers' resistance, the fight for self-governance is situated within the well-documented tradition of fierce legal professional independence in those countries[63] compared to the relatively weak resistance staged by European and other (as in Japan and Australia) legal professional associations. Associations outside of North America took part in the initial resistance to gatekeeping.[64] However, their resistance largely faded away when met with strong pushback from governments and judiciaries.[65]

The discussion so far shows that institutional factors – namely, threats to the *image* and the *administration* of the legal profession – have fuelled lawyers' resistance to the gatekeeping initiative, lying beneath the official narrative of concern for liberal democracy. The self-image of legal professionals as guardians of public interest, and their need for administrative independence and self-governance of the profession, meant that both 'being regulated by' and 'working for' the government are anathema and ill-fitting for actors who claim to monitor the state's disciplinary power.

Implications of institutional consciousness for gatekeeping: banking vs. legal professionals

Legal professionals' perception that gatekeeping rules threaten the status and self-governance of their profession, particularly within the North American context, affects how they apply AML/CTF rules. To see this even more clearly, legal professionals' perceptions towards gatekeeping can be contrasted with that of another professional group – namely, the banking sector. Whereas legal professionals characterise the imposition of gatekeeping obligations as intrusive micro-management of the profession by governments, bankers see it as a burdensome entrustment of governmental power into their hands. Consequently, lawyers demanded greater implementation discretion and less collaboration with

61 Shepherd (fn 11), 98.

62 ABA, *Resolution 300* (11–12 August 2008).

63 See Kronman, A.T., *The Lost Lawyer: Failing Ideals of the Legal Profession* (Harvard University Press, 1993); Gordon, R., 'A new role for lawyers? The corporate counselor after Enron' (2002–2003) 35 *Connecticut Law Review* 1185; Gordon, R., 'The return of the lawyer-statesman?' (2017) 69 *Stanford Law Review* 1731.

64 Kirby, D., 'The European Union's gatekeeper initiative: The European Union enlists lawyers in the fight against money laundering and terrorist financing' (2008) 37 *Hofstra Law Review* 261.

65 See Ali, N.T., 'States' varied compliance with international anti-money laundering standards for legal professionals' (2019) 88 *Nordic Journal of International Law* 280.

the state, whilst bankers pushed for less discretionary power, ever-more defined tasks, and greater collaboration with the state.

The professional service company, KPMG, undertakes global AML surveys which provide key sources of insight into the perceptions of financial institutions regarding the implementation of AML rules.[66] These reports find that banks are not comfortable when executing their gatekeeping roles on a risk-based approach. The report from 2014 identifies that the top-three AML compliance costs for financial institutions are automated transaction monitoring systems, KYC exercises (creating, updating, reviewing data), and personnel recruitment and retention.[67] This report underscores that risk-based control of dirty money is very expensive for banks; other commentators further claim that this regime would eventually force 'second-tier' banks out of the market.[68]

Bankers' aversion to the risk-based approach in gatekeeping is not the only cost. The other crucial issue they face is a lack of information and fear of exercising their independent judgement when the law is ambiguous. The risk-based approach leaves much of the information gathering and decision-making work to the ground-level executors, in this case banks. Unlike in the case of, for example, international sanctions list where banks have to execute mechanically the freezing of assets of already specified individuals and entities,[69] the risk-based approach requires banks themselves to decide when to act, requiring them to devise and apply various criteria corresponding with the varying degrees of risk posed by their clients.

Making such lists demands thorough customer due diligence work by banks. In doing so, one core element poses a great challenge: identifying beneficial owners. Bank officials consistently regard this element as the most difficult task, as it is involves complex and time-consuming financial intelligence work.[70] The key difficulties raised by bankers are obtaining adequate information about clients and being able to identify risk and take measure against it.[71] Assessing risk requires (financial) intelligence on clients and their associations, for which banks are furnished less than perfect intelligence from official sources.[72] Furthermore, in identifying and tackling risk, banks increasingly report that automated risk-management

66 The reports are generally available at the KPMG website (<http://www.kpmg.com>).

67 KPMG, *Global Anti-Money Laundering Survey* (2014) (<https://assets.kpmg.com/content/dam/kpmg/pdf/2015/03/global-anti-money-laundering-survey-latest.pdf>). In addition, see Gadinis, S. and Mangels, C., 'Collaborative gatekeepers' (2016) 73 *Washington & Lee Law Review* 797.

68 Simons, E.L., 'Anti-money laundering compliance: Only mega banks need apply' (2013) 17 *North Carolina Banking Institute* 249.

69 Even then, this involves a degree of human decision-making – e.g., names on sanctions lists have various aliases and involve linguistic and cultural insight to identify. For example, if we enter the name 'Sadam Hussein' into the Lexis Nexis © WorldCompliance sanctions database, it turns up six aliases and alternative spellings (English and Arabic) of the name that are in use.

70 KPMG (fn 67), 25.

71 *Ibid.*, 26–27.

72 See, e.g., UK Law Commission, *Anti Money Laundering: The SARs Regime* (Consultation Paper No. 236, 2018).

techniques fail to deliver adequate results. Consequently, banks have to rely more on human decision making, which actively positions their personnel on the frontlines of interpreting and policing crime.[73] Vanessa Iafolla has shown how front-office bank personnel engage in empirical and moral judgement starting from the very initial steps of SAR processing, whether by associating certain monetary instruments with particular AML/CTF risk or determining customers' vulnerability to predicate crimes by their spending habits and social status.[74] The responsibility that comes with such positioning as an interlocutor of the AML/CTF regime has often led banks to adopt a de-risking approach, which involves risk avoidance altogether, instead of risk management, resulting in grave financial exclusion consequences for the global poor by disrupting remittances and trade.[75]

For both of these informational and risk-management needs, bankers seek the state's close collaboration. The KPMG survey shows that 63% of survey respondent bankers said that 'regulators should provide additional guidance' on how to execute risk-based AML, and 43% indicated that 'stronger relationship with regulators' is needed.[76] Yet this demand goes against the very idea espoused by the risk-based approach of devolving decision-making power to local actors. Bankers are, in other words, demanding less regulatory responsibility and more detailed guidance from governments. When such detailed guidance from governments is not forthcoming, banks resort to a hyper-cautious execution of their gatekeeping role.[77]

This reaction from bankers starkly contrasts with that of lawyers. The latter positions their profession as a public-interest function and hence in principle have fewer objections to assuming public responsibility. However, due to the institutional factors outlined earlier, lawyers object to detailed gatekeeping obligations as if 'mere businesses' and to close collaboration with the state. Therefore, lawyers have argued for the most expansive application of the risk-based approach in executing their gatekeeping role. At times, lawyers even explicitly stated their fear of governments imposing 'bank-style obligations' on lawyers.[78]

73 *Ibid.*; Isa, Y.M., Sanusi, Z.M., Haniff, M.N. and Barnes, P.A., 'Money laundering risk: From the bankers' and regulators perspectives' (2015) 28 *Procedia Economics and Finance* 7.

74 Iafolla, V., 'The production of suspicion in retail banking: An examination of unusual transaction reporting' in King et al. (fn 37), 81–107.

75 Stanley, R.L. and Buckley, R.P., 'Protecting the West, excluding the rest: The impact of the AML/CTF regime on financial inclusion in the pacific and potential responses' (2016) 17 *Melbourne Journal of International Law* 83; Ramachandran, V., Collin, M. and Juden, M., 'De-risking: An unintended negative consequence of AML/CTF regulation' in King et al. (fn 37) 237–271.

76 KPMG (fn 67), 36–38.

77 Dean, A., Thompson, E. and Keatinge, T., 'Draining the ocean to catch one type of fish: Evaluating the effectiveness of the global counter-terrorism financing regime' (2013) 7 *Perspectives on Terrorism* 62; De Koker, L. and Jentzsch, N., 'Financial inclusion and financial integrity: Aligned incentives?' (2013) 44 *World Development* 267; Davies, H., 'The dilemma of defining risk appetite in banking' *Financial Times* (9 September 2014).

78 Terrill, J.A. and Breslow, M.A., 'The role of lawyers in combating money laundering and terrorist financing: Lessons from the English approach' (2015) 60 *New York Law School Law Review* 433, 454.

Bankers, on the other hand, perceive the risk-based approach in gatekeeping as burdensome commandeering by the government or as being deputised to act in place of the government, whilst they profess to be mere businesses that should only be deployed as executors.

Conclusion

This analysis of the legal professionals' receptivity to the gatekeeping obligations shows how the international AML/CTF regime impacts the institutional consciousness of its professional interlocutors. In particular, the legal community's anxiety over gatekeeping revolves around the perceived threat to two specific institutional issues: one is the position or reputation of legal professionals as public-interest actors, and the other is the independence or self-governance of the profession. Consequently, the local reception, transposition, and implementation of the FATF-led international gatekeeping rules has been negotiated and shaped by the legal profession's exceptional resistance, at least in the United States and Canada. Elsewhere, such strategies have not succeeded.

This chapter further shows how the institutional impact of the gatekeeping initiative is not uniform across professional sectors, as could be gleaned from the contrast between legal and banking professionals. Whilst lawyers perceive gatekeeping obligations as unwelcome micro-management of the profession, bankers reflect an understanding of gatekeeping as an entrustment of public power or deputation into a governmental role, which they considered equally unwelcome. Upon realising that resistance had failed and that gatekeeping obligations are here to stay, legal professionals advocated for open-ended rules that would allow them greater discretion in implementation. Bankers, on the other hand, requested that the rules be as detailed as possible so that they, as private actors, bear less discretionary responsibility of interpreting a public law.

In order to enhance collaboration with professional, organised groups, such as lawyers, therefore, governments and the FATF need to address the fit of new regulatory initiatives with the institutional cultures of those professions. In comparing lawyers and bankers, we see that lawyers' institutional consciousness resulted in a resistance to gatekeeping regulations that frustrated states' compliance with FATF standards, whereas the response from bankers was an overzealous execution of gatekeeping regulations that resulted in a wave of financial exclusion to the global poor. This shows that professional gatekeepers indeed act as interlocutors of AML/CTF rules, meaning that they translate and shape the regulatory process on the ground and that in doing so, their institutional context shapes the implementation and the consequences of such rules.

8 Occupation, organisation, and opportunity

Theorising the facilitation of money laundering as 'white-collar crime'

Katie Benson

Introduction

Within official discourse in the United Kingdom, individuals who facilitate money laundering on behalf of others, either knowingly or unwittingly, by means of their legitimate occupational position are characterised as 'professional enablers.' The term 'professional enabler' emerged in the 2013 United Kingdom's *Serious and Organised Crime Strategy*, which stated that '[o]rganised crime cannot function without the legitimate economy' and suggested that 'complicit or negligent professional enablers, such as bankers, lawyers and accountants, can act as gatekeepers between organised criminals and the legitimate economy'.[1] More recently, United Kingdom threat and risk assessments have concentrated on the role of 'professional enablers' in relation to economic crimes rather than 'traditional' organised crime, with a particular focus on their involvement in 'high-end' money laundering, which is distinguished from 'cash-based' money laundering. High-end money laundering is associated primarily with serious frauds and major corruption, and it is characterised in part by its reliance on access to the professional skills of lawyers and accountants, amongst others.[2]

The involvement of legitimate professionals in the facilitation of money laundering, therefore, is primarily framed in terms of the nature of the predicate criminality: the professional's role is conceptualised in relation to the serious and/or organised crime that it is 'enabling.' Similarly, much of the academic literature in this area considers the facilitation of money laundering as one of a number of ways in which professionals can provide assistance to 'organised criminals',[3]

1 Home Office, *Serious and Organised Crime Strategy* (Home Office, 2013) 48.

2 National Crime Agency (NCA), *High End Money Laundering: Strategy and Action Plan* (2014); NCA, *National Strategic Assessment of Serious and Organised Crime* (2015); HM Treasury/Home Office, *UK National Risk Assessment of Money Laundering and Terrorist Financing* (HM Treasury/Home Office, 2015).

3 For example, Lankhorst, F., and Nelen, H., 'Professional services and organised crime in the Netherlands' (2004) 42(2/3) *Crime, Law and Social Change* 163; Middleton, D. and Levi, M., 'The role of solicitors in facilitating "organized crime"': Situational crime opportunities and their regulation' (2004) 42(2/3) *Crime, Law and Social Change* 123.

and empirical examination of cases of facilitation refers primarily to professionals' role in the laundering of the proceeds of drug trafficking and other organised criminal activities.[4] The limited criminological attention given to professionals' involvement in the facilitation of money laundering means that the nature of this involvement has been under-theorised, leaving a significant gap in our understanding of the contexts of this involvement and the factors that shape it. Furthermore, the use of the singular concept of 'professional enabler(s)' acts to conflate a whole range of actors, actions, and relations and decontextualises the individual behaviours and decision making that lead to professionals playing a role in money laundering on behalf of others.

This chapter aims to address this gap by conceptualising the facilitation of money laundering as a form of 'white-collar crime,' thus shifting the focus from the nature of the predicate criminality to the nature of professionals and their particular occupational and organisational contexts. The chapter focuses on the facilitation of money laundering by legal professionals; whilst different types of legitimate professionals may play similar roles in facilitating laundering, contexts specific to legal professionals bear further consideration. Conceptualising the facilitation of money laundering by legal professionals as a form of 'white-collar crime' emphasises the professional status of these actors and draws attention to their specific *occupational* context (i.e. the legal profession) and the *organisational* setting in which they are located (i.e. the nature of their firm or practice). Following a brief overview of the empirical research on which this chapter is based, the chapter explains how the facilitation of money laundering by legal professionals fits within the conceptual framework of 'white-collar crime,' 'organisational crime,' and/or 'occupational crime' and draws attention to the need to consider multiple (micro, meso, and macro) levels of analysis when trying to understand occupational and organisational misconduct. Then, taking meso-level occupational and organisational contexts as its focus, the chapter explores how the structures, processes, and transactions of the legal profession can create opportunities for the facilitation of money laundering. The chapter goes on to discuss the characteristics of law firms which may shape these opportunities and considers how the culture of particular legal practices (or types of practice) may be more or less conducive to involvement in money laundering.

Methodology

This chapter is based on the findings from a research project that examined the role of legal professionals in the facilitation of money laundering and the criminal

4 For example, Cummings, L. and Stepnowsky, P., 'My brother's keeper: An empirical study of attorney facilitation of money laundering through commercial transactions' (2011) 1(1) *Journal of the Professional Lawyer* 1; Schneider, S., 'Organized crime, money laundering, and the real estate market in Canada' (2004) 21(2) *Journal of Property Research* 99.

justice and regulatory responses in the United Kingdom.[5] The research involved the analysis of cases of solicitors convicted of money laundering offences for actions taken on behalf of clients which can be considered to have in some way facilitated money laundering, alongside interviews with members of law enforcement and other criminal justice bodies, professional and regulatory bodies, and the legal profession. Twenty cases of solicitors who had been convicted of various money laundering offences between 2002 and 2013[6] were identified from a range of sources, including the Westlaw legal database and transcripts of hearings from the disciplinary tribunals of relevant United Kingdom professional or regulatory bodies. The offences related to their professional position or role and involved the solicitor facilitating the retention, use, or control of criminal proceeds by others or failing to disclose knowledge or suspicion of money laundering by their client(s). Data were collated on these cases from multiple sources (including court of appeals transcripts, Solicitors Disciplinary Tribunal transcripts, and media reports) and analysed alongside the interview data.

The facilitation of money laundering as 'white-collar crime'

The concept of 'white-collar crime' was introduced by Edwin Sutherland, who defined it as 'a crime committed by a person of respectability and high social status in the course of his occupation'.[7] Sutherland's aim was to draw attention to crimes not usually included within the scope of criminology at that time and thus challenge traditional explanations of criminal behaviour that focused on poverty or social disadvantage. However, the centrality which his definition gives to the social status of the offender has been widely criticised for creating 'an imprisoning framework that confuses the offender with the offence'.[8] Instead, it is argued, the focus should be on the nature and characteristics of certain offences rather than on those carrying them out, leading to the use of the terms 'organisational crime' and 'occupational crime' as alternatives to 'white-collar crime.' Croall, however, considers 'white-collar crime' to be a useful umbrella term, defining it broadly as 'an abuse of a legitimate occupational role which is regulated by law'.[9]

'Occupational crime' refers to offences committed by individuals for their own benefit in the course of activity in a legitimate occupation, or offences committed

5 Full details of this research and its findings can be found in Benson, K., *Lawyers and the Proceeds of Crime: The Facilitation of Money Laundering and Its Control* (Routledge, 2020). See also Benson, K. 'Money laundering, anti-money laundering and the legal profession' in King, C., Walker, C., and Gurulé, J. (eds.), *The Palgrave Handbook of Criminal and Terrorism Financing Law* (Palgrave MacMillan, 2018).

6 Under the Proceeds of Crime Act 2002, the Drug Trafficking Act 1994, or the Criminal Justice Act 1993, depending on when the offence was committed.

7 Sutherland, E., *White Collar Crime* (Dryden, 1949) 9.

8 Pontell, H. and Geis, G., *International Handbook of White-Collar and Corporate Crime* (Springer, 2007) xiv.

9 Croall, H., *Understanding White-Collar Crime* (Open University Press, 2001) 17.

by employees against their employers.[10] The key feature of this concept is the location of the offence, with the legitimate occupation providing the context in which the offence occurs. The *occupational context* provides opportunities for criminal activity, which can be exploited regardless of the specific motivation of the offender[11] and can also provide a degree of 'invisibility' to the offence because the offender is 'legitimately present at the scene.'[12] The occupational role can play a part in the commission of the offence, with the offender making use of 'some form of technical or 'insider' knowledge' or professional expertise.[13] The concept of 'organisational crime' refers to 'crime committed by a legal organisation or a member of that organisation in the course of his occupation in favour of the organisation'.[14] Its defining features, therefore, are the *organisational setting* of the behaviour and its purpose – at least in part – of serving the goals of the organisation. Organisational crime can include violations of laws or regulations in small, medium, and large businesses; corporations (corporate crime); and public or voluntary organisations, as well as those committed for the benefit of the state or its agencies (state crime).

Lawyers who facilitate money laundering fall within the definitions of 'white-collar crime' highlighted earlier and can be considered to have committed both 'occupational crime' (as the actions that constitute a criminal offence take place within, and are facilitated by, the context of their legitimate occupational role) and 'organisational crime' (as these actions take place within an organisational setting of some form). Their actions may not necessarily be carried out 'in favour of the organisation', however, and whether the lawyer's role in the laundering leads to, or is driven by, personal or organisational benefit (or both) can vary. It is their technical knowledge and professional expertise, and employment in an occupation that provides expert services and facilitates complex financial transactions, that has led to lawyers (and other similar professionals) being positioned as 'gatekeepers' in the fight against money laundering and is said to provide the means and opportunity for them to help criminals launder the proceeds of their crimes.[15] Conceptualising the facilitation of money laundering by legal professionals within the framework of 'white-collar crime,' therefore, emphasises the professional status of these actors and draws attention to their specific *occupational context* and the *organisational setting* in which they are located and allows the use of theories and findings from the extensive existing body of white-collar

10 See Clinard, M. and Quinney, R., *Criminal Behavior Systems: A Typology* (Holt, Rinehart and Winston, 1973); Clinard, M. and Yeager, P., *Corporate Crime* (Free Press, 1980).

11 Clinard, M. and Meier, R., *Sociology of Deviant Behavior* (Wadsworth, 2011).

12 Croall (fn 9) 8.

13 *Ibid.*

14 Huisman, W. and van de Walle, G., 'The criminology of corruption' in De Graaf, G., von Maravic, P., and Wagenaar, P. (eds.), *The Good Cause: Theoretical Perspectives on Corruption* (Barbara Budrich Publishing, 2010).

15 For example, World Economic Forum, *Organized Crime Enablers: A Report for the Global Agenda on Organized Crime* (2012); Europol, *EU Serious and Organised Crime Threat Assessment: SOCTA 2013* (2013); Financial Action Task Force, *Money Laundering and Terrorist Financing Vulnerabilities of Legal Professionals* (Financial Action Task Force, 2013).

crime research and scholarship to provide new insights into the nature of their involvement in money laundering.

Various theoretical perspectives have been developed to explain occupational and organisational offending.[16] Whilst many of these explanations focus on either individual, organisational, or wider social-structural contexts, there is increasing consensus on the need to consider multiple levels of analysis (micro, meso, and macro) and the interconnections and interactions between them in order to fully explain this form of offending behaviour.[17] Though individual characteristics and personality traits may influence the likelihood of involvement in offending, offending choices will also be shaped by the nature of the organisation in which the individual is based (such as organisational culture, structure, and strategy) and the wider environment. Certain organisational characteristics will create opportunities for offending which, as well as allowing offending to take place, may also cause white-collar crime by 'provoking criminal behaviour'.[18] In addition, the nature of organisations, their cultures, and the opportunities for white-collar crime that occur within them are shaped by their wider social, political, cultural, and economic contexts. For example, cultures of competition and enterprise that are endemic to capitalist systems may drive white-collar offending: the 'enterprise culture' which stresses the values of individualism and financial success can lead to business practices that 'bend the rules' in the pursuit of profit or personal gain,[19] and a culture of competition leads organisations and individuals to seek a competitive advantage over each other, sometimes by illegitimate means. The characteristics of organisations within certain industry sectors will be shaped by the wider industry culture, as well as the nature of the regulatory environment; for example, weak forms of regulatory governance may increase the presence of opportunities for offending.

Various micro-, meso-, and macro-level contexts shape the decision making of legal professionals in relation to their involvement in the management of criminal proceeds generated by others. These contexts include the regulatory and competitive environments of the legal profession, its policy environment in relation to the anti-money laundering regime, and, at the micro-level, the nature of the relationship between the legal professional and the predicate offender.[20] The remainder of this chapter focuses on the meso-level, considering both the characteristics

16 For an overview, see Huisman, W., 'Criminogenic organizational properties and dynamics' in Van Slyke, S., Benson, M., and Cullen, F. (eds.), *The Oxford Handbook of White-Collar Crime* (Oxford University Press, 2016); Benson (fn 5).

17 See, for example, Vaughan, D., 'Rational choice, situated action, and the social control of organizations' (1998) 32(1) *Law and Society Review* 23; Vaughan, D., 'Beyond macro- and micro-levels of analysis, organizations, and the cultural fix' in Pontell, H. and Geis, G. (eds.), *International Handbook of White-Collar and Corporate Crime* (Springer, 2007); Huisman 2016 (fn 16).

18 Madensen, T., 'Opportunities for crime' in Van Slyke, S., Benson, M., and Cullen, F. (eds.), *The Oxford Handbook of White-Collar Crime* (Oxford University Press, 2016) 382.

19 Sikka, P., 'Enterprise culture and accountancy firms: new masters of the universe' (2008) 21(2) *Accounting, Auditing and Accountability Journal* 268.

20 Benson (fn 5).

of the firms or practices in which lawyers work (their *organisational* setting) and the nature of the legal profession itself (the *occupational* context).

The occupational context

Analysis of 20 cases of lawyers who were convicted of money laundering showed how the structures, processes, and transactions of the legal profession can create opportunities for the facilitation of laundering.

'Normal' transactions

Most of the transactions that served to launder criminal proceeds in the cases examined were 'normal' transactions. In other words, the transactions were those that legal professionals carry out or facilitate on behalf of clients for legitimate reasons on a regular basis as part of their normal occupational role. For example, the most common transactions in the cases analysed were (i) the purchase of residential property using the proceeds of crime, or sale of property that had been bought using the proceeds of crime and was thus considered to be a criminal asset, and (ii) various transactions involving the passing of criminal proceeds through the firm's client account.[21]

The role of the convicted solicitor in cases involving the purchase or sale of property was in the conveyancing process: conducting the legal and administrative work required for the transfer of property. The Solicitors Regulation Authority's (SRA) *Risk Assessment on Anti-Money Laundering and Terrorist Financing* (issued in March 2018) considers conveyancing as one of the services provided by solicitors that pose the highest risk for money laundering (along with client account services and trust and company formation).[22] It reports that approximately half of the suspicious activity reports (SARs) that are submitted by the legal sector in the United Kingdom relate to property transactions, suggesting that purchasing property is an attractive means of money laundering 'because of the large amounts of money that can be laundered through a single transaction, and the fact that property will tend to appreciate, or can be used to generate rental income'.[23] The purchase of commercial or residential property provides an ideal method of laundering criminal funds, offering two points at which the funds can be legitimised: firstly, as deposits are moved through a law firm's client account and, secondly, as the funds are exchanged for the ownership of the property. Furthermore, as the SRA points out, rental income or profit

21 Client accounts (or trust accounts) are bank accounts held by a legal practice for the purpose of holding and transferring client money. They are used to, for example, receive fees and deposits, issue or cash cheques, facilitate funds transfers or purchases, and make disbursements to or on behalf of the client. For regulations, see Solicitors Regulation Authority (SRA), *Handbook* (Version 21, 2018 <http://www.sra.org.uk/solicitors/handbook/>).

22 SRA, *Risk Assessment on Anti-Money Laundering and Terrorist Financing* (2018) (<http://www.sra.org.uk/sra/how-we-work/reports/aml-risk-assessment.page#>)

23 *Ibid.*

made by the sale of the property also provides legitimate income from initially illegitimate funds.

In the transactions involving the purchase of property, the deposits paid (which were considered to have been earned through illegal activity) will have passed through the solicitor's firm's client account. In a number of other cases, it was the use of the client account for passing money from one location to another that was the primary means by which the criminal proceeds were laundered, and it was the solicitor's actions in facilitating this that resulted in his or her conviction. Client accounts provide a 'façade of legitimacy' to funds that pass through them and transactions that originate from them; they can be used as a way of 'moving money from one individual to another through a legitimate third party under the guise of a legal transaction without attracting the attention of law enforcement agencies'.[24] Furthermore, because of the principle of lawyer-client confidentiality,[25] banks are unaware of the identity of the client whose funds are being moved through client accounts, and so their use can help to circumvent banks' anti-money laundering procedures.[26] Within the cases analysed, client accounts were used as a conduit for funds being transferred between company or personal bank accounts; to purchase cars, yachts, or jets, thus obscuring the owner of the funds/purchaser of the assets; and as one part of a complex series of accounts for money to pass through.

In addition to property purchases or sales and the movement of funds through client accounts, other transactions evident in the cases included the transfer of the ownership of assets and use of corporate vehicles and offshore accounts. These are all transactions that legal professionals provide to legitimate clients on a regular basis as part of their occupational role. With 'clean' money, they would be considered as normal business transactions, but with 'dirty' money originating from illegal activity, these same transactions constitute money laundering.[27] This means that non-legitimate transactions (i.e. transactions with non-legitimate funds) will be hidden amongst the legitimate transactions that lawyers will also (and usually primarily) be carrying out in their day-to-day work. In many cases, these will essentially be the same transaction: the non-legitimate transactions will look the same as legitimate transactions, and the actions and behaviours of the lawyer carrying them out will be the same. As such, transactions conducted by lawyers involving criminal proceeds can be seen as being 'parasitical' on the legitimate transactions they carry out as a function of their regular occupational role.[28] The proximity of legal professionals' occupational structures and processes

24 *Ibid.*

25 The general principle of confidentiality for solicitors in the United Kingdom is set out in the SRA, *Handbook* (fn 21) Chapter 4.

26 Middleton, D., 'Lawyers and client accounts: Sand through a colander' (2008) 11(1) *Journal of Money Laundering Control* 34.

27 The principal money laundering offences are set out in the Proceeds of Crime Act 2002, ss.327–329.

28 Benson, M., Madensen, T., and Eck, J., 'White-collar crime from an opportunity perspective' in Simpson, S. and Weisburd, D. (eds.), *The Criminology of White-Collar Crime* (Springer, 2009) 185.

to funds of criminal origin – as well as to those of legitimate origin – therefore provides opportunities for money laundering, as they can hide non-legitimate transactions amongst their legitimate transactions (it also creates vulnerabilities for those working in the profession, as transactions involving criminal funds can also be hidden from them).

Legitimate and specialised access

Opportunities for crimes within an occupational context arise in part because the offender 'has legitimate access to the location in which the crime is committed,' helping to provide their actions with 'a superficial appearance of legitimacy.'[29] They have access to the 'target,' or situations that can be taken advantage of for personal (or organisational) gain, and are more likely to encounter or become aware of these situations as they 'move through familiar places.'[30] Where money laundering is facilitated by legal professionals, this access may also need to be specialised, requiring certain skills and expertise that are available to such professionals and allow them to take advantage of opportunities that they encounter. For example, lawyers who play a role in the purchase or sale of property bought with the proceeds of crime have legitimate 'access' to the conveyancing process that acts to launder the criminal proceeds and have the expertise and required qualifications to facilitate this process, and their access to a client account allows them to move funds from illicit sources as required and gives the funds the necessary veneer of legitimacy.

Lawyers' positions as 'respected' professionals and the status that this confers may also enhance their ability to take advantage of situations that can facilitate money laundering. For example, the cases analysed included a solicitor who helped his brother manage the proceeds of mortgage frauds by witnessing an email related to a transfer of title and using headed paper to forge a document to support a funds transfer (amongst other actions). Another solicitor used his position to try and convince a bank that funds obtained through fraud had been earned legitimately so that they would release the funds from a frozen account. These individuals were thereby making use of their position as solicitors and playing on the trust and status that this imparts.

Confidentiality and privilege

A central feature of the relationship between the legal professional and the predicate offender whose criminal proceeds are being laundered is that it is a lawyer-client relationship, which confers on it principles of confidentiality and legal professional privilege (LPP). The nature and scope of these principles and

29 Benson, M. and Simpson, S., *Understanding White-Collar Crime: An Opportunity Perspective* (Routledge, 2018) 101.

30 Madensen, T. (2016) 'Opportunities for crime' in Van Slyke, S., Benson, M., and Cullen, F. (eds.), *The Oxford Handbook of White-Collar Crime* (Oxford University Press, 2016) 396.

their application to issues relating to money laundering vary between countries and depend on the constitutional and legal framework within a country (and, in some federal systems, within each state).[31] Legal professionals are required, both professionally and legally, to keep the affairs of present or former clients confidential, 'unless otherwise allowed or required by law and/or applicable rules of professional conduct'.[32] LPP protects the client against disclosure; it recognises the right of individuals to be open and candid with their lawyers without fear that their communications will later be disclosed to their prejudice.[33] However, there are limits to the protections provided by LPP; in the United Kingdom, the 'crime/fraud exception' to the principle states that LPP 'does not extend to documents which themselves form part of a criminal or fraudulent act, or communications which take place in order to obtain advice with the intention of carrying out an offence'.[34]

Despite this exception, the protections provided by the duty of confidentiality and LPP may create challenges for investigations which require access to documents or details of discussions and have implications for oversight of client account transactions (as discussed earlier). The scope and application of principles of confidentiality and privilege[35] in relation to money laundering are complex and open to misunderstanding and divergent interpretations by legal professionals and law enforcement.[36] The need to ensure that privilege is respected can increase the time and resources required in a criminal investigation, and claims of LPP can cause delays to investigations and impede the gathering of evidence.[37] Furthermore, the United Kingdom's 2017 *National Risk Assessment of Money Laundering and Terrorist Financing* states that there have been instances of lawyers falsely or incorrectly claiming LPP to prevent the disclosure of certain documents,[38] and the Financial Action Task Force (FATF) suggests that individuals involved

31 FATF (fn 15).

32 IBA, *International Principles on Conduct for the Legal Profession* (International Bar Association, 2011) 6.

33 LPP does not apply to all communications between client and lawyer and is, therefore, not as broad in its coverage as the principle of confidentiality. Within the United Kingdom, for example, it covers only confidential communications that fall under the categories of 'advice privilege' and 'litigation privilege.' Advice privilege covers communications between a lawyer and his or her client for the purpose of giving or receiving legal advice. Litigation privilege protects confidential communications between a client or his or her lawyer and third parties made in relation to litigation that has commenced or is in reasonable prospect (see Thanki, B., Carpenter, C., Cutress, J., Goodall, P., King, H., Loveridge, R., Oppenheimer, T., Yeo, N., and Phelps, R., *The Law of Privilege* (3rd ed., Oxford University Press, 2018).

34 Legal Sector Affinity Group, *Anti-Money Laundering Guidance for the Legal Sector* (2018), para. 7.4.5.

35 In addition to and distinct from LPP, POCA 2002 provides an exemption from reporting requirements for solicitors when communications have been received in 'privileged circumstances.' Again, an exception applies when the communication was given with a view to furthering a criminal purpose. See POCA 2002, ss.330(6)(b) and (10).

36 FATF (fn 15).

37 FATF (fn 15); Middleton (fn 26).

38 HM Treasury/Home Office 2015 (fn 2).

in criminal activity may believe that they are protected by LPP, without understanding the limitations of this protection.[39] This perception of protection would make lawyers attractive to individuals with criminal proceeds to launder and thus increase their vulnerability to exploitation or provide opportunities for them to become involved in money laundering.

The organisational setting

The organisational context has long been seen as an important factor in the commission of white-collar offences. Organisational characteristics and dynamics, including structure, culture, and strategy, shape the behaviours of those within and so must be seen as crucial in shaping offending behaviour within and by organisations.[40] The structure of a law firm could refer to its size and complexity; the way that authority, accountability, roles, responsibilities, information flows, and decision-making processes are structured or allocated; the organisation of compliance processes and management; the levels of autonomy of different members; and the extent and nature of oversight processes and procedures. As with other forms of organisational misconduct, the nature and characteristics of the firms or practices in which lawyers work may provide opportunities for them to facilitate money laundering (or create vulnerabilities which could be exploited by those in possession of criminal proceeds). The culture of particular legal practices (or types of practice) may produce environments that are more or less conducive to the involvement of their employees in money laundering (as well as other forms of misconduct).

Size and complexity

The size and structure of law firms within the United Kingdom vary widely from large international city firms to small 'high-street' practices with much lower turnovers and fewer employees. In addition, many solicitors in the United Kingdom work as 'sole practitioners', providing legal services from practices in which they are the only lawyer. The 2017 United Kingdom *National Risk Assessment of Money Laundering and Terrorist Financing* reported that there were over 14,000 firms providing legal services in the United Kingdom in 2016, with 72% of those employing fewer than 10 employees.[41]

Evidence from research on organisational crime provides no consensus on the relationship between size or complexity and illegal behaviour or compliance with

39 FATF (fn 15).

40 See, for example, Huisman (fn 16) for an overview of the criminogenic properties and dynamics of organisations; Vaughan (fn 17) for how the nature of the organisational setting can influence individuals' decisions to take such opportunities; Campbell, J.-L. and Göritz, A., 'Culture corrupts! A qualitative study of organizational culture in corrupt organizations' (2014) 120 *Journal of Business Ethics* 291 for a summary of research on the role of organisational culture in misconduct by employees.

41 From Office for National Statistics, 'Business population estimates 2016' (<https://www.gov.uk/government/statistics/business-population-estimates-2016>, 2016).

laws or regulations. Some suggest that large firms are more likely to engage in illegal behaviour, often on multiple occasions, due in part to more complex business processes and management structures.[42] However, large firms also have the resources to invest in training, preventive systems, and compliance programmes; may put a greater emphasis on compliance; and may be more visible to regulatory agencies.[43] Complex organisations, with several layers of management or consisting of multiple sub-divisions, may create more opportunities for misconduct or regulatory non-compliance.[44] On the other hand, smaller firms might lack the ability or expertise to comply with required standards. For example, sole practitioners and small legal practices may find it much more difficult than larger firms to keep up with anti-money laundering regulations and guidance provided by their supervisors or professional bodies due to lower exposure to guidance documents and necessary expertise or a lack of resources to enable staff to attend training. Interviews with law enforcement personnel suggested that individuals looking to launder criminal proceeds would be more likely to use small 'high-street' legal practices than larger firms, as they provide a 'lower-risk' option, with sole practitioners being seen as particularly attractive due to the lack of oversight from others in the practice. However, the nature (based on type, frequency, or scale) of the transactions conducted and services provided by lawyers in large, multinational law firms may provide opportunities for those wishing to move or conceal the origins of particular forms or large amounts of illicit funds or those requiring more complex financial constructions. Therefore, rather than concluding that firms of a certain size or complexity are more or less likely to provide opportunities for money laundering, it seems probable that different types of firms provide different types of opportunities.

Autonomy and oversight

A degree of autonomy and lack of internal oversight in relation to particular activities or transactions may allow legal professionals to take advantage of opportunities to facilitate money laundering. The level (and effectiveness) of oversight within law firms will vary, influenced by the size, structure, organisational strategy, and culture of the firm. For example, the autonomy enjoyed by sole practitioners may allow them to conduct transactions or act for clients without scrutiny from partners or other colleagues. However, a lack of effective oversight can also exist in larger organisations, especially those with more decentralised structures.[45] The case data highlighted a certain level of autonomy and possible lack of oversight in several cases where passing money through the firm's client account

42 For example, Simpson, S. and Rorie, M., 'Motivating compliance: Economic and material motives for compliance' in Parker, C. and Lehmann Nielsen, V. (eds.), *Explaining Compliance: Business Responses to Regulation* (Edward Elgar Publishers, 2011).

43 Huisman (fn 16) 448.

44 *Ibid.*, 447.

45 *Ibid.*

was the means of facilitation, even though the solicitors involved were not sole practitioners. This category included a solicitor who, whilst only one of four partners in his firm, was noted to have 'had in fact *sole operational control* over the [client] account' through which he transferred £8 million of criminal proceeds.[46] Another example was a solicitor who was the sole principal partner in his firm (though the size and structure of the firm is not clear) and so may have been in a position to avoid scrutiny over the transactions he was conducting through the client account. Two solicitors convicted of money laundering offences due to their roles in the movement of criminal proceeds through their firms' client accounts were the designated Money Laundering Reporting Officers for their firms (as well as being managing partner and senior partner) and so may not have been subject to the same degree of oversight or scrutiny as they might have been without occupying these roles.[47]

Organisational form

Organisations which provide legal services can take various forms. This variety continues to grow in the United Kingdom with the opening up of the legal services market and introduction of, for example, alternative business structures (ABS). ABSs are a new form of law firm,[48] which allow non-lawyers to be involved in owning and becoming partners in law firms. The purpose of the introduction of ABSs was to increase competition within the legal services market, and there were initial concerns about the impact this would have on the provision of legal services in the United Kingdom. However, a 2017 Legal Services Board report showed that only a minority of the ABSs licensed since their introduction were new firms, with the majority being existing legal services providers that had converted to ABSs.[49]

Concerns were raised, however, by solicitors interviewed for this project about the emergence of particular formats of legal services providers. A number of the solicitors highlighted what they referred to as 'conveyancing farms' or 'conveyancing factories' as posing particular risks in relation to money laundering. These were described as 'big companies that do really cheap conveyancing' (Solicitor 1), with large teams of non-qualified staff (paralegals) carrying out the conveyancing and being supervised by a small number of qualified lawyers. This system was described as 'conveyancing by numbers' (Solicitor 1), with staff having 80–100 cases to manage at any given time and minimal supervision of their work. This raises concerns about the standard of due diligence that can be carried out, as one solicitor pointed out, 'If you're dealing with that volume, then it's very difficult to even make sure you've seen all the proper bank statements, never mind had

46 *R v Paul Winter Morris* [2009] EWCA Crim 9 (emphasis added).

47 For wider discussion of such instances, see Benson (fn 5).

48 Legal Services Act 2007, Part V.

49 Legal Services Board, *Evaluation: ABS and Investment in Legal Services 2011/12–2016/17: An Analysis of Investment in Legal Services since the Introduction of ABS Licensing* (2017).

a chance to read them properly and check them' (Solicitor 3). Such firms were, therefore, considered to pose much higher risk in relation to money laundering.

Conclusion

This chapter has shown how conceptualising the facilitation of money laundering by legal professionals within the framework of 'white-collar crime' provides new insights into the ways that the organisational characteristics of legal practices and the nature of the legal profession itself can create opportunities for money laundering. For example, high levels of autonomy and a lack of effective oversight within a legal practice can allow lawyers to conduct transactions involving illicit funds with relative impunity. The degree of autonomy and level of oversight experienced by a legal professional may be shaped by the size and structure of his or her practice and the legal professional's role within that practice. Whilst sole practitioners will enjoy very little or no oversight of their actions, effective oversight can also be lacking in larger firms due to the status or position of individual lawyers or the nature of internal structures. Sole practitioners and small 'high-street' practices may be particularly vulnerable to exploitation by those with criminal proceeds to launder due to being seen as 'lower risk' and less visible to regulators and having fewer resources to invest in anti-money laundering training and compliance processes. However, the nature of transactions conducted and services provided by lawyers in large, multinational law firms could be used to hide the kinds of complex financial arrangements required to move or conceal large-scale illicit funds, and complex, multi-layered management structures may create opportunities for misconduct or regulatory non-compliance.

Legal professionals have legitimate and specialised access to a range of processes, transactions, and structures that can be used to launder or otherwise manage the proceeds of criminal activity. For example, the use of client accounts by the legal profession provides the opportunity to move funds from one individual or organisation to another or make purchases on behalf of clients whilst providing the funds/transactions with the necessary veneer of legitimacy to avert the attention of law enforcement or financial institutions. The role played by legal professionals in property purchase and sale processes places them in potential proximity to funds of illegal origin, providing opportunities to facilitate money laundering, as well as making them vulnerable to exploitation by those seeking to purchase property with criminal proceeds. Other services that legal professionals provide for clients as part of their 'normal', legitimate occupational role include the formation and administration of companies and other corporate vehicles. As with property transactions and the use of client accounts to transfer funds, these services can be used for illicit as well as licit purposes (or they can involve 'dirty' money in the same way that they can be used with 'clean' money) and so, when involving criminal proceeds, can be seen as being 'parasitical' on the legitimate processes, transactions, and structures of the legal profession.

The construction of those who become involved in the facilitation of money laundering as 'professional enablers' acts to decontextualise this involvement, and a lack of criminological attention in this area means that the nature of professionals' involvement in facilitating money laundering remains under-theorised. Considering the individual, organisational, occupational, and wider environment-level contexts of professionals' actions enables a more effective understanding of the factors that shape them and so provides opportunities for developing strategies for preventing the facilitation of money laundering, as well as avenues for further research.

9 New payment systems

Potential counter-terrorist financing risks and the legal response in the United Kingdom

*Doron Goldbarsht**

Introduction

New payment systems (NPSs) are an alternative to the traditional financial services that are typically offered by regulated financial institutions, such as banks. They are characterised by the innovative ways in which they initiate payments through, or extend the reach of, traditional retail electronic payment systems. NPSs are increasingly interconnected, not only between themselves but also with traditional payment methods.[1] One of the greatest (positive) impacts of NPSs has been the inclusion of individuals from developing countries in which basic financial services have not been sufficiently available.[2]

However, the development of NPSs also poses threats for the control of terrorist financing (TF) funds generation and transfer.[3] Methods of TF continue to evolve in response to emerging changes in technology or deliberate attempts to circumvent law enforcement counter-terrorist financing (CTF) efforts. NPSs pose risks that may increase over the short term as overall use of these systems grows. Many NPSs can be accessed globally and used to transfer funds quickly across borders. Some online payment systems and digital currencies are also anonymous by design, making them attractive for TF – particularly when the payment system is based in a jurisdiction with a comparatively weak CTF regime.[4]

In order to mitigate these risks, technological advances in financial services require constant monitoring, along with appropriate legislation and enforcement,

* The author wishes to thank Ms Carolina Jimenez Molina for excellent research assistance.

1 Financial Action Task Force (FATF), *Guidance for a Risk-Based Approach: Prepaid Cards, Mobile Payments and Internet-Based Payment Services* (2013) 10. See also Górka, J. (ed.), *Transforming Payment Systems in Europe* (Springer, 2016).

2 Winn, J. and de Koker, L., *Introduction to Mobile Money in Developing Countries: Financial Inclusion and Financial Integrity Conference Special Issue* (University of Washington School of Law Research Paper No. 2013-01, 2013); Malady, L., Buckley, R.P., and Arner, D.W., *Developing and Implementing AML/CFT Measures Using a Risk-Based Approach for New Payments Products and Services* (CIFR Paper No. 028/2014 and University of Hong Kong Faculty of Law Research Paper No. 2014/021, 2014).

3 FATF, *Guidance for a Risk-Based Approach* (fn 1) 13–20.

4 FATF, *Emerging Terrorist Financing Risks* (2015) 20–21.

in a manner that ensures financial prosperity and inclusion.[5] The structure, functioning, and risks of NPSs require effective regulation and operational measures in order to ensure that financial integrity risks are addressed effectively so that bringing more people into the formal financial framework does not come at the expense of effective controls that mitigate the TF risks posed by these emerging payment methods.

This chapter considers the changes in the UK NPS legal regime in the light of the two Financial Action Task Force (FATF) reports that have reviewed the United Kingdom's implementation of the international standards: the first report was published in June 2007[6] and the second in December 2018.[7] This examination will assist in answering two critical questions. The first is whether the CTF regime for NPSs is consistent with the international instruments with which it was ostensibly enacted to comply. The second is whether the UK CTF responses are sufficiently tailored to the United Kingdom's NPS risks, paying attention to the government's ambition to create a world-leading environment for the development of innovative payments and financial technology.[8]

Following this introduction, the first part of the chapter will introduce the features and risks of three main types of NPSs. The second part will discuss the FATF Recommendations, which represent the international standards to be applied in CTF – in particular, the recommendations that are key to NPSs. The third part will examine the UK responses to the international standards. The chapter will then offer some concluding remarks, answering the questions posed earlier and contending that the UK efforts to comply with the international standards are not precisely aligned with the risks posed by the NPSs in the United Kingdom.

How new payment systems work

NPSs include a variety of services that apply groundbreaking technological solutions to the provision of financial services. This section will focus particularly on the three NPSs that are considered most relevant from the perspective of TF: prepaid cards, mobile payment services, and Internet-based payment services. It will first describe the payment system and explain how it works, the entities that are involved, and their roles or activities. The section will then detail the potential risks involved in each of the three NPSs.

5 Zerzan, A., *New Technologies, New Risks? Innovation and Countering the Financing of Terrorism* (World Bank Working Paper No. 174, 2009) 1–2.

6 FATF, *Third Mutual Evaluation Report: Anti-Money Laundering and Combating the Financing of Terrorism: The United Kingdom of Great Britain and Northern Ireland* (2007).

7 FATF, *Fourth Round Mutual Evaluation Report: Anti-Money Laundering and Counter-Terrorist Financing Measures – United Kingdom* (2018). See further Keatinge, T. et al., *No Rest for the Wicked: Driving Change in the UK's Post-FATF Evaluation AML Regime* (RUSI, 2019).

8 HM Treasury, *Digital Currencies: Response to the Call for Information* (2015) 19.

Prepaid cards

Prepaid cards, which are a type of electronic money, are physical cards that are increasingly marketed by small and medium enterprises and retail merchants. Whilst credit cards and debit cards, respectively, draw money from a line of credit or from a checking account, the value of a prepaid card comes from money given to the card issuer prior to the use of the card.[9] That preloaded value is encoded on a magnetic stripe or an electronic chip.[10] Consumers can easily access a prepaid card by buying it from a distributor (a retail store). The issuer does not need to conduct any analysis of the cardholder's credit standing and does not bear the costs of opening and managing a payment account.[11]

A wide spectrum of prepaid cards is available.[12] Closed-system prepaid cards, which are limited to buying goods or services only from the merchant issuing the card, are usually sold at fixed amounts and cannot be redeemed for cash. A common example is gift cards. Anonymous customers can buy closed-system cards with cash, without needing to identify sources, and the card can then be used to transfer its value to a merchant without recording the identity of the person making the transaction.[13] In spite of allowing concealed money transfers, these cards are considered to pose a lower risk for TF because of their closed usage spectrum.[14] Semi-closed-system prepaid cards, such as mall cards, have a similar structure but can be used to pay multiple associated merchants or service providers. These cards are issued by third parties, such as banks.[15] In contrast, open-system prepaid cards, such as charged travel cards, can be used at almost any credit-card-accepting merchant. They are reloadable and can also be used to retrieve cash from automated teller machines (ATMs).

Potential CTF risks of prepaid cards

Identifying the individual who uses a prepaid card can be difficult because providers are not necessarily subject to customer due diligence (CDD) requirements.[16]

9 Gurung, J., Wijaya, M., and Rao, A., 'AML/CTF compliance and SMEs in Australia: A case study of the prepaid card industry' (2010) 13(3) *Journal of Money Laundering Control* 184, 193; Sienkiewicz, S., *Prepaid Cards: Vulnerable to Money Laundering?* (Federal Reserve Bank of Philadelphia Payment Cards Center Discussion Paper No. 07–02, 2007) 1.

10 FATF, *Money Laundering Using New Payment Methods* (2010) 16. See also Choo, K.-K.R, 'New payment methods: A review of 2010–2012 FATF mutual evaluation reports' (2013) 36 *Computers & Security* 12.

11 FATF, *Emerging Terrorist Financing Risks* (fn 4), 5–6.

12 Linn, C.J., 'Regulating the cross-border movement of prepaid cards' (2008) 11(2) *Journal of Money Laundering Control* 146, 148–150; Choo, K.-K. R., *Money Laundering Risks of Prepaid Stored Value Cards* (Trends and Issues in Crime and Criminal Justice No 363, Canberra, 2008) 3.

13 Linn (fn 12), 147.

14 FATF, *Emerging Terrorist Financing Risks* (fn 4), 5; Sienkiewicz (fn 9), 9–16.

15 Choo (fn 12), 2–4; Furletti, M., *Prepaid Card Markets and Regulation* (Federal Reserve Bank of Philadelphia Payment Cards Center Discussion Paper No. 04–01, 2004) 2–8.

16 FATF, *Emerging Terrorist Financing Risks* (fn 4) 13.

Moreover, some funding methods for the purchase of the prepaid card can be tracked and linked to the individual responsible, but the cards can also be acquired anonymously with cash or other NPSs that are not linked to a bank account.[17] Another risk associated with prepaid cards is that one common fund may be accessed with multiple cards, meaning that the funding can be established via one card, but the beneficiaries can obtain additional cards that are also linked to the account. In addition, any third party abroad – even one that is unknown to the issuer – can easily receive a shipped card and access the value stored in it, provided they know the personal identification number.[18] Some cards allow global reach payments, cash access, and fund transfers. Their compact size facilitates discrete physical cross-border transportations of value – features that can be taken advantage of by criminals.[19] Current security systems and regulations, which are primarily focused on identifying bulk cash, are not designed to detect the movement of prepaid cards.[20] This failure makes prepaid cards vulnerable to exploitation by terrorist organisations.

Mobile payment services

The term 'mobile payment services' refers to various types of transactions where a mobile phone is used in the payment process.[21] Non-traditional financial institutions, such as telecom operators, facilitate the transactions by taking advantage of mobile telecommunications networks or proximity technologies.[22] In post-paid systems, the telecom operator allows the phone owner to charge certain transactions to the phone bill, and in prepaid systems, the phone owner uses the phone as a payment system access device to authorise the deduction of value from the prepaid account held by the telecom operator or other service provider.[23] Technologies used to set these services in motion include text messaging, mobile Internet access, near-field communication, programmed subscriber identity module cards, and unstructured supplementary service data.[24] Mobile transactions are also facilitated by financial institutions, which include banks, depository institutions, and money or value transfer services (MVTS).[25]

17 *Ibid.*, 20.
18 Sienkiewicz (fn 9), 36–37.
19 The FATF has evidenced that ISIL has used prepaid cards to receive funds: *Financing of the Terrorist Organization Islamic State in Iraq and the Levant (ISIL)* (2015) 24.
20 Linn (fn 12), 160.
21 Krueger, M., 'Mobile payments: The second wave' in Górka, J. (ed.), *Transforming Payment Systems in Europe* (Springer, 2016) 214–235.
22 Dahlberg, T., Mallat, N., Ondrus, J., and Zmijewska, A., 'Past, present and future of mobile payments research: A literature review' (2008) 7(2) *Electronic Commerce Research and Applications* 165.
23 FATF, *Report on New Payment Methods* (2006) 6–8; FATF, *Emerging Terrorist Financing Risks* (fn 4), 9.
24 Merritt, C., *Mobile Money Transfer Services: The Next Phase in the Evolution in Person-to-Person Payments* (Retail Payments Risk Forum White Paper, Federal Reserve Bank of Atlanta, 2010) 13–14; FATF (fn 4), 9.
25 FATF, *Report on New Payment Methods* (fn 23) 6–8.

Two main types of mobile payment models can be identified: bank-centric and mobile network operator-centric.[26] In the bank-centric model, users have bank accounts from the entity that provides the mobile payment. Through their accounts, users can access electronic money that is not tied to a payment account, or they can access innovative financial services through their mobile phones with lower transaction limits. In this model, the input of mobile network operators is limited to solely providing the telecommunication network facility that enables the transfer of payment messages. In contrast, the mobile network operator-centric model usually works with the customer's prepaid accounts that are held by the mobile network operator or its subsidiaries. The user does not need a bank account. Depending on the size of the mobile network operator company and the legal framework, international payment services are also offered – including the ability of the recipient to withdraw cash from an ATM.[27]

Potential CTF risks of mobile payments

The two main risks associated with mobile payments are also latent in prepaid cards. The first is due to the methods that can be used to fund accounts and transactions: cash and non-bank payment options are risky because the origin of the funds is not identified, and third-party funding poses a threat of anonymity because the holder of the funding account is sometimes not properly identified. The second is that mobile payment services usually allow for transfers over long distances, and some can cross national borders. This geographical reach is attractive to terrorist organisations. Moreover, different CTF controls are enforced in each jurisdiction, leaving the areas with deficient regulation especially vulnerable.[28] Elusiveness is also perceived as a risk. This can happen when mobile phones are shared amongst many individuals or where an agent operates a mobile phone on behalf of the owner – all leading to the concealment of the true initiator and recipient of a transaction.[29] In addition, new mobile payments services are developed every day, including new products associated with other NPSs, and there is also the opportunity for cash withdrawals, which makes transaction monitoring more arduous.[30]

Internet-based payment services and virtual currencies

With Internet payment services, users can add money to their online accounts and can transfer electronic money to other individuals who hold accounts with the

26 *Ibid.*

27 *Ibid.*, 9; Chatain, P.L. et al., *Protecting Mobile Money against Financial Crimes: Global Policy Challenges and Solutions* (World Bank Publications, 2011) 28.

28 FATF, *Emerging Terrorist Financing Risks* (fn 4) 6–9.

29 Chatain, P. et al., *Integrity in Mobile Phone Financial Services Measures for Mitigating Risks from Money Laundering and Terrorist Financing* (World Bank Working Paper No 146, 2008) 12–13.

30 FATF, *Emerging Terrorist Financing Risks* (fn 4) 9.

same provider, or they can pay sellers (such as through PayPal). Some accounts are pre-funded, with customers holding accounts directly with the payment service provider.[31] Accounts to receive digital currency can be created by any individual with a web connection. In the process, some Internet payment providers may require recipients to link their accounts to a bank account or credit card. Remittances can cross national borders and, once conveyed, recipients can pay online with the electronic currency or withdraw it.

National currencies can be exchanged with the electronic currency through buying or selling digital currency. Payment for online auctions can be executed through pre-funded accounts, with or without recipients being required to register. Internet-based payment also happens in online gambling and in virtual worlds, where participants buy a proxy currency or token with their national currency and can make transactions with the proprietor, other participants, or retailers inside the system.[32] Clients can also purchase or sell a digital representation of precious metals by paying intermediaries who claim to hold the commodities on behalf of the online owner – all with little or no identity verification.[33] The derivatives can be exchanged, like traditional commodity or securities derivatives, between account holders.

Potential CTF risks of Internet-based payment services and virtual currencies

The system of virtual currencies has no central server or service provider, and it generates no historical records of transactions.[34] The original cryptocurrency purchase can be identified, but all succeeding transactions are usually anonymous or very difficult to detect.[35] In some cases, anonymous transfers and funding are possible, and customer relationships are typically not face-to-face.[36]

Virtual currencies could be used for TF when the user buys digital currency from a currency exchanger. The purchase could be made by cheque, credit card, wire transfer, cash, or other value transfer. The virtual currency can then be transferred to another account holder located anywhere in the world. The recipient

31 FATF, *Report on New Payment Methods* (fn 23) 15–16.

32 FATF, *Emerging Terrorist Financing Risks* (fn 4) 10. According to the FATF, only convertible virtual currencies pose a TF threat: *Guidance for a Risk-Based Approach: Virtual Currencies* (2015), 6. For more on virtual money (rather than digital money), see Chambers-Jones, C., 'Money laundering in a virtual world' in King, C., Walker, C., and Gurule, J. (eds.), *The Palgrave Handbook of Criminal and Terrorism Financing Law*, Vol. 1 (Palgrave, 2018) 165. For more on gambling and digital currencies, see Chambers-Jones, C.L. and Hillman, H., *Financial Crime and Gambling in a Virtual World* (Edward Elgar, 2014).

33 Hett, W., 'Digital currencies and the financing of terrorism' (2008) 15(2) *Richmond Journal of Law and Technology* 4, 4–9; FATF, *Report on New Payment Methods* (fn 23) 9; FATF, *Emerging Terrorist Financing Risks* (fn 4) 11.

34 Hett (fn 33), 6–13.

35 FATF, *Emerging Terrorist Financing Risks* (fn 4) 35–36.

36 FATF, *Virtual Currencies: Key Definitions and Potential AML/CFT Risks* (Paris, 2014) 7–8; Brantly, A., 'Financing terror bit by bit' (2014) 7(10) *CTC Sentinel* 1.

could use that value by converting it to cash through a currency exchanger. The money is sometimes transferred to banks that are subject to jurisdictions with lighter banking regulations and reporting requirements in order to lessen the possibility of being tracked.[37]

The system has been relatively reliable regarding the effectiveness of transactions, and it is certainly fast.[38] Furthermore, segmentation and the complexity of transactions complicate supervision, regulation, and enforcement.[39] As observed by Kaiser, virtual currencies are issued and maintained by dissociated individuals who run the system virtually. They are detached from any state government or institution, signifying that no established body could have control over them, which entails high levels of anonymity in transactions.[40] These characteristics, most emphatically the possibility of anonymity (or, more appropriately, 'pseudonymity,' since although a user's actual identity is not visible, information about their transactions is recorded publicly)[41] for both users and transactions, ease the transfer of funds and pose a risk of TF.

CTF and the international standards

Whilst the headline norms about CTF can be found in United Nations (UN) backed conventions and resolutions,[42] the detailed international standards which are observed today in the field of CTF have been set by FATF, a classic example of an inter-governmental body formulating non-binding (but effective) norms.[43] These norms are known as 'recommendations,' being detailed technical standards that cover regulatory, supervisory, law enforcement, and legal issues.[44] The recommendations have been revised nine times, with the most recent update in October 2018, to ensure that they remain up to date, relevant, and capable of universal application (assuming that they have been implemented

37 Hett (fn 33), 6–13.

38 Brantly (fn 36), 3–5.

39 FATF, *Virtual Currencies: Key Definitions and Potential AML/CFT Risks* (fn 36) 9.

40 Kaiser, C., 'The classification of virtual currencies and mobile payments in terms of the old and new European anti-money laundering frameworks' in Gimigliano, G. (ed.), *Bitcoin and Mobile Payments: Constructing a European Union Framework* (Palgrave Macmillan, 2016) 203.

41 Keatinge, T., Carlisle, D., and Keen, F., *Virtual Currencies and Terrorist Financing: Assessing the Risks and Evaluating Responses* (European Parliament, PE 604.970, 2018) 30–31.

42 For the former, see International Convention for the Suppression of the Financing of Terrorism 1999 (974 *U.N.T.S.* 177). For resolutions, see <http://www.un.org/counterterrorism/ctitf/en/resolutions> (the output continues with UNSCR 2462 of 28 March 2019 and UNSCR 2482 of 19 July 2019).

43 Goldbarsht, D., 'Who's the legislator anyway? How the FATF's global norms reshape Australian Counter Terrorist Financing Laws' (2017) 45(1) *Federal Law Review* 127; Abbott, K.W., Snidal, D., and Zangl, B. (eds.), *International Organizations as Orchestrators* (Cambridge University Press, 2015) 289.

44 FATF, *Methodology for Assessing Technical Compliance with the FATF Recommendations and the Effectiveness of AML/CFT Systems* (2013) 2.

in national law).[45] The FATF Recommendations also apply to NPSs where TF vulnerabilities exist.

Of particular relevance for NPSs is FATF Recommendation 15 dealing with new technologies, which requires countries and financial institutions to identify and assess the TF risks that may arise in relation to the development of new products and business practices and the use of new or developing technologies for both new and pre-existing products. In the case of financial institutions, such a risk assessment should take place prior to the launch of new products or business practices or the use of new or developing technologies.

According to FATF Recommendation 10, financial institutions are prohibited from keeping anonymous accounts and are required to undertake CDD measures when, *inter alia*, establishing business relations or when there is a suspicion of TF.[46] Further, financial institutions are required to verify the identity of the customer and beneficial owner before or during the course of establishing a business relationship or conducting transactions for occasional customers. This task is relevant to NPSs that involve the establishment of business relations – commonly, an NPS operates in similar ways to an account, and the holding and management of an account on behalf of a customer represents the establishment of a business relationship, which is a circumstance that requires the conduct of CDD measures.

When an NPS is used as a payment system to effect a person-to-person wire transfer, the transaction is similar to a wire transfer and is subject to FATF Recommendation 16. This recommendation requires countries to ensure that financial institutions include required information on wire transfers and related messages and that the information remains with the wire transfer or related message throughout the payment chain.

According to FATF Recommendation 26, all providers of financial services should be subject to adequate regulation and supervision. However, FATF Recommendation 14 focusing on MVTSs amplifies this requirement, stating that countries should take measures to ensure that providers of MVTSs – including agents – are licensed or registered and are subject to effective systems for monitoring and enforcing compliance with national CTF requirements.[47] It should be noted that agents are more common amongst NPS providers than traditional financial services since they are required as intermediaries between conventional and virtual payment services. Countries should take action to identify natural or legal persons that carry out MVTSs without a licence or registration and to apply appropriate sanctions. Therefore, where an NPS falls within the definition of an MVTS, the provider should be licensed or registered, supervised, and subject to CTF measures.

With regard to cash couriers, countries are required by FATF Recommendation 32 to have measures in place to detect the physical cross-border transportation

45 FATF, *International Standards on Combating Money Laundering and the Financing of Terrorism and Proliferation: The FATF Recommendations* (2018).

46 For the relationship between the TF risk and the CDD measures required, see Malady, L., Buckley, R.P. and Arner (fn 2), 17.

47 FATF, *Money Laundering Using New Payment Methods* (fn 10) 68.

of currency and bearer negotiable instruments (BNIs), including through a declaration or disclosure system. Countries should ensure that their competent authorities have the legal authority to stop or restrain currency or BNIs that are suspected to be related to TF. This recommendation was developed with the objective of ensuring that terrorists and other criminals cannot finance their activities through the physical cross-border transportation of currency and BNIs.

The NPS legal regime in the United Kingdom, which will be detailed next, is intended to comply with the international standards set by the FATF.

The legal response in the United Kingdom to terrorist financing via new payment systems

The United Kingdom has substantial experience in responding to terrorist threats and pursuing the support networks that make terrorist acts possible.[48] For many years, terrorism in Northern Ireland constituted a significant threat to security in the United Kingdom; it has, in fact, resulted in more deaths than the attacks in the US on September 11, 2001, albeit over a much longer period.[49] The threat to the United Kingdom from international terrorism is still assessed as 'severe,' which means that an attack is highly likely (the threat level was briefly raised to 'critical' – meaning that an attack is expected imminently though nowadays from Islamist rather than Irish causes.[50] According to Europol, the UK experiences the highest number of terrorism attacks in Europe.[51]

Before September 11, 2001, the United Kingdom already had a wide range of legislative measures in place to counteract terrorist activity. The centrepiece of this legislative framework was the Terrorism Act 2000. The UK Parliament, nevertheless, enacted the Anti-Terrorism, Crime and Security Act 2001 in time to report to the UN Security Council's Counter-Terrorism Committee at the end of

48 See Walker, C., *Terrorism and the Law* (Oxford University Press, 2011) chap. 9; Walker, C., *Blackstone's Guide to the Anti-Terrorism Legislation* (3rd ed., Oxford, 2014).

49 For different statistics (for example, overall death by year, by location, or by type), see McKittrick, D. et al., *Lost Lives* (Mainstream, Edinburgh, 1999). For why casualty figures for terrorism can be misleading, see Greer, S., 'Terrorism and counter-terrorism in the UK: From Northern Irish troubles to Global Islamist Jihad' in Lennon, G., King, C., and McCartney, C. (eds.), *Counter-Terrorism, Constitutionalism and Miscarriages of Justice: A Festschrift for Professor Clive Walker* (Hart, 2018) 46.

50 HM Treasury and Home Office, *National Risk Assessment of Money Laundering and Terrorist Financing 2017* (2017) 26.

51 In 2017, a total of 205 foiled, failed, and completed terrorist attacks were reported by nine European Union (EU) Member States: the United Kingdom (107), France (54), Spain (16), Italy (14), Greece (8), Belgium (2), Germany (2), Finland (1), and Sweden (1): EUROPOL, *European Union Terrorism Situation and Trend Report 2018* (2018) 9; see also Kirk, A., 'How many people are killed by terrorist attacks in the UK?' *The Daily Telegraph* (5 October 2017); Walker, C., *Blackstone's Guide to the Anti-Terrorism Legislation* (3rd ed., Oxford University Press, 2014) 276; Roach, K., *The 9/11 Effect: Comparative Counter-Terrorism* (Cambridge University Press, 2011) 244.

2001,[52] taking the 90-day period for reporting back to the committee as a deadline for enacting new CTF laws. The United Kingdom technically implemented all the international standards. However, despite this implementation and despite having modern legislation with regard to CTF,[53] the United Kingdom needed to enact additional legislation in order to comply with the international standards and to respond to the risks posed by NPSs.[54]

In 2015, the United Kingdom published a national assessment of TF risks in order to better understand those risks, to inform the efficient allocation of resources, and to mitigate the risks.[55] It found little evidence to indicate that the use of NPSs has been adopted in TF – whether as a means by which to raise funds, to pay for infrastructure, or to transfer funds – and there were no case studies upon which any solid conclusions could be drawn that NPSs are used for TF. Therefore, it determined that the TF risks associated with NPSs are low. In its second risk assessment, published in 2017, the United Kingdom analysed the current TF risks with regard to different vulnerabilities (including, *inter alia*, accountancy and legal services, property and estate agency services, trusts and corporate structures, and cash). It found that, except in the case of e-money (for which the risk assessment was changed to medium), there remains little evidence of the use of NPSs for TF and the risks from NPSs remain low.[56]

The impression thus created is that whilst, in theory, digital currencies could be used to purchase items to execute a terror attack, or to otherwise fund such an act, there is a lack of evidence that this is actually occurring in the United Kingdom. In fact, because other financing methods are more attractive to those financing terrorism, the TF risks from digital currencies are low, and terrorist use of digital currencies is 'unlikely to increase significantly in the next five years.'[57] Prepaid cards remain a possible method for moving terrorist funds or for purchasing weapons, in particular because they are much less bulky than cash. However, prepaid cards as a substitute for cash are more appealing to money launderers than they are to terrorist financers, since TF generally involves lower amounts of money and, therefore, the cash funds tend to be relatively compact.[58] Nonetheless, increasing the international reach of CTF measures by working with

52 S/RES/1373 (2001) and S/RES/1624 (2005).

53 For a full survey, see Walker, C.P., *The Anti-Terrorism Legislation* (3rd ed., Oxford University Press, 2014) chap. 3; Ryder, N., *The Financial War on Terror: A Review of Counter-Terrorist Financing Strategies since 2001* (Routledge, 2015).

54 For a general discussion on the CTF regime in the United Kingdom, see Ryder, N. et al., 'The financial war on terrorism: A critical review of the United Kingdom's counter-terrorist financing strategies' in King, C., Walker, C., and Gurule, J. (eds.) (fn 32), 783; Donohue, L., 'Anti-terrorist finance in the United Kingdom and United States' (2006) 27(2) *Michigan Journal of International Law* 303.

55 HM Treasury and Home Office, *National Risk Assessment of Money Laundering and Terrorist Financing* (London, 2015) 79.

56 HM Treasury and Home Office, *National Risk Assessment of Money Laundering and Terrorist Financing 2017* (2017) 41.

57 *Ibid.*, 39.

58 *Ibid.*

international groups, such as the FATF, remains a major concern in the United Kingdom.[59] Consequently, the UK legislation (mainly based on EU initiatives) dealing with NPSs has been bolstered in recent years, bringing it into compliance with the FATF standard.

The EU implements the FATF Recommendations through EU directives that Member States are required to transpose into national law. The (revised) Payment Services Directive (PSD2)[60] is the principal EU legislation that sets regulatory requirements for those who wish to provide payment services. The UK Payment Services Regulations 2017 were enacted to comply with the obligation to implement PSD2 by January 13, 2018.[61] The relevant financial crime provisions of the Payment Services Regulations 2017 and the Electronic Money Regulations 2011[62] focus on the registration of prepaid card issuers, describe who can issue electronic money in the United Kingdom,[63] and provide for imprisonment, a fine, or both for anyone in breach.[64] Further important legislation under PSD2 includes the Money Laundering, Terrorist Financing and Transfer of Funds (Information on the Payer) Regulations 2017 (ML Regulations 2017),[65] which transposed the EU Fourth Money Laundering Directive[66] into UK law. In general, these regulations place requirements on regulated entities (and a range of high-value dealers, which is not required under the FATF standards)[67] to undertake risk assessments in order to identify, assess, understand, and mitigate the risks of money laundering and TF affecting the United Kingdom (regulations 16–25); to apply CDD (regulations 27–38), whilst allowing reliance on a third party to apply CDD measures (regulations 39–40); and to comply with a range of supervision and registration requirements with regard to money laundering and TF.

When dealing with new technologies as applied to NSPs, the United Kingdom has – as required by the FATF standards – identified and assessed the risks. Financial institutions are asked to ensure that appropriate measures are taken before and during the adoption of new technologies in order to identify and,

59 Home Office and HM Treasury, *Action Plan for Anti-Money Laundering and Counter-Terrorist Finance* (2016) 3.

60 Directive (EU) 2015/2366 of the European Parliament and of the Council of November 25, 2015, on payment services in the internal market, repealing Directive 2007/64/EC.

61 Payment Services Regulations 2017, SI 2017/752, reg. 1(6). These regulations replaced the Payment Services Regulations 2009, SI 2009/209.

62 SI 2011/99.

63 *Ibid.*, regs. 5 (authorised electronic money institution), 12 (small electronic money institution).

64 *Ibid.*, reg. 63; Payment Services Regulations 2017, reg. 138.

65 SI 2017/692. These regulations replaced the Money Laundering Regulations 2007 and the Transfer of Funds (Information on the Payer) Regulations 2007, SI 2007/3298.

66 Directive (EU) 2015/849 of the European Parliament and of the Council of May 20, 2015, on the prevention of the use of the financial system for the purposes of money laundering or terrorist financing.

67 ML Regulations 2017, regs. 8(g) and 14(1)(a).

if necessary, mitigate any TF risks.[68] However, under the UK regime, there is no binding requirement for financial institutions to similarly assess the risks of new products, business practices, and delivery mechanisms.[69] Therefore, in the 2018 FATF evaluation, the United Kingdom was rated largely compliant with this requirement.[70]

Regarding CDD, financial institutions are prohibited in the United Kingdom from setting up an anonymous account for any new or existing customer. In addition, they must apply CDD measures to all anonymous accounts that are already in existence before such accounts are used in any way.[71] It seems that the United Kingdom has not been fully compliant with FATF Recommendation 10, which specifies that the requirement for financial institutions to undertake CDD should be set out in primary legislation rather than in secondary legislation, such as the Money Laundering Regulations. This shortcoming, it seems, will also not be rectified by the Sanctions and Anti-Money Laundering Act 2018, which provides the legislative basis for the United Kingdom's CTF regime after its exit from the EU, as it leaves the implementation of this requirement to future regulations.[72] However, aside from this relatively insignificant formalistic issue, most of the CDD measures put in place by the United Kingdom meet the FATF standards. Nonetheless, minor deficiencies relevant to NPSs still exist. According to the ML Regulations 2017, financial institutions must conduct ongoing monitoring of a business relationship, including scrutinising transactions undertaken throughout the course of the relationship to ensure that they are consistent with the financial institution's knowledge of the customer, the customer's business, and its risk profile.[73] Yet there is no explicit requirement to understand the ownership and control structure of customers, as demanded under the FATF standard. In addition, the ML Regulations 2017 state that financial institutions must obtain and verify the customer's name, its company number, and the address of its registered office,[74] but this duty is restrained with regard to the board of directors and senior personnel responsible for the customer's operations. Instead, financial institutions are obliged to take 'reasonable measures' only: the duty is not absolute, as required by the international standard. In its Third Mutual Evaluation Report (MER), the United Kingdom was rated only partially compliant with the

68 *Ibid.*, reg. 19(4)(c).

69 The industry guidance published by the Joint Money Laundering Steering Group, which comprises the leading UK trade associations in the financial services industry, advises firms to comply fully with the FATF standard. This guidance, however, is non-binding. See Joint Money Laundering Steering Group, *Prevention of Money Laundering/Combating Terrorist Financing: Guidance for the UK Financial Sector, Part I* (2017) para. 4.23.

70 FATF, *Fourth Round Mutual Evaluation Report* (fn 7) 201.

71 ML Regulations 2017, regs. 29(6), 29(7).

72 Sanctions and Anti-Money Laundering Act 2018, s. 49. See also the Explanatory Notes relating to the Sanctions and Anti-Money Laundering Bill [HL] as brought from the House of Lords on January 25, 2018, 19.

73 ML Regulations 2017, reg. 28(11)(a).

74 *Ibid.*, reg. 28(3).

requirements. The United Kingdom subsequently improved its implementation of this standard and, in its Fourth MER, was rated largely compliant with the standard.[75]

As for providers of MVTSs, they are required to be registered by either the Financial Conduct Authority or Her Majesty's Revenue and Customs (HMRC).[76] Both entities have a range of enforcement powers when assessing non-compliance, including non-compliance with the requirement for MVTS providers to be registered in order to operate. These include the civil power to fine or publicly censure, the power to impose temporary or permanent prohibitions on management, and the power to issue injunctions.[77] Criminal sanctions are also available for contravening the requirements.[78] The United Kingdom was rated largely compliant with this standard in the Third MER but achieved a rating of compliant in the Fourth MER.[79]

With regard to cash couriers – travellers entering or leaving the United Kingdom – the United Kingdom applies a declaration system. However, this does not apply to those travelling to or from an EU Member State. A false declaration is subject to an administrative fine (of £5,000) from HMRC.[80] Persons transporting funds or BNIs in relation to TF may be subject to penalties for these offences: natural persons are subject to 14 years' imprisonment, or an unlimited fine, or both.[81] It is worth noting that the Criminal Finances Act 2017 extended the definition of 'cash' in the Anti-Terrorism, Crime and Security Act 2001 to include gaming vouchers, fixed-value casino tokens, and betting receipts but not prepaid cards.[82] In its Fourth MER, the United Kingdom retained a rating of largely compliant with this standard, mainly because the fines available for false declarations are not sufficiently dissuasive.[83]

Another important piece of legislation is the EU Funds Transfer Regulation,[84] which has been in effect since June 26, 2017, and which aims to ensure the traceability of payment transactions. Financial institutions are required to ensure that all cross-border wire transfers of €1,000 or more are accompanied by information, including the originator's name, account number, address, official personal

75 FATF, *Third Mutual Evaluation Report* (fn 6), 127; FATF, *Fourth Round Mutual Evaluation Report* (fn 7) 97.

76 ML Regulations 2017, regs. 54, 56, 58.

77 *Ibid.*, regs. 76, 78, 80.

78 *Ibid.*, regs. 54, 56, 86.

79 FATF, *Third Mutual Evaluation Report* (fn 6) 138; FATF, *Fourth Round Mutual Evaluation Report* (fn 7) 200.

80 Control of Cash (Penalties) Regulations 2007, SI 2007/1509, reg. 3.

81 Proceeds of Crime Act 2002, ss.327–329 (concealing; arrangements; and acquisition, use and possession), 334 (penalties); Terrorism Act 2000, s.15 (fundraising).

82 Criminal Finances Act 2017, s.38; FATF, *Fourth Round Mutual Evaluation Report* (fn 7) 72.

83 FATF, *Third Mutual Evaluation Report* (fn 6) 105; FATF, *Fourth Round Mutual Evaluation Report* (fn 7), 228.

84 Regulation (EU) 2015/847 of the European Parliament and of the Council of May 20, 2015, on information accompanying transfers of funds.

document number, and customer identification number or date and place of birth, as well as the beneficiary's name and account number.[85] Transfers below €1,000 must be accompanied by the names and account numbers of the originator and the beneficiary.[86] These obligations also apply to MVTS providers and their agents.[87] The regulation is, therefore, a powerful tool in the prevention, detection, and investigation of TF. Consequently, the rating of the UK wire transfer regime was upgraded dramatically from partly compliant to fully compliant with the FATF standard.[88]

Other more general legislation is also relevant. The Terrorism Act 2000 represents an attempt to fulfil the role of a modern code against terrorism.[89] The act specifies offences, including fundraising, use and possession, funding arrangements, and failure to disclose.[90] It also extends the jurisdiction to apply to specified action done outside the United Kingdom as if it had been done in the United Kingdom.[91] Also significant are Part 5 of the Proceeds of Crime Act 2002, which provides for the confiscation or civil recovery of the proceeds from crime; the Counter-Terrorism Act 2008,[92] which, *inter alia*, extends the basis for financial restrictions to countries which are blacklisted by the FATF and deals with procedures for making objections to designations; and the Criminal Finances Act 2017, which increases the state powers for the purpose of countering terrorism.[93] NPS institutions operating in the United Kingdom are also subject to the various pieces of legislation that implement the United Kingdom's financial sanctions regime.[94]

Concluding remarks

Terrorist activity, especially grand showcase attacks, would be made much more difficult if the organisations responsible could be prevented from accessing funds. Financial sources are, therefore, an important focus when attempting to limit terrorism. The basic premise is deceptively simple: smother the source of fuel and a

85 *Ibid.*, art. 4.
86 *Ibid.*, art. 6(2).
87 *Ibid.*, art. 2(1).
88 FATF, *Third Mutual Evaluation Report* (fn 6) 138; FATF, *Fourth Round Mutual Evaluation Report* (fn 7) 203.
89 Walker, C., *Blackstone's Guide to the Anti-Terrorism Legislation* (Oxford University Press, Oxford, 2011) 289. According to Walker, this attempt fails to meet the desired standards in all respects.
90 Terrorism Act 2000, ss.15–17, 21A.
91 *Ibid.*, s.63.
92 ss.62, 63 and Sched 7.
93 ss.35–43.
94 ISIL (Da'esh) and Al-Qaida (Asset-Freezing) Regulations 2011, SI 2011/2741, reg. 10; Terrorist Asset-Freezing, etc., Act 2010, ss.11, 12, 13, 14, 15, 18. These provisions are being replaced by Sanctions and Anti Money Laundering Act 2018; ISIL (Daesh) and Al Qaida (United Nations Sanctions) EU Exit Regulations 2019, SI 2019/466; Counter Terrorism (Sanctions) (EU Exit) Regulations 2019, SI 2019/577.

terror cell will die. Yet this is not an easy task in an innovative financial environment. Taking this point into account, it is important to highlight the expectations and challenges that confront the UK regulator – like other regulators globally – around NPSs. On the one hand, regulators arguably must create norms that comply with the FATF standard. On the other hand, they cannot block innovation. How to balance these two competing considerations is neither easy nor static in a sector that is particularly dynamic.[95]

Digital technology has revolutionised the way people buy, sell, and transfer funds. The growth in the use of digital payments is rapid.[96] The expansion of NPSs is an exciting opportunity because, in a strong NPS ecosystem, TF risks will be reduced whilst simultaneously improving the lives of individuals in the general community.

As we have seen, the TF risks posed by NPSs in the United Kingdom in general are assessed as being low. Despite that assurance, the United Kingdom has adopted a very robust CTF policy when dealing with NPSs. The regulator has designed controls that target threats without unnecessarily preventing communities from accessing NPSs. It seems that the United Kingdom has made a strong effort both to implement EU legal obligations and to comply with the international standards set by the FATF. The challenge always is that complying blindly with the standards, where they do not align with the risks posed by the NPSs in the United Kingdom, can impede the development of NPS ecosystems and hinder the inclusiveness of the formal financial framework.

95 See further Arner, D.W. et al., 'The evolution of FinTech: A new post-crisis paradigm' (2015–16) 47 *Georgetown Journal of International Law* 1271.

96 Contactless payments made each month grew by nearly 20 times in the 3 years to June 2017: HM Treasury, *Cash and Digital Payments in the New Economy: Call for Evidence* (2018) 2.

10 The use of cryptocurrencies in the UK real estate market

An assessment of money laundering risks

*Ilaria Zavoli**

Introduction

In December 2017, for the first time in the history of the UK real estate market, residential properties were sold using bitcoins.[1] This event sparked debate about the money laundering risks of the use of cryptocurrencies for property transactions in the United Kingdom. Some think that cryptocurrencies have revolutionary effects on national economies,[2] and they might bring benefits to the real estate market.[3] However, the use of cryptocurrencies raises concerns for their compatibility with the existing UK anti-money laundering (AML) legislation. In particular, cryptocurrency transactions can create issues for the customer due diligence (CDD) checks that the 2017 Money Laundering Regulations impose on real estate agents.[4] These actors are key gatekeepers in the UK AML regime, and they play an essential role in property transactions, acting either on behalf of the buyer or the seller. As such, it is important to critically evaluate the risks that real estate agents might face when dealing with transactions involving the use of cryptocurrencies.

This chapter addresses these issues and concerns, examining the money laundering risks of the use of cryptocurrencies in the UK real estate market. In particular, this three-part study seeks (i) to understand how cryptocurrencies can pose

* This research was supported by a British Academy 'Tackling the UK's International Challenges' grant (ref: IC160112).

1 See Harley, N., 'First bitcoin homes sell in the UK' *The Telegraph* (<http://www.telegraph.co.uk/news/2017/12/16/first-bitcoin-homes-sell-uk/>, 16 December 2017).

2 See Nica, O., Piotrowska, K. and Schenk-Hoppé, K.R., 'Cryptocurrencies: Economic benefits and risks' (2017) Working Paper No. 2 *FinTech* 1; Swan, M., 'Anticipating the economic benefits of Blockchain' (2017) 7(10) *Technology Innovation Management Review* 6.

3 See Onibalusi, A., 'Benefits of using cryptocurrency to buy real estate' *Huffington Post* (<http://www.huffingtonpost.co.uk/entry/benefits-of-using-cryptocurrency-to-buy-real-estate_uk_5a1edd64e4b0e37da0447b7e?guccounter=1&guce_referrer=aHR0cHM6Ly93d3cuZ29vZ2xlLmRlLw&guce_referrer_sig=AQAAALSkewpyxGVU7ktXwfL5Jb86K9–7Lumm9_zNTQe2idwUYdF-LscQRv386uK5Vl6WkzAz72av90cfBYJ_IbVM2K69nJnfHQRh21kj_wJRJF1wUdUYtB_e4JmxIyHV89GibjuoSH4e0gHjblXhgV_sAYmYirnffkw-knHrZghuLLb_>, 30 November 2017).

4 Money Laundering, Terrorist Financing and Transfer of Funds (Information on the Payer) Regulations 2017, SI 2017/692, regs. 8(2)(f), 13, 27–38.

money laundering risks to the property sector, (ii) to examine the UK money laundering obligations imposed on real estate agents and determine the approach of these professionals to the issue, and (iii) to propose some regulatory changes to effectively address concerns by arguing that there is a need for shared governance, with a better and more informed involvement of real estate agents as gatekeepers of the UK property market. To this end, the chapter includes an analysis of the relevant literature and draws upon the findings of the author's interviews with real estate agents. Given the current policy interest in this topic, including a recent parliamentary report on the role of digital currencies in various sectors,[5] this chapter is particularly timely, as it provides some innovative perspectives for future legislative and policy actions.

Money laundering and the use of cryptocurrencies: concerns for the UK real estate market

Despite its growing popularity, the phenomenon of cryptocurrencies is not new to the world of global finance and technology. Its origins can be traced back to 1983 when the cryptographer David Chaum created the first type of cryptocurrency called 'ecash.'[6] What is more recent is the association of cryptocurrencies with illicit activities and their alleged involvement in the commission of crimes, particularly money laundering.[7] This section examines some key aspects of cryptocurrencies to identify potential money laundering risks in property transactions.

At present, more than 1,900 cryptocurrencies exist.[8] Not all cryptocurrencies share the same features, and only some of them have become increasingly popular due to their appeal as lucrative forms of investment in the global market.[9] For instance, this fate applies to the bitcoin system. There is no universally accepted definition of cryptocurrencies, but some guidance is provided by two reports from the European Central Bank.[10] Here, cryptocurrencies are identified as one of three possible virtual currency schemes: closed, unidirectional, or

5 See House of Commons Treasury Committee, *Crypto-assets* (2017–19 HC 910).

6 On the development of cryptocurrencies, see Clarke, J., 'The long road to Bitcoin' in Narayanan, A. et al. (eds.), *Bitcoin and Cryptocurrency Technologies: A Comprehensive Introduction* (Princeton University Press, 2016).

7 For instance, see Jones, C., 'Digital currencies and organised crime update' *Financial Regulation International* (30 April 2018); van Wegberg, R., Oerlemans, J.J. and van Deventer, O., 'Bitcoin money laundering: mixed results? An explorative study on money laundering of cybercrime proceeds using bitcoin' (2018) 25(2) *Journal of Financial Crime* 419.

8 An updated list is available at <http://www.coinlore.com/all_coins>.

9 Some authors talk about a 'cryptocurrencies' revolution.' See Pak Nian, L. and Lee Kuo Chuen, D., 'Introduction to Bitcoin' in Lee Kuo Chuen, D. (ed.), *Handbook of Digital Currency: Bitcoin, Innovation, Financial Instruments, and Big Data* (Academic Press/Elsevier, 2015) 25.

10 See European Central Bank, 'Virtual currency schemes: A further analysis' (<http://www.ecb.europa.eu/pub/pdf/other/virtualcurrencyschemesen.pdf>, February 2015) and 'Virtual currency schemes' (<http://www.ecb.europa.eu/pub/pdf/other/virtualcurrencyschemes201210en.pdf>, October 2012).

bidirectional. Specifically, bitcoins are a form of 'bidirectional' virtual currency scheme because they can be purchased using legal tender and can be converted into legal tender.[11] For example, cryptocurrencies like bitcoins can be purchased using pounds sterling and can be converted into pounds sterling, depending on the needs of the owner.

This definition of cryptocurrencies shows how, by their very nature, these virtual currencies can potentially be used as a tool for money laundering purposes. As an example, because cryptocurrencies can be exchanged for legal tender, they can be easily involved in different phases of money laundering (placement, layering, and integration).[12] Moreover, some cryptocurrencies like bitcoins have significantly increased in value.[13] Although subject to some fluctuations, this high value increases the risk of their use in illicit activities like money laundering because they might represent a viable and profitable medium for criminals who need to launder large sums.[14] Both of these features are relevant in real estate transactions. Indeed, given their high value, cryptocurrencies might be used to purchase high-end properties for money laundering purposes. Moreover, due to their versatility as financial tools (that is, the possibility to be exchanged for legal tender), they might be easily used to integrate the proceeds of money laundering activities into sources of legitimate wealth, such as real estate properties.

In recent years, there has been an increasing recourse to cryptocurrencies for money laundering.[15] A famous case was that of Charlie Shrem, founder of BitInstant, who was convicted for having facilitated money laundering involving bitcoin through the dark-web, online-market Silk Road.[16] Research by Foley et al. confirms the use of cryptocurrencies for the commission of crimes (including money laundering).[17] This research estimates that 'approximately one-quarter of all users (26%) and close to one-half of bitcoin transactions (46%) are associated with illegal activity.'[18] This finding sheds a further negative light on cryptocurrencies and their potential use for illicit activities.

There are two aspects of the use of cryptocurrencies that pose particular risks for the control of money laundering activities in the UK real estate market. These

11 See *ibid.* (2015, 23–28) and (2012, 13–20).

12 See Brenig, C., Accorsi, R., and Müller, G., 'Economic analysis of cryptocurrency backed money laundering' (2015) Paper 20 *ECIS 2015 Completed Research Papers* 1.

13 On December 17, 2017, bitcoin reached the value of $19,783 per bitcoin.

14 See Brown, S.D., 'Cryptocurrency and criminality: The Bitcoin opportunity' (2016) 89(4) *Police Journal: Theory, Practice and Principles* 327.

15 See Dostov, V. and Shust, P., 'Cryptocurrencies: An unconventional challenge to the AML/CFT regulators?' (2014) 21(3) *Journal of Financial Crime* 249.

16 See Hern, A., 'Bitcoin entrepreneur sentenced to two years in prison' *The Guardian* (<http://www.theguardian.com/technology/2014/dec/22/bitcoin-entrepreneur-sentenced-jail>, 22 December 2014).

17 See, for instance, Foley, S., Karlsen, J.R., and Putniņš, T.J. 'Sex, drugs, and bitcoin: How much illegal activity is financed through cryptocurrencies?' (2019) 32 *Review of Financial Studies* 1798.

18 *Ibid.*, 1800.

are the anonymity linked to cryptocurrency transactions and the lack of traditional intermediaries, such as financial institutions and banks.

As for the first aspect, digital currencies transactions are characterised by a high-level of anonymity.[19] Their configuration ensures the anonymity of the individuals involved independently from the type of transaction and the amount of money concerned. Generally speaking, cryptocurrency transactions are based on a peer-to-peer system where there is a person who acts as the sender of the currency and another user as the receiver.[20] In the majority of cases (including the bitcoin system), the transactions are publicly available because they are registered in a public ledger called blockchain, but the identities of the users involved are hidden. Some talk about 'pseudonymity' rather than anonymity because the real identities of the users are unknown, but they are still identified in the cryptocurrency transaction with a public key.[21]

The anonymity of cryptocurrencies is one of the most concerning features with regard to money laundering potential[22] and the challenges that real estate agents might encounter when performing AML checks. Indeed, money launderers could potentially hide their identities behind the technical features of cryptocurrency transactions and try to avoid attempts by enforcement authorities to identify them.[23] In this regard, four elements of risk need to be considered. First, although the transactions are publicly available, it is very difficult (although not impossible) for AML enforcement agents to discover the identities of the users involved.[24] Therefore, this becomes an issue of traceability of transactions involving cryptocurrencies and the identification of the users of this system. Second, the level of anonymity of a cryptocurrency transaction varies depending on the type of cryptocurrency involved (some cryptocurrencies, such as Monero, guarantee higher anonymity than others)[25] and on the use of specific routers (such as Tor) that permit users to hide their IP addresses.[26] This last element is becoming an increasingly problematic barrier for the identification of money launderers involved in a transaction. Third, money launderers can also rely on a variety of

19 See Narayanan, A. et al., *Bitcoin and Cryptocurrency Technologies: A Comprehensive Introduction* (Princeton University Press, 2016) 138ff.

20 On this mechanism, see *ibid.*, 51–75; Pak Nian, L. and Lee Kuo Chuen, D., 'Introduction to Bitcoin' in Lee Kuo Chuen, D. (ed.), *Handbook of Digital Currency: Bitcoin, Innovation, Financial Instruments, and Big Data* (Academic Press/Elsevier, 2015) 15ff.

21 See Brito, J. and Castillo, A., *Bitcoin: A Primer for Policy Makers* (2nd ed., Mercatus Centre George Mason University, 2013) 7.

22 See Reynolds, P., 'Tracking digital footprints: Anonymity within the bitcoin system' (2017) 20(2) *Journal of Money Laundering Control* 172.

23 See *ibid.*, 177.

24 See Irwin, A.S.M. and Turner, A.B., 'Illicit Bitcoin transactions: Challenges in getting to the who, what, when and where' (2018) 25(1) *Journal of Money Laundering Control* 1.

25 See O'Driscoll, A., 'Monero vs zcash vs dash: Which is the most anonymous cryptocurrency?' *Comparitech* (<http://www.comparitech.com/crypto/anonymous-cryptocurrency-monerto-zcash/>, 4 April 2018).

26 See Girasa, R., *Regulation of Cryptocurrencies and Blockchain Technologies: National and International Perspectives* (Palgrave MacMillan, 2018) 152.

services that permit them to achieve an even higher level of anonymity, concealing not only their identities (and IP addresses) but also the transactions in which they are involved.[27] For instance, 'mixing' is a viable method that guarantees to break down the transaction into multiple parts and to mix the cryptocurrencies used amongst other users.[28] Fourth, the technical features mentioned earlier necessitate the public and private actors involved in AML to modify their strategies substantially, relying on financial and logistic resources (such as IT services and personnel) that might not be available and up to the task.[29] This means that traditional methods to prevent and fight money laundering are not always effective, and only a minority of AML actors have the capacity to tackle money laundering involving cryptocurrencies. All the aforementioned issues are apparent in the context of property transactions, especially when real estate agents need to conduct checks on the identities and sources of funds of the users.

The second important aspect of cryptocurrencies that creates money laundering risks, especially in real estate transactions, is the lack of pivotal traditional intermediaries, such as banks or financial institutions.[30] Usually, no other individuals are involved in a cryptocurrency transaction, except for the sender and the receiver, and so the transfer of cryptocurrencies is immediate and direct. This fact raises concerns for AML for three reasons. First, AML CDD checks on the transaction can be null or very limited. Indeed, the subjects involved in the transaction are fewer than in ordinary transactions (since banks might be excluded), and the transaction is then evaluated from an AML perspective only by some actors (such as real estate agents and solicitors). This fact reduces the possibilities to verify the legitimacy of the transaction, the identities of the individuals involved, and the sources of funds.

Second, the fewer the subjects involved, the less information can be shared. Although sharing information is already problematic in conventional transactions, with the use of cryptocurrencies, this becomes even more complicated. This deficiency might be detrimental for setting up effective AML strategies that require intelligence cooperation amongst different sectors and subjects. Moreover, it might create additional problems for those subjects (including real estate agents) who do not have deep knowledge about cryptocurrency transactions and how to gather useful information on the individuals involved.

Finally, sometimes in cryptocurrency transactions, traditional intermediaries are substituted by other subjects that perform collateral activities necessary for the completion of the transaction.[31] As an example, in the bitcoin system, all transac-

27 On the various services available, see Narayanan (fn 19) 138ff.

28 See (fn 19) 151ff.

29 See Tziakouris, G., 'Cryptocurrencies: A forensic challenge or opportunity for law enforcement? An INTERPOL perspective' (2018) 16(4) *IEEE Security & Privacy* 92.

30 See Harwick, C., 'Cryptocurrency and the problem of intermediation' (2016) 20(4) *The Independent Review* 569.

31 See Motsi-Omoijiade, I.D., 'Financial intermediation in cryptocurrency markets: Regulation, gaps and bridges' in Lee Kuo Chuen, L. and Deng, R. (eds.), *Handbook of Blockchain, Digital Finance, and Inclusion* (vol. 1, Academic Press/Elsevier, 2017) 207.

tions are verified through the work of 'miners.'[32] Alternatively, there might be the intervention of subjects that act as exchange or online wallet providers to support the users of the transaction, providing them with online services that enhance cryptocurrency exchanges.[33] As will be discussed in the following section, some of these subjects pose additional challenges to the application of AML legislation in the UK real estate market because not all of them are regulated by the relevant legislation.

Cryptocurrency transactions in the UK real estate market: approaches and issues

Based on the foregoing risk features, this section will discuss the significant and distinct challenges that anonymity and the lack of traditional intermediaries pose to real estate agents when conducting the CDD checks required by the 2017 Money Laundering Regulations. Real estate agents have to deal with very similar issues that other actors encounter when involved in cryptocurrency transactions (including financial institutions) but with the additional burden of performing CDD checks in a sector (the real estate market) that is not fully prepared for this task.

As part of a wider project on AML, 17 interviews have been conducted with UK real estate agents and compliance officials about their AML obligations, with a specific question about the use of cryptocurrencies in real estate transactions. The interviews revealed some interesting findings on the topic, which can be divided into three categories: (i) awareness of the issue and understanding of the phenomenon, (ii) general approach to the use of cryptocurrencies, and (iii) specific approach in light of AML obligations.

Real estate agents are generally aware of the use of cryptocurrencies in various sectors, including their own, and they have knowledge of the existence of a plurality of cryptocurrencies.[34] The interviewees consider the use of cryptocurrencies a huge issue for the UK property sector, and they see it as a growing phenomenon that requires careful consideration, both from a legislative and policy point of view.[35] However, this generic awareness is not accompanied by a full understanding of what cryptocurrencies are and how they work. For instance, few interviewees know the specifics of the blockchain system and how a transaction is conducted using bitcoins.[36] The majority of the real estate agents interviewed have only a vague understanding of the phenomenon, and this shallow knowledge is often linked to indirect information gathered through the media rather than a specific technical knowledge or training.[37]

32 When a transaction is verified, these miners are rewarded with the issue of 50 'new' bitcoins.

33 For an analysis, see Motsi-Omoijiade (fn 31).

34 Interviews 2; 7; 8; 9; 10; 12; 13; 14; 15.

35 Interviews 7; 10; 13; 14.

36 Interview 7.

37 Interview 13.

This first finding is significant because it indicates that (although not representing the whole sector) the interviewees have no comprehensive knowledge of this complex phenomenon. Despite the broad range of information that they might have gathered directly or (mostly) indirectly on the topic, their understanding of cryptocurrencies is quite vague and imprecise. This first worrying element needs to be considered carefully when analysing the money laundering risks posed by cryptocurrencies in the UK real estate market. Indeed, with no comprehensive information and proper knowledge, real estate agents are at risk of being targeted by money launderers infiltrating the system by relying not only on willing facilitators but also on less informed actors in the sector.[38]

The earlier finding is linked to the general approach adopted by real estate agents towards the use of cryptocurrencies in property transactions. In this regard, the interviewees' opinions varies, and there is a clear dichotomy between those who have not dealt with cryptocurrency transactions (the majority of interviewees) and those who have concluded or are in the process of concluding such transactions – for instance, with the use of bitcoins. In this sense, many interviewees say that they have not had any experience yet of the use of cryptocurrencies to conclude real estate transactions,[39] and they have not heard of other real estate professionals involved in these transactions.[40] A minority of interviewees recall cases in which they have been directly involved in real estate transactions where cryptocurrencies have been used, but they all refer to the need to use 'considerable caution'[41] when involved in these transactions. Some talk of a case-by-case approach to be adopted.[42]

This varied approach is an interesting aspect of the relationship between cryptocurrencies and real estate agents because it indicates that the phenomenon is still in its embryonic phase, and it is not widespread as in other sectors, such as the financial or the luxury goods markets.[43] However, despite the few property cryptocurrency transactions concluded, the growing interest in the cryptocurrencies market and their use for illicit purposes might become a heightened concern in the future in the UK real estate market, as has occurred in the United States and Canada.[44] Moreover, the lack of experience of real estate agents with

38 This is similar to the lack of information and appropriate training that can affect financial investigators. See Chave, D., 'Proceeds of crime training: Bringing it up to date' (2017) 24(3) *Journal of Financial Crime* 437.

39 Interviews 8; 12.

40 Interview 2.

41 Interview 10.

42 Interview 7.

43 For an analysis on the use of cryptocurrencies in the real estate sector, see Wolfson, R., 'Bitcoin won't encourage cryptocurrency for real estate, but Cryptoeconomics will' *Forbes* (<http://www.forbes.com/sites/rachelwolfson/2018/05/21/bitcoin-wont-encourage-cryptocurrency-for-real-estate-but-cryptoeconomics-will/>, 21 May 2018).

44 See in the United States, 'Bitcoin fever hits US real estate market' *The Straits Times* (<http://www.straitstimes.com/world/united-states/bitcoin-fever-hits-us-real-estate-market>, 14 January 2018); in Canada, Dingman, S., 'Ontario regulator probes cryptocurrency use in real estate' *The Globe and Mail* (<http://www.theglobeandmail.com/real-estate/toronto/ontario-regulator-probes-cryptocurrency-use-in-real-estate/article38029116/>, 22 February 2018).

this type of transaction indicates the existence of another gap in the UK AML system: the risk of having untrained, inexperienced professionals dealing with property transactions that are more complex due to the different, more challenging medium involved.

A further relevant point that emerges from the interviews relates to the reasons given by real estate agents who have decided not to be involved in cryptocurrency transactions. A major explanation here is the lack of trust in the system of cryptocurrencies and, in some cases, the fear of being involved in illicit activities. Some say that 'it is better to be safe than sorry';[45] others talk of a 'minefield'[46] and something 'terrifying.'[47] At first sight, all the negative opinions expressed seem to suggest a clear opposition of real estate agents towards the use of cryptocurrencies. In particular, these views indicate a strong negative connotation of cryptocurrencies in property transactions. However, a closer analysis reveals that the negative comments might be due to the two points previously considered: a lack of full understanding of the phenomenon and a lack of engagement with it. In other words, the opposition and carefulness attached to cryptocurrency transactions might be caused by a fear of the 'unknown' rather than a proper evaluation of the pros and cons of these transactions.[48] This aspect is pivotal for understanding a second issue of the UK AML system: the rejection *a priori* of a viable tool for transactions (cryptocurrencies) that is not necessarily linked to crime but that is treated as such because of a lack of knowledge and experience. The significance of this gap becomes even clearer when considering the specific approach that real estate agents adopt when dealing with these transactions.

Real estate agents who have been involved or are willing to be involved in property transactions with cryptocurrencies generally think that the use of these currencies is a red flag for money laundering.[49] In particular, the transaction might become suspicious when large non-fully traceable sums are transferred with cryptocurrencies, such as bitcoins.[50] Some interviewees consider these transactions to be 'dodgy,'[51] and they think that there might be many money laundering challenges arising from the use of digital currencies in the real estate market. Major concerns are expressed in relation to two aspects: (i) the anonymity of the transactions[52] and (ii) the increasing digitalisation of the market and the lack of personal interaction with real estate professionals.[53]

45 Interview 12.
46 Interview 8.
47 Interview 8.
48 Similarly, this happens with regulation choices made by governments worldwide. See the Law Library of Congress, *Regulation of Cryptocurrency around the World* (<http://www.loc.gov/law/help/cryptocurrency/cryptocurrency-world-survey.pdf>, June 2018).
49 Interviews 10; 13.
50 Interview 7.
51 Ibid.
52 Ibid.; 9.
53 Interview 10.

Several interviewees are worried about the impossibility of fulfilling their AML obligations, especially the CDD checks that require the identification of the parties involved in real estate transactions and the assessment of the nature and purpose of the transactions.[54] They argue that with certain digital currencies (such as Ripple), identifying the customers involved and 'evidencing the source of funds' would be impossible.[55] As for the lack of personal contact in the transaction, some real estate professionals fear that 'this might actually assist money launderers in the future'[56] because it will reduce the need for 'physical' lawyers and valuers.[57]

This fact creates issues for those obliged to carry out CDD checks under the UK Money Laundering Regulations 2017, as they face many difficulties in knowing the real identities of those behind a transaction. In particular, two main factors negatively affect the checks by real estate agents over digital currency transactions. First, real estate agents do not necessarily have the technical skills to deal with these transactions. At present, UK legislation does not regulate cryptocurrencies (whether in the property market or other sectors); therefore, there is no obligation to undergo specific training or employ a dedicated money laundering officer for digital currency transactions.

Second, real estate agents do not necessarily have the resources to perform in-depth CDD checks on the identities of parties that want to buy real estate with digital currencies. The checks over cryptocurrency transactions require specialised IT software and personnel, which might be available only at a high cost for real estate agencies. Although the identities of customers might be traceable, following the chain of transactions linked to a certain public address, many users disguise their identities using routers (such as Tor) that hide their IP addresses. Thus real estate agents cannot fully assess and verify the identities of customers who use cryptocurrencies, thereby increasing the risk of money laundering for the entire property sector.

As discussed in the previous section, cryptocurrency systems avoid the use of mediators and financial institutions or banks as third parties in transactions. The underpinning idea is to create 'peer-to-peer' systems (like bitcoin), where there are no costs associated with the involvement of a third party and no intermediate passages between the main parties.

The absence of traditional third parties in cryptocurrency transactions has a major effect in relation to AML CDD checks and the role of real estate agents. Indeed, real estate agents (alongside solicitors) would be the only subjects who conduct the checks over the customers' identities for property transactions. In normal property transactions, real estate agents act in a multilateral AML system in which the same transaction and customer are subject to checks by a plurality of actors, including banks and real estate professionals. With cryptocurrencies, real estate agents are one of the few actors doing CDD checks, and the possible

54 Interviews 7; 8; 9; 10.

55 Interview 9.

56 Interview 10.

57 Ibid.

information gaps cannot be filled by AML agencies through cross-references amongst different sectors. In other words, AML national agencies could not use the additional information gathered by the actors of other sectors (like banks) because those actors would not be involved in any 'business relationship' with the parties that want to trade in digital currencies. This is a relevant issue for real estate agents because the burden of the CDD is only partially shared with other actors (for instance, solicitors), and, in this sense, they become one of the last standing actors of the AML system. This fact increases the level of responsibility of real estate agents and their importance as key gatekeepers of the UK real estate market, albeit national agencies do not offer the necessary, consequential increase of support (financial, logistic, informative).

In conclusion, the use of cryptocurrencies in the UK property sector is still a relatively new phenomenon, and few real estate agents have been involved in these transactions. However, the fact that cryptocurrencies are not yet properly regulated[58] and carry a negative reputation is a dissuasive factor for real estate agents to become involved in them. The approach of real estate agents is cautious, and it seems to be strictly linked to the unfulfilled need to receive more guidance and information from relevant national agencies and supervisory bodies. This aspect will be discussed in the next section of this chapter.

Some considerations on future legislation and shared governance

It is clear that there are still many gaps and unanswered questions that need to be considered by the UK legislator. These gaps also involve considerations of appropriate legislative and policy actions that should be taken in the near future to tackle the phenomenon effectively and reduce the possibility of cryptocurrencies being used to facilitate money laundering in the UK property market.

As for the legislative response, comprehensive regulation of cryptocurrencies that would cover all sectors of the UK economy, including the real estate market, should be delivered. Real estate agents think that, at present, there is a problematic lack of regulation and that substantial work is required by the government.[59] Despite the general concerns associated with the use of cryptocurrencies in the sector, future legislation should not include a blanket ban on them since they can also provide some benefits.[60] On the contrary, cryptocurrency transactions need to be regulated with effective and discerning provisions, especially in light of the possible future challenges (including Brexit) for the UK AML system.

58 See European Parliament, *Virtual Currencies and Terrorist Financing: Assessing the Risks and Evaluating Responses*, PE604.970, May 2018; Directive (EU) 2018/843 of the European Parliament and of the Council of 30 May 2018, OJ L156/43; Egan, M., 'A Bit(Coin) of a problem for the EU AML framework' in King, C., Walker, C., and Gurulé, J. (eds.), *The Palgrave Handbook of Criminal and Terrorism Financing Law* (Palgrave MacMillan, 2018).

59 Interview 10.

60 Interviews 9; 10.

Any future legislation on the topic should also include training requirements for real estate professionals. Some interviewees suggest that more guidance should be provided on the topic by the government, Her Majesty's Revenue and Customs (HMRC), National Crime Agency (NCA), and other national agencies that deal with the real estate market.[61] This guidance should clarify important aspects of the use of digital currencies to buy real estate, such as how real estate agents can perform CDD checks effectively and how they can trace the source of funding. Moreover, national agencies should not simply urge real estate agents to avoid these types of transactions, but they should be able to provide more help to real estate professionals who want to advance transactions using cryptocurrencies.[62]

Regarding the future perspectives, not all real estate agents interviewed have a clear idea of the future of cryptocurrencies in the UK economy in general and the property market specifically. Some argue that this will be a huge issue for the real estate market.[63] Others think that the blockchain technology might be an important tool to improve the sector and speed up transactions.[64] Others are waiting to see how things will develop and how the government will regulate the phenomenon.[65] These opinions indicate that there are two points of interest for real estate agents that will be relevant in the future of cryptocurrency transactions in the UK property market.

First, real estate agents are keen to understand what will happen with an increased use of cryptocurrencies in property transactions. Some professionals seem to be more positive than others, but there is a certain level of growing expectation linked to the future of these transactions. Moreover, despite the negative comments mentioned previously, there persists positive interest in these types of transactions, especially for the benefits that they might bring to the sector and the professionals involved in it. This perspective indicates the need for a balanced approach in the future regulation of cryptocurrencies in the real estate market (and in other sectors). This means that there is a need, on the one hand, to guarantee adequate checks on the transactions carried out in the sector to avoid illicit activities and prevent money launderers from profiting from it and, on the other hand, to allow the use of innovative methods of payment that might facilitate transactions and create a more streamlined process for the business.

Second, attention should be directed to the legislative approach that the UK government should take with regard to cryptocurrencies in general and their use in the real estate market specifically. As discussed earlier, real estate agents have expressed many concerns about the legislative gaps existing in the UK AML system on the topic and the lack of clarity on the issue by institutional agencies. Whilst at present, estate agents are left in a legislative limbo, there are certain

61 Interviews 8; 13; 14.
62 Interview 9.
63 Interview 14.
64 Interview 10.
65 Interview 9.

expectations that in the future, the phenomenon will be properly regulated, and precise guidelines will be provided to all those involved in the sector. This requires not only a legislative response that will address the obligations of real estate agents when dealing with cryptocurrencies but also adequate policies that will act as points of reference for the professionals to avoid inconsistency and loopholes.

Detailed regulation of cryptocurrencies is needed in specific sectors of the UK economy, including the real estate market. Future regulation should not ban the use of cryptocurrencies, but it should provide for a balanced legislative and policy framework where these currencies can be used following precise provisions and under the control of AML supervisory bodies.[66] Future legislation should address the two main problems of the use of cryptocurrencies in the real estate market: (i) the anonymity of the transactions, where the parties' identities are unknown or difficult to verify, and (ii) the limited number of traditional intermediaries subjected to AML obligations (such as banks) and the challenges arising for AML checks.

Given the lack of knowledge about the phenomenon, the diffidence that accompanies real estate transactions involving cryptocurrencies, and the complexity of these transactions (particularly to conduct CDD checks), training should be provided for real estate agents (for instance by HMRC). These activities should be designed to improve the technical skills and capacities of real estate professionals (especially real estate agents) to deal with cryptocurrency transactions and to carry out proper CDD checks in these cases by identifying the parties and assessing the nature and sources of funds. Moreover, the government and relevant national agencies should guarantee financial and logistic assistance to real estate agents who do not have the necessary resources by way of personnel and IT services to conduct AML CDD checks over real estate transactions in which cryptocurrencies are used (particularly to identify the customer, the source of funds, the beneficial owner in these highly anonymous and IT-complex transactions). This further aid should be tailored, considering the size and financial status of the real estate agencies requiring such assistance and the existence of IT services that could be used by the agencies in support of their activities.

The regulation of property transactions involving cryptocurrencies should also become the occasion for developing a model of shared governance.[67] In the United Kingdom, a good model of governance should include both the action of national agencies involved in AML activities and the direct participation of real estate agents who conduct the CDD checks provided in the Money Laundering Regulations 2017. Shared governance does not mean that real estate agents will be put at the same level as the legislator in the norm-making process, but it refers

66 Interestingly, similar considerations are made by the House of Commons Treasury Committee, *Crypto-assets* (2017–19 HC 910) 16ff.

67 On governance and cryptocurrencies, see Campbell-Verduyn, M., 'Bitcoin, crypto-coins, and global anti-money laundering governance' (2018) 69(2) *Crime, Law and Social Change* 283.

to the possibility to be heard and to have their views properly considered. This regime would be similar to what happens, for instance, in the financial sector, where the relevance of private actors is growing, and 'the agents in charge of the 'doing' end up shaping the content of governance too.'[68]

In this regard, it is posited that real estate agents might make two distinct contributions to the UK AML system. On the one hand, real estate agents should be consulted by national authorities in different phases of the development of the AML system. In particular, they should be involved in the pre-legislative phase (as already happens with the opening of public consultations) but also in the concrete implementation stage. This means that there should be a process of consultation with relevant stakeholders (the real estate professionals) on a regular basis, in which there is an assessment of the practice of AML in the specific sector of relevance. On the other hand, real estate agents should be actively involved in the policy-making process as effective gatekeepers of the property sector. In contrast to what happens with the 2017 Regulations, AML obligations should be conceived not as top-down provisions but as shared-responsibility norms that identify private actors (including real estate agents) as 'active' and not 'passive' recipients of national legislation. Consequently, real estate agents should be able to inform the provisions that relate to their sector and activities, and they should be able to influence the decisions taken at the national level with their practices.

The shared governance model should apply to all property transactions in the United Kingdom, but, as explained in this chapter, it would be particularly relevant for real estate transactions involving cryptocurrencies. Indeed, here the complexity of the operation requires direct control by real estate agents as the first subjects money launderers encounter in the transaction (alongside solicitors). Therefore, there is a need for more cooperation between national authorities and the professionals who deal with property transactions on a daily basis.

Conclusion

This chapter has critically analysed the use of cryptocurrencies in the UK real estate market and discussed some of the money laundering risks associated with these transactions. In particular, it has examined relevant points that have emerged from the literature on cryptocurrencies, pointing out their most problematic features that might be of concern for the UK AML system. Moreover, attention has been given to the specific issues emerging from the perspective of real estate agents interviewed for this study, considering important aspects of their AML obligations that might be undermined or complicated by the use of cryptocurrencies.

From the foregoing study, the author advances two ideas. First of all, the use of cryptocurrencies in the UK real estate market is a complex phenomenon that

68 Tsingou, E., 'New governors on the block: the rise of anti-money laundering professionals' (2018) 69(2) *Crime, Law and Social Change* 191, 204.

cannot be either disregarded or overestimated given the lack of official data on its extent.[69] It requires necessary attention by national authorities with a balanced approach, meaning regulation capable of promoting the positive aspects of cryptocurrency transactions and limiting possible abuses and illicit activities. To this end, the national legislator should carefully assess the features of cryptocurrencies that make them attractive to money launderers, with a specific focus on the real estate sector. In particular, attention should be given to two aspects discussed in the chapter. The first aspect concerns the structural elements of cryptocurrencies. These include the issue of anonymity and the lack of traditional intermediaries involved in the transaction. These elements should be tackled by the legislator to avoid loopholes and help real estate professionals deal with cryptocurrencies. The second aspect relates to the practical approaches of real estate agents to transactions that include cryptocurrencies. In this regard, the legislator should consider various aspects: from the procedures to be followed to the training; and from the financial and logistic sources at the disposal of real estate agents to the guidance provided by the HMRC and NCA.

Second, the approach to property transactions involving cryptocurrencies should become the occasion for developing a model of shared governance. This model would see both the participation of national agencies and real estate agents that have to perform the CDD checks provided in the 2017 AML Regulations. This model of shared governance should not create equal obligations and level of responsibilisation for the institutional actors and the real estate professionals. On the contrary, it should lead to a distribution of functions and duties between the two, but with the possibility for real estate agents to have their practice and opinion properly considered. In so doing, the fight against money laundering would see a better, more informed legislation and policy system put in place, with a combination of theoretical and practical considerations. As a final caveat, it is worth noting that the shared governance model proposed is not intended as a substitute of the existing UK AML framework but as a part of it. So, the model should work as a defined part of the AML framework, integrated as an additional section or regulation to the 2017 AML Regulations. In other words, the new model of shared governance would improve the UK AML framework with a suitable transition from *lex lata* (the law as it exists) to *lex ferenda* (the law as it should be).

69 A general analysis on the use of cryptocurrencies in other sectors and some data can be found in the House of Commons Treasury Committee, *Crypto-Assets* (2017–19 HC 910) 5–7; 12–15.

11 Criminal money and antiquities

An open-source investigation into transnational organised cultural property crime

Samuel Andrew Hardy

Introduction

Policy discourse now regularly emphasises that antiquities are used both for financing terrorism and laundering criminal money.[1] Legal reforms, to categorise art and antiquities as commodities at high risk of exploitation by money launderers, are being implemented or considered around the world.[2] Yet stakeholders also recognise that there are 'hardly any . . . data on illicit commerce' in cultural objects or 'instruments for measuring' it, regardless of the participant.[3] In terms of policing (international) cultural property crime, there is a counterproductive leaning towards easier, quicker, cheaper seizure, forfeiture, and repatriation rather than indictment, conviction, and punishment,[4] even when shipments of cultural goods display indicators of terrorist financing.[5] So, there continue to be comparatively few well-documented, successfully prosecuted criminal cases by which to assess the necessity and effectiveness of traditional and innovative assemblages of governance.[6]

1 See, e.g., European Commission, *Commission Staff Working Document Accompanying the Document Report from the Commission to the European Parliament and to the Council on the Assessment of the Risks of Money Laundering and Terrorist Financing Affecting the Internal Market and Relating to Cross-Border Situations.* SWD (2017) 241 final, 124–128.

2 For example, in the EU Fifth Money Laundering Directive (Directive 2018/843 of May 30, 2018) and the US Illicit Art and Antiquities Trafficking Prevention Bill (HR 5886–115th Congress (2017–2018)).

3 European Commission (fn 1) 124.

4 St. Hilaire, R., 'Seize and send v. investigate and indict: Focusing on cultural heritage criminal investigations and prosecutions' *Cultural Heritage Lawyer Blog* (<http://culturalheritagelawyer.blogspot.com/2012/03/seize-and-send-v-investigate-and-indict.html>, 5 March 2012).

5 For example, St. Hilaire, R., 'Newly Obtained Documents Reveal Suspected Ties to Terrorism and Money Laundering in Antiquities Trafficking Investigation; "Seize and Send" Outcome Flags Urgent Need for Specially Designated Prosecutors to Bring Criminals to Justice' *Cultural Heritage Lawyer Blog* (<http://culturalheritagelawyer.blogspot.com/2015/09/newly-obtained-documents-reveal.html>, 30 September 2015).

6 For a US-based survey, see Vlasic, M.V. and DeSousa, J.P., 'The illicit antiquities trade and terrorism financing' in King, C., Walker, C., and Gurulé, J. (eds.), *The Palgrave Handbook of Criminal and Terrorism Financing Law* (Palgrave MacMillan, 2018). One of the few

Indeed, there are many who advocate against the application of anti-money laundering (AML)/counter-terrorist financing (CTF) requirements on this basis. For example, the International Confederation of Art and Antique Dealers' Associations (CINOA) uses 'the absence of recurring evidence of terrorism financing' through art market transactions within the European Union (EU) to argue that heavier regulation would put an 'enormous,' 'disproportionate,' and 'unacceptable burden' on the trade, which mostly comprises small- and medium-sized enterprises that 'do not have the resources to fund the same compliance services' as businesses in other sectors.[7] Perversely, it justifies this claim precisely by highlighting how 19% of fine arts that are auctioned in Europe change hands for USD 10,000+ and 26% that are sold around the world change hands for USD 50,000+.

The market-aligned Committee for Cultural Policy (CCP) claims success in preventing (or at least delaying) the extension of AML measures to dealers in art and antiquities in the United States.[8] To challenge the campaign for stricter AML regulation, the CCP advances the fact that there have been 'no convictions for pure money laundering in the art trade.'[9] The underlying logic would seem to suggest that, because the convicted criminals have committed two crimes instead of one, states should not try to make it more difficult for them to commit one of those two.

Encapsulating the market position, the president of the Art Dealers' Association of America (ADAA) asserts that money laundering is 'simply not . . . pervasive.'[10] Yet a British money laundering suspect told an American undercover agent that art was such a 'profitable investment' precisely 'because of "money laundering"', because it was 'the only market that [was] unregulated.'[11] An American money laundering suspect told another undercover agent, 'You don't have to worry about it. . . . We can do it any way, any way you want. . . . No receipt, no invoice. . . . That's the way I like to do business.'[12]

---

documented cases in recent years involved art that was 'smuggled out of [Brazil] to hide illegal profits' by banker Edemar Cid Ferreira. See Carrigan, M., 'US anti-money-laundering bill could reappear early next year' *The Art Newspaper* (11 December 2018).

7 Confédération Internationale des Négociants en Oeuvres d'Art, 'CINOA Position Paper (April 2018) on the Proposed Revision of the 4th EU Anti Money Laundering Directive' *CINOA* (<http://www.cinoa.org/cinoa/perspectives?action=view&id=AWJwp9yN1B8GfYskag3i>, 3 April 2018).

8 Fitz Gibbon, K., 'Committee for cultural policy 2018 year-end report' *Cultural Property News* (<https://culturalpropertynews.org/committee-for-cultural-policy-2018-year-end-report/>, 30 December 2018).

9 Committee for Cultural Policy, 'Anti-money laundering campaign trips . . . over the truth' *Cultural Property News* (<https://culturalpropertynews.org/anti-money-laundering-campaign-trips-over-the-truth/>, 25 October 2018).

10 Carrigan, M., 'US anti-money-laundering bill could reappear early next year' *Anti-Money Laundering Association* (<https://theamla.com/news/us-anti-money-laundering-bill-could-reappear-early-next-year/>, 12 December 2018).

11 *US v Kyriacou and others*, Indictment No. CR 18 0102, 28 February 2018 (Eastern District of New York) 16.

12 St. Hilaire, R., '"No invoices? Cool." Art, Artifacts, and Money Laundering' *Cultural Heritage Lawyer Blog* (<https://culturalheritagelawyer.blogspot.com/2019/01/art-artifacts-money laundering.html>, 8 January 2019).

As this chapter demonstrates, terrorist financiers (as well as other conflict financiers) and organised criminals are not only capable of exploiting the market; they are already exploiting it.[13] Meanwhile, observers continue to suggest that 'expertise' is necessary to exploit the market. This claim may have limited their estimation of the threat of exploitation by terrorist financiers and organised criminals, which the European Commission judged to be 'moderately significant' in June 2017.[14] For instance, the ransoming of stolen paintings was already known to have profited the terrorist network that attacked Paris in November 2015 and Brussels in March 2016.[15]

Formal partnerships and informal collaborations are emerging to overcome the obstacles to effective policing of this activity, whether by conducting due diligence checks to establish the facts of a case, producing previously unobtainable evidence that is admissible in court, monitoring previously untouchable actors who may then be investigated, tracing previously obscured networks that may then be analysed, or assessing otherwise fragmented pieces of evidence that may then inform analysis. Thus this chapter also shows how innovative assemblages of governance are making distinct contributions to policing. This chapter is particularly important in light of ongoing efforts to regulate this important sector.

Using open-source intelligence to inform policy and practice

One developing field for the gathering of intelligence to analyse risks and trends in cultural property crime, if not also for the collection of evidence to ground criminal investigations and legal proceedings, is open-source research.[16] Such research may somewhat compensate for the dearth of well-documented criminal cases. Consequently, intelligence-led policing – and, equally importantly, evidence-led policy – may achieve greater success in the disruption of trafficking.

Open science is founded on practices of 'open access, open data and open methods,' on the provision of permanent, free online access to the publication, its data sets (ideally, the raw data), and its 'methods of data collection, analysis,

13 Campbell, P., 'The illicit antiquities trade as a transnational criminal network: Characterizing and anticipating trafficking of cultural heritage' (2013) 20(2) *International Journal of Cultural Property* 113; Paul, K.A., 'Ancient artifacts vs. digital artifacts: New tools for unmasking the sale of illicit antiquities on the dark web' (2018) 7(2) *Arts* 12.

14 European Commission (fn 1) 125.

15 Loore, F., 'Trafic d'art et terrorisme: cambriolage du Musée Van Buuren à Uccle en 2013; les policiers avaient identifié Khalid El Bakraoui' (trans: Trafficking of art and terrorism: robbery of the Van Buuren Museum in Uccle in 2013; the police have identified Khalid El Bakraoui) *Paris Match* (24–30 November 2016) 57.

16 Berry, D.M., 'Internet research: Privacy, ethics and alienation: An open source approach' (2004) 14(4) *Internet Research* 323; Podbregar, I. and Ivanuša, T., 'Open source intelligence and intelligence analytics' (2010) 61(2) *Journal of Criminal Investigation and Criminology* 191; Hribar, G. et al., 'OSINT: A "Grey Zone"?' (2014) 27 *International Journal of Intelligence and CounterIntelligence* 529.

and visualization' so that research is accessible, assessable, and reproducible.[17] There may be significant constraints on the implementation of open science in criminology for the protection of sources and subjects. Notwithstanding those constraints, the fullest possible implementation is increasing the volume, complexity, and reliability of data that researchers can collect, as well as expanding the number of analysts and the range of their expertise.

To give one example of how open science works, combining techniques from digital humanities, biological anthropology, and criminology whilst collaborating across North America, Europe, and Asia-Pacific, one team has performed a scoping review of the 'red market' in human remains,[18] developed methods of research into the online trade,[19] and produced a text analysis of online communities.[20] Therein, they have traced transnational networks from extractor to dealer to collector. To give another example, a study has found testimony from a treasure hunter that he transports his metal detector into and out of restrictive jurisdictions by carrying its components in different containers.[21] In both cases, this knowledge is already being mobilised in capacity-building programmes, through which it may refine training of cultural heritage professionals and law enforcement agents and thereby increase prevention of unlicensed activity. Currently, the evidence base is so limited that it is difficult, if not impossible, to conduct a systematic review of the effectiveness of policy on cultural property crime. However, there have been foundational studies of evidence in relation to the functioning of cultural property crime and responses to it. These studies include systematic reviews of tomb robbing in Italy,[22] interfaces between legal and illegal operators in the antiquities trade,[23] and the effects of politics on the resolution of legal disputes over cultural property.[24]

17 Marwick, B. et al, 'Open science in archaeology' (2017) 17(4) *SAA Archaeological Record* 8.

18 Huffer, D. and Chappell, D., 'The mainly nameless and faceless dead: an exploratory study of the illicit traffic in archaeological and ethnographic human remains' (2014) 62 *Crime, Law and Social Change* 131.

19 Huffer, D. and Graham, S., 'Fleshing out the bones: Studying the human remains trade with Tensorflow and Inception' (2018) 1(1) *Journal of Computer Applications in Archaeology* 55.

20 Huffer, D. and Graham, S., 'The insta-dead: The rhetoric of the human remains trade on Instagram' (2017) 45 *Internet Archaeology* (<http://intarch.ac.uk/journal/issue45/5/toc.html>).

21 Hardy, S.A., 'To get a good price, "You have to sell in international bidding sites": Trafficking of metal-detected cultural goods from South Asia' in Hufnagel, S. and Moiseienko, A. (eds.), *Criminal Networks and Law Enforcement: Global/International Perspectives on Illicit Enterprise* (Routledge, 2019).

22 Balcells Magrans, M., *Contemporary Archaeological Looting: A Criminological Analysis of Italian Tomb Robbers* (PhD, City University of New York, 2018) 31–70.

23 Tijhuis, E., *Transnational Crime and the Interface between Legal and Illegal Actors: The Case of the Illicit Art and Antiquities Trade* (Wolf Legal Publishers, 2006) 205.

24 Shehade, M. and Fouseki, K., 'The politics of culture and the culture of politics: Examining the role of politics and diplomacy in cultural property disputes' (2016) 32 *International Journal of Cultural Property* 357.

By exploiting the amount and accessibility of evidence on the web, open-source research is enabling quantitative and qualitative analyses that are testing received opinion, opening new avenues of research, and compiling an evidence base that will be the foundation for policy analysis. Open-source research may be key in corroborating novel studies that document new evidence for long-disputed phenomena.[25] Thereby, it may change approaches to policing, which, for instance, long denied the possibility of theft-to-order, thus hamstringing investigations into cases of theft-to-order.[26] Critically, then, it may contribute to risk analyses for money laundering and terrorism financing/conflict financing with art and antiquities.

The limits and possibilities can be seen in the following summary review of organised cultural property crime. Whilst even its *existence* remains controversial in international discussion, the functioning of collaboration between Italian mafia and 'Russian mafia' (or 'Eurasian organised crime') in crimes involving antiquities (including the trafficking of antiquities, murder, and robbery of collectors) has been documented in Russian since at least 1997.[27] Russian mafia boss Semion Mogilevich's handling of antiquities, which ranged from trafficking of 'stolen icons'[28] to 'advance fee fraud' that fraudulently appropriated cultural assets,[29] has been documented in English since 1998.[30]

Practical difficulties, however, arise. Even if knowledge is, nowadays, not unidentifiable due to the language of the record, it may be inaccessible due to the geographical location of the record. Alternatively, it may be identifiable and geographically accessible, yet remain unknown due to the intellectual location of the record outside the field of cultural property crime. Nonetheless, it is becoming *much more* identifiable and *much more* accessible due to the archiving of historical documents and the publication of contemporary documents online, as well as the

25 For example, Al-Azm, A. and Paul, K.A., 'The Middle East's other Facebook revolution: Antiquities trafficking in the digital age' *World Politics Review* (<http://www.worldpoliticsreview.com/articles/25532/the-middle-east-s-other-facebook-revolution-antiquities-trafficking-in-the-digital-age>, 14 August 2018).

26 Hardy, S.A., 'Is looting-to-order "just a myth"? Open-source analysis of theft-to-order of cultural property' (2015) 1 *Cogent Social Sciences* (<https://doi.org/10.1080/23311886.2015.1087110>). See other discussions of policing in Chappell, D. and Hufnagel, S. (eds.), *Contemporary Perspectives on the Detection, Investigation and Prosecution of Art Crime* (Ashgate Publishing, 2014).

27 Maksimov, A., *Rossiskaya Prestupnost: Kto Est Kto* (trans: *Russian Crime: Who's Who*) (EKSMO-Press, Moscow, 1997) (<http://www.kulichki.com/moshkow/POLITOLOG/r-prest.txt>).

28 Harding, L., 'Russia's most notorious Mafia Boss arrested in Moscow' *The Guardian* (<http://www.theguardian.com/world/2008/jan/25/russia.lukeharding>, 25 January 2008).

29 Sweeney, J., 'Mr Bigski's dirty money grows fat in UK Banks' *The Observer* (5 December 1999).

30 Friedman, R.I., 'The most dangerous mobster in the world' *The Village Voice* (<http://www.villagevoice.com/1998/05/26/the-most-dangerous-mobster-in-the-world>, 26 May 1998).

refinement of machine translation and the expansion of the range of languages that may be subjected to machine translation. As detailed here and elsewhere in relation to multi-commodity trafficking and money laundering by organised criminals from Eastern Europe and Latin America, open-source research can demonstrate the existence and functioning of criminal phenomena, which can then inform the activities of police and customs. Furthermore, law enforcement agencies may be aware of traffickers of cultural objects, yet only as traffickers of other commodities; law enforcement agencies are 'increasing[ly] regular[ly]' searching for drugs and finding 'vast' quantities of antiquities.[31] So, such open-source evidence can identify suspects, routes, and networks, which can then be targeted in law enforcement operations.

How innovative assemblages can facilitate traditional governance

Public investigators can often only 'reveal' risk that is already known to someone or another in some way or another, even if that knowledge is difficult for others to identify and access. Sometimes, they may reconstruct networks that are otherwise only visible as isolated sets of nodes. Yet when private actors monitor the market, they may be able to identify suspects and suspect goods and then present cases to law enforcement agents for forensic investigation.

Due to the different requirements and norms of police procedure and private investigation, as well as the different knowledge of police officers and cultural-historical experts, private actors may be able to identify *previously unknown* suspects and networks. For instance, cultural-historical experts may identify suspect goods, investigative journalists may then (justify that they) devote resources to targeting people and exposing their activities, and law enforcement agents may then (justify that they) investigate forensically. Even if such cases are shelved, fear of prosecution (or simply bad publicity) may lead to restitution of cultural property.

One recent case clearly demonstrates the key role of private actors in monitoring the trade in (il)licit antiquities and combatting crimes against cultural property and thus the potential of greater information sharing and closer collaboration between cultural property law enforcement agents and cultural heritage workers. This case concerned the 'bronze Buddha,' and involved a representative of the Association for Research into Crimes Against Art (ARCA) in Italy, a representative of the India Pride Project (IPP) in Singapore, a retiree from the Archaeological Survey of India (ASI) in India, a representative of the International Council of Museums (ICOM) in France, and an anonymised expert in an undisclosed

31 With regard to known narcotics traffickers who are also antiquities traffickers, see Acar, Ö. and Kaylan, M., 'The Hoard' *Connoisseur* (July 1988) 74. With regard to the commonality of finds of antiquities in searches for narcotics, see Bowman, B.A., 'Transnational crimes against culture: looting at archaeological sites and the "grey" market in antiquities' (2008) 24(3) *Journal of Contemporary Criminal Justice* 225, 231.

location, who cooperated with an officer of the National Police in the Netherlands and an officer of the Metropolitan Police in the United Kingdom.[32]

Due to the comparative ease of laundering antiquities that have been looted from archaeological sites through the art market with false collecting histories and no contradictory paperwork, the CEO of ARCA undertook voluntary monitoring for looted antiquities at the European Fine Arts Fair in the Netherlands in 2018. There, she found a suspect object for sale that was ultimately proved to have been 'stolen from the Nalanda Archaeological Museum' in India in 1961.[33]

ARCA and the IPP compared photographs that had been taken by ARCA with records that were provided by an ASI retiree. They identified a match and notified the head of the Art and Antiques Crime Unit in the Netherlands (and other relevant authorities and institutions). Then when the dealer from the United Kingdom revealed to the police in the Netherlands that they were handling the object for a consignor, ARCA and the IPP shared their documentation with an officer of the Art and Antiques Unit in the United Kingdom.[34]

The Metropolitan Police contacted the director of programmes and partnerships for ICOM, who 'arranged for a neutral external expert opinion,' which reaffirmed the opinion of ARCA and the IPP.[35] Then, finally, the bronze Buddha was 'voluntarily relinquish[ed]' by its possessor and repatriated to India.[36]

Albeit that this Internet-mediated process seems encouraging, it must be borne in mind that the Internet is equally an everyday tool for criminals as it is for crime fighters.[37] Much private online trading may be practically invisible to crime fighters and thus practically impossible to disrupt before laundered objects appear on the open market.

Identified evidence of money laundering and conflict financing

Traditionally, it has been difficult to demonstrate concrete evidence of money launderers using art and antiquity items. Indeed, empirical research had previously found 'very little evidence' of money laundering with '*stolen* works of art, or *looted* and *smuggled* antiquities.'[38] However, that was a product of the (rigorously) restricted research design and the sporadic evidence base.[39] Such research

32 Albertson, L., 'Repatriation: The case of the stolen TEFAF Buddha' *Association for Research into Crime against Art (ARCA)* (<https://art-crime.blogspot.com/2018/08/repatriation-case-of-stolen-tefaf-buddha.html>, 5 August 2018).

33 *Ibid.*

34 *Ibid.*

35 *Ibid.*

36 *Ibid.*

37 Hardy, S.A., 'Heritage crime: Criminological perspectives' in Mitsilegas, V., Hufnagel, S. and Moiseienko, A. (eds.), *Research Handbook on Transnational Crime* (Edward Elgar Publishing, 2020).

38 For example, Tijhuis (fn 23) 205 – emphasis added.

39 *Ibid.*

can also be a tortuous and comparatively unproductive process. Thus illicit activity may be discussed yet not documented by one source[40] and then only corroborated by the subsequent discovery of a leaked document from one other source.[41] Nevertheless, today, exceptional political situations, such as the crises in Ukraine, can generate significant direct documentation.[42] There is also significant direct documentation of conflict antiquities trafficking to finance warfare, espionage, oppression, or terrorism. Whether state forces and anti-state forces in Syria and Turkey (occupying), state forces in Indonesia-occupied East Timor/ Timor-Leste, China-occupied Tibet, warlords in Afghanistan and Somalia, or terrorist financiers in Germany and Egypt, there has been evidence of trafficking of (or profiteering off) cultural objects to finance (or incentivise) political violence within the last 20 years.[43]

Such open-source research also documents the peculiar utility of cultural assets *as* laundering assets, which is most clearly demonstrated by the antiquities-for-methamphetamine economy in the United States. It is 'often' impossible for law enforcement agents to seize cultural objects that have been bought with the proceeds of drug sales (or bartered for drugs) by multi-commodity dealers because there is 'no [forensic] proof' that they were 'acquired illegally.'[44] As observed by a forensic archaeologist, 'When you have an artifact in your hand, you might as well have a packet of cash.'[45] Highlighting another benefit of cultural assets, investigative journalists in North Macedonia wryly note that government ministers

40 For example, BBC Panorama, 'An in-depth investigation of leaked documents reveals Ukrainian gangsters, their families and associates taking advantage of offshore secrecy and ineffective money laundering controls to buy luxurious property and works of art.' Watch Tonight at 8.30 pm on @BBCOne #BBCPanorama (<https://twitter.com/BBCPanorama/status/988468378561064960>, 23 April 2018). This tweet indicates that investigative journalists had evidence of money laundering with art by organized criminals, yet it was cut from the broadcast programme (*Gangsters' Dirty Money Exposed*, <http://www.bbc.co.uk/programmes/n3ct3v2w>). Thus that evidence was not published and archived in a way that could be identified and assessed. In this case, searches for the excised material found an alternative source of similar information.

41 Cf. Servizio Centrale Operativo di Polizia di Stato, 'Mafia Ucraina [Ukrainian Mafia]' (Servizio Centrale Operativo di Polizia di Stato, 7–8 October 1998) (<http://www.occrp.org/images/stories/Exhibit_10_ItalianReport.pdf>).

42 For example, Taylor, A., 'What did Yanukovych take with him when he fled his mansion? Paintings, guns and a small dog, according to new video' *The Washington Post* (12 March 2014); Lindsay, I., 'How will the Crimean crisis affect the Russian art market?' *Russian Art Dealer* (<http://www.russianartdealer.com/journal/crimean-crisis-affect-russian-art-market/>, 2 April 2014).

43 Hardy, S.A., 'Antiquities trafficking and conflict financing: the fight against looting and smuggling of cultural property goods in a global perspective of peace' in Caracciolo, I and Montuoro, U. (eds.), *Preserving Cultural Heritage and National Identities for International Peace and Security* (G. Giappichelli Editore, 2019).

44 Patel, S.S., 'Drugs, guns and dirt' (<http://archive.archaeology.org/0903/etc/drugs.html>, 1 March 2009).

45 Martin McAllister, cited by Thomas, M., 'Why are people looting clear lake?' (<http://www.psmag.com/nature-and-technology/why-are-people-looting-clear-lake>, 16 September 2015).

with extraordinary wealth have 'modest vehicles,' which the public can see, 'but expensive paintings,' which the public cannot see.[46]

As already noted, there is growing concern about the risk of money laundering in the art and antiquities market in significantly consuming market countries, such as the United States[47] and the United Kingdom,[48] and primarily trading market countries, such as Switzerland.[49] Trade associations persist in asserting that the art market is 'erroneously believed to be . . . a high risk sector for money laundering,' whilst there is 'little evidence to suggest' that it is 'linked to money laundering.'[50] Yet due to legal research and the accumulation of other resources on the web, open-source research now identifies wide-ranging evidence to suggest that money is laundered through the art market, by organized criminals,[51] by politically exposed persons (PEPs),[52] and by other criminals.[53] For instance, according to the indictment in a recent case involving the 1965 painting of *Personnages* by Pablo Picasso, two individuals (Kyriacou and Aristodemou) met with a third individual (who happened to be an undercover FBI agent) and proposed

46 Scoop, 'The six richest Minsters are worth 35 Million Euros' *Inbox* (<http://en.inbox7.mk/?p=2741>, 19 November 2018).

47 Rubenfeld, S., 'Art world's response to money-laundering concerns draws critics' *Dow Jones* (<http://www.dowjones.com/insights/art-worlds-response-money-laundering-concerns-draws-critics/>, 3 March 2017).

48 Porter, T., 'Criminals seeking to launder millions through art market, warn experts' *International Business Times* (<https://www.ibtimes.co.uk/criminals-seeking-launder-millions-through-art-market-warn-experts-1567027>, 25 June 2016).

49 Bradley, S., 'Can the art market regulate itself against illicit activity?' *SwissInfo* (9 February 2017) (<http://www.swissinfo.ch/eng/responsible-art_can-the-art-market-regulate-itself-against-illicit-activity/42943258>).

50 For example, Confédération Internationale des Négociants en Oeuvres d'Art, 'New measures threaten to damage the art trade' *CINOA* (<http://www.cinoa.org/cinoa/perspectives?action=view&id=AWJJONIyqkC4eatYdKj1>, 19 March 2018).

51 In countries from Colombia to Russia. See, e.g., Cawley, M., 'Colombia artifact smuggling case shows links between drugs and culture' *InSight Crime* (<http://www.insightcrime.org/news/brief/colombia-artifact-smuggling-case-shows-links-between-drugs-and-culture/>, 2 September 2014); Russian Mafia, 'Russian Mafia legalize criminal money under the guise of contemporary art exhibitions' *Russian Mafia* (<http://www.rumafia.net/en/material/11?hl=RUE>, March 2010).

52 In countries from Brazil to the Philippines: Salcedo-Albarán, E., Jorge Garay, L., Santos, D., Macías, G., and Guerra, N., 'The "Lava Jato" network: Corruption and money laundering in Brazil' (2018) 29 *Global Observatory of Transnational Criminal Networks* 1, 13, 25; United States Attorney's Office, New York County District, 'DA Vance: Former secretary to Imelda Marcos convicted on all counts at trial involving disappearance of Monet and other artworks' *Stolen Asset Recovery Initiative* (<https://star.worldbank.org/corruption-cases/sites/corruption-cases/files/Marcos_Bautista_Conviction_NY_District_Attorney_PR_Nov_18_2013.pdf>, 18 November 2013).

53 In countries from the United Kingdom to Israel: Borschel-Dan, A., 'Arrest of Jerusalem antiquities dealers opens a smuggling Pandora's Box' *The Times of Israel* (<http://www.timesofisrael.com/arrest-of-israeli-antiquities-dealers-opens-a-smuggling-pandoras-box/>, 1 August 2017); Kinsella, E., 'UK Art Dealer Matthew Green charged in a $9 million Picasso money-laundering scheme' *Artnet News* (<https://news.artnet.com/art-world/matthew-green-charged-money-laundering-us-1236929>, 6 March 2018).

laundering proceeds of stock manipulation deals through the purchase and sale of art. It was proposed that the *Personnages* painting could be purchased for £6.7 million and then later sold in order to 'clean the money.'[54] It was Aristodemou who characterised the art trade as 'the only market that is unregulated' and albeit hyperbolically advertised that 'art was a profitable investment because of "money laundering."'[55]

In 2018, Paul Manafort, a prominent US lobbyist, pled guilty to conspiracy through money laundering, tax fraud, and obstructing justice. In the course of those activities, he had successfully converted at least USD 1,690,160 in offshore bank accounts in Cyprus through purchases of antiques and art in the United States.[56] Amongst other places, Manafort converted income from services for political actors in Ukraine. In that country, there is a longer history of illicit handling of cultural goods by PEPs. For instance, former prime minister Pavlo Lazarenko was convicted of money laundering in the United States in 2004, whereafter a lithograph by Picasso and a vase of unspecified origin were seized in 2013.[57]

High-value transactions for cultural goods from around the world by drug smugglers, paramilitary fighters, and political associates in Latin America and participation by lower-level as well as higher-level criminals there serve to demonstrate the risk of handling criminal money in the art market more broadly. The everyday tone of discussion in Latin America also serves as an antidote to protestations of naivety in North America and Europe. Elsewhere, evidence has been presented that demonstrates the existence of multi-commodity trafficking of antiquities with drugs, wildlife, and other commodities in Belize, Guatemala, Honduras, and Mexico, which has been committed by organised crime groups, corrupt networks within state agencies, and transnational organised crime.[58] In this chapter, evidence is presented from Colombia and Mexico that shows how members and associates of organised crime groups and paramilitary organisations have laundered money with art and antiquities.

Colombia

In the transatlantic narcotics trade that pivots on Colombia, different trafficking/terrorist organisations have been implicated in the handling of art since (if not

54 *US v Kyriacou* (fn 11) 16.

55 *Ibid.*

56 United States Attorney's Office for the District of Columbia, 'Superseding Criminal Information [Document 525–1, Case 1:17-cr-00201-ABJ]' (<https://assets.documentcloud.org/documents/5747661/Manafort-Sentencing-USA-Attachments-A-F.pdf>, 23 February 2019).

57 Rubenfeld, S., 'US seizes Ex-Ukrainian Prime Minister's mansion' *Wall Street Journal* (<https://blogs.wsj.com/riskandcompliance/2013/11/07/us-seizes-ex-ukrainian-prime-ministers-mansion-picasso-lithograph/>, 7 November 2013).

58 Hardy (fn 37).

the 1970s then) the 1980s,[59] through the 1990s[60] and the 2000s,[61] and into the 2010s.[62] As explained by his brother, notorious Medellín cartel boss Pablo Escobar 'bought magnificent art . . . , antique furniture, and other very desirable items that could be sold easily for cleaned money with no questions asked'; since laundering could drain 'as much as 50 percent or 60 percent' of the proceeds of the drugs crime, 'there were always people willing to do deals.'[63] According to his son, Escobar's wife, María Victoria Henao Escobar, also handled fine art[64] and 'valuable antiques such as Chinese vases and pre-Columbian pieces made of gold and clay.'[65] Medellín narcotrafficker Rafael Cardona Salazar had at least one Ming porcelain vase.[66]

As well as Cali cartel bosses Justo Pastor Perafán and Victor Patiño Fómeque,[67] Cali cartel trafficker Carlos Alberto Mejía had an entire 'art collection,'[68] which included at least one pre-Columbian vase.[69] A financial channel between the Cali cartel and the Liberal Party intermediary, Elizabeth Montoya de Sarria, resulted in her investing proceeds in fine art.[70] In the same vein, narcotraffickers and paramilitaries, who are not notorious enough to have been named, have bought 'artwork[s]' and other cultural objects that indicate an interest in antiquities, such as 'golden replicas of Egyptian relics and some elaborate bronze sculptures.'[71] This appears to have been due to ignorance rather than price, as they bought many fakes in the belief that they were masterpieces. For instance, one drug trafficker

59 Escobar, R., *Escobar: The Inside Story of Pablo Escobar, the World's Most Powerful Criminal* (Hodder, 2010) 75.

60 Dudley, S., 'Hector Beltran Leyva, the BLO's gentleman operator, captured in Mexico' *Insight Crime* (<http://www.insightcrime.org/news/analysis/hector-beltran-leyva-blo-political-operator-captured-mexico/>, 2 October 2014).

61 Cawley (fn 51).

62 Tóth, M., 'Police in Spain and Bulgaria bust drug smuggling, money laundering and burglary gang' *Illicit Trade News* (<http://www.illicit-trade.com/2018/05/police-in-spain-and-bulgaria-bust-drug-smuggling-money-laundering-and-burglary-gang/>, 26 May 2018).

63 Escobar (fn 59) 75.

64 Guarnizo Álvarez, J., 'Las Joyas Perdidas de la Mafia [The lost jewels of the Mafia]' *El Colombiano* (<http://www.elcolombiano.com/historico/las_joyas_perdidas_de_la_mafia-EKEC_78936>, 20 February 2010).

65 Escobar, J.P., *Pablo Escobar: My father* (Ebury Publishing, 2016).

66 Guarnizo Álvarez (fn 64).

67 Carreres, A., 'Así Es Como Pablo Escobar Logró Esconder 1,500 Millones Durante Años (trans.: This Is How Pablo Escobar Managed to Hide 1,500 Million for Years') *Vice* (<http://www.vice.com/es_mx/article/jmzae3/asi-es-como-pablo-escobar-logro-esconder-1500-millones-durante-anos>, 17 October 2016).

68 Saviano, R., *Zero* (Penguin, 2016) 234–235.

69 Guarnizo Álvarez (fn 64).

70 *Ibid.*

71 Brodzinsky, S., 'Escobar's Rolex and other items seized from Colombia's drug lords are sold' *The Guardian* (29 October 2013) (<http://www.theguardian.com/world/2013/oct/29/escobar-rolex-seized-colombia-drug-lords-farc>).

and money launderer for the Norte del Valle cartel, Luis Hernando Gómez Bustamante ('Rasguño'), bought works that had been attributed to Rubens.[72]

Indeed, some narcotraffickers have been 'pathological accumulators (*acumuladores patológicos*)' of cultural objects.[73] At least at one time, narcotrafficker consumption was so great that it created a 'speculative bubble (*burbuja especulativa*)' in artworks,[74] yet perhaps only 25% of seized works were authentic.[75] The art has been used as an asset to secure an inheritance for the families of traffickers and has been stolen by paramilitaries in their campaigns against traffickers.[76] Paramilitary leader Fidel Castaño, who 'bartered drugs for art (*cambió las drogas por el arte*)' in the United States and Israel,[77] boasted that 'trafficking art was more lucrative' than trafficking drugs.[78] Contradicting rumours of his death that had persisted since 1994, in 2004, the United States indicated that he was alive and well and 'continuing his work as a dealer of art (*continúa su trabajo como dealer de arte*)' in France or Israel.[79] In other cases, one money launderer for drug traffickers smuggled antiquities from Colombia to Spain,[80] whilst 'poly-criminal' drug traffickers laundered the proceeds of their own activity in Spain and their suppliers' activity in Colombia through the art market.[81]

Mexico

In the transatlantic narcotics trade that pivots on Mexico, Sinaloa cartel boss Joaquín Guzmán, 'el Chapo', had 'a collection of exotic art – some of which was illegal to possess – some stolen works (*una colección de arte exótico – algunos de los cuales era ilegal poseer – algunas obras robadas*).'[82] It included 'sculptures, works of art (*esculturas, obras de arte*).'[83] Although there are other factors, such

72 Revista Arcadia, 'Los Rubens de Rasguño (trans.: Scratch's Rubens)' *Revista Arcadia* (<http://www.revistaarcadia.com/impresa/portada/articulo/pinturas-rubens-del-narcotraficante-rasguno/44270>, 16 September 2015).

73 Salamanca, F., 'Cuevas de la Casa Medina [Caves of the house of Medina]' *El Malpensate* 185 (<http://www.elmalpensante.com/articulo/3768/cuevas_de_la_casa_medina>, 2017).

74 Salamanca (fn 73).

75 Guarnizo Álvarez (fn 64).

76 Carreres (fn 67).

77 Olea, D.M., 'El narco y su relación con el arte (trans.: The drug trafficker and his relationship with art)' *Cultura Colectiva* (<https://culturacolectiva.com/arte/el-narco-y-su-relacion-con-el-arte/>, 17 July 2015).

78 Dudley (fn 60).

79 Olea (fn 77).

80 Cawley (fn 51).

81 Tóth (fn 62).

82 MiMundo Motor, '¿Quién Compró la Lujosa Colección de Autos de "el Chapo" Guzmán? (trans.: Who Bought the Luxurious Collection of Cars of "el Chapo" Guzmán?)' *Mundo Hispánico* (<https://mundohispanico.com/auto/quien-compro-la-lujosa-coleccion-de-autos-de-el-chapo-guzman-fotos>, 29 August 2017).

83 MiMundo Motor (fn 82).

as the functionality of the legislation and the skittishness of innocent market actors, it is notable that the flow of money into the art market reduced significantly when Mexico imposed AML measures.[84] Further examples abound, such as jailed Beltrán Leyva cartel boss Héctor Beltrán Leyva, who momentarily operated as property developer and art dealer 'Alonso Rivera Muñoz,' and Beltrán Leyva's alleged partner in crime, 'alleged financial operator (*presunto operador financier*)' Germán Goyeneche Ortega,[85] who was a property developer and art collector who was 'into antiquities, especially of the pre-Colombian variety.'[86]

Further examples range way beyond Colombia and Mexico. Russian mafia boss Alexander Naumov ('Naum') had an iconic collection.[87] In at least three massive operations against Eurasian organised crime in Spain,[88] cultural goods were seized as proceeds of crime.[89]

Conclusion

As has been shown in this chapter, the market for art and antiquities is not only vulnerable to exploitation but also already being exploited for the laundering of criminal money and the financing of political violence. Market(-aligned) campaigning against restrictive regulation might appear to indicate that the market itself believes that AML regulation would significantly affect the operation of the business.

However, the market might only fear an increase in administration and be right in fearing an increase in administration without any decrease in crime. After all, the United Kingdom's implementation of the Dealing in Cultural Objects (Offences) Act 2003 was supposed to facilitate the prosecution of dishonest dealers who knew or could be expected to believe that they were handling cultural objects that had been 'tainted' by illegal extraction. It faced a mixed reception, though it was approved by the British Art Market Foundation.[90] Yet, in the end, market opinion held that the regulation was simply 'ineffective' and had caused

84 Partlow, J., 'Mexican Art galleries suffer as drug-money law ends anonymous cash buys,' *The Washington Post* (<http://www.washingtonpost.com/world/mexican-art-galleries-suffer-as-drug-money-laws-end-anonymous-cash-buys/2014/09/16/4e5dc6c4-3d41-11e4-a430-b82a3e67b762_story.html?noredirect=on>, 18 September 2014).

85 Ureste, M., '5 Preguntas para Conocer a "el H," el Rey de la Cocaína que Vendía Arte' (trans.: 5 Questions to Become Acquainted with "el H," the King of Cocaine that Sold Art)' *Animal Político* (<http://www.animalpolitico.com/2014/10/quien-es-es-hector-beltran-leyva-y-en-que-zonas-operaba/>, 3 October 2014).

86 McGahan, J., 'Trading dime bags for Salvador Dali' *The Daily Beast* (<http://www.thedailybeast.com/trading-dime-bags-for-salvador-dali>, 19 October 2014).

87 Maksimov (fn 27).

88 Operation Wasp in 2005, Operation Malaya in 2006 and Operation Troika in 2008.

89 Pluzhnikov, S., 'Mafia Ruso v Marbele (trans.: Russian Mafia in Marbella)' *Skandaly* (<https://scandaly.ru/2018/04/02/mafia-ruso-v-marbele/>, 2 April 2018).

90 Bailey, M., 'A new UK law to fight the illicit trade: It is now an offence to handle an object if you know that it was illegally removed from a site anywhere in the world after 2003' *The Art Newspaper* (9 January 2004).

'no change' whatsoever beyond 'cosmetic' changes for a few and location changes for a very few (who might be suspected of being the very worst actors for whom even generally useless legislation constituted a threat to their businesses).[91] The first conviction was secured 13 years after the passage of the law.[92]

Conversely, Germany's implementation of the Cultural Property Protection Act of 2016 established a requirement for export licences from the country of origin for import of ancient artefacts into Germany and demonstrable observation of due diligence in the handling of other high-value cultural assets.[93] It thus faced intense market-aligned protests against the 'bureaucratic burden (*Bürokratieaufwand*)'[94] and its 'high implementation costs.'[95] Yet it led to the arrest of one coin dealer and four coin collectors within a matter of months[96] and left the market 'alive (*lebt*)'[97] and well.

Given these divergent examples, the requirements of the law may ultimately have little practical impact when customs checks and police investigations are so limited that illegal conduct is rarely identified to enable the application of the law.[98] This practical freedom to operate unmonitored is only expanded by the explosion of the online market and particularly the private online market that functions through private communications in online fora and social networks and encrypted communications with smartphone apps. To make a significant impact, state and civil society need to move from the law's refinement to its enforcement.

91 Mackenzie, S. and Green, P., 'Criminalising the market in illicit antiquities: An evaluation of the dealing in cultural objects (offences) Act 2003 in England and Wales' in Mackenzie, S. and Green, P. (eds.), *Criminology and Archaeology: Studies in Looted Antiquities* (Hart Publishing, 2009), 145, 149.

92 Herman, A., 'Conviction at last under 2003 Act' *Institute of Art and Law* (<https://ial.uk.com/1448-2/>, 11 May 2016).

93 Federal Republic of Germany, Act on the protection of cultural property ((Federal Law Gazette [BGBl.] Part I p. 1914), <http://www.gesetze-im-internet.de/englisch_kgsg/englisch_kgsg.pdf>, 31 July 2016).

94 Habermalz, C., 'Ausnahmeregelungen Verhindern die Wirksamkeit (trans.: Exceptions prevent effectiveness)' (<http://www.deutschlandfunk.de/ein-jahr-kulturgutschutzgesetz-ausnahmeregelungen.724.de.html?dram:article_id=391526>, 19 July 2017).

95 Neuendorf, H., 'Germany ratifies controversial cultural heritage legislation' *Artnet News*, (<https://news.artnet.com/art-world/germany-ratifies-cultural-heritage-legislation-547412>, 8 July 2016).

96 CoinWeek, 'Cultural property law leads to arrests of coin collectors in Munich' *CoinWeek* (<https://coinweek.com/ancient-coins/cultural-property-law-leads-to-arrests-of-coin-collectors-in-munich/>, 7 April 2017).

97 Habermalz (fn 94).

98 *Ibid.*; see other discussions of law in Desmarais, F. (ed.), *Countering Illicit Traffic in Cultural Goods: The Global Challenge of Protecting the World's Heritage* (ICOM, 2015).

Part III

Country-specific insights or rebellion

12 UK corporate corruption

A regulatory paradox

Nicholas Mills

Introduction

The seminal works of Edwin Sutherland highlighted the notion and dilemmas of corporate criminality. Perhaps most noteworthy of his claims was the concept that 'white-collar' corporate criminals are recidivist offenders.[1] This view, and the intentions it assigns, presents the question of how best such a problem can and should be policed. For, if this intent or habitual desire is left unchecked, it presents detrimental consequences for the commercial world and for society. This problem nestles itself within the reality that multinational corporations have become an unavoidable fact of life with prominent economic centrality. As producers of wealth, they hold a key role within international economies and raise fundamental questions over where global power lies.[2]

But what happens when these powerful corporations decide to abuse their influence for financial gain? Especially within recent years, large businesses have attracted attention for their criminal misconduct, accelerating global discussion over bribery and corruption. Within the United Kingdom, a stark moment occurred in January 2017 when Rolls-Royce admitted to its part in a global corruption scandal.[3] Ultimately, a Deferred Prosecution Agreement (DPA) was approved whereby Rolls-Royce is to pay a penalty of over £497 million – inclusive of a 50% discount based on the professed 'extraordinary cooperation' of the company.[4] This case not only served as a reminder of the extremities of corporate wrongdoing but also reinforced key research issues: how corporate wrongdoing in the United Kingdom should best be efficaciously challenged, whether the current reliance on self-regulatory approaches is correct, and whether the current law offers all bark and no bite.

1 Sutherland, E., *White-Collar Crime: The Uncut Version* (Yale University Press, 1983).

2 Strange, S., 'Big business and the state' (1991) 20(2) *Millennium Journal of International Studies* 245.

3 Evans, R., Pegg, D., and Watt, H., 'Rolls-Royce to pay £671m over bribery claims',' *The Guardian* (<http://www.theguardian.com/business/2017/jan/16/rolls-royce-to-pay-671m-over-bribery-claims>, 16 January 2017).

4 *Serious Fraud Office v Rolls Royce PLC; Rolls Royce Energy Systems Inc*, Southwark Crown Court, Case No: U20170036, January 17, 2017.

This chapter examines the UK Bribery Act 2010 and illustrates how it has incorporated self-regulation as a tactic. The origins of self-regulation are then briefly discussed before identifying how this regulatory philosophy has become a primary approach of corporate crime regulation and enforcement. This chapter will argue that by being too reactive, the self-regulatory regime imposed by the Bribery Act 2010 does not offer the benefits proclaimed, ultimately lacking the desired and intended substance to control and deter corporate criminality.

Context

The Bribery Act 2010

With a trail of serious commercial scandals in the United Kingdom, public discontent and increasing international pressure prompted successive governments to update legislation against corruption.[5] The legislation which existed prior to the 2010 Act gained political attention for being 'unduly complicated and confusing as a result of . . . piecemeal development to deal with specific issues or problems.'[6] The need for legislative reform was highlighted by the Organisation for Economic Co-operation and Development's (OECD) Working Group on Bribery which noted that it was 'disappointed and seriously concerned' with the 'UK's continued failure to address deficiencies in its laws' and to fall in line with international obligations.[7] After its ratification of the OECD Anti-Bribery Convention in 1998, the United Kingdom failed to bring a single criminal case against any commercial entity until 2008[8] – a matter which reinforced concerns surrounding legislative inadequacies.[9] Following an investigation into corruption claims against BAE Systems in 2010,[10] international pressure pointed towards legislative modification as 'a matter of political priority.'[11]

Soon after, alongside calls for increased corporate liability, the Bribery Act 2010 was enacted and proclaimed as a global leader in prevention, 'intended to

5 Anwar, A. and Deeprose, G., 'The Bribery Act 2010' (2010) *Scots Law Times* 23(1), 125.

6 CMS Cameron McKenna, *Law Now: A Guide to Existing Bribery and Corruption Offences in England and Wales* (CMS Cameron McKenna LLP, 2010).

7 Organisation for Economic Co-operation and Development, *United Kingdom: Phase 2bis. Report on the Application of the Convention on Combating Bribery of Foreign Public Officials in International Business Transactions and the 1997 Recommendation on Combating Bribery in International Business Transactions*, 4 (<http://www.oecd.org/unitedkingdom/41515077.pdf>, 16 October 2008).

8 There were some investigative actions, for instance, *R (Energy Financing Team Ltd and others) v Director of the Serious Fraud Office* [2005] EWHC 1626 (Admin).

9 Organisation for Economic Co-operation and Development (fn 7) paras 23–35.

10 Lee, D. and Evans, R., 'BAE admits guilt over corrupt arms deal,' *The Guardian* (<http://www.theguardian.com/world/2010/feb/05/bae-systems-arms-deal-corruption>, 6 February 2010).

11 Organisation for Economic Co-operation and Development (fn 7), Executive Summary, 4.

make Britain's anti-corruption laws fit for purpose and fit for regulating international business.'[12] Through consolidation and repeals, it created a package of sanctions, extending to both domestic and overseas activities, and, significantly, took direct aim at corporations through the section 7 'failure to prevent bribery' offence whereby a company could become liable for the corrupt activities of its employees, subsidiaries, and third parties. Within the 2010 Act, corporations have a full defence to any section 7 charge if they can demonstrate that they have in place adequate procedures designed to prevent bribery.[13] With no prescriptive advice given to companies, the responsibility is placed on each corporation itself to create and impose its own compliance procedures. This provision illustrates how self-regulation has become an intrinsic element of the 2010 Act and its desire to effectively regulate corporate bribery.

The rise of corporate self-regulation

A now common corporate regulatory and governance strategy, self-regulation places itself between two diametrically opposite theoretical concepts of liability attribution and effective deterrence advancement: that of punishment versus persuasion[14] and deterrence versus compliance.[15] That is, there are those who feel that there must be a fundamental basis of deterrence through the use of prosecution and sanctioning, whereas for others, positive persuasion, amenability, and agreement are better suited to achieve compliance within the environment of a corporation given their ability to adapt and evolve.[16] When Ayres and Braithwaite proposed self-regulation within their pyramid of escalating enforcement strategies for regulators,[17] they placed self-regulation at its base, departing from the stereotypical state-led 'command and control' regimes and igniting an attempt to make regulation work with low-level intervention. Thus self-regulatory capacities were advocated as a satisfactory preference for regulation to facilitate economic efficiency, with intervention only occurring to correct market failure. By adopting self-regulation, direct enforcement and state intervention are seen as a last resort, to be saved for rare cases, with businesses to instead take primary

12 Aaronberg, D. and Higgins, N., 'The Bribery Act 2010: All bark and no bite?' (2010) 5(1) *Archbold Review* 6.

13 Bribery Act 2010 s.7.

14 Ayres, I. and Braithwaite, J., *Responsive Regulation: Transcending the Deregulation Debate* (Oxford University Press, 1992) 24.

15 Reis, A., 'Consequences of compliance and deterrence models of law enforcement for the exercise of police discretion' (1984) 47(4) *Law and Contemporary Problems* 83; Scholz, J.T. 'Cooperation, deterrence, and the ecology of regulatory enforcement' (1984) 18(1) *Law and Society Review* 179.

16 Micklethwait, J. and Wooldridge, A., *The Company: A Short History of a Revolutionary Idea* (Weidenfeld, 2003) 173.

17 Ayres and Braithwaite (fn 14) 35.

responsibility for their own legal compliance.[18] With the additional endorsement of self-regulation in the *Cadbury Report*,[19] the reduction of state-led approaches reinforces how regulation effectively became acquired by the private sector, echoing Stigler's earlier observation of how regulation appeared to be 'designed and operated primarily for its benefit.'[20] With inadequate state resources, the then UK political policy of Better Regulation[21] paved the way for 'a material and ideological assault on regulation'[22] whereby less resource-intensive options have come to the forefront of business regulation.

Consequently, a 'regulatory orthodoxy' has developed.[23] This firstly posited a state-led punitive outlook as unsustainable[24] due to a lack of governmental capacity and expertise to regulate the market. Second, with such a regulatory orthodoxy, a targeted ('risk-based') approach is required to ensure optimal efficacy and efficiency. Finally, it requires that overall management of corporate compliance ultimately be left to the commercial entities themselves (or associated third parties) because they should have a moral commitment to ethical operation and are not, contrary to common perception, amorally motivated actors driven by profit.[25] This ideology[26] has since proceeded to transcend state-oriented regulation and governance agendas, subsequently metastasising itself within a variety of fora, including the corporate criminal landscape,[27] as a normative principle favouring industry autonomy. Thus,

> in business regulation circles these days, there is not much contesting of the conclusion that consistent punishment of business non-compliance would be a bad policy, and that persuasion is normally the better way to go when there is reason to suspect that cooperation with attempting to secure compliance will be forthcoming.[28]

18 Tombs, S., 'Crisis, what crisis? Regulation and the academic orthodoxy' (2015) 54(1) *Howard Journal of Criminal Justice* 57, 58.
19 Cadbury, A., *Report of the Committee on The Financial Aspects of Corporate Governance* (Gee, 1992), 3.13–3.15.
20 Stigler, G., 'The theory of economic regulation' (1971) 2(1) *Bell Journal of Economics* 3.
21 Better Regulation Task Force 1997. This has been replaced since 2006 by the Better Regulation Commission and then, in 2008, by the Better Regulation Executive (see <http://www.gov.uk/government/groups/better-regulation-executive>).
22 Tombs, S. and Whyte, D., 'Transcending the deregulation debate? Regulation, risk, and the enforcement of Health and Safety Law in the UK' (2013) 7(1) *Regulation and Governance* 61, 65.
23 Almond, P. and Colover, S. 'The criminalization of work-related death' (2012) 52(1) *British Journal of Criminology* 997, 1010; S Tombs (fn 18) 57.
24 Almond and Colover, (fn 23); Tombs (fn 18).
25 Tombs (fn 18) 59.
26 Moran, M., *The British Regulatory State: High Modernism and Hyper-Innovation* (Oxford University Press, 2001).
27 Braithwaite, J., 'Enforced self-regulation: A new strategy for corporate crime control' (1982) 80(7) *Michigan Law Review* 1466.
28 Braithwaite, J., 'Rewards and regulation,' (2002) 29(1) *Journal of Law and Society* 12, 20.

Adequate procedures: self-regulation in practice

The foregoing philosophies, which favour self-regulatory methods, gain real influence on corporate criminality through their permeation within section 7 of the Bribery Act 2010. The very nature and reliance of having in place 'adequate procedures' promotes responsible self-rule, whereby the state (regulator/enforcement agency) predominantly takes a back seat, placing primary onus on the regulatee. The creation of one's own compliance policies and/or procedures represents an outsourcing of the regulatory responsibilities usually held by the state so that regulation and compliance instead become subjective matters for the commercial entity. Therefore, the adequate procedures provision in section 7(2) demands that corporate entities self-regulate and self-control.

This compliance-oriented model reflects a 'generalised rejection of deterrence-based approaches.'[29] The stipulations of the 2010 Act, whilst seeking to balance the interests of market freedom and the realistic abilities of state enforcement agencies, have thereby followed previous precedents in maintaining this model of self-regulation, notwithstanding instances of corporate abuse. This direction towards self-governance is further advocated within the associated Ministry of Justice guidance.[30] Despite the guidance advocating a zero-tolerance approach, the Serious Fraud Office (SFO) has in practice been seen to express a too highly proclaimed value in the importance of self-regulation and the deemed integrity of corporations,[31] even though UK and international policymakers had previously suggested that self-regulation should not be used for matters which pose high risk or are of significant public interest.[32]

The reliance placed on such self-regulatory philosophies has compromised the efficacy of the 2010 Act, as it has lowered the level of corporate oversight. As later illustrated, this approach has created a regulatory paradox which proclaims the objective to prevent these serious crimes but seemingly cultivates them.[33] Exemplified by decades of corporate corruption cases, the subjective approach which arises through allowing corporate institutions to self-regulate reduces the vigilance of outside state oversight by affording a notable degree of trust to entities that have proven themselves to be all too often untrustworthy.

29 Tombs (fn 18).

30 Ministry of Justice, 'The Bribery Act 2010: Guidance' (<http://www.justice.gov.uk/downloads/legislation/bribery-act-2010-guidance.pdf>, 2011).

31 Memorandum of Understanding between the Association of the British Pharmaceutical Industry, the Prescription Medicines Code Of Practice Authority and the Serious Fraud Office 2011 (<http://www.pmcpa.org.uk/aboutus/Documents/Memorandum%20of%20Understanding%20between%20the%20ABPI,%20PMCPA%20AND%20SFO%20Final%20June%202011.pdf>).

32 Better Regulation Taskforce, *Alternatives to State Regulation* (2000).

33 Weismann, M., 'The Foreign Corrupt Practices Act: The failure of the self-regulatory model of corporate governance in the global business environment' (2009) 88(4) *Journal of Business Ethics* 615; Weismann, M., Buscaglia, C., and Peterson, J., 'The Foreign Corrupt Practices Act: Why it fails to deter bribery as a global market entry strategy' (2014) 123(4) *Journal of Business* Ethics 591.

Critique

The weaknesses of self-regulation

A self-regulatory style and the responsibility it permits can present benefits to averting corporate misconduct. While not only preventing the government from holding a regulatory monopoly, it offers the attraction of greater inspectorial depth and understanding from familiarity, knowledge, and proximity on the part of internal compliance teams and their ability to 'know where the bodies are buried.'[34] Monitoring a corporation can incur cost and difficulty, which external state regulators struggle to overcome. Following the recent DPA with Rolls-Royce,[35] the SFO openly admitted that, but for the cooperation and information provided by Rolls-Royce, they would have been unable to access the level of detail provided to them by the corporation.[36] This raises questions about the efficacy and scope of the United Kingdom's approach to cases of commercial bribery given its reliance on the candour of the regulatee. As a result of adopting a self-regulatory approach, although it addresses the limitations of 'centralised' state regulation, there are obvious restrictions from placing trust, oversight, and responsibility onto the regulatee.

Consequently, the state suffers a decreased ability to monitor commerce due to the dependence and promotion of a self-regulatory regime. This hinderance has recently been evidenced in the SFO's decision to curtail its prosecutions of individuals in the case against Rolls-Royce and against GlaxoSmithKline.[37] Despite each involving fundamentally deep-rooted allegations (and even admissions) of bribery and corruption, the SFO felt there was either insufficient evidence to prosecute or that their pursuance was not in the public interest.[38] These terminations illustrate, firstly, the state's heavy reliance on the promise (or hope) of corporations to effectively self-regulate; secondly, the state's inability to effectively oversee and/or ensure compliance; and thirdly, that even when in possession of substantial evidence, a DPA is more likely than prosecution. Contrary to the ominous discourse of the SFO,[39] state regulators are left in a weakened position

34 Ayres and Braithwaite (fn 14) 104; Douglas, M., 'The use of audited self-regulation as a regulatory technique' (1995) 47(1) *Administrative Law Review* 181.

35 Serious Fraud Office News Releases, 'SFO completes £497.25m deferred prosecution agreement with Rolls-Royce PLC' (17 January 2017).

36 Morgan, B., 'The future of deferred prosecution agreements after Rolls-Royce' (<http://www.sfo.gov.uk/2017/03/08/the-future-of-deferred-prosecution-agreements-after-rolls-royce/>, 8 March 2017).

37 Wallace, T., 'SFO abandons probes into Rolls-Royce and Glaxo,' *The Telegraph* (<http://www.telegraph.co.uk/business/2019/02/22/sfo-abandons-probes-rolls-royce-glaxo/>, 22 February 2019).

38 Serious Fraud Office, Statements, 'SFO closes GlaxoSmithKline investigation and investigation into Rolls-Royce individuals' (<http://www.sfo.gov.uk/2019/02/22/sfo-closes-glaxosmithkline-investigation-and-investigation-into-rolls-royce-individuals/>, 22 February 2019).

39 Ruddick, G., 'Serious fraud office boss warns big names to play ball – or else,' *The Guardian* (<http://www.theguardian.com/business/2017/apr/01/serious-fraud-office-deferred-prosecution-agreements>, 2 April 2017).

ever to sustain a prosecution. This predicament, therefore, detracts from the aims of self-regulation since an escalating scale of state enforcement is not an eventual reality. Progressing through the regulatory pyramid if self-regulation fails not only helps satisfy the functional goal of achieving or enforcing compliance but also satisfies broader goals of meta-regulation for there to be a purposeful mix of instruments used to attain compliance.[40]

A predominant problem is that cases of commercial corruption are usually driven by the rational calculation of costs and opportunity, often undeterred by public policy and the threat of legal penalties unless the costs of compliance outweigh the costs of defection.[41] With this mentality, the attributes of self-regulatory oversight often prove ineffective. Whilst self-regulation may improve internal monitoring, there are inherent tensions within this approach. As Grabosky and Shover state,

> There is currently a remarkably optimistic consensus in some academic quarters about how to reduce the harm caused by privileged predators. The heart of it lies in the presumed promise of pluralistic, cooperative approaches. . . . These assumptions highlight the need for enhanced prevention, more diverse and more effective internal oversight and self-monitoring, and more efficient and effective external oversight. . . . They make sense theoretically, and we endorse them. We do so not because they have a record of demonstrable success but principally because sole or excessive reliance on state oversight and threat of criminal prosecution is difficult, costly, and uncertain. Still, we are mindful, as others should be, that the onset of the Great Recession occurred during and despite the tight embrace of self-regulation, pluralistic oversight, and notions of self-regulating markets by policy makers.[42]

The earlier view raises a significant problem when considering cases of commercial disobedience. The potential limitations of a self-regulatory approach become repeatedly apparent given the lack of 'demonstrable success.'[43] Despite supporting rhetoric that it will help streamline the regulatory process, self-regulation within the commercial sector has been associated with the exploitation of legal loopholes,[44] which results in sizeable crimes, social harms, and regulatory failures. What becomes clear are alarming shortcomings, which question the empirical

40 Gunningham, N. and Grabovsky, P., *Smart Regulation: Designing Environmental Policy* (Oxford University Press, 1998), ch 6.

41 Kagan, R. and Scholz, J., 'The "criminology of the corporation" and regulatory enforcement strategies' in Hawkins, K. and Thomas, J.M. (eds.), *Enforcing Regulation* (Kluwer-Nijhoff, 1984).

42 Grabosky, P. and Shover, N., 'Editorial conclusion forestalling the next epidemic of white-collar crime: Linking policy to theory' (2010) 9(3) *Criminology & Public Policy Special Issue: The Global Economy, Economic Crisis, and White-Collar Crime* 641, 641–642.

43 Tombs (fn 18) 65.

44 Nelken, D., 'White-collar and corporate crime' in Maguire, M. et al., (eds.), *The Oxford Handbook of Criminology* (5th ed., Oxford University Press, 2012) 623.

and conceptual legitimacy of subjective controls,[45] thereby implying a somewhat glorified view of self-regulation and potential for cosmetic compliance[46] (as per the 'Potemkin Villages' phenomenon[47]). From banking scandals to environmental disasters, the problematic correlation which arises is that the voluntary 'trust us' approach, as now imported into the 2010 Act, clearly supports the arguments that voluntary regulation without adequate enforcement simply does not work,[48] not least given the known naiveties and dangers of self-rule[49] which may simply satisfy self-serving interests.[50]

Whilst there would undoubtedly be counter-examples that show virtuous behaviour by British companies, there can be no reliable guarantee of effective subjective regulation to the strength as presented and relied upon within the 2010 Act. According to Tombs and Whyte, this is not just a problematic aberration but rather more a threat to stability governed by a hegemonic common sense led from the rise in neoliberal deregulation.[51] Critically then, the evidence which challenges the efficacy of self-regulation runs counter to the approach adopted in the 2010 Act. Worryingly, if this responsibility is not matched with impactive compliance strategies and ethics, self-regulatory approaches may be ineffective at dealing with problems such as bribery and corruption,[52] despite the 'fervent belief' in its power and effectiveness as institutionalised within the section 7 defence.[53]

The regulatory approach

With the state too often taking a reactive rather than proactive approach to serious corporate crime as a result of failed self-regulation, crimes such as bribery and corruption are inadequately regulated. Therefore, if the aim of the 2010 Act

45 Gibbs, C., 'Corporate citizenship and corporate environmental performance' (2012) 57(4) *Crime, Law and Social Change* 345; Almond, P. and van Erp, J., 'Regulation and governance versus criminology: Disciplinary divides, intersection and opportunities' (2018) *Regulation and Governance* (<https://doi.org/10.1111/rego.12202>); King, C. and Lord, N., *Negotiated Justice and Corporate Crime* (Palgrave MacMillan, 2018).

46 Almond and van Erp (fn 45) 18.

47 Gray, G.C., 'The regulation of corporate violations: Punishment, compliance, and the blurring of responsibility' (2006) 46(5) *British Journal of Criminology* 875.

48 US Securities and Exchange Commission, Chairman Cox announces end of consolidated supervised entities program (<http://www.sec.gov/news/press/2008/2008-230.htm>, 26 September 2008).

49 Ayres and Braithwaite (fn 14) 106.

50 Braithwaite, J. and Fisse, B., 'Self regulation and the costs of corporate crime' in Shearing, C.D. and Stenning, P.C. (eds.), *Private Policing* (Sage Publications, 1987).

51 Tombs, S. and Whyte, D., 'Counterblast: crime, harm and the state-corporate nexus' (2015) 54(1) *Howard Journal of Criminal Justice* 91.

52 Weismann (fn 33); Weismann et al., (fn 33).

53 Scanlan, G., 'Offences concerning directors and officers of a company: Fraud and corruption in the United Kingdom: The present and the future' (2008) 15(1) *Journal of Financial Crime* 22, 25.

was to prevent such crimes, success will arguably be limited if proactive and independent steps are not installed. The concepts of 'proactive' or 'intelligence-led' policing, for instance, are hardly new phenomena[54] but have proven successful in other aspects of criminal justice, including organised crime.[55] Additionally, using historical case data to identify previous weaknesses and adopting a proactive and imaginative outlook surrounding known vulnerabilities would reduce the current reliance on effective self-regulation alone. To complement the 'failure to prevent' landscape, as well as UK regulators beginning to use existing laws more forcefully,[56] further proactive measures could even extend to considerations of precursor offences surrounding system and control failures. Whilst funding and resources remain important constraints to these prospects, tools such as intrusive audit and inspection (on a random and unanticipated basis), as well as the increasing use of artificial intelligence and data analytics,[57] could undoubtedly help spot-check compliance.

Only when self-regulation fails and the state intervenes have corporations been prompted to reactively amend, compensate, or realign their activities to a more publicly acceptable concept of moral behaviour.[58] In other words, the fact that the 2010 Act requires private actors to effectively self-regulate (and state regulators become dependent on compliance) is alone insufficient to deter acts of bribery and corruption. Despite the House of Lords Bribery Act 2010 Committee concluding that the 2010 Act should be used as a gold standard for other legislators, its report fails to fully comprehend or discuss the lack of enforcement to date.[59] Whilst the section 7 offence and the proposed corporate liability expansions (of a similar nature) are necessary to encourage ethical business, without the 'absolutely critical'[60] element of external enforcement against those playing an active or complicit role in corrupt activity, there remains over-reliance

54 Heaton, R., 'The prospects for intelligence-led policing: Some historical and quantitative considerations' (2000) 9(4) *Policing and Society* 337; Ratcliffe, J. H. and Guidetti, R., 'State police investigative structure and the adoption of intelligence-led policing' (2008) 31(1) *Policing: An International Journal of Police Strategies and Management* 109.

55 Alvesalo, A. and others, 'Re-imagining crime prevention: Controlling corporate crime?' (2006) 45(1) *Crime, Law & Social Change* 14.

56 Wessing, T., 'The FCA's new approach to market abuse reminds business leaders of their obligations' (<https://united-kingdom.taylorwessing.com/en/insights/fsr-update/the-fcas-new-approach-to-market-abuse-reminds-business-leaders-of-their-obligations>, 23 May 2017).

57 Serious Fraud Office, 'AI powered "Robo-Lawyer" helps step up the SFO's fight against economic crime' (<http://www.sfo.gov.uk/2018/04/10/ai-powered-robo-lawyer-helps-step-up-the-sfos-fight-against-economic-crime/>, 10 April 2018).

58 Hauser, C. and Hogenacker, J. 'Do firms proactively take measures to prevent corruption in their international operations?' (2014) 11(3–4) *European Management Review* 223.

59 House of Lords Select Committee on the Bribery Act 2010, *The Bribery Act 2010: Post-Legislative Scrutiny* (2017–19 HL 303) para 319.

60 Sir Brian Leveson, *House of Lords Select Committee on the Bribery Act 2010: Corrected Oral Evidence* (<http://www.parliament.uk/documents/lords-committees/Bribery-Act-2010/Bribery-written-evidence-volume.pdf>, 13 November 2018), Q44, 298.

on corporations to self-regulate and self-report wrongdoing. Without the necessary external enforcement and individual prosecutions, the section 7 offence, and the self-regulation it permits, cannot become the 'very effective tool' it is hailed to be.[61]

The need for enhanced oversight

Whilst it may reflect a desirable goal of self-policing, self-regulation alone does not ensure that a commercial entity is willing or ready to regulate itself in line with the desires of government and/or public will.[62] Therefore, without impactful procedures to diagnose and mitigate risk through internal commitments,[63] adequate incentives to comply,[64] and, ultimately, the clear threat of enforcement backed by the state's actual capacity to do so (as a benign big gun[65]), the aim of preventing corruption appears to be destined to founder. A primary reason is the context of self-regulation within a commercial setting, that its utilisation is taking place in an environment of corporatisation and conservationism which serve private interests at public expense.[66] The shortcoming which arguably becomes apparent is that only when under outside interrogation or inquiry is there a need to make sense of the surrounding or governing expectations.[67] Indeed, according to a former senior executive of Siemens, when it comes to any contestation towards commercial needs, 'keeping the business unit alive' and 'not jeopardising thousands of jobs overnight' is crucial.[68] In this position, by evoking an ability to self-manage, self-regulation can even fend off more strenuous state intervention,[69] especially when the regulator believes it is working,[70] in turn creating a lack of

61 von Dadelszen, H., *House of Lords Select Committee on the Bribery Act 2010–Corrected Oral Evidence* (<http://www.parliament.uk/documents/lords-committees/Bribery-Act-2010/Bribery-written-evidence-volume.pdf>, 23 October 2018), Q112–118, 221.
62 Omarova, S., 'Wall street as community of fate: Toward financial industry self-regulation' (2011) 159(1) *University of Pennsylvania Law Review* 442.
63 Parker, C., *The Open Corporation: Effective Self-Regulation and Democracy* (Cambridge University Press, 2002).
64 Kolieb, J., 'When to punish, when to persuade and when to reward: Strengthening responsive regulation with the regulatory diamond' (2015) 41(1) *Monash University Law Review* 136.
65 Ayres and Braithwaite (fn 14).
66 Black, J., 'Decentering regulation: Understanding the role of regulation and self regulation in a "post-regulatory" world' (2001) 54(1) *Current Legal Problems* 123.
67 Gunningham, N. and Rees, J., 'Industry self-regulation: An institutional perspective' (2002) 19(4) *Law and Policy* 379.
68 Transparency International, 'Incentivising ethics: Managing incentives to encourage good and deter bad behaviour' *TIUK* (<http://www.transparency.si/images/publikacije/Incentivising_Ethics_TIUK.pdf>, 2016).
69 Ayres and Braithwaite (fn 14).
70 Memorandum of Understanding between the Association of the British Pharmaceutical Industry, the Prescription Medicines Code of Practice Authority and the Serious Fraud Office 2011 (fn 31).

involvement and oversight.[71] This point was recently reinforced by the Financial Reporting Council's investigation into the auditing activities of KPMG (regarding Rolls-Royce) and its declared inability through particular auditing practices to probe deep enough to uncover any evidence of corrupt activity. The investigation exemplified the apparent existence of self-regulation in creating cosmetic compliance where what tends to become important is that a policy/procedure exists and not what actually is achieved. Such scepticism arises from the fact that the process in practice is copiously operationalised by the regulatees themselves. Citing the financial crash, Lapavitsas summarised this self-regulatory landscape as follows:

> The characteristic feature of the new regulation is that it has been shaped by the financial institutions . . . its purpose has been to ensure the ability of the financial system to grow and extract profits. It has not contributed in the slightest to avoiding financial bubbles nor to imposing the costs of financial crises onto those responsible for them. On the contrary, contemporary regulation has led to society bearing the brunt of financial disasters, while private individuals associated with finance have reaped the benefits of expansion.[72]

With this self-governed responsibility comes the risk of outcomes which reinforce a regulatory orthodoxy and not the objectives of self-regulation. Self-regulation as a method for corporate crime control can in reality offer the perfect haven to deceive the state into thinking an irresponsible actor is in fact acting responsibly. With the acknowledged difficulty in uncovering corrupt activity without the cooperation of the regulatee (as evident in the four DPAs to date), the requirement of having adequate procedures to prevent misdeeds may indeed excuse inefficient governments[73] whose roles should ultimately reduce risks through legal frameworks.[74] Yet despite increased SFO funding,[75] with both budget[76] and staffing[77] less than any UK police force, the SFO cannot help but be highly selective in its actions, leaving the Bribery Act as an endorsement of the neoliberal approach to control and governance via self-regulation, thereby supporting the disingenuous claim that corporate crime is sufficiently deterred.

71 Tombs and Whyte (fn 51) 91–95.

72 Polychroniou, C.J., 'Costas Lapavitsas discusses the financialization of capitalism,' *Truthout* Wcapitalism/>, 26 January 2014).

73 Braithwaite, J., 'Responsive business regulatory institutions' in Coady, C.A.J. and Sampford, C.J.G. (eds.), *Business, Ethics and the Law* (Federation Press, 1993).

74 Haines, F., *The Paradox of Regulation: What Regulation Can Achieve and What It Cannot* (Edward Elgar Publishing, 2011).

75 Serious Fraud Office, 'Changes to SFO funding arrangements' (<http://www.sfo.gov.uk/2018/04/19/changes-to-sfo-funding-arrangements/>, 19 April 2018).

76 Home Office, *Police Funding for England & Wales 2015–2019* (Statistical Bulletin 13/18, 2018).

77 House of Commons Library, *Police Service Strength* (Briefing Paper 00634, UK Parliament, 2018).

The lack of deterrence was exemplified in a global fraud, bribery, and corruption study by Ernst & Young over the period of October 2017 to February 2018, which canvassed 2,550 executives from 55 countries.[78] Despite being undertaken during a period where enforcement efforts were perceived to be increasing and corruption awareness to be at an all-time high since the financial crash,[79] the study revealed some less than encouraging results. Whilst 97% of respondents recognised the importance of business integrity, 38% still felt corruption occurs widely within businesses in their countries (including 34% for the United Kingdom), 11% felt bribery was commonplace to obtain and retain business, and 13% would justify cash payments if required.[80] Furthermore, a study by PricewaterhouseCoopers for 2018 conveyed an increased reporting of bribery and corruption by 17% compared to 2016,[81] and Ministry of Justice statistics highlighted a near fourfold increase in fraud-related offences since 2011.[82] These studies illustrate a lack of improvement towards the prevention of corruption within the United Kingdom and represent a 20% increase in the perception of corruption compared to previous findings.[83] The results demonstrate that, despite the changes in the 2010 Act, amplified regulatory rhetoric and increased enforcement activity, cases of corruption, and risks and perceptions have risen.

This approach of allowing companies to 'police' themselves not only invites a conflict of interest but also places trust in entities which have proven themselves to be unreliable. Clearly, there exists a conflict of interest. As Douglas states,

> Self-regulation seems to be self-contradicting. If government regulation of an industry or problem is considered necessary, how can that responsibility then be returned to those from whom it was taken?[84]

The extant self-regulatory approach would suggest that changes are needed to the institutional structures and the actual provision of policies and laws. Such a transformation should not rely on faith in self-regulation as a regulatory philosophy and should offer external interventions when necessary. To do so, it needs to be demonstrated that the commission of such acts will readily be treated as a serious crime.[85] However, it is not reassuring that civil methods – such as the

78 Ernst & Young, 'Integrity in the spotlight – The Future of Compliance–15th Global Fraud Survey' (<http://www.ey.com/Publication/vwLUAssets/ey-jbs-15th-global-fids-fraud-survey-eng/$FILE/ey-jbs-15th-global-fids-fraud-survey-eng.pdf>, 2018).

79 Transparency International, 'United Kingdom Corruption Index' *Tradingeconomics.com* (<https://tradingeconomics.com/united-kingdom/corruption-index>, 2018).

80 Ernst & Young (fn 78).

81 PricewaterhouseCoopers (Professional services network), *PwC's 2018 Global Economic Crime and Fraud Survey* (<http://www.pwc.com/gx/en/services/advisory/forensics/economic-crime-survey.html#cta-1>, 2018).

82 Binham, C., 'White collar prosecutions plummet even as crime rises' (<http://www.ft.com/content/8751e754-6e3e-11e7-bfeb-33fe0c5b7eaa>, 24 July 2018).

83 Ernst & Young (fn 78).

84 Douglas (fn 34) 173.

85 Alvesalo et al., (fn 55) 13.

use of DPAs – are used with growing frequency since organisations (and their officers) are not only able to elude prosecution but also may well be faced with a financial penalty which they are capable of responding to through their financial prowess.[86] This position underplays the premeditated impact of criminal wrongdoing and undermines the way in which serious economic crimes are regulated.[87]

Conclusion

This chapter has illustrated how self-regulation has become the primary philosophy upon which corporations are held accountable for corruption within the United Kingdom. Under the Bribery Act 2010, commercial entities are able to control their adherence to governing legislation. To pursue an effective culture where corrupt practices are restrained, the aforementioned 'orthodoxy' illustrates that a significant regulatory dilemma remains. How should the state seek a synergy between when and whether such crimes should be punitively enforced or be dissuaded by agreement and what roles the state and commercial entities themselves should play in choosing a solution? This chapter by no means concludes that self-regulation has totally failed, but it does reinforce the need at least to seek more pragmatic approaches and/or solutions to address the reality, which is the prevalence and severity of corporate crime. Doing so will help to discover how the promulgation of ethical business free from corruption can be better achieved than through corporate self-regulation.

The beginning of this chapter identified how self-regulation has developed into widespread use for the regulation of corporate crime. During its growth, this self-regulatory culture has simultaneously brought notable increases in cases of commercial bribery and corruption.[88] Without adequate funding, resources, and efforts to pursue the difficult and costly task of individual prosecutions when other regulatory methods do not succeed, there will remain a stark inequality in the application of the criminal law to corporate crimes.[89] With the SFO currently having 40 active cases,[90] any claim that this figure may reflect beneficially improved regulation and enforcement should be balanced with the realisation that corporate crime is thriving. Permitting corporations to self-regulate has demonstrated a regulatory paradox: corporations which blatantly fall foul of such rules, principles, and procedures are subject to, and express, self-imposed adherence towards those very guidelines.

86 Despite the alleged bribes and contractual/financial gains of Rolls-Royce covering 24 years (1989 to 2013), less than 1 year after the DPA was secured – with 5 years to repay – they reported a pre-tax profit of £1.9 billion. See Grote, D., 'BP and Rolls-Royce top FTSE after swinging into profit' (<https://citywire.co.uk/wealth-manager/news/bp-and-rolls-royce-top-ftse-after-swinging-into-profit/a1038763>, 1 August 2017).

87 Wells, C., 'Containing corporate crime: Civil or criminal controls?' in Gobert, J. and Pascal, A.-M. (eds.), *European Developments in Corporate Criminal Liability* (Routledge, 2011).

88 Binham (fn 81).

89 Braithwaite, J. and Fisse, B., *Corporations, Crime and Accountability* (Cambridge University Press, 1993) ch 5.

90 Serious Fraud Office, 'Our cases' (<http://www.sfo.gov.uk/our-cases/#aza>).

Despite its repeated abuse, the paradigm of self-regulation is imprinted within the 2010 Act. As the primary piece of commercial anti-bribery legislation in the United Kingdom, the Bribery Act 2010 seeks to change regulatory cultures but has pursued this objective by placing too high a reliance on the institutions to achieve this goal themselves, thereby diminishing the potential effectiveness. Instead, what seems to be required is a departure from economically driven self-regulation towards a greater emphasis on empowered regulators who have the tools and finances to pursue a more frequent utilisation of enforcement.[91] Building upon the failure to prevent offences already in force,[92] it is contended that an increased focus on proactive regulation and enforcement is necessary to monitor the arguably disjointed nature towards economic crimes.[93] Additionally, if the state is indeed solely unable to provide sufficient oversight, provisions should be considered for the greater use of third parties (such as non-governmental organisations and societal groups) to publicise corporate criminal activity and/or poor social responsibility[94] and for stakeholders to be in an immediate position where they can challenge corporations so as to push them towards more ethical and less criminal pathways.

91 The lack of advice to businesses from the Ministry of Justice and embassies is also a major criticism of the House of Lords Select Committee on the Bribery Act 2010, *The Bribery Act 2010: Post-Legislative Scrutiny* (2017–19 HL 303).

92 Bribery Act 2010, s.7, and Criminal Finances Act 2017, Part 3.

93 Transparency International UK, *Don't Look Won't Find: Weaknesses in the Supervision of the UK's Anti-Money Laundering Rules* (<https://transparency.eu/wp-content/uploads/2016/11/TI_UK_Dont_Look_Wont_Find.pdf>, November 2015).

94 See, for instance, the Israeli Maala Index, which creates standards and then ranks companies according to their ethical practice: 'Maala Index 2018' (<https://en1.maala.org.il/maala-index/maala-index-2018/>, 2018).

13 Corporate criminal liability and the failure to prevent offence

An argument for the adoption of an omissions-based offence in AML

Steven Montagu-Cairns

Introduction

Of the 38.8 billion payments made in the United Kingdom in 2017,[1] the overwhelming majority were entirely legitimate.[2] The United Kingdom's role as the world's largest centre for cross-border banking does, however, make it vulnerable to corruption. Corruption is the abuse of entrusted power for private gain, and the economic and social implications of corruption are enormous. Reports have estimated that corruption adds up to 10% to business costs globally.[3] A recent estimate put the annual cost of bribery alone at $1.5 to $2 trillion,[4] though there are obvious difficulties in accurately quantifying the costs.

Corruption and serious organised crime go hand in hand. For organised crime to be effective, criminals generally use corrupt means to gain access to their ill-gotten gains. The UK financial markets can provide this access with the National Crime Agency (NCA) believing that 'many hundreds of billions of international criminal money is laundered through UK banks, including their subsidiaries, each year.'[5] Serious and organised crime affects more UK citizens more often than any other national security threat and leads to more deaths in the United Kingdom each year than all other national security threats combined.[6]

1 UK Finance, *UK Payment Markets Summary 2018* (<http://www.ukfinance.org.uk/system/files/Summary-UK-Payment-Markets-2018.pdf, 2018>, 2019) 2.

2 Dell, G. and McDevitt, A., *Exporting Corruption Report* (Transparency International, <http://files.transparency.org/content/download/2318/14294/file/2018_Report_ExportingCorruption_English.pdf>, 2018).

3 Bray, J. (Director (Analysis) Control Risk) and Simmons & Simmons (law firm), 'Facing up to Corruption: A Practical Business Guide' (<http://www.giaccentre.org/documents/CONTROLRISKS.CORRUPTIONGUIDE.pdf>, 2007) 10.

4 International Monetary Fund, *Corruption: Costs and Mitigating Strategies* (<http://www.imf.org/external/pubs/ft/sdn/2016/sdn1605.pdf>, 2016).

5 See National Crime Agency, 'Money laundering' (<http://web.archive.org/web/20151002092736/www.nationalcrimeagency.gov.uk/crime-threats/money-laundering>, 2015).

6 National Crime Agency, *National Strategic Assessment of Serious and Organised Crime 2018* (<https://nationalcrimeagency.gov.uk/who-we-are/publications/173-national-strategic-assessment-of-serious-and-organised-crime-2018/file>, 2018); HM Government, *National*

Corruption scandals are front-page news around the world. Scandals have stretched from South America and the Caribbean in the form of the Panama[7] and Paradise[8] Papers, through to Germany and the United States and the actions of major corporations, such as Volkswagen.[9] The United Kingdom is not immune from its own corruption scandals. The mis-selling of payment protection insurance (PPI) to victims (who did not need it, would not be able to claim on it, or did not know they had been sold it) is just one example. Fines and claims relating to the mis-selling have resulted in repayment of around £36 billion to those who were mis-sold.[10] The LIBOR rigging scandal was another example of a corrupt culture within the financial system that saw significant fines imposed on guilty parties.[11] Furthermore, as the recent case of Rolls-Royce[12] has shown, corruption can permeate even the largest and most renowned of corporate institutions.

Developing new and innovative ways to combat corruption has been at the forefront of legislative efforts for some time. Whilst UK prosecutors have had some measure of success,[13] their difficulties in holding companies to account, as in the case of the phone-hacking scandals, have arguably undermined public confidence in the UK criminal justice system. As a result, the UK legislature has introduced an alternative form of liability through an omissions-based offence. This 'failure to prevent' model has been developed in two specific areas – namely, bribery and tax evasion, with proposals to extend it further. The intention of this chapter is twofold. First, it will critically examine the viability of the failure to prevent (FTP) offence and the benefits of omissions-based offences in corporate criminal liability. Subsequently, the chapter will offer an argument for the expansion of the offence to other areas of financial crime, in particular, anti-money laundering (AML) offences. Whilst rejected in recent legislation, the Sanctions and Anti-Money Laundering Act 2018, it is argued that the implementation of a failure to prevent money laundering offence would offer significant advantages in

---

Security Capability Review (<https://assets.publishing.service.gov.uk/government/uploads/system/uploads/attachment_data/file/705347/6.4391_CO_National-Security-Review_web.pdf>, 2018).

7 Led by the International Consortium of Investigative Journalists (ICIJ) (<http://www.icij.org/investigations/panama-papers/>).

8 Also led by the ICIJ (<http://www.icij.org/investigations/paradise-papers/>).

9 The Volkswagen emissions scandal was exposed in 2015 when the US Environmental Protection Agency discovered that Volkswagen had intentionally programmed its diesel engines with a 'defeat device' to change the emissions output of its engines. See Ewing, J., *Faster, Higher, Farther: The Inside Story of the Volkswagen Scandal* (W.W. Norton, 2018).

10 FCA, Monthly PPI refunds and compensation (<https://www.fca.org.uk/data/monthly-ppi-refunds-and-compensation>, 2019).

11 BBC News, 'UBS fined $1.5bn for Libor rigging' (<https://www.bbc.com/news/business-17904674>, 19 December 2012).

12 *Serious Fraud Office v Rolls-Royce Plc* [2017] Lloyd's Rep. F.C. 249.

13 For example, in 2014, British banks paid £12.6 billion in penalties to settle corporate regulatory disputes; see Fortado, L., 'British banks pay £12bn in penalties' (<https://www.ft.com/content/3389707c-0790-11e5-a58f-00144feabdc0>, 31 May 2015).

combatting economic crime and align with the UK government's anti-corruption strategy.[14]

Identification principle

The identification principle governs almost all areas of corporate financial crime in the United Kingdom, with some exceptions.[15] Currently, where an offence requires proof of *mens rea*, the law seeks to identify who is the controlling mind and will of the company and then assesses whether they had knowledge of the alleged criminal event to secure a conviction against the company itself. Only 'the acts and state of mind of those who represent the directing mind and will [are to] be imputed to the company.'[16] The threshold for the test is extremely high and difficult to meet. In December 2015, for example, the Crown Prosecution Service (CPS) announced that they could not prosecute News Group International for phone hacking carried out by multiple employees, including the then editor of one of its newspapers:

> The law on corporate liability in the United Kingdom makes it difficult to prove that a company is criminally liable if it benefits from the criminal activity of an employee, conducted during their employment. The company will only be liable if it can be proved that the individual involved is sufficiently senior, usually close to or at board level, to be the 'controlling mind and will' of the company. . . . The present state of the law means it is especially difficult to establish criminal liability against companies with complex or diffuse management structures.[17]

As Alun Milford commented, 'Had the CPS had recourse to a failure to prevent offence; it would not have had this problem.'[18] Commentators have called the identification principle 'dated,'[19] 'deficient,'[20] and 'inadequate,'[21] particularly in relation to larger corporations that have sophisticated managerial structures.

14 HM Government, *UK Anti-Corruption Strategy 2017 to 2022* (<http://www.gov.uk/government/publications/uk-anti-corruption-strategy-2017-to-2022>, 2017).
15 These exceptions include bribery under the Bribery Act 2010 and tax evasion following the enactment of the Criminal Finances Act 2017.
16 Crown Prosecution Service, 'Corporate Prosecutions: Legal Guidance' (<www.cps.gov.uk/legal-guidance/corporate-prosecutions>).
17 Saunders, A., *Statement from the Crown Prosecution Service: No further action to be taken in Operation Weeting or Golding* (<https://web.archive.org/web/20151218214838/www.cps.gov.uk/news/latest_news/no_further_action_to_be_taken_in_operations_weeting_or_golding/>, 11 December 2015).
18 Milford, A., 'Control liability: Is it a good idea and does it work in practice?' Speech at Cambridge Symposium on Economic Crime (<http://www.sfo.gov.uk/2016/09/06/control-liability-good-idea-work-practice/>, 6 September 2016).
19 Copp, S. and Cronin, A., 'New models of corporate criminality: The development and relative effectiveness of "failure to prevent" offences' (2018) 39 *Company Lawyer* 104, 107.
20 Campbell, L., 'Corporate liability and the criminalisation of failure' (2018) 12(2) *Law and Financial Markets Review* 57, 58.
21 Copp and Cronin (fn 19).

Most criminal offences, including financial crime offences, such as bribery, fraud, and money laundering, require both *mens rea* and *actus reus* to be proven. In a corporate context, whilst the *actus reus* may be committed by any of the company's employees or agents, the *mens rea* must be that of the directing mind and will of the corporation. Established in *Asiatic Petroleum*,[22] the courts expanded on the separate legal personality principle established in the earlier case of *Salomon v A Salomon Ltd*[23] in concluding that the owner of a vessel was the 'directing mind and will of the company' because 'he was the alter ego of the company.'[24] If the *mens rea* is not found amongst the directing mind of the company, then the company is not guilty of a criminal offence. The identification principle requires proof that a senior corporate officer is involved in the offence before the corporation can be held liable.[25] When identifying *mens rea*, the degree of delegation is paramount. If a director delegates a particular duty to an individual, it is the amount of this delegation that will determine whether the action is seen as being from the corporation. The identification principle serves as an incentive to directors and senior management to 'turn a blind eye' to questionable or dubious practices and equally as a disincentive for the internal reporting of suspected illegality.[26] One of the main criticisms of the identification principle is the difference in the treatment of prosecutions for small- and medium-sized enterprises (SMEs) as opposed to multinational organisations. Large companies with complex management structures are able to decentralise and diffuse responsibilities to avoid liability. Identifying senior company directors who qualify as the 'directing mind and will' is extremely difficult to prove in the larger corporation.[27] In direct contrast to News Group International, *R v Smith & Ouzman Ltd*[28] involved a small company that specialised in printing documents. In January 2016, the company, along with two of its employees, were found guilty of making corrupt payments to influence the award of business contracts in Africa and ordered to pay £2.2 million following sentences of imprisonment against two employees. Here the judge was able to identify the 'controlling mind' of the corporation due to the small size of the business.

Whilst there are significant advantages for larger organisations, they may not entirely escape the ascription of liability. For example, the courts may attempt to attribute to a company the actions of an employee when to decide otherwise

22 *Lennard v Asiatic Petroleum* [1915] AC 705.

23 [1896] UKHL 1.

24 *Asiatic Petroleum* (fn 22) at 715.

25 *Tesco Supermarkets Ltd v Nattrass* [1972] AC 153.

26 Her Majesty's Revenue and Customs, *Tackling Offshore Tax Evasion* (<http://www.gov.uk/government/consultations/tackling-offshore-evasion>, 2015).

27 Wells, C., *Corporations and Criminal Responsibility* (2nd ed., Oxford University Press, 2001) chap. 5.

28 Southwark Crown Court (<https://www.sfo.gov.uk/2016/01/08/convicted-printing-company-sentenced-and-ordered-to-pay-2-2-million/>, 8 January 2016).

would defeat the intentions of a statutory duty. In *Meridian*,[29] the chief information officer (CIO) of an investment management company breached a statutory duty by not declaring a substantial purchase of shares in a public issue. In this case, the CIO had corporate authority but without the direct knowledge of the directors. The Privy Council upheld the lower court's decision to hold the corporation liable on the basis that the CIO was the directing mind of the corporation. Lord Hoffman stated,

> There would be little sense in deeming such a *persona ficta* to exist unless there were also rules to tell one what acts were to count as acts of the company. It is therefore a necessary part of corporate personality that there should be rules by which acts are attributed to the company.[30]

However, in *Regis Paper Co Ltd*,[31] the court of appeals considered *Meridian* but, ultimately, held that where a false entry was made on a record required for environmental pollution control, culpability could not be attributed to the corporation unless the requirements from *Tesco v Nattrass* were satisfied.

Outside of financial crime, the identification principle has already been identified as inadequate. In the case of corporate manslaughter, the Corporate Manslaughter and Corporate Homicide Act 2007 replaced the identification principle. Under s.1, an organisation can be guilty of the offence if the way that its activities are managed or organised by senior management is a substantial element in the breach. This substantially lowers the threshold from the director level, as it does not require the prosecution to show specific failings on the part of an individual director.[32]

Omissions and corporate liability

Given the clear failings of the identification principle, there has been some legislative movement towards the introduction of omissions-based liability for corporations. It is generally accepted law that a person must not cause harm by a positive act.[33] Furthermore, it is accepted that a person or body will not (normally) be liable if they omit to prevent the harm.[34] There are exceptions, however, where the criminal law is drafted expressly to penalise an omission on exceptional grounds.[35]

29 *Meridian Global Funds Management Asia Ltd v Securities Commission* [1995] UKPC 5. See New Zealand Securities Amendment Act 1988, ss.20, 30.

30 *Ibid.*, para 7.

31 *R v St Regis Paper Company* Ltd [2011] EWCA Crim 2527.

32 For further discussion of this legislation, see Dobson, A., 'The corporate manslaughter and Corporate Homicide Act 2007: A symbolic response' (2009) 17(2) *Asia Pacific Law Review* 185.

33 For discussion, see Simester, A.P. and von Hirsch, A., *Crimes, Harms and Wrongs: On the Principles of Criminalisation* (Bloomsbury Publishing, 2011).

34 See Kugler, I., 'Two concepts of omission,' (2004) 14 *Criminal Law Forum* 421.

35 Ormerod, D. and Laird, K., *Smith and Hogan's Criminal Law* (14th ed., Oxford University Press, 2015), 72–73.

The use of omissions-based offences has experienced fierce debate with views veering between the 'conventional view' and the 'social responsibility view.'[36] The conventional view states that the criminal law should be reluctant to impose any liability for omissions except in clear and serious cases. Under the 'conventional view,' the duties to other people should be confined to duties towards those for whom some responsibility has been voluntarily undertaken. The 'social responsibility view' instead argues that we live in a cooperative society, and so it would be fair to place citizens under obligations to render assistance to other individuals in certain situations.[37]

Whilst historically the judiciary have attempted to limit the use of omissions-based offences,[38] the UK legislature has instead been more proactive in extending the scope of omissions-based offences. These offences fall into a number of different categories. The 'failure to disclose' offences can be found within the Proceeds of Crime Act (POCA) 2002[39] and the Terrorism Act.[40] The 'failure to protect' offence[41] criminalises an adult 'member of a household' who knew or ought to have been aware that there was a significant risk of serious physical harm being caused to a child in that household, and the child died. Finally, there are the 'failure to prevent' offences, which are the key concern of this chapter.

FTP and the Bribery Act 2010

The FTP was first introduced by the Bribery Act 2010 (BA 2010). The BA 2010 was intended to bring the United Kingdom in line with the OECD Anti-Bribery Convention[42] and contained multiple primary offences. Whilst the BA 2010 provided for offences of active[43] and passive[44] bribery, as well as bribing a foreign public official,[45] the reform that garnered the most attention in both Parliament and the media was the offence of a failure of a commercial organisation to prevent bribery under section 7.[46]

36 Ashworth, A. 'The scope of criminal liability for omissions' (1989) 105 *Law Quarterly Review* 424.
37 *Ibid.*, 425.
38 For discussion, see Mead, G., 'Contracting into crime: A theory of criminal omissions,' (1991) 11(2) *Oxford Journal of Legal Studies* 147 and Ashworth, A., *Positive Obligations in Criminal Law* (Hart, 2013).
39 Proceeds of Crime Act 2002, ss.330, 331.
40 The Terrorism Act 2000 contains multiple 'failure to disclose' type offences under ss.19, 21A and 38B. See Walker, C., 'Conscripting the public in terrorism policing: Towards safer communities or a police state?' [2010] *Criminal Law Review* 441.
41 Domestic Violence, Crime and Victims Act 2004, s.5.
42 Organisation for Economic Co-operation and Development Convention on Combating Bribery of Foreign Public Officials in International Business Transactions 1997 (<www.oecd.org/corruption/oecdantibriberyconvention.htm>).
43 BA 2010, s.1.
44 BA 2010, s.2.
45 BA 2010, s.6.
46 BA 2010, s.7.

Section 7 is a strict liability offence that can only be committed by a commercial organisation.[47] The organisation is liable where employees or agents engage in conduct that would amount to a bribery offence unless they can show that they have in place 'adequate procedures designed to prevent'[48] bribery. This allows for corporate responsibility to be assigned to acts carried out at the lower, 'rogue' employee, level.[49]

It is interesting to note that the failure to prevent offence is a reverse burden of proof offence, where the organisation needs to show a balance of probabilities that it had the adequate procedures in place to prevent bribery occurring. The detailed requirements to prevent offending are contained in guidance documentation.[50]

Hailed at the time as the toughest anti-corruption legislation in the world, it should be determined whether the omissions-based offence has been successful. The Serious Fraud Office (SFO) has been able to secure a number of high-profile successes. For example, in November 2015, a Deferred Prosecution Agreement (DPA) was approved by Lord Justice Leveson between Standard Bank PLC and the SFO[51] in relation to an indictment alleging an offence under section 7 of the BA 2010.[52] Under the terms of the DPA, Standard Bank agreed to pay financial orders of US$25.2 million and was required to pay the Government of Tanzania a further US$7 million in compensation, as well as costs to the SFO of £330,000. The first conviction under section 7 was in 2016 when Sweett Group PLC pleaded guilty to a charge of failing to prevent an act of bribery intended to secure and retain a contract with Al Ain Ahlia Insurance Company (AAAI).[53] The result was a £1.4 million fine, a confiscation order of £851,152.23, and, additionally, a cost order of £95,031.97. During the sentencing hearing, His Honour Judge Bedoe commented,

> The whole point of section 7 is to impose a duty on those running such companies throughout the world properly to supervise them. Rogue elements

47 BA 2010, s.7(5).

48 BA 2010, s.7(2).

49 Copp, S.F. and Cronin, A., 'New models of corporate criminality: The problem of corporate fraud- prevention or cure?' (2018) 39 *Company Lawyer* 139, 145.

50 Serious Fraud Office, *Guidance on Facilitation Payments and Hospitality* (<https://web.archive.org/web/20121009233452/www.sfo.gov.uk/bribery – corruption/the-bribery-act/business-expenditure.aspx>, 2012). See now <http://www.sfo.gov.uk/publications/guidance-policy-and-protocols/bribery-act-guidance/>, 2019.

51 For discussion on the UK DPA regime, see King, C. and Lord, N., *Negotiated Justice and Corporate Crime: The Legitimacy of Civil Recovery Orders and Deferred Prosecution Agreements* (Palgrave, 2018).

52 *SFO v Standard Bank*, Case No: U20150854, Southwark Crown Court, (<https://www.judiciary.uk/wp-content/uploads/2015/11/sfo-v-standard-bank_Final_1.pdf>, 30 November 2015).

53 See Serious Fraud Office, 'Sweett group,' (<http://www.sfo.gov.uk/cases/sweett-group>, 12 May 2016).

> can only operate in this way, and operate for so long, because of a failure properly to supervise what they are doing and the way they are doing it.[54]

Further cases have resulted in a £6.5 million DPA with an anonymised SME, 'XYZ,'[55] and, perhaps, the highest profile of all, a DPA with Rolls-Royce. In January 2017, following a four-year investigation, the SFO and Rolls-Royce entered into a DPA to the value of £497.25 million.[56] The SFO found evidence of a conspiracy to corrupt or failure to prevent bribery by Rolls-Royce in China, India, South America, and other markets over a period of almost 25 years, including numerous payments of cash and other rewards handed over in return for assistance in obtaining government contracts. The DPA covered multiple charges, including five separate allegations of failing to prevent bribery contrary to section 7 of BA 2010.

The first contested case under section 7 was held in April 2018 at Southwark Crown Court. Skansen Interiors Ltd (SIL)[57] was accused of failing to prevent the managing director from bribing real estate agents DTZ to secure two office refurbishment contracts worth £6 million in 2013. Despite having carried out an internal investigation and self-reported to the UK National Crime Agency, SIL faced a section 7 prosecution before a jury. At the time of trial, SIL was a dormant company. Therefore, the presiding judge questioned why it was being prosecuted, as no financial penalty could be imposed and the only judgement which could be given by the Court would be an absolute discharge. The CPS argued, however, that the public interest test for a prosecution was satisfied in this case, as it could send a message to other companies. SIL was found guilty.

It would appear, then, that the failure to prevent offence under the BA 2010 has garnered some success. Furthermore, the then director of the SFO was keen to expound the merit of such an offence following the Sweett Group case:

> Acts of bribery by UK companies significantly damage this country's commercial reputation. This conviction and punishment, the SFO's first under s.7 of the Bribery Act, sends a strong message that UK companies must take full responsibility for the actions of their employees and in their commercial activities in accordance with the law.[58]

54 Serious Fraud Office, 'News release, Sweett Group PLC sentenced and ordered to pay £2.25 million after Bribery Act conviction' (<http://www.sfo.gov.uk/2016/02/19/sweett-group-plc-sentenced-and-ordered-to-pay-2-3-million-after-bribery-act-conviction/>, 19 February 2016).

55 *Serious Fraud Office v XYZ*, Case No: U20150856, Southwark Crown Court (<http://www.sfo.gov.uk/2016/07/08/sfo-secures-second-dpa/>, 8 July 2016).

56 *Serious Fraud Office v Rolls-Royce Plc* [2017] Lloyd's Rep. F.C. 249.

57 *R v Skansen Interiors Limited*, Southwark Crown Court, unreported, February 2018 (<http://www.cps.gov.uk/cps/news/company-directors-jailed-bribery>).

58 Serious Fraud Office (fn 55).

The House of Lords Bribery Act 2010 Committee was established in 2018 to consider and report on the effectiveness of the 2010 Act;[59] their evidence and findings have confirmed the efficacy of the section to be 'remarkably successful.'[60]

Criminal Finances Act 2017 and omissions-based offences

The Criminal Finances Act (CFA) 2017 came into force on September 30, 2017, representing the most significant overhaul of the United Kingdom's AML regime in over a decade. It was also the second expansion of corporate criminal liability for omissions-based offences following the BA 2010.

The most important provision for the purposes of this chapter is the development of two new corporate criminal offences of failing to prevent the facilitation of tax evasion, a stand-alone provision found under Part 3 of the Act. The two offences relate to the corporate failure to prevent either domestic[61] or foreign[62] tax evasion. It is a defence to both offences to show that the firm had in place reasonable prevention procedures.[63] Penalties for the offences include an unlimited fine and, in severe cases, the potential loss of licence for a financial services firm or the disqualification of an individual director.[64] As no cases have yet been brought, it is difficult to comment on the capability of the CFA 2017 to hold persons to account. However, it is interesting to note that there are some subtle differences between the omissions-based offences contained in the CFA 2017 and the BA 2010. Under the CFA 2017, there are two separate offences for domestic and foreign tax evasion predicate offences[65] rather than a single offence under the BA 2010.[66] Furthermore, the prevention procedures need to be 'reasonable in all the circumstances'[67] rather than 'adequate,'[68] as in the BA 2010. This could potentially cause some alarm; however, both offences are subject to Her Majesty's Revenue and Customs (HMRC) guidelines which have gone some way to relieve the worry.[69] There is also no need for a benefit to be intended or accrue in respect of the taxation offence, unlike the bribery offence. Whilst subtle in difference, this

59 House of Lords Select Committee on the Bribery Act 2010, *The Bribery Act 2010: Post Legislative Scrutiny* (2017–2019 HL 303).
60 *Ibid.*, para 171.
61 CFA 2017 s.45 (5).
62 CFA 2017, s.46(6).
63 CFA 2017, ss.45(2), 46(3).
64 CFA 2017, ss.45(8), s.46(7).
65 CFA 2017, s.45(5), 46(6).
66 BA 2010, s.7(1).
67 CFA 2017, ss.45(2), 46(3).
68 BA 2010, s.7(2).
69 Her Majesty's Revenue & Customs, 'Tackling tax evasion: Government guidance for the corporate offences of failure to prevent the criminal facilitation of tax evasion' (<https://assets.publishing.service.gov.uk/government/uploads/system/uploads/attachment_data/file/672231/Tackling-tax-evasion-corporate-offences.pdf>, 1 September 2017).

will further increase corporate accountability, compared to the bribery offence, by incentivising the introduction of robust compliance and preventive policies.[70]

Sanctions and Anti-Money Laundering Act 2018: a missed opportunity?

The past few decades have witnessed a cavalcade of legislative activity within the area of money laundering.[71] The two most important pieces of legislation being the POCA 2002, which sets out the principal money laundering offences,[72] and more recently the Money Laundering Regulations 2017 ('ML Regs 2017').[73] Part 2 of the ML Regs 2017 requires that regulated firms have policies, controls, and procedures to mitigate and manage risks of money laundering and terrorist financing. In addition, the Crime and Courts Act 2013 allows for the use of DPAs for specified economic crimes, including money laundering,[74] and provides a new mechanism for information sharing between POCA regulated entities (such as banks and financial institutions) in relation to suspected money laundering.[75] Finally, the Sanctions and Anti-Money Laundering Act (SAML) 2018 was introduced in anticipation of Brexit to enable the United Kingdom to continue to implement United Nations (UN) sanctions regimes without reliance on European Union legislation.[76] For the purposes of the chapter, it is not what is contained within SAML that is the most interesting part of the legislation but instead what was omitted.

During a House of Lords stage of the SAML bill, a proposal was put forward to introduce a new offence of failing to prevent money laundering.[77] Clause 9 sought to create an offence if a relevant body failed to put in place adequate procedures to prevent a person associated with it from carrying out a money laundering facilitation offence.[78] Alongside, clause 15 proposed a process for disqualification for those at the top level who had failed to prevent money laundering. Both clauses were narrowly voted down.[79] However, it is argued here that the clauses merit some further analysis as follows.

70 Campbell (fn 20) 61.
71 See Herlin-Karnell, E. and Ryder, N., 'The robustness of EU financial crimes legislation: A critical review of the EU and UK anti-fraud and money laundering scheme' (2017) 27(4) *European Business Law Review* 427; Ryder, N., *Money Laundering: An Endless Cycle? A Comparative Analysis of the Anti-Money Laundering Policies in the United States of America, the United Kingdom, Australia and Canada* (Routledge, 2012).
72 Proceeds of Crime Act 2002, ss.327, 328, 329.
73 Money Laundering, Terrorist Financing and Transfer of Funds (Information on the Payer) Regulations 2017.
74 Courts Act 2013 sch. 17 pt. 2.
75 CFA 2017, s.10.
76 For discussion, see Gordon, R., Smyth, M., and Cornell, T., *Sanctions Law* (Hart, 2019).
77 Hansard (House of Lords) vol. 637, cols. 156, 157 6 March 2018.
78 A money laundering facilitation offence would include concealing, disguising, converting, transferring, or removing criminal property under the POCA 2002, s.327.
79 Hansard (House of Lords) vol. 637, cols. 180, 181, 6 March 2018.

The UK government has been committed to strengthening prosecutors' tools for combatting corruption. There has been a general upward trend in volume of regulation over the past 20 years. The Senior Managers and Certification Regime (SMCR)[80] was introduced to reduce harm to consumers and strengthen market integrity by making individuals more accountable for their conduct and competence. Under the SMCR, senior officers can be held accountable for the wrongdoings of their junior staff if that senior management has failed to put in place reasonable steps to prevent wrongdoing. The SMCR provides for strict liability offences coupled with reverse burden 'reasonable prevention procedures' defences, akin to the Bribery Act 2010. Further to the SMCR, there has also been the development of a 'super regulator' in the Office for Professional Body Anti-Money Laundering Supervision (OPBAS).[81] OPBAS is a new regulator set up in 2018 by the government to strengthen the United Kingdom's anti-money laundering (AML) supervisory regime and to ensure the professional body AML supervisors provide consistently high standards of AML supervision. Alongside this body, the new Economic Crime Strategic Board was formed in January 2019,[82] which will meet twice a year and set priorities, direct resources, and scrutinise performance against the economic crime threat, which is set out in the Serious and Organised Crime (SOC) Strategy.[83] With such a depth of regulation, is a further offence (as in Clause 9 of the SAML bill) really required?

Regulators are getting tougher on financial crime; authorities issued £2.45 billion worth of fines between 2013 and 2015.[84] The United Kingdom already has significant AML policies, controls, and procedures that have allowed regulators to impose significant fines for AML weaknesses and failings. For example, in November 2015, Barclays Bank was fined £72 million for failing to adhere to their duty of skill, care, and diligence when dealing with a politically exposed person (PEP).[85] Furthermore, Deutsche Bank was fined £163 million in January 2017 for failing to oversee the formation of new customer relationships and the

80 Financial Services (Banking Reform) Act 2013 with amendments made by the Bank of England and Financial Services Act 2016.

81 Oversight of Professional Body Anti-Money Laundering and Counter Terrorist Financing Supervision Regulations 2017, SI 2017/1301.

82 Her Majesty's Treasury et al., 'New taskforce to tackle economic crime' (<http://www.gov.uk/government/news/new-taskforce-to-tackle-economic-crime>, 14 January 2019).

83 Her Majesty's Government, *Serious and Organised Crime Strategy* (<https://assets.publishing.service.gov.uk/government/uploads/system/uploads/attachment_data/file/752850/SOC-2018-web.pdf>, November 2018).

84 Ernst & Young (professional service firm), 'Fines and prison sentences issued by UK regulators are increasing, EY's Investigations Index reveals' (<http://www.ey.com/uk/en/newsroom/news-releases/15-11-30-fines-and-prison-sentences-issued-by-uk-regulators-are-increasing>, 30 November 2015).

85 See Financial Conduct Authority, 'FCA fines Barclays £72 million for poor handling of financial crime risks-Press Release' (<http://www.fca.org.uk/news/press-releases/fca-fines-barclays-£72-million-poor-handling-financial-crime-risks>, 26 November 2015).

booking of global business in the United Kingdom.[86] This was the largest ever financial penalty for AML controls failings by the Financial Conduct Authority (FCA). The FCA appears to be much more proactive when dealing with AML breaches than their predecessor, the Financial Services Authority.[87]

The work of the FCA continues to find widespread weaknesses in key AML controls.[88] Notwithstanding the previous activity, significant criticisms of the effectiveness of the UK regulator have persisted.[89] In its 2018 Evaluation of the United Kingdom, the Financial Action Task Force (FATF) identified a number of areas for criticism in relation to AML supervision.[90] The FATF identified inconsistencies in the use of serious activity reports (SARs).[91] Analysis of the annual report of the NCA shows that the number of SARs submitted is increasing; for example, in 2017 alone, just over 300,000 SARs were made. The main practical issue is the high volume of SARs, some of which are submitted defensively to avoid criminal liability, and many of which are of little intelligence value and/or are of poor quality.[92] Furthermore, the FATF was critical of the variation in AML supervision dependent on the sector.[93] It recognised the intensity of supervision was not consistent across 22 different sectors and identified that the United Kingdom should ensure that supervision of all entities is fully in line with the significant risks that the United Kingdom faces. Whilst recognising OPBAS's potential new role in reducing the inconsistency, it is argued that developing a more holistic approach to liability by adopting a single failure to prevent offence that covers all areas would offer significant advantages over the disconnect that is currently being observed through the myriad of professional bodies. The UK government has also identified the need to develop a single, whole-system approach as an important strategy when tackling SOC.[94]

86 See Financial Conduct Authority, 'FCA fines Deutsche Bank £163 million for serious anti-money laundering controls failings-Press Release' (<http://www.fca.org.uk/news/press-releases/fca-fines-deutsche-bank-163-million-anti-money-laundering-controls-failure>, 31 January 2017).

87 See Ryder, N., '"Too scared to prosecute and too scared to jail" A critical and comparative analysis of enforcement of financial crime legislation against corporations in the USA and the UK' (2018) 82 *Journal of Criminal Law* 245, 260.

88 Financial Conduct Authority, *Thematic Review: How Small Banks Manage Money Laundering and Sanctions Risk* (TR14/16, <http://www.fca.org.uk/publication/thematic-reviews/tr14-16.pdf>, November 2014) 5.

89 See Corruption Watch, 'Corporate crime gap: How the UK lags the US in policing corporate financial crime' (<https://docs.wixstatic.com/ugd/54261c_0c851a40156e4b17adc44c9bee2fda66.pdf>, March 2019).

90 Financial Action Task Force, 'Anti-money laundering and counter-terrorist financing measures: United Kingdom, Fourth Round Mutual Evaluation Report' (<http://www.fatf-gafi.org/media/fatf/documents/reports/mer4/MER-United-Kingdom-2018.pdf>, December 2018).

91 Ibid., 5.

92 Law Commission, *Anti-Money Laundering: the SARs Regime Consultation Paper* (Law Com. No. 236, 2018) para. 1.29.

93 FATF (fn 91).

94 Her Majesty's Government, *Serious and Organised Crime Strategy* (fn 84).

The ML Regs 2017 apply to persons identified under Part 2 as acting in the course of business carried on by them in the United Kingdom and listed under Regulation 8. The advantage that the FTP offence would have over the ML Regs 2017 is that it is not concerned with the nature of the business being carried out. The business need not be identified under Regulation 8; the only requirement is that the entity has a 'demonstrable business presence.'[95]

The substantive benefits of the BA 2010 have already been identified.[96] However, perhaps the most important reason for using an FTP offence is the informal positive impact the BA 2010 is already having on the markets. The overall perceptions of bribery and corruption are that they have fallen since 2014, with 91% of those surveyed stating that their companies' management were clear in their condemnation of the practice.[97] The influence of FTP stretches further than the jurisdiction of England and Wales, with the BA 2010 used as a benchmark and exemplar for other jurisdictions. For example, Australia is considering adopting a similar offence to section 7.[98]

Corporate failure to prevent economic crime proposal

In recent years, there has been some parliamentary traction for the further development of FTP offences. In January 2017, the Ministry of Justice issued a call for evidence to seek information and opinions on the viability of a general corporate offence of failing to prevent any economic crime.[99] The call made particular reference to the inclusion of 'FTP' fraud, false accounting, and money laundering offences:

> [T]he consultation will explore whether the 'failure to prevent' model should be extended to complement existing legal and regulatory frameworks. The consultation follows the recent announcement by the Prime Minister to bring forward a criminal offence for corporations who fail to stop their staff facilitating tax evasion and two recent prosecutions for the offence of failure of a commercial organisation to prevent bribery on its behalf.[100]

95 Ministry of Justice, *Bribery Act 2010: Guidance to Help Commercial Organisations Prevent Bribery* (<http://www.gov.uk/government/uploads/system/uploads/attachment_data/file/181762/bribery-act-2010-guidance.pdf>, February 2012).

96 House of Lords Bribery Act 2010 Committee (fn 60).

97 PricewaterhouseCoopers (professional services network), 'Global economic crime and fraud survey' (<https://www.pwc.com/gx/en/economic-crime-survey/pdf/GlobalEconomicCrimeSurvey2016.pdf>, 2016) 38.

98 Crimes Legislation Amendment (Combatting Corporate Crime) Bill 2017 (Bills Digest No. 105, 2017–18).

99 Ministry of Justice, 'Corporate liability for economic crime: Call for evidence' (<https://consult.justice.gov.uk/digital-communications/corporate-liability-for-economic-crime/>, 13 January 2017).

100 Ministry of Justice, 'Press release: New plans to tackle corporate fraud' (<http://www.gov.uk/government/news/new-plans-to-tackle-corporate-fraud>, 12 May 2016).

The solicitor general, Robert Buckland, has said there is a 'strong case' for the implementation of a new corporate offence of failing to prevent economic crime. He went further, alluding to the dire implications of a situation where 'weaknesses in our current law' result in foreign jurisdictions holding British companies to account where UK law has not.[101] In 2016, Attorney General Jeremy Wright also emphasised difficulties with the current law:

> Our current system of limited corporate liability incentivises a company's board to distance itself from the company's operations. In this way, it operates in precisely the opposite way to the Bribery Act 2010, one of whose underlying policy rationales was to secure a change in corporate culture by ensuring boards set an appropriate tone from the top.[102]

The Ministry of Justice is currently considering the responses received to the 2017 call for evidence and is analysing the impacts of the government's range of recent reforms in this area. It is expected to respond to its call for evidence in due course. Furthermore, the recent Bribery Act review also called upon the government to 'delay no more in analysing the evidence'[103] and outlined the support for an offence more generally.[104]

Conclusion

Money laundering harms society by enabling criminal activity and can affect the reputation of the UK financial system.[105] Both David Green, the former director of the SFO, and Lisa Osofsky, the current director of the SFO, believe a reform of corporate criminal liability law in favour of the failure to prevent offence is necessary in order to fulfil public expectations.[106] There are two primary governmental responses to corporate crime: legislation to prevent future occurrences of the behaviour and enforcement activity with the intention of punishing those responsible for financial misdeeds. To be effective, both options must be utilised by

101 Buckland, R., 'Solicitor general's speech at Cambridge Symposium on Economic Crime 'Speaking at the 35th Annual Cambridge International Symposium on Economic Crime (<http://www.gov.uk/government/speeches/solicitor-generals-speech-at-cambridge-symposium-on-economic-crime>, 4 September 2017). For example, see the work of Corruption Watch (fn 90).

102 Wright, J., 'Attorney General Jeremy Wright speech to the Cambridge Symposium on Economic Crime' (<http://www.gov.uk/government/speeches/attorney-general-jeremy-wright-speech-to-the-cambridge-symposium-on-economic-crime>, 5 September 2016).

103 House of Lords Bribery Act 2010 Committee (fn 60) 231.

104 Bribery Act 2010 Committee (fn 60) 227.

105 FCA, Anti-money laundering Annual Report 2017/18 (19 July 2018) 4.

106 See Bentham, M., 'Fraud chief calls for tougher corporate prosecution laws,' *London Evening Standard* (<http://www.standard.co.uk/news/uk/fraud-chief-calls-for-tougher-corporate-prosecution-laws-a3150011.html>, 6 January 2016) and Bribery Act 2010 Committee, Oral evidence volume: *The Bribery Act 2010: Post Legislative Scrutiny* (14 March 2019) Q 157.

governmental agencies. The identification principle is an archaic construct that is no longer fit for modern-day corporate criminal liability. Indeed, it has been described as a 'dated,'[107] 'deficient,'[108] and 'inadequate'[109] approach which creates an imbalance between large and small corporate bodies. An omissions-based offence, such as FTP, thus offers significant advantages to resolve these deficiencies. Furthermore, the current myriad of professional bodies that are vested with the obligations of ensuring that policies, controls, and procedures are appropriate for preventing money laundering are failing to deliver a consistent approach.[110] A single FTP offence spanning all sectors would allow for greater consistency.

The principal arguments for the proposed failure to prevent offence are similar to those articulated for the Corporate Manslaughter and Corporate Homicide Act 2007, the Bribery Act 2010, and the Criminal Finances Act 2017. The FTP offence offers an innovative means of legislative redress that has proven to be effective in those areas; it has brought about a shift in British corporate attitudes to business. For example, Mark Gregory, general counsel for Rolls-Royce, singled out section 7 specifically in his evidence to the House of Lords Committee on the Bribery Act.[111] The FTP offence would ensure that boards set an appropriate AML tone, ensure overhauls of the current AML compliance systems, and increase the likelihood of self-reporting wrongdoing. It is important to recognise the limits of corporate criminal liability. Ultimately, there will always be criminal activity, and no new offence is truly a panacea to resolve all corporate crime.[112] Nevertheless, the implementation of a failure to prevent money laundering offence would offer significant advantages over the current provisions in combatting economic crime.

107 Copp and Cronin. (fn 19).
108 Campbell (fn 20).
109 Copp and Cronin (fn 19).
110 FATF (fn 91).
111 Bribery Act 2010 Committee (fn 107) at Q63.
112 Tombs, S. and Whyte, D., *The Corporate Criminal: Why Corporations Must Be Abolished* (Routledge, 2015).

14 The development of laws in Kuwait to combat corruption

A work in progress

Noura T. A. Al-Oumi

Introduction

Kuwait is a constitutional monarchy and has the oldest directly elected parliament amongst Arab Gulf states, being first elected in 1963.[1] The 1962 Constitution guarantees independent courts and executive audit.[2] Yet Transparency International's Corruption Perception Index report indicated that, out of 180 countries, Kuwait's ranking had dropped to 85th in 2017 from 75th in 2016.[3] The level of corruption in Kuwait is escalating, and so this chapter considers its responses to corruption and particularly those responses that might be viewed as innovative. The enhancement of anti-corruption policies in both private and public sectors is an essential pillar to facilitate the country's social and legal progress. Concerted efforts are needed in Kuwait society to tackle corruption, particularly public-sector corruption.[4]

The first part of this chapter sheds light on the background of corruption in Kuwait, focusing mainly on the public sector. The second part deals with the general setting for legal responses to corruption in Kuwait. The third part focuses on the Anti-Corruption Law No.2 of 2016 regarding the Establishment of the Kuwait Anti-Corruption Authority (NAZAHA), with special emphasis on the innovative illicit enrichment offence in Article 22(6). The chapter compares Kuwaiti domestic law with international anti-corruption standards. The last part of this chapter outlines the effectiveness of the illicit enrichment law. Here the chapter recommends the adaptation of civil measures to tackle corruption.

1 See Al Saleh O, *The Constitutional System and Political Institutions in Kuwait* (vol. 1, 2nd ed., Dar Alkotob Press, 2003); Al-Hamedah, K., *Kuwait's Constitutional System* (University of Kuwait Press, 2010).

2 Articles 162–173 (the Judiciary) of the Kuwait Constitution 1962.

3 Transparency International Report, Corruption Perception Index 2017: Global Score (<http://www.transparency.org/country/KWT>).

4 Al-Jazeera, 'Protesters storm Kuwaiti parliament' (<http://www.aljazeera.com/news/middleeast/2011/11/20111116204038300676.html11>, 17 November 2011); Ulrichsen, K.C., 'Kuwait: Political crisis at critical juncture' (<http://www.bbc.com/news/world-middle-east-20026581>, 23 October 2012).

Overview of Kuwaiti corruption by reference to case studies

Legislation in Kuwait about corruption has developed over time in response to specific circumstances and needs. For instance, the Protection of Public Funds Law no. 1 of 1993 derives from the public assets and funds stolen during the Iraqi invasion of 1990–1991. The Money Laundering Regulation no. 106 of 2013 was a political response to the 9/11 attacks. Recently, the Anti-Corruption Law no. 2 of 2016 introduced the illicit enrichment offence as a result of the multi-million-dollar Kuwaiti Parliament scandal of late 2011. These background events will now be explained as key catalysts for change.

The cases of the Kuwait Investment Authority (KIA) and Kuwait Oil Tanker Company (KOTC)

During the Iraqi invasion of Kuwait in August 1990, around $6 billion was stolen from publicly held investment accounts run by the KIA in London.[5] The KIA was established in Kuwait by Amiri Decree, Law No. 47 of 1982, with responsibility for managing the funds of the Government of Kuwait.[6] The KIA was meant to supplement revenue from oil sales and invest surplus money, so it was made responsible for the management of Kuwait's General Funds and Future Generation Funds (FGF).[7] Officials and trustees of the public funds, including two members of the ruling Al-Sabah family, were accused of stealing investment money. This scandal provoked a wave of public anger.[8]

Criminal proceedings began on 26 October 1992 for misappropriation of public funds in violation of the (now repealed) Articles 44–45 of the Law No.31 of 1970 Amending Certain Provisions of the Penal Code No. 16 of 1960.[9] However, the defendants had to be tried *in absentia*, and their full trial remains pending.[10] Therefore, civil law actions were the necessary route for asset recovery, and these took place in 19 jurisdictions, including the Bahamas, Cayman Islands, Jersey, Kuwait, Spain, Switzerland, and the United Kingdom. In 1993, the Kuwaiti Investment Organization (a branch of the KIA based in London) initiated civil

5 Cases No. 137 and 138/1997 Supreme Criminal Court, December 22, 1997.

6 See Kuwait Investment Authority Law No. 47 of 1982.

7 The FGF was established under the Reserves for Future Generation Law No. 106 of 1976.

8 Al Husaini, W., *The Kuwait Investment Office (KIO) Scandal: A Study of Auditing and Audit Expectation in an International Context* (PhD University of Sheffield, 2000).

9 By Article 44 of Law No. 31 of 1970 stated, 'Every public employee, servant, or worker who embezzles money, papers, effects or others delivered to him/her because of his/her job, shall be punished by temporary imprisonment which is not less than three years.' By Article 45 of Law No. 31 of 1970 stated, 'Every public employee, servant, or worker who without right steals public funds . . . , or facilities such for others, shall be punished by temporary imprisonment which is not less than three years.' These Articles have been repealed under the Law No. 1 of 1993 Regarding the Protection of Public Funds but without prejudice to prior actions.

10 Case No. 176/2005 Supreme Criminal Court, May 9, 2006.

proceedings, which resulted in a 1999 judgment in the UK commercial court for $687 million in damages.[11]

In addition to the KIA scandal, the minister of public funds discovered in 1992 that large-scale embezzlement and fraud had been perpetrated in 1988 and early 1991 by four public officials and others employed by KOTC. They had been receiving illegal profits through unlawful commissions and forged contracts. They later transferred millions of dollars of public funds into their secret private accounts outside Kuwait, based in London, Switzerland, and the Bahamas. The former KOTC chairman appeared in the Kuwait criminal court and was sentenced to 55 years imprisonment, whilst the other defendants fled Kuwait and were tried *in absentia*.[12] In 1995, the Kuwait government commenced civil proceedings, once again in London, which resulted in $137 million in damages.[13]

In these two cases, the government encountered several legal challenges. The paramount issue was that the offences had been committed outside Kuwait's territory. Second, most suspects in both cases had to be tried *in absentia* for the offences of committing embezzlement and stealing public funds under the repealed Articles 44–48 of the Law No.31 of 1970 in relation to Amending Certain Provision of the Penal Code No.16 of 1960. That law gave insufficient power for the prosecution to restrain suspects from leaving the jurisdiction or to follow the stolen funds, especially in relation to family members' who received the proceeds of crime.

As a legal reaction, Law No. 1 of 1993 related to protecting public funds was introduced to add several measures lacking in the previous Law No.31 of 1970 in relation to amending certain provisions of the Penal Code No.16 of 1960.[14] For instance, the 1993 law grants the attorney general a warrant power to restrain the accused from leaving the country and to follow public funds in both internal and external jurisdictions in addition to tracing the proceeds of public funds crimes through family members, as mentioned in Articles 24 and 25. In addition, the law introduced for the first time an enhanced asset recovery penalty, as stipulated in Article 16.[15] Moreover, the law made as criminal offences causing grave damage to the public funds or interests, whether such damage is a result of negligence or failure in preforming public employment (Article 14). Next, the 1993 law

11 *Grupo Torras SA & Ors v Sheikh Fahad & Ors* [1999] EWHC 300 (Comm). The UK judgment was the basis for proceedings in the Bahamas, Cayman Islands, and Jersey where trusts and other assets belonging to the main defendant Sheikh Fahad Al-Sabah were located.

12 Case No. 333/2012 Supreme Criminal Court, July 21, 2013.

13 *Kuwait Oil Tanker Company SAK & Anor v Al Bader & Ors*, [2000] EWCA Civ 160.

14 For details, see Al-Dhfiry, F., *The Criminal Protection to the Public Funds in Law No. 1 of 1993: A Critical Legal Analysis Study* (Kuwait University, 2006); Al-Kandry, F., 'The criminal protection of the public funds: A critical legal analysis study of the law no. 1 of 1993' (1994) 18(2) *Kuwait Journal of Law* 271–317.

15 By Article 16 , 'in addition to the penalty stipulated for the crimes mentioned in Articles 9, 10, 11, and 12, the culprit shall be sentenced to dismissal and a fine equal twice the amount of what he/she has embezzled or seized or facilitated for others of money, interest or profits.'

created a new monitoring system in Article 6, whereby it obliged public bodies to notify the State Audit Bureau of Kuwait (Diwan) regarding transactions or actions relevant to the investment relating to funds inside and outside the country. Moreover, Article 23 requires verdicts for any of the crimes in violation of its provision to take effect immediately. Finally, the rule of limitation is curtailed under Article 21: 'The penal action shall not abate for the crimes stipulated upon this law.'[16]

The case of Kuwait's Public Institution for Social Security (PIFSS)

Another major violation of Kuwait's public funds involved the corruption and embezzlement of public pensions by Fahad al-Rajaan, the former head of the PIFSS. The defendant faced accusations, including the embezzlement of public funds, betrayal of public trust, and money laundering, relating to when he was the head of the PIFSS. The accused is now a fugitive, as he was sentenced to a ten-year prison term *in absentia* for the misappropriation of public funds; an international arrest warrant has been issued.[17] A Swiss judge ordered in December 2014 that $100 million in 15 bank accounts (out of the $390 million suspected to have been embezzled) belonging to the defendant be frozen. In 2017, the Westminster Magistrates' Court ruled that there is no legal barrier to prevent his extradition to Kuwait.[18] This ruling is based on the (unpublished) memorandum of agreement signed in 2016 between the Crown Prosecution Service and the Kuwaiti Public Prosecution.[19] The PIFSS case is one of the successful cases executed through Law no. 1 of 1993 mentioned earlier. Nonetheless, up to this moment, the defendant has not been extradited, and his money is merely frozen and has not been recovered.

The Parliament scandal

In 2011, corruption in Kuwait reached another nadir after the political crises over allegations of corruption involving 15 members of Parliament (MP; out of 50 MPs in total) and the former prime minister. The scandal, as exposed by the *Alqabas* newspaper, claimed that 25 million dinars (around £50/$92 million) had been deposited into several MPs' bank accounts by the former prime minister, allegedly in return for supporting government policies.[20] The public prosecution

16 The normal periods of limitation are, for felonies, ten years and, for misdemeanours, five years under Articles 4 and 6 of the Kuwaiti Penal Code No. 16/1960.

17 Subdivision Criminal Court 28 April 2016, No. 159/2015 in the Public Funds Prosecution Department.

18 Westminster Magistrates Court, 5 April 2017 (unpublished).

19 Kuwaiti Attorney General Dherar Al-Assousi, Statement on 6 April 2017 (<https://alqabas.com/379033/>).

20 Alqabas Newspaper, '"The 17 Million deposits into MPs accounts confuse the Banks"' (20 August 2011).

of the 15 MPs on suspicions of committing money laundering offences was then commenced.[21]

However, this political scandal never went to trial, the suspicious illicit money was never recovered, and the public prosecution was ordered to shelve the case due to the absence of evidence. According to the attorney general's statement justifying the termination, despite a thorough investigation, there was an 'absence of bribery or assault of public funds or money laundering offences . . . the Public Prosecution came to the conclusion that further regulation is needed to oblige public officials to disclose their income, and illicit enrichment offence will be implemented.'[22]

The scandal led to the promulgation of the Amiri Decree No. 24 of 2012, 'Setting up the Public Authority to Combat Corruption and the Pertinent Provision for Financial Disclosure.' However, in December 2015, the Constitutional Court ruled that the Amiri Decree No. 24 of 2012 was unconstitutional.[23] Later, the Council of Ministers approved a new anti-corruption bill, which was subsequently approved by the National Assembly in January 2016; the Law No. 2 of 2016 regarding the NAZAHA was then issued.[24]

One of the significant outputs of the 2012 and 2016 anti-corruption laws is the introduction of illicit enrichment as an offence in Article 22(6). Criminalising the unjustifiable increase in the wealth of high-profile public officials was deemed necessary and led to the promulgation of the Amiri Decree no. 24 of 2012.[25] This form of criminal conduct is recognised in Article 20 of the United Nations Convention against Corruption (UNCAC), which describes it as a 'significant increase in the assets of a public official that he or she cannot reasonably explain in relation to his or her law- full income.'

Against this background, this chapter next evaluates the Kuwaiti Anti-Corruption Law no. 2 of 2016 in order to identify where Kuwait's laws fall below the standards of the UNCAC. Special emphasis is placed on the illicit enrichment offence due to its supposed strength and innovation.

Legality principle

Before moving on to study the illicit enrichment provision, it is crucial to understand more fully why the pre-existing criminal justice system failed to secure convictions in most of these political misconduct cases.

21 Criminal complaints to the Kuwaiti Public Funds Prosecution Department by local banks of Kuwait case numbers: 1283/2011, 1281/2011, 1282/2011, 1287/2011, 1285/2011, 1355/2011, 1284/2011, 1353/2011, 1457/2011, 1288/2011, 1352/2011, 1449/2011, 1280/2011.

22 The Attorney General's statement in the press conference on October 18, 2012, is available at <http://www.alraimedia.com/Home/Details?Id=bdfdcbd0-6dca-4a80-aea3-96b85e4dc1a1>.

23 Constitutional Court ruling No. 24/2015, December 20, 2015.

24 Kuwait Anti-Corruption Authority (<http://www.nazaha.gov.kw/EN>).

25 Commentary Statement on the Amiri Decree No. 24 of 2012 (19 November 2012).

Kuwait recognises the following right under Article 32 of the Constitution, repeated also in Article 1 of Criminal Law no. 16 of 1962: 'No crime and no penalty may be established except by virtue of law.' In respect to this legality principle, the prosecution in the Parliament scandal of 2011 came to the conclusion that there was a lack of clear criminal legislation that condemns MPs for accepting gifts from the then prime minister. Their conduct was perceived as unethical but not criminal.

Difficulties in enforcement also arose under the Bribery Law No. 42 of 1971 which prohibits public officials from requesting, accepting, or taking a promise for performing or abstaining from performing an inherent function of his or her position, even if he or she mistakenly believes such a function falls within the scope of his or her official duties.[26] Hence, the fundamental conditions under the Bribery Law are as follows: the recipient must be a public official abusing his or her 'official duty'; there must be a benefit or promise that constitutes the material element of the crime; there must be criminal intent. In principle, no conviction would result if there were an absence of proof that the public official had requested or agreed to receive a financial or non-financial advantage. Hence, according to this restriction, the Bribery Law cannot be applied in the hypothetical situation of a significant increase in the wealth of public officials.

As for Law no. 1 of 1993 Regarding the Protection of Public Funds, two conditions must be fulfilled: first, the perpetrator is a public official, and, second, the stolen money must comprise public funds. The foundation of the crime requires two further elements. First, the public official must commit one of the criminal offences stipulated in Articles 9, 10, 11, 12, and 14 – namely, the 'embezzlement of public funds,' 'stealing or facilities stealing,' 'improper preferment to gain interest,' or 'grave damage to public funds due to negligence.' Second, the intent element must also be fulfilled.[27] Clearly, this law merely remedies the embezzling or stealing of public funds by public officials, but it lacks a comprehensive response to fight more subtle forms of corruption.

As far as money laundering is concerned, the provision of this law is also insufficient to criminalise MPs' corruption.[28] According to Article 2 of the Law No. 106 of 2013 Regarding Combating Money Laundering and the Financing of Terrorism, 'a person shall be considered a perpetrator of the money laundering crime if he or she knew that these monies were obtained from a crime and deliberately

26 Article 35 states, 'Any public official who asks or accepts for himself or for third party a promise or a gift to perform or to abstain from any of the activities of his office shall be penalized.'

27 Articles 9, 10, 11, and 12 of Law No. 1 of 1993 Regarding the Protection of Public Funds.

28 On March 10, 2002, following the 9/11 attacks, the government of Kuwait enacted Law No. 35 of 2002 for Combating Money Laundering Operations, believing that it would comply with all international obligations. However, this Law excluded financing terrorism. This 2002 Law was abolished and substituted by Law No. 106 of 2013 Money Laundering and Financing Terrorism, which responded to the FATF's later criticism and monitoring process: (see FATF, 'Improving Global AML/CFT Compliance: on-going process – 27 February 2015' <http://www.fatf-gafi.org/countries/j-m/kuwait/documents/fatf-compliance-february-2015.html>).

undertook the following.'[29] The element of money laundering requires the conversion or transfer of property that derives from proceeds of crimes for concealing illicit gain, as described in the UNCAC. Hence, the prosecution must initially determine that criminal conduct has occurred and must establish a link between the property being laundered and that criminal conduct.[30] For this purpose, the money laundering offence could not be imposed on Kuwaiti MPs due to the absence of criminal conduct.

Following the serious ongoing corruption incidents, criminal legislation has been developed in response to each occurrence but has remained deficient in various ways.

Emergence of new anti-corruption law in Kuwait

According to Transparency International,

> Corruption involves behaviour on the part of officials in the public sector, whether politicians or civil servants, in which they improperly and unlawfully enrich themselves, or those close to them, by the misuse of the public power entrusted to them.[31]

In line with this concept and to deal with deficiencies in law as already outlined, anti-corruption legislation has now appeared in Kuwait under Law No. 2 of 2016 regarding the NAZAHA. Article 22 identifies the crimes of corruption which make up the illicit enrichment offence as follows:

1 Offences against the public funds stipulated in Law No. 1 of 1993 regarding the protection of public funds.
2 Bribery and abuse of influence stipulated in Law No. 31 of 1970 amending some provisions of the Penal Code No. 16 of 1960.
3 Crimes stipulated in Law No. 16 of 2013 regarding combating money laundering and the financing of terrorism.
4 Falsification and forgery offences stipulated in Law No. 16 of 1960 regarding the Penal Code.
5 Offences relating to the administration of justice stipulated in the Penal Code.
6 Crimes of Illicit Gain stipulated in the Penal Code.
7 Crimes of smuggling stipulated in Law No. 10 of 2003 regarding the Common Customs Law of the Gulf Cooperation Council States.

29 Article No. 2 of the Kuwaiti Money Laundering and Financing Terrorism Law No. 106 of 2013 is compatible with Article No. 23 of the UNCAC that stipulates: '(a) (i) The conversion or transfer of property, knowing that such property is the proceeds of crime.'

30 Alldridge, P., *Money Laundering Law* (Hart Publication, 2003) 4.

31 OECD Glossaries: Corruption: A Glossary of International Standards in Criminal Law (<https://securitysectorintegrity.com/publication/oecd-glossaries-corruption-glossary-international-standards-criminal-law/>).

8 Crimes of tax evasion stipulated in Decree No. 3 of 1955 regarding Kuwait Income Tax.
9 Crimes of impeding the work of the authority, putting pressure upon it to hinder the performance of its duties, interfering in its terms of reference, or refraining from providing it with the required information stipulated by that law.
10 The crimes stipulated in Law No. 10 of 2007 regarding the protection of competition.
11 The crimes stipulated in Law No. 25 of 1996 regarding the disclosure of commissions in connection with state contracts.
12 Any other crimes stipulated in other law, which are considered corruption offences.

Given this non-exhaustive list, it should be considered why the additional illicit enrichment offence is viewed as necessary. It seems to be merely a repetition of offences that were already deemed as insufficient to counter corruption. For this reason, this study will now explain illicit enrichment and assess its potential to fight corruption by public officials in Kuwait.

Analysing illicit enrichment under Kuwait law

Illicit enrichment was defined as a potential crime which states should consider adopting in Article 20 of the UNCAC 2003 as 'a significant increase in the assets of a public official that he or she cannot reasonably explain in relation to his or her lawful income.' At the regional level, illicit enrichment is also mentioned in the Arab Convention on Anti-Corruption 2010, Article 4(7). Kuwait ratified the UNCAC by Law no. 47 of 2006, which led to the Amiri Decree Law no. 24 of 2012 and the establishment of an independent body to prevent corruption – namely, the NAZAHA.

The Amiri Decree no. 24 of 2012, as mentioned earlier, considered illicit enrichment to be a criminal offence; however, that law did not provide a clear definition of the offence.[32] On this matter, Article 1 of the No. 2 of 2016 law specifically defines illicit enrichment in the general rules and glossary as follows:

> [An] increase in the assets owned by the person subject to the provision of this law, his or her minor children, and those under his or her guardianship, custodianship or curatorship that he or she cannot reasonably explain in relation to his or her lawful income.

This offence is built on the requirement that certain public officials disclose their financial statements to the NAZAHA within a timely manner, as stipulated by

32 Al-Oumi, N., 'Illicit enrichment: Comparative analysis study to the Decree-Law No. 24 of 2012 setting up the public authority to combat corruption and the pertinent provision for financial disclosure' (2015) 39(4) *Kuwait Journal of Law* 65.

Article 32 of Law No. 2 of 2016. The NAZAHA examines these financial statements. If it suspects an unjustifiable increase in wealth, then the case is transferred to the Public Prosecution department to commence a criminal investigation.[33] In this context, the legislator has adopted a zero-tolerance rule. The statute itself does not provide criteria or a threshold level, but it embraces a broad concept to determine illicit gain – namely, the increase in wealth, whether trivial or significant, compared with the official income level. In contrast, Article 20 of the UNCAC requires a significant increase in the assets of public officials.

The word 'significant' aims to provide further reassurance that Article 20 would not be used unjustly.[34] However, there is some uncertainty as to the meaning of 'significant.' Some countries, such as India, have set a threshold of a 10% unjustified increase in income.[35] Specifying a threshold for illicit enrichment in statutes may prevent prosecutions for trivial amounts; however, it may then be interpreted that a level of corrupt conduct will be tolerated.

The Kuwaiti 2016 law further specifies the public officials who are subjected to the provision of this law. They are also legally obliged to report their financial affairs and those of their minor children and those under their guardianship, custodianship, or curatorship inside and outside Kuwait. The scope of this law is exclusively applied to public officers who hold leadership positions, such as the prime minister and ministers (executive authority), the 50 MPs (legislative authority), members of the Supreme Court, judges, the attorney general, and members of the prosecution department (judicial authority). Any other public officers who do not hold such a position are exempt from financial disclosures and not subjected to the 2016 law.[36] In addition, the public officials' spouse(s) and associates are not required to report their financial affairs. The law also applies to

> representatives of the State in the membership of the boards of directors of companies in which the state or one of the government agencies, public bodies or institutions or other public legal entities, directly contribute not less than 25% of their capital.[37]

This limitation in identifying relevant public officials in Kuwait law does not comply with the meaning of 'public officials' in the UNCAC, who are more broadly identified in Article 2(a) as comprising

33 The public prosecutors are constitutionally obliged to watch over the application of the Penal Code, the pursuit of offenders, and the execution of sentences, as stipulated under Article 167 of the 1962 Constitution. See also Kuwaiti Criminal Procedure Code No. 17 of 1962, Art.9; Al-Nweibt, M., *Explaining the General Rules of the Kuwaiti Criminal Procedurals and Penalty Code* (2nd ed., Kuwait University Press, 2008).

34 Berger, T., Mathias, M., Morales, M., and Muzila, L., *On the Take: Criminalizing Illicit Enrichment to Fight Corruption Stolen Asset Recovery (StAR) Initiative* (World Bank Group, 2012) 18–19.

35 See *Saran v. State of M.P.*, CRA 1060/2004 (2006), INMPHC 274 (11 November 2006).

36 Article 2 of the Anti-Corruption Law No. 2 of 2016, the public officials list is available at: <http://www.nazaha.gov.kw/en/Pages/financialdisclosure.aspx>.

37 Article 2(10) of Law No. 2 of 2016 (emphasis added).

> (i) any person holding a legislative, executive, administrative or judicial office of a State Party . . . irrespective of that person's seniority; (ii) any other person who performs a public function, including for a public agency or public enterprise, or provides a public service; . . . foreign public officials.

A further issue in Kuwait arose regarding the 25% threshold of the state's 'direct' contribution to the company as stated in Article 2(10) of the Anti-corruption Law No.2 of 2016. What if the state contributes a mere 24% of company capital? Or what if the 25% is indirectly related to a third party? The principle of criminal legality should require strict interpretation in these circumstances.[38]

In addition, the 2016 Law can also be criticised in relation to its omission of family members and associates from the financial disclosures requirement. There is thus a legal gap that should be rectified to meet the UNCAC's standards, especially Article 52, which requires the following:

> Each State Party shall take such measures as may be necessary, in accordance with its domestic law, to require financial institutions within its jurisdiction to verify the identity of customers, to take reasonable steps to determine the identity of beneficial owners of funds deposited into high-value accounts and to conduct enhanced scrutiny of accounts sought or maintained by or on behalf of individuals who are, or have been, entrusted with prominent public functions and their ***family members and close associates*** (emphasis added).

Moreover, recommendation No. 6 of the Financial Action Task Force (FATF) requires enhanced monitoring schemes of the family and associates of public officers:

> Countries should implement targeted financial sanctions regimes to comply with United Nations Security Council resolutions. . . . The resolutions require countries to freeze without delay the funds or other assets of, and to ensure that no funds or other assets are made available, directly or indirectly, to or for the benefit of, any person or entity.[39]

The failure to include members of the family in the financial statement requirement hinders tackling the proceeds of crime, as the criminal law in Kuwaiti does not recognise a connected individual wrongdoer as an accessory.[40] There

38 The Supreme Court of Kuwait ruled on December 4, 2007, in relation to non-state company capital that all private companies, regardless of the state's percentage contribution to that company capital, either 'directly' or 'indirectly' through a third part contractor shall be protected under the protection of Public Funds Law No. 1 of 1993: judgment no. 78 of 14 November 2000 (vol. 7(4) July 2004 p. 247 rule no. 4).

39 FATF (2012–2018), 'International Standards on Combating Money Laundering and the Financing of Terrorism & Proliferation' (<http://www.fatf-gafi.org/recommendations.html>).

40 Under Article 49 of Kuwait's Penal Code no 16/1960, if a person offers assistance to the principal offender after committing the crime, that person can be held responsible as a

are some alternative offences which can be committed by those who assist a principal offender – namely, the offence to impede apprehension or prosecution of arrestable offenders or counselling offences – but family members of a principal offender are exempt from these applications.[41] As a result, public officials may violate the criminal law and then conceal stolen money in their wives' private accounts, which weakens the law in fighting corruption by public officials.[42]

Illicit enrichment and fairness

The criminalisation of illicit enrichment next raises concerns about reversing the burden of proof and the related protection against self-incrimination.[43] It is a system built on reasonable grounds for suspecting that a person has obtained proceeds from criminal activities; once established, rebuttal then lies on the defendant to show the legitimacy of the acquisition.[44] The reversal of the burden of proof in a criminal trial is a radical change to the individual's fundamental rights that gives rise to concerns under Article 14(3)(g) of the UN International Covenant on Civil and Political Rights (and equivalents such as Article 6 of the European Convention on Human Rights).[45] Hence some countries, such as the United States and Canada, have rejected this provision as an infringement of constitutional rights.[46]

Several scholars have argued that illicit enrichment reverses the burden of proof by requiring defendants to prove that their assets are legal.[47] In general criminal proceedings, the prosecutor must set forth all the elements of the crime and prove the charges beyond reasonable doubt.[48] When the basic fact is constructed, the burden of producing evidence shifts to the defendant who must produce sufficient evidence to rebut the presumed fact. If the defendant fails to

---

post-accessory. However, in 2008, according to the constitutional judgment no. 6 of 2007, April 22, 2008, and the judgment no. 1 of 2009, Article 49, was abolished, as it was deemed unconstitutional.

41 Articles 132 and 132 of Kuwait's Penal Code No. 16/1960.

42 See Al-Oumi, N. (fn 32) 91–93.

43 The presumption of innocence is emphasised under Article 43 of the Kuwait Constitution of 1962 and under Article 16 of the Arab Charter on Human Rights 2004.

44 Booz Allen Hamilton (consulting firm), *Comparative Evaluation of Unexplained Wealth Orders: Prepared for the US Department of Justice* (National Institute of Justice, 2011) 126.

45 King, C., 'Civil forfeiture and Article 6 of the ECHR: Due process implication from England and Wales and Ireland' (2014) 34 *Legal Studies* 371.

46 Henning, P.J., 'Public corruption: A comparative analysis of international corruption conventions and United States law' (2001) 18 *Arizona Journal of International and Comparative Law* 793, 814. See also Low, A., Andria, K., Bjorklund, Kathryn, C., and Atkinson, K., 'The inter-American convention against corruption: A comparative with United States Foreign Corrupt Practice Act.' (1998) 38 *Virginia Journal of International Law* 243.

47 Kofela-Kale, N., *Combating Economic Crimes Balancing Competing Rights and Interests in Prosecuting The Crime of Illicit Enrichment* (Routledge, 2012) 9.

48 Article 102 of the Kuwait Criminal Procedure Code No. 17 of 1961 states the investigator authority is obliged based on its investigation and gathered evidence to submit the case to the court.

produce sufficient evidence, the court will rule in accordance with the proven legal grounds and evidence.[49] Yet it can be argued that the provision of illicit enrichment upholds a permissive presumption and, therefore, does not undermine individual rights.[50] As far as illicit enrichment is concerned, the burden of proof of an illicit enrichment offence must be satisfied by prosecutors by at least providing convincing evidence that exhibits an increase in wealth beyond lawful income; this requires the prosecutor to establish its case in detail. Only then is the defendant put in jeopardy if no further explanation is offered.

A similar argument was expressed in the European Court of Human Rights case of *Salabiaku v. France* that set forth the principle of 'reasonable presumption,' arguing that where the law applies instead an almost irrefutable presumption, it will be incompatible with Article 6.[51] It was held that the state must confine presumptions 'within reasonable limits which take into account the importance of what is at stake and maintain the right of the defence.'[52] Hence, the court balances the state's interests with the right of the accused to rebut the claim but within the context of a requirement that, overall, the trial must be fair.

The impact provided by the illicit enrichment offence can be perhaps justified on the basis that a public official has been granted and accepted a position of trust and, hence, can in turn be subjected to specific regulatory requirements to protect the public sector from the abuse of that trust. In this context, the obligation to disclose the source of income and assets to the authorities (the NAZAHA under Kuwait law) reflects a specific legal obligation upon those subjected to the law and does not appear to be a general breach of fundamental rights. The failure to disclose relevant information regarding an increase in assets is a breach of trust and, therefore, properly considered to be a criminal offence.[53]

Therefore, the offence of illicit enrichment, as applied to a limited target (official) population who have willingly assumed a highly privileged position with some conditions attached, does not violate the privilege of the presumption of innocence or self-incrimination rights. It is a law built on reasonable legal grounds for suspecting public officials who either directly or indirectly possess property and have gained wealth incompatible with their lawful income. The

49 Cassella, S., 'The case for civil forfeiture: Why in rem proceedings are an essential tool for recovering the proceeds of crime' (2008) 11(1) *Journal of Money Laundering Control* 8; Cassella, S., 'Civil asset recovery: The American experience' (2013) 3 *European Criminal Law Associations' Forum* 98.

50 See, for instance, the case of *Phillips v United Kingdom* App. No. 41087/98 5 July 2001.

51 *Salabiaku v. France,* Application No. 10519/83, Ser A 141-A, October 7, 1988, para. 26.

52 *Salabiaku v. France* (fn 51) para. 28.

53 The penalty for failure to submit the financial disclosure is stipulated in Article 46 of the Anti-Corruption Law No. 2 of 2016. For incomplete or incorrect disclosure with the subject's prior knowledge, or not submitting a disclosure for his or her minor children, or those under his or her guardianship, custodianship or curatorship, despite being already warned, the penalty is imprisonment for a term not exceeding three years and/or a fine of not less than 3,000 K.D. and not more than 30,000 K.D. Dismissal from office can be ordered by the court.

shifted burden of proof relates to important societal concerns and, therefore, requires that the accused shows the legitimacy of his or her possessions, which could be said to be a fair imposition relating to facts and evidence readily within the person's control.

Recommendations

Illicit enrichment is an innovative criminal measure for tackling corruption which targets the proceeds derived from criminal activities. Its primary objective is to deprive criminals from acquiring or benefiting from unlawful activities. However, prosecutors must first prove an increase in the assets and wealth of public officials that is incompatible with their lawful income. In detail, illicit enrichment differs from conventional criminal conduct in another important respect: the law shifts part of the burden of proof to the property owner, who must prove a legitimate source for his or her wealth, and so the failure to justify the legitimacy of the alleged wealth is one of the criminal elements of the illicit enrichment offence. These seemingly radical features of illicit enrichment cover the loopholes in prior criminal law in Kuwait.

Despite the augmented developments in monitoring and assessment programmes related to disclosure by selected public officials, considerable challenges remain. Moreover, there is limited evidence from completed inquiries and prosecutions for judging the merits of this legal development due to a combination of legal factors. In Kuwaiti corruption cases, most of the accused have absconded, and so their alleged wrongdoing awaits full examination by criminal trial. As for civil law, there have been modest results in asset recovery and offender sanctions. With the KIA case, for example, the offenders have yet to face justice, though their illicit assets have been frozen for more than two decades. The case of PIFSS is similar. The process of confiscation in criminal law amounts to determining whether a person is to be charged as manifested in Article 78 of the Kuwait Penal Code No. 16 of 1960. This provision states that confiscation is a permissive measure determined by the judge as an additional (optional) penalty along with imprisonment and fines.

Paradoxically, trial *in absentia* is not a criminal conviction: the defendant is not at that point fully charged with a criminal offence within Article 78 of the Penal Code. Therefore, the absconding defendant continues to enjoy the fruits of his or her criminal deeds outside Kuwait's jurisdiction for as long as mutual legal assistance and even political diplomacy may take. Clearly, further legal development, particularly related to asset recovery, is required. Thus, there might be value in other unconventional legal tools in the fight against corruption and illicit gain – namely, through civil proceedings (so-called non-conviction confiscation)[54] or unexplained wealth orders (UWOs).[55]

54 See Goldsmith, A., Gray, D., and Smith, R., 'Criminal assets recovery in Australia' in King, C. and Walker, C.P. (eds.), *Dirty Assets: Emerging Issues in the Regulation of Criminal and Terrorist Assets* (Ashgate, 2014).

55 See Booz Allen Hamilton (consulting firm) (fn 44).

The civil approach to the confiscation of criminal property can be applied without the need for criminal conviction and based on the civil standard of proof namely the balance of probabilities.[56] Hence, non-conviction-based confiscation is recommended as a promising approach for Kuwait, especially for those high officials with plentiful resources and a seemingly endless supply of lawyers to defend their interests and assets. In addition, Kuwait must also improve the mutual legal assistance instruments so as to strengthen international cooperation. It is therefore gratifying to note that both extradition[57] and mutual legal assistance arrangements[58] with the United Kingdom are now in the process of being strengthened, though the time being taken to achieve this goal might be said to be inordinate even for the world of diplomacy.[59]

Conclusion

Corruption by public officials has been a prominent and destructive phenomenon in Kuwait. In response, many criminal measures have been promoted, with illicit enrichment as the latest and most innovative resort. This chapter briefly introduces the issue and questions the likelihood of the measure being effective. This chapter has argued that the illicit enrichment offence is justifiable but remains of uncertain impact. If, however, the offence is eventually condemned as disproportionate because of the issues of shifting the burden of proof and self-incrimination, then the civil law approach ought to be pursued more vigorously, though its gain in effectiveness is still at some cost to fairness.

Postscript: events that occurred whilst writing this chapter in Kuwait.

First: In March 2018, the Parliament passed a new law No.13/2018 concerning Banning Conflict of Interest. Accordingly, it is prohibited for public official to carry out any activity, which is directly linked to their job, or own a share in any activity or financial transaction related to their job. This also applied to the employee's adolescent kids, wife, partners, or those under their guardianship or custody. The Constitutional Court abolished this law, as it failed to provide a clear explanation of what constitutes a conflict of interest deed to warrant the ban, which involve a breach of the legality principle. In addition, the law infringes the constitutional right of

56 Cassella, S., 'Civil asset recovery: The American experience' (fn 49); Al-Oumi, N., 'In pursuit of non-conviction based confiscation asset recovery: Comparative analysis study of the Kuwaiti criminal law' (2018) 42(2) *Kuwait Journal of Law* 89.

57 See Extradition Treaty between the Government of the United Kingdom of Great Britain and Northern Ireland and the Government of the State of Kuwait (Cm. 9657, 2018).

58 See Treaty on Mutual Legal Assistance in Criminal Matters between the Government of the United Kingdom of Great Britain and Northern Ireland and the Government of the State of Kuwait (Cm. 9658, 2018).

59 No comprehensive convention exists, so coordination on criminal matters is based on a reciprocal MLA basis, such as with Switzerland and USA (October 7, 2017) (see, for the latter, <http://www.cbp.gov/newsroom/national-media-release/united-states-signs-customs-mutual-assistance-agreement-kuwait>, 7 September 2017).

private ownership, which renders the law unconstitutional (Constitutional Court, Appeal No.7/2018, May 1, 2019).

Second: Regarding to the PIFSS case, a second *absentia* conviction issued by the Criminal Court that sentenced Fahed Al-Rajaan and his wife to life in prison for public funds embezzlement. The court also ordered the convicts to refund $82 million and fined them twice the amount they stole; in addition, the court ordered confiscation of their properties, real estates, companies and shares, and movable assets that were used for money laundering (Criminal Court case No.49/2015, June 27, 2019).

15 Proceeds of corruption crime

The Kuwaiti legal response

Khaled S. Al-Rashidi

Introduction

Kuwaiti law has long taken action against 'dirty money.' The Protection of Public Funds Act (PPFA) 1/ 1993 included interim measures that aimed to protect public funds that are at the disposal of the suspect from being dissipated or hidden.[1] Furthermore, the Anti-Corruption Authority Act (ACAA) 2/2016 introduced sophisticated provisions related to corruption crimes. The ACAA requires specific categories of public officials and politicians to submit a financial disclosure of their own and their spouse's property, a measure that facilitates the detection of unexplained wealth. In this context, the ACAA establishes an illicit enrichment offence (IEO) and designates investigative provisions to deal with such an offence. Finally, money laundering (ML) is deemed to be a corruption crime and is, therefore, subject to strict measures set out in the Anti-Money Laundering and Combating Finance of Terrorism Act (AML/CFT Act) 106/2013. When there are reasonable grounds to suspect that a corruption crime has occurred, the prosecutorial authorities can take interim measures to restrain proceeds of crime.[2] Within this context, the chapter will focus on three Kuwaiti corruption offences: public money offences, IEO, and ML. These three legal responses lend themselves to being examined in the light of innovative approaches to combat corruption. These forms of offences are ideal examples in which criminals can potentially generate illicit gains and to which applying innovative approaches to proceeds of crime could instil a deterrent effect.

To this end, this chapter will examine the extent to which Kuwaiti laws combat a deep-seated problem in Kuwait. Building on analysis of existing laws, this chapter advances two arguments. First, although Kuwait has responded by law to proceeds of corruption crimes, the development of this response does not match up to the deep-seated problem of corruption. Second, civil forfeiture and unexplained wealth orders (UWOs) are two innovative legal tools that ought to be adopted in Kuwait. This chapter is arranged as follows. The first section analyses the corruption problem in Kuwait in the light of the state's political and economic characteristics and identifies 'grand corruption' as the prevalent pattern. Second, it focuses on the financial arrangements of anti-corruption cases, including interim and asset recovery

1 PPFA, s.24.
2 ACAA, s.36.

measures. This section aims to illustrate the current legal powers available to law enforcement authorities, highlighting the shortcomings in Kuwaiti law. Third, it addresses innovative approaches to proceeds of corruption, including whether they can be applied to Kuwait, and the challenges impeding their adoption. This section helps to assess the effectiveness/adequacy of the current Kuwaiti laws to deal with grand corruption and identifies civil forfeiture and UWOs as two extra international best practices that could potentially fight grand corruption in Kuwait.

The problem of corruption in Kuwait

Corruption is a form of crime. Factors that contribute to common crimes may also affect the incidence of corruption. However, whilst there is a correlation between several forms of 'common' crimes in a cross-section of counties, there is not a 'significant' correlation between them and corruption.[3] This may indicate that corruption is a crime that has its own characteristics and causes. Therefore, it has been said that 'corruption *is* a government problem'[4] and is largely an internal flaw of the state institutions, including the social, political, and economic institutions. This applies to the problem of corruption in Kuwait, which derives, as elsewhere, from the state's characteristics.[5] In that context, a brief analysis of the political and economic situation in Kuwait will help to identify the corruption problem.

Politically, although Kuwait adopts a democratic system of government,[6] its democracy is 'precarious' and faces many challenges.[7] For example, the ruling classes in Kuwait – as (political) corporate groups – are said to dominate the state institutions,[8] where they derive their dominance from their membership in the royal family. This leads to an imbalance in power relations and has inevitable effects on democracy, which is rated internationally as relatively weak.[9] Other corporate groups in the state also dominate the political scene. The socio-political organisation in Kuwait comprises distinct components, and this construct can be analysed as *corporatism*: a comparative politics approach that provides a perspective on several socio-political phenomena, such as the 'relations between society as represented by interest groups and the state or government, and hence on the dynamics' of

3 Lederman, D., Loayza, N., and Soares, R., 'Accountability and corruption: Political institutions matter' (2005) 17(1) *Economics and Politics* 1–2.

4 Moene, K. and Søreide, T., 'Corruption control' (2016) 66(2) *Crime, Law and Social Change* 148.

5 World Bank, *Helping Countries Combat Corruption: The Role of the World Bank* (World Bank, 1997) 12.

6 Kuwait Constitution, art.6 (the English version of the constitution can be found at <http://www.constituteproject.org/constitution/Kuwait_1992.pdf?lang=en>).

7 See Al-Najjar, G., 'The challenges facing Kuwaiti democracy' (2000) 54(2) *Middle East Journal* 242.

8 Herb, M., 'A nation of bureaucrats: Political participation and economic diversification in Kuwait and the United Arab Emirates' (2009) 41(3) *International Journal of Middle East Studies* 376.

9 Economist Intelligence Unit, 'Economist Intelligence Unit's Democracy Index' (2018) (<https://infographics.economist.com/2018/DemocracyIndex/>); Global Democracy Ranking, 'The Democracy Ranking of the Quality of Democracy 2016' (2016) (<http://democracyranking.org/wordpress/rank/democracy-ranking-2016/>).

state-society relations.[10] There is a powerful directing state, with different interest groups (as corporate units) forming that organisation and incorporated into the political structure of state institutions. The government has the central role in identifying, recognising, and integrating these corporate units in the policy decision making of the state.[11] The pivotal role played by the government in its relations with interest groups explains why societies such as Kuwait place power in the hands of a small ruling group who usually derive their right to reign from ties of kinship and 'social position.'[12] This form of social organisation is found in Kuwait where interest groups exist and are premised on the basis of kinship, tribalism, and sectarianism.[13]

Economically, and as rehearsed, the 'resource curse' literature, corruption, and political dysfunction are observed to be intrinsic problems in countries rich in natural resources like oil.[14] In this regard, Kuwait is a rentier state that depends on oil remittances, which make up the bulk of the government revenues.[15] Oil revenues directly accrue to the government treasury,[16] which encourages a centralised and state-dominated economy.[17] Furthermore, such state-dominated economy lacks a taxation system, including tax on consumption and tax on individuals' income.[18] The absence of a taxation-based economic system contributes to corruption one way or another. This argument is supported by the fact that the moral and political considerations which underlie both the management of tax and oil revenues differ depending on the nature of the revenue itself. The illegal disposal of public money by the government through misappropriation or general mismanagement is more difficult and challenging in the context of revenues from taxes.[19] The literature regarding 'tax morality' emphasises the moral commitment behind paying taxes, which entails a commitment on the part of the government to impose strict fiscal oversight to 'encourage greater transparency and accountability in taxation affairs, which can lead to broader, more equitable and [more] fair fiscal outcomes.'[20]

10 Wiarda, H.J., *Corporatism and Comparative Politics: The Other Great ISM* (ME Sharpe, 1996) 5.

11 Adams, P., 'Corporatism and comparative politics: Is there a new century of corporatism?' in Wiarda, H.J. (ed.), *New Directions in Comparative Politics* (3rd ed., Westview Press, 2002) 20.

12 Collier, M.W., 'Explaining corruption: An institutional choice approach' (2002) 38(1) *Crime, Law and Social Change* 8.

13 Al-Tarrah, A., 'Rulers, merchants and shaikhs in Gulf politics' in Al-Sharekh, A. (ed.), *The Gulf Family: Kinship Policies and Modernity* (SAQI in association with London Middle East Institute, SOAS, 2007) 121.

14 See Ross, M.L., 'What have we learned about the resource curse?' (2015) 18 *Annual Review of Political Science* 239.

15 Herb (fn 8) 376.

16 El-Katiri, L., Fattouh, B., and Segal, P., 'Anatomy of an oil-based welfare state: Rent distribution in Kuwait' in Held, D. and Ulrichsen, K. (eds.), *The Transformation of the Gulf: Politics, Economics and the Global Order* (Routledge, 2012) 167.

17 Kinninmont, J., *Kuwait's Parliament: An Experiment in Semi-Democracy* (Chatham House, 2012) 4.

18 Eltony, M.N., 'The economic development experience of Kuwait: Some useful lessons' (2007) 23(1) *Journal of Economic and Administrative Sciences* 80. According to the Income Tax Act 3/1995, tax is limited to foreign corporate entities.

19 Sala-i-Martin, X. and Subramanian, A., 'Addressing the natural resource curse: An illustration from Nigeria' (2013) 22(4) *Journal of African Economies* 608. Like Kuwait, the government revenues of Nigeria mainly depend on oil.

20 Chohan, U., 'The Panama papers and tax morality' (6 April 2016) (<https://ssrn.com/abstract=2759418>) 3–4.

In contrast, the situation is different for states based overwhelmingly on oil revenues. The challenge is that 'there is no final consumer to whom [oil revenues] "naturally" accrue.'[21] Therefore, governments have stronger discretionary authority in managing oil revenues. The management of oil revenues then is subject to opaque considerations, which facilitates corruption. The spending of oil revenues is prone to vested political considerations, particularly when revenues come from oil wells directly to a government's treasury.[22] Governments in this position can rely on oil revenues to dilute social pressures for the demands of more representation, transparency, and accountability regarding the use of public funds.[23] Governments which obtain tremendous revenues from oil exports do not endeavour to levy taxes on people as a responsible means to win people's satisfaction and relieve popular claims about fair treatment and accountability.[24] The wealth accumulated by oil revenues does not require persistent efforts and the undertaking of risks; thus, the appeals for accountability tend to fade away.[25] Whilst governments distract the people's focus through the partial distribution of oil revenues to them, and whilst people prefer to keep the situation as it is rather than demand good governance of oil revenues and, hence, the levying of taxes, corruption finds an opportunity to permeate the upper domain of state bodies.

These political and economic characteristics suggest a high-level corruption pattern, leading to the inference that the problem in Kuwait is one of 'grand corruption' (the involvement of state high-rank officials in corrupt practices).[26] Indeed, Kuwait has witnessed several grand corruption cases involving millions of Kuwaiti dinars, such as, for example, the Kuwaiti investments in Spain,[27] the scandal of oil tankers,[28] the investments of the Public Institution for Social Security,[29] and the scandal of the expenses of the Ministry of Interior.[30] Grand corruption, due to its intrinsic nature, is also said to be responsible for the lack of progress in the counter-corruption field in Kuwait, an issue subject to analysis next. Kuwait's score in the Transparency International Corruption Perception Index (CPI) may indicate the extent of the corruption problem (Table 15.1).

21 El-Katiri, Fattouh and Segal (fn 16) 168.

22 *Ibid.*

23 Ross, M., 'Does oil hinder democracy?' (2001) 53(3) *World Politics* 325, 332–334.

24 *Ibid.*, 328.

25 Hafez, Z., 'The culture of rent, factionalism, and corruption: A political economy of rent in the Arab world' (2009) 2(3) *Contemporary Arab Affairs* 466.

26 World Bank, *Anticorruption in Transition: A Contribution to the Policy Debate* (World Bank, 2000) 16.

27 There are several decisions that dealt with the case of Kuwaiti investments in Spain. For the details of the litigation in general, see *Grupo Torras SA v Al-Sabah* (No. 5) [1999] CLC 1469. See also Garton, J., 'Grupo Torras v Al-Sabah' (2001) 15 *Tolley's Trust Law International* 93.

28 See Case No 275/1993 and 8/1993, 28/6/2009 (Kuwaiti First Instance Court – Criminal Division).

29 See Case No 1200/2016, 27/3/2017 (Kuwaiti Supreme Court – Criminal Division).

30 Kuwait News Agency, 'Kuwaiti Parliament refers interior ministry spending the public prosecution' (2018) (<http://www.kuna.net.kw/ArticleDetails.aspx?id=2689507&language=en>).

Table 15.1 CPI of Kuwait[31]

Year	*2014*	*2015*	*2016*	*2017*
Score	44	49	41	39

Kuwaiti laws on proceeds of corruption

Kuwaiti law defines proceeds of crime[32] and identifies specific measures directed at such ill-gotten benefits – the main thrust of this chapter. These measures can be classified into two categories: interim and provisional measures and confiscation and forfeiture.

Interim and provisional measures

Illicit assets can be hidden or moved outside a jurisdiction. Thus, it is critical that expeditious, preventive actions are taken when an investigation begins to preserve assets (liable to confiscation) from dissipation, loss, or transfer to third parties. Law enforcement authorities can apply several preservation methods, most importantly freezing and seizure orders that are directed at natural and legal persons or properties.[33] According to Kuwaiti law, the power to issue such restraint orders is granted to the Public Prosecution Office (PPO), which is a judicial actor.[34]

In general, the Anti-Corruption Authority (hereinafter NAZAHA) is responsible for receiving reports related to all forms of corruption offences and for conducting an initial investigation. If it can be inferred from this investigation that a public money offence or IEO has been committed, NAZAHA then passes the dossier of the case to the PPO, which has the authority of investigation and prosecution.[35] For the IEO, special investigation measures (commensurate with its nature) have been established.[36] In relation to ML, the Kuwait Financial Intelligence Unit (KFIU) was re-established in 2013 as an independent administrative body that is responsible for requesting, receiving, and analysing suspicious transactions reports (STRs) that are suspected to be proceeds of crime and are related and linked to, or could be used in, ML.[37]

31 On the scale, '0' is highly corrupt, and '100' is very clean. (See <http://www.transparency.org/research/cpi/overview>). Of course, it is important to acknowledge that the CPI is based on 'perceptions.'

32 See AML/CFT Act 106/2013, s.1.

33 Greenberg, T.S., Samuel, L.M., Grant, W., and Gray, L., *Stolen Asset Recovery: A Good Practices Guide for Non-Conviction Based Asset Forfeiture* (World Bank, 2009) 51.

34 PPFA, s.24; ACAA, s.36. See further <http://www.nazaha.gov.kw/EN/Pages/default.aspx>.

35 Statutory Instrument No. 300/2016 of the ACAA, s.56.

36 ACAA, ss.30–36.

37 The KFIU was first established in 2003. Jusic, A., 'Kuwait's administrative risk-based model for the prevention of money laundering: Costs and benefits of compliance with the Financial Action Task Force (FATF) Standards' (2017) 31(2) *Arab Law Quarterly* 101, 108–109.

If there are reasonable grounds to suspect that offences against public funds,[38] IEO,[39] or ML have been committed,[40] the PPO can take any provisional measure to restrain the suspect from disposal and administration of the relevant property, whether it is in the possession of the suspect or other individuals. These provisional measures will not be discharged until the financial sanctions are enforced (or the case is dismissed).[41] Alongside the PPO, victim state institutions may take any type of provisional measures to prevent the disposal, dissipation, and movement of assets, whether in Kuwait or abroad.[42]

Confiscation and forfeiture

Beside the pre-conviction provisional measures, Kuwaiti laws have long recognised forfeiture and confiscation as post-conviction legal tools to prevent offenders from benefiting from their criminal enterprises. In all criminal cases, the courts are empowered to forfeit any property that was used, or could be used, in committing an offence. Forfeiture extends to the assets derived from that criminal property.[43] In public funds offences, each judgement shall include an order to confiscate the assets as part of the sentence.[44] The PPFA opts for a value-based confiscation where the convicted person is obliged to pay 'an amount of money equivalent to the value of their criminal benefit.'[45] To facilitate confiscation, transactions that were carried out with assets associated with crimes to prevent the authorities from recovering them shall be rendered invalid.[46]

In the case of IEO, the judgement shall include a forfeiture order in relation to the ill-gotten gains, whether in the possession of the offender or his or her spouse and minors.[47] The courts, however, can extend the order to cover any individual or legal entity that has benefited from IEO so that the confiscation or forfeiture order can be effective against them.[48] The court can, in IEO and other corruption cases, exempt the offender from punishment if the offender enables the authorities during the investigation process to identify or locate the assets.[49]

For the ML crime, the courts shall order the forfeiture of the following funds and instrumentalities: (a) proceeds of crime and the funds intermingled with, or derived from, or exchanged for these proceeds; (b) income and other gains from

38 PPFA, s.24.
39 ACAA, s.36.
40 AML/CFT Act, s.22.
41 PPFA, s.27.
42 *Ibid.*, s.24.
43 Criminal Law Act 16/1960, s.78.
44 PPFA, s.16.
45 UNODC, *Manual on International Cooperation for the Purposes of Confiscation of Proceeds of Crime* (UN, 2012) 19.
46 PPFA, s.28.
47 ACAA, s.48.
48 *Ibid.*, s.55.
49 *Ibid.*, s.44.

proceeds of crime; and (c) the objects of crime.[50] If the forfeiture of funds and instrumentalities is not possible because they cannot be located or are no longer available, the court shall issue a confiscation order equivalent in value to the tainted funds and instrumentalities.[51] In this way, any hard boundary between the nature of forfeiture and confiscation orders is avoided in Kuwaiti law.

Innovative approaches to proceed of corruption

Kuwait has achieved some notable progress in two relevant areas: its counter-corruption law,[52] and its AML law.[53] However, the adequacy of the existing criminal-based measures to deal with the problem of corruption in Kuwait is questionable. The Stolen Asset Recovery Initiative (StAR) asserted that criminal forfeiture is not always an effective tool for proceeds of corruption and recommended that there should be alternatives for the asset recovery process, particularly civil forfeiture and UWOs.[54] Thus, this section is focused on two issues. First, it identifies civil forfeiture and UWOs and their features as two innovative tools that are missing in the Kuwaiti counter-corruption laws. Second, it discusses the potential effectiveness of these two tools in Kuwait and what may impede their adoption.

Civil forfeiture

Generally, two regimes are used in the asset forfeiture process: non-conviction-based forfeiture (civil forfeiture) and criminal forfeiture (following conviction).[55] Both regimes aim to capture the proceeds and instrumentalities of crimes, but they differ in their procedures. First, criminal forfeiture requires initiating criminal proceedings and obtaining a conviction, whilst civil forfeiture does not.[56] Second, criminal forfeiture is an action against a person (*in personam)* and is part of the sentence, whilst civil forfeiture is an action against the property and asset itself (*in rem)*.[57] Third, criminal forfeiture often requires the heightened standard of proof that is used in criminal cases (beyond reasonable doubt), whilst civil forfeiture requires the lower standard of proof used in civil cases – that is, the

50 AML/CFT Act, s.40.

51 *Ibid.*, s.40.

52 See UNODC, *Review of Implementation of the United Nations Convention against Corruption: Kuwait Executive Summary* (UN Fourth Session, 27–31 May 2013) 9.

53 See MENAFATF, *Mutual Evaluation Report: 3rd Follow-Up Report for State Of Kuwait: Anti-Money Laundering and Combating the Financing of Terrorism* (MENAFATF, 2015).

54 Gray, L., Hansen, K., Recica-Kirkbride, P., and Mills, L., *Few and Far: The Hard Facts on Stolen Asset Recovery* (World Bank and OECD, 2014) 68.

55 Greenberg, Samuel, Grant, and Gray (fn 33) 13.

56 UNODC, *Manual on International Cooperation for the Purposes of Confiscation of Proceeds of Crime* (fn 45) 20.

57 Greenberg, Samuel, Grant and Gray (fn 33) 13–14.

balance of probabilities.[58] Fourth, criminal forfeiture is either 'object-based' (the prosecution should prove that the assets are proceeds of the crime committed) or 'value-based' (allowing the forfeiture of benefits accrued to the offender from crime), whilst civil forfeiture is only object-based.[59]

Despite being a recent and 'under-theorised' means of combatting crime,[60] civil forfeiture is provided for in Article 54(1)(c) of the UNCAC 2003, which requires all States Parties to consider forfeiting proceeds of crime without a conviction. Civil forfeiture derives its significance from the policy rationales that lie behind it. The perceived 'failure' of criminal law caused by due process safeguards to combat serious criminality has led to the resort to the civil technique to target criminal assets.[61] Moreover, in the realm of organised crime, especially corruption, offenders can be leaders or high-ranking officials who tend to be far from the criminal enterprise, meaning that it may be impossible to bring them to justice.[62] Thus civil forfeiture is able to overcome two types of difficulties: first, difficulties raised by the procedural safeguards of criminal law and, second, difficulties raised by the complexity of corruption crimes as a white-collar crime.[63]

Although civil forfeiture represents itself as 'an alternative approach that made use of civil processes to target criminal assets,'[64] it is not necessarily more effective. For example, there have been occasions where assets were suspected to be proceeds of crime, but law enforcement authorities were not able to seize or forfeit them under the provisions of civil forfeiture because of the impossibility to obtain evidence to undertake civil action to forfeit the illicit property.[65] Therefore, even if the standard of proof is lower in civil forfeiture, finding sufficient evidence still impedes any potential forfeiture in the future. This exposes the deficiency of civil forfeiture and the need for additional innovative tools, such as the UWOs (as discussed next).

Despite the commitment of Kuwait to the UNCAC, its laws lack a civil forfeiture regime. However, some legal provisions bring the forfeiture regime in Kuwait closer to civil forfeiture, though not fully. Criminal forfeiture proceedings

58 *Ibid.*

59 For detailed distinctions, see *ibid.*

60 See Hendry, J. and King, C., 'How far is too far? Theorising non-conviction-based asset forfeiture' (2015) 11(4) *International Journal of Law in Context* 398–411.

61 *Ibid.*, 398–399.

62 Simser, J., 'Perspectives on civil forfeiture' in Young, S.N.M. (ed.), *Civil Forfeiture of Criminal Property: Legal Measures for Targeting the Proceeds of Crime* (Edward Elgar Publishing, 2009) 13–14.

63 Ryder, N., 'To confiscate or not to confiscate? A comparative analysis of the confiscation of the proceeds of crime legislation in the United States of America and the United Kingdom' (2013) 8 *Journal of Business Law* 767.

64 Hendry and King (fn 60) 399.

65 In the United Kingdom, the Home Office proposed that the existing provisions of Proceeds of Crime Act (POCA) 2002 that allow for civil forfeiture were not helpful in these cases. See Sproat, P., 'Unexplained wealth orders: An explanation, assessment and set of predictions' (2018) 82(3) *Journal of Criminal Law* 232.

are allowed in cases in which the convicted has died after the criminal charge was instituted. In offences against the public purse,[66] IEO,[67] and ML,[68] the death of the convicted shall not preclude the confiscation of proceeds of the crime, and the victim state institutions can ask the court to issue a confiscation order in regard to the assets and claim compensation. Also, the absconding of the defendant does not constitute an impediment to a confiscation order, as section 122 of the Criminal Justice Act 17/1960 allows for a criminal trial to proceed *in absentia* for many reasons, *inter alia*, when the court has ascertained that the suspect is a fugitive and is not expected to be arrested in a timely manner. In this context, the confiscation order will be immediately enforceable and effective against both the inheritors and any individual that has actually benefited from the crime committed.[69] However, these provisions do not technically transform the existing confiscation regime into a fully civil law asset forfeiture process. Even though securing a criminal conviction is not required in the scenarios mentioned (because of the suspension or termination of the criminal procedures), it is still required that at an earlier point the authorities initiate criminal proceedings against the person. Confiscation is limited in these cases because a criminal charge must have been instituted whilst the offender was alive.[70] Thus the cases mentioned are not separated from the criminal proceedings, a condition prevailing in truly civil forfeiture.[71]

UWOs

UWOs are a recent development in civil enforcement against corruption. They aim to strengthen the state powers to fight organised crime and deprive criminals of the gains and benefits derived from criminal activities without a predicate crime.[72] In the United Kingdom, for example, section 362A of the Criminal Finances Act (CFA) 2017 stipulates that the High Court can grant a UWO order to a law enforcement authority in relation to any property when the court is satisfied that certain requirements are met. This order requires the respondent to, *inter alia*, explain how he or she obtained the property at issue.[73] Failure to satisfy the requirements of a UWO can be used as an evidence for investigators to support any subsequent civil forfeiture action against the property in question.[74] As such, UWOs are 'investigative orders' that can be used as a means to

66 PPFA, s.22.
67 ACAA, s.48.
68 AML/CFT Act, s.40.
69 PPFA, ss.22, 23.
70 UNODC, *Manual on International Cooperation for the Purposes of Confiscation of Proceeds of Crime* (fn 45) 80.
71 Greenberg, Samuel, Grant, and Gray (fn 33) 14.
72 Booz Allen Hamilton (consulting firm), *Comparative Evaluation of Unexplained Wealth Orders: Prepared for the US Department of Justice* (National Institute of Justice, 2011) 9.
73 CFAs, s.362A(3).
74 Sproat (fn 65) 232–233.

achieve the recovery of proceeds of crime.[75] However, UWOs also have their own distinctive features.[76] First, the UWO system introduces the concept of unexplained wealth.[77] Second, it does not have to be proven that the property liable to forfeiture is the proceeds or an instrument of crime (the lack of a nexus between crime and property); what is required is that the property the person holds is unexplained wealth.[78] Third, the onus of proof is on the owner of the property, who is legally obliged to demonstrate the legal provenance of this property.[79]

Kuwaiti law does not deploy UWOs. However, in accordance with Article 20 of UNCAC, Kuwait has legislated for IEO.[80] This crime has some elements of the UWO laws in that it is directed at proceeds of corruption and reverses the burden of proof to the offender, though it differs in some respects. For example, IEO applies only to public officials; the IEO is dependent on the financial disclosure system; the criminal liability of an official cannot be raised on the basis of IEO unless he or she has submitted the financial disclosure required.[81] However, although Kuwaiti law does not provide for UWOs, many of their features might find some echoes in the ACAA. First, the AACA has criminalised illicit enrichment, which is defined as 'a significant increase in the wealth of an official or his/her minors that cannot be reasonably explained in relation to their lawful income.'[82] To that end, the same act established the financial disclosure system to monitor the wealth of specific officials, according to which high-ranking officials are obliged to declare their own and their spouse's wealth.[83] This system enables NAZAHA to identify IEO suspects proactively.[84] Consequently, irrespective of the requirements of IEO (such as prosecution), 'unexplained wealth' is reflected in Kuwaiti counter-corruption laws. For the second feature (the lack of a nexus between crime and targeted property), though the forfeited property should be the proceeds or instrumentalities of crime, the IEO under the ACAA does not necessitate proving a direct nexus between crime and property. The mere lack of justification of the legitimate source of the wealth can be a reason to secure the forfeiture of assets.[85] For the third feature (the reverse of burden of proof), reversing the burden of proof has been established in IEO. The burden of proof

75 *Ibid.*, 235.
76 Booz Allen Hamilton (fn 72) 11.
77 *Ibid.*, 1.
78 *Ibid.*
79 *Ibid.*
80 See further the chapter by Al-Oumi in this book.
81 Al-Oumi, N., 'Illicit enrichment: Comparative analysis study to the Decree-Law No. 24 of 2012 setting up the public authority to combat corruption and the pertinent provision for financial disclosure' (2015) 39(4) *Kuwait University Law Journal* 65, 96.
82 ACAA, s.1.
83 Al-Oumi (fn 81) 95.
84 ACAA, s.30.
85 Al-Oumi (fn 81) 98.

is first placed on the public prosecutor, who should prove that there is unexplained wealth that cannot be reasonably explained in relation to the legal income of the suspect and then the burden is transferred to the suspect, who can refute this rebuttable presumption.[86] In line with the characteristics mentioned, the pathway to adoption of UWOs is, to large extent, paved in Kuwait. What seems to be novel to Kuwaiti law is that UWOs – as in the case of the UK laws – in order to be used, require civil forfeiture that does not require a criminal conviction, a tool that is absent in Kuwait laws.

Innovation in Kuwait: importance and challenge

Civil forfeiture and UWOs are innovative approaches that have, alongside each other, the potential to deal with the grand corruption pattern prevalent in Kuwait. Such *in rem* innovative forfeiture regimes derive their importance from their functions. The UWOs, for instance, enable the enforcement authorities to trace the source of any unexplained wealth,[87] belonging either to a public official or an individual. According to the current Kuwaiti laws, the unexplained wealth is restricted to specific types of officials, and it is impossible to identify any unexplained wealth without submitting the financial disclosures. UWOs, therefore, have the potential to perform a significant function for Kuwait where the corruption problem lies within political elites, whether they hold a public office or not.

The nature of grand corruption makes combatting it inherently challenging. Building sufficient evidence to investigate and convict those involved in grand corruption cases is difficult because corruption in such cases consists of acts committed by political elites (including those who are responsible for decision making) and involves complex techniques of hiding assets. Therefore, the current financial arrangements to combat grand corruption through the traditional tools of criminal law are inadequate, in particular in regard to dealing with proceeds of grand corruption. Where corruption pervades the high-level officials of the state and is not just a problem amongst low-rank officials, the financial arrangements regarding proceeds of corruption (reliant on criminal proceedings against the individuals, securing the conviction of elites and rendering them criminals, and, hence, recovering illicit assets derived from corruption) are unrealistic and less functional.

In order to overcome these difficulties, an emphasis on the financial aspects of crime should be central to counter-corruption strategies.[88] In addition to traditional criminal tools, there should also be an innovative approach to combat

86 *Ibid.*, 99–101.

87 Sproat (fn 65) 236.

88 King, C. and Walker, C., 'Emerging issues in the regulation of criminal and terrorist assets' in King, C. and Walker, C. (eds.), *Dirty Assets: Emerging Issues in the Regulation of Criminal and Terrorist Assets* (Routledge, 2016) 4.

corruption – namely, civil-based asset forfeiture measures that are targeted, first and foremost, at the dirty money rather than individuals.[89] In grand corruption cases, counter-corruption policies – that are more concerned with stripping the offenders from the illicit benefits than stigmatising them – might be prove relatively palatable and effective compared to criminal sanctions. Therefore, when criminal prosecution is impossible for any reason, such as the impunity of the offenders or the inability to obtain evidence, the civil forfeiture measure (with the help of UWOs) is a plausible alternative. In that case, the Kuwaiti policymakers ought to prioritise the deprivation of the corrupt from the benefits of their crimes over securing the criminal conviction of the corrupt criminals. But when a criminal prosecution is possible, and there is robust evidence that a corruption crime has been committed, the enforcement authorities should seek the deprivation of the convicted of their illicit assets based on a fair criminal trial due to the safeguards that the criminal law provides.

Grand corruption raises more complex difficulties, however. The lack of progress in dealing with proceeds of crime (such as introducing innovative forfeiture regimes) is not attributable, as has been said, to the traditional or technical standards surrounding criminal law and the constitutional considerations regarding guilt and innocence and the standard of proof.[90] In general, the lack of political will, to be exerted by political actors of the state, forms a key barrier to combatting corruption and recovering stolen assets.[91] As corruption permeates through the layer of policymakers, those political elites lack incentives and the political will to improve the law and prefer to maintain the current situation.[92] It is understandable, then, that the grand corruption which characterises the problem in Kuwait hampers potential progress in the infrastructure of counter-corruption laws. The extent of Kuwaiti counter-corruption legislation adopted so far does not invalidate the argument here since its adoption has not been fully voluntary. Sharman explained the diffusion of AML policies amongst different countries and argued that the national policies in the developing counties are often not determined on a rational thinking or voluntary basis, but by 'power-based mechanisms,' such as international coercion through blacklisting.[93] The FATF blacklisting system is a coercive mechanism to impose AML standards, and this, indeed, has 'elicited instrumental compliance by states.'[94] Kuwait has

89 Young, S.N.M., *Civil Forfeiture of Criminal Property: Legal Measures for Targeting the Proceeds of Crime* (Edward Elgar Publishing, 2009) 1.

90 UNODC, *Manual on International Cooperation for the Purposes of Confiscation of Proceeds of Crime* (fn 45) 80.

91 Stephenson, K.M., Gray, L., Power, R., Brun, J.-P., Dunker, G., and Panjer, M., *Barriers to Asset Recovery: An Analysis of the Key Barriers and Recommendations for Action* (World Bank, 2011) 24.

92 Martini, M., *Fighting Grand Corruption: Challenges and Successes* (Transparency International, 2015) 2.

93 Sharman, J.C., 'Power and discourse in policy diffusion: Anti-money laundering in developing states' (2008) 52(3) *International Studies Quarterly* 635.

94 *Ibid.*, 636.

provided the Middle East and North Africa FATF (MENAFATF) with full reports about the progress of AML laws and then applied for removal from the regular follow-up (being monitored).[95] Added to this problem is the limitation that the UNCAC does not impose 'firm obligations' on States Parties.[96] Yet without external factors to galvanise Kuwait to develop its domestic laws, the Kuwaiti policymakers will not spontaneously opt for innovative approaches to combat corruption effectively.

Conclusion

This chapter has argued that Kuwait law has long responded to proceeds from corruption crimes. This response has included a wide range of measures that can be classified into two categories: provisional measures, such as freezing and seizure orders, and post-conviction measures, such as forfeiture and confiscation. However, these measures are of a criminal nature; namely, they are triggered in, and confined to, criminal cases either on the basis of suspicion or conviction. Reflection on the non-traditional, innovative approaches to proceeds of crime, such as those stipulated by the UNCAC and the UNTOC, exposes a lack of civil-based measures within Kuwaiti laws. It is argued that grand corruption, a pattern that prevails in Kuwait because of its characteristics as a state, hinders any progress in civil laws related to forfeiture. This is because grand corruption can be linked to the corporate group layer that is responsible for the development of laws; these policymakers are not willing to develop counter-corruption laws. This lack of progress will persist unless there are international mechanisms that impose specific standards about corruption to mirror those imposed by the FATF in the arena of AML.

In Kuwait, and in all jurisdictions, civil measures are of particular importance for corruption crimes, especially when these crimes involve grand corruption that permeates the upper echelon of public officials who dominate the state institutions. Gathering robust evidence and the subsequent prosecution and, ultimately, conviction of those officials is difficult due to the impunity they may enjoy. Therefore, it is concluded here that existing forfeiture mechanisms cannot deal with a phenomenon like grand corruption. The focus of any future financial arrangements should be on the assets arising from corrupt activities rather than the corrupt actors. Taken together, these results suggest that the law enforcement authorities should be vested with more powers in relation to asset forfeiture. In particular, there should be a 'shift from a criminal legal strategy to a civil model' in regard to forfeiture.[97] The Kuwaiti policymaker must prioritise targeting the assets rather than the corrupt as this step is more realistic in grand

95 MENAFATF (fn 53) 3–8.

96 Rose, C., *International Anti-Corruption Norms: Their Creation and Influence on Domestic Legal Systems* (Oxford University Press, 2015) 97.

97 Ryder (fn 63) 2.

corruption cases. Given that prosecuting high-profile offenders for corruption crimes inevitably raises political sensitivity, targeting the assets might encounter less severe objections. The targeting of assets rather than persons might also be more attainable when the assets are abroad (as they often are). In that eventuality, civil actions against assets might be more feasible (and rewarding) than extradition warrants against high officials.

16 The suspension of Nigeria from the Egmont Group and its re-admittance

Olufemi Olaoye

Introduction

In response to the often-interwoven crimes of money laundering and terrorism financing (ML/TF) many political, legal, and institutional initiatives have been geared towards combatting those crimes. The Financial Action Task Force[1] (FATF) and other international organisations, such as the Egmont Group of Financial Intelligence Units ('the Egmont Group'),[2] have been at the international forefront of setting standards to combat ML/TF. These actors have enjoined the international community to domesticate the set standards through national legislation but without taking into consideration the local peculiarities of individual countries. Whilst ML/TF are often perpetuated on a cross-border basis, their immediate regulation and control remain matters for individual countries. In recognition of the adverse effects of ML/TF, the Nigerian government has taken countermeasures through its elaborate anti-money laundering/ combating the financing of terrorism (AML/CFT) legal frameworks and ratification of international instruments.[3] However, the country still experiences ML/TF

1 See Financial Action Task Force, *International standards on combatting money laundering and the financing of terrorism and proliferation* (<http://www.fatf-gafi.org/media/fatf/documents/recommendations/pdfs/FATF%20Recommendations%202012.pdf>, updated 2019). For further discussion, see Nance, M.T., 'Re-thinking FATF: An experimentalist interpretation of the Financial Action Task Force' (2018) 69 *Crime, Law and Social Change* 131.

2 See Egmont Group of Financial Intelligence Units, *Egmont Group Strategic Plan 2018–2021* (<https://egmontgroup.org/sites/default/files/filedepot/EG_Strategic_Plan_2018-2021/2018-2021%20Egmont%20Group%20Strategic%20Plan%20-%20Approved%20by%20the%20HoFIU%20in%20Sydney%20%28Sep%202018%29%20-%20Public%20website.pdf>, 2018). See also International Monetary Fund, Legal Dept., Monetary and Financial Systems Dept., *Financial intelligence units: An overview* (World Bank, <https://www.imf.org/external/pubs/ft/FIU/fiu.pdf>, 23 July 2004); Thony, J.-F., 'Processing financial information in money laundering matters: The financial intelligence units' (1996) 4(3) *European Journal of Crime, Criminal Law and Criminal Justice* 257.

3 Nigeria has ratified the United Nations (UN) Convention against Illicit Traffic in Narcotic Drugs and Psychotropic Substances (Vienna Convention) (3 October 1989), the UN Convention against Transnational Organised Crime (Palermo Convention) (29 March 2001), and the UN Convention against Corruption in 2003 (14 December 2004).

activities. According to Okogbule, the pervasiveness of these crimes in Nigeria lies in the fact that those charged with responsibility for dealing with them are themselves often either directly involved or beneficiaries of such criminal activities.[4] Nigeria also experiences lax and ineffective enforcements mechanisms,[5] reflected by the suspension of Nigeria from the Egmont Group on July 5, 2017, and its eventual re-admittance in September 2018.

This chapter examines Nigeria's AML/CFT legal framework (and its inadequacies) in the light of international standards. The chapter also considers the suspension of Nigeria from the Egmont Group and the Nigerian Financial Intelligence Unit Act, 2018 (NFIU Act), enacted in direct response to the suspension. The chapter advocates for more efficient implementation of the NFIU Act and other AML/CFT legal instruments.

Nigeria's AML/CFT legal frameworks

The Nigerian government has put in place various legislative and regulatory measures to address ML/TF in line with relevant international instruments. There are six key pieces of legislation, complemented by a range of regulations, circulars, and guidelines issued by the respective financial supervisory authorities.[6] The key legislative measures are (a) National Drug Law Enforcement Agency (NDLEA) Act, 1989; (b) Money Laundering (Prohibition) Act 2011 (as amended) (MLPA); (c) Economic and Financial Crimes Commission Act, 2004 (EFCC Act); (d) Independent Corrupt Practices and Other Related Offences Commission Act, 2000 (Independent Corrupt Practices Commission Act); (e) Terrorism (Prevention) (Amendment) Act, 2013 (TPAA); and (f) the Nigeria Financial Intelligence Unit Act, 2018 (NFIU Act). These statutory enactments form the thematic preoccupation of this chapter, and their salient provisions will be discussed to convey an understanding of the context for the NFIU Act.

The National Drug Law Enforcement Agency (NDLEA) Act 1989

The NDLEA Act (Decree No. 48) of 1989 was enacted following Nigeria's ratification of the Vienna Convention (UN Convention Against Illicit Traffic

4 Okogbule, N.S., 'Official corruption and the dynamics of money laundering in Nigeria' (2007) 14(1) *Journal of Financial Crime* 49.

5 US Department of State, 'Countries/Jurisdictions of Primary Concern – Nigeria' (<https://2009-2017.state.gov/j/inl/rls/nrcrpt/2015/vol2/239096.htm>, 2017).

6 See the Central Bank of Nigeria, Anti-Money Laundering and Combating the Financing of Terrorism in Banks and Other Financial Institutions in Nigeria Regulations, 2013 SI 16; Securities and Exchange Commission Nigeria, Anti-Money Laundering/Combating Financing of Terrorism (AML/CFT) Compliance Manual for Capital Market Operators 2010; the Special Control Unit Against Money Laundering of the Federal Ministry of Industry Trade and Investment, Anti-Money Laundering/Combating the Financing of Terrorism (AML/CFT) Regulations for Designated Non-financial Business and Professions in Nigeria, 2013 SI 16.

in Narcotic Drugs and Psychotropic Substances of 1988). On that basis, the NDLEA Act restricted the money laundering offences to the laundering of the proceeds of drug trafficking. Yet it soon became clear that other economic and financial crimes, for example human trafficking, were escalating and contributing to the growth in the incidence of money laundering. These apparent gaps in the NDLEA Act led to the enactment of the Money Laundering Decree No 3 of 1995, which has gone through chains of amendment culminating in the Money Laundering Prohibition Act 2011 (as amended).

Money Laundering Prohibition (MLPA) Act 2011

The primary AML law in Nigeria is the MLPA (Harmonized Act no.11), which repealed the Money Laundering (Prohibition) Act, 2004.[7] The MLPA provides appropriate penalties and expands the scope of supervisory and regulatory authorities.[8] The Act also requires financial institutions to observe customer due diligence (CDD) for any transaction involving just $1,000 or its equivalent.[9] However, this relatively low threshold for financial transactions has not been very effective because of the cash-based economy of Nigeria.[10]

Section 6(10) of the MLPA provides immunity for directors, officers, and employees of financial institutions and designated non-financial institutions from any civil or criminal liability in suits that might be brought against them by their customers as a result of the performance of their duties under the Act.[11] Prior to the enactment of the MLPA, the duty of confidentiality hindered steps against money laundering. In addition to performing normal CDD, section 3(7) of the MLPA requires the financial institution or designated non-financial institution to put in place an appropriate risk-management system regarding politically exposed persons (PEPs).[12]

The relevance of the provisions on PEPs cannot be overemphasised given Nigeria's political climate, where political office holders and their allies are regularly found misappropriating state assets. Following the military administration of the late General Sanni Abacha (1993–1998), his successor in office commissioned

7 MLPA, s. 24. See, generally, Ikpang, A., 'A critical analysis of the legal mechanisms for combating money laundering in Nigeria' (2011) 1 *African Journal of Law and Criminology* 118, 130.

8 Section 2(5) of the MLPA spells out the penalty for failure to declare or making a false declaration to the Nigerian Customs with regard to international transfers as required by the provisions of s.12 of the Foreign Exchange (Monitoring and Miscellaneous Provisions) Act 1995. On conviction, violators will either forfeit the undeclared funds or be imprisoned for at least two years or both.

9 MLPA, ss.3(1)(b), (5).

10 Amali, M.O., *Curbing money laundering: Global reception and implementation of international anti money laundering standards a case study on Nigeria* (PhD, University of Huddersfield) (<http://eprints.hud.ac.uk/id/eprint/31396/1/__nas01_librhome_librsh3_Desktop_FINAL THESIS.pdf>, 2016).

11 See Rec.21 of the FATF (fn 21).

12 FATF, Rec.12.

a probe into allegations of corruption levelled against Abacha. These investigations revealed that Abacha and his 'kitchen cabinet' stashed away in foreign bank assets estimated between USD 5–6 billion.[13] By May 2007, USD 2 billion had been repatriated.[14] In April 2018, the sum of USD 322 million, forming part of the Abacha loot, was repatriated from Switzerland.[15]

Regardless of the provisions of the MLPA, misappropriation of public funds by political office holders has not significantly declined, which brings to question the effectiveness of the MLPA.[16] How could transactions involving huge sums of money be made without detection from the regulatory authorities and especially the financial institutions? The answer lies in the connivance between money launderers and regulatory authorities.[17]

The MLPA divides the regulatory regime between financial institutions (FIs) and designated non-financial institutions (DNFIs). Section 1 (a) and (b) of the Act provides:

> No person or body corporate shall, except in a transaction through a Financial Institution, make or accept cash payment of a sum exceeding Nigerian Naira (₦) 5,000,000.00 or its equivalent, in the case of an individual; or ₦ 10,000,000.00 or its equivalent, in the case of a body corporate.

A transfer to or from a foreign country of funds or securities by a person or body corporate including a money service business of a sum exceeding US$10,000 or its equivalent shall be reported to the Central Bank of Nigeria (CBN), Securities and Exchange Commission (SEC), or EFCC in writing within seven days from the date of the transactions.[18]

This strengthening of regulations within the financial industry seems to have displaced crimes to the non-financial business sectors. In response, sections 5 and 25 of the MLPA regulate DNFIs, which include dealers in jewellery, cars and luxury goods, chartered accountants, audit firms, tax consultants, clearing and settlement companies, legal practitioners, hotels, casinos, supermarkets, and such other businesses as the Federal Ministry of Industry, Trade, and Investment

13 Enweremadu, D.U., 'Nigeria's quest to recover looted assets: The Abacha affair' (2013) 48(2) *Afrika Spectrum* 51. For wider discussion, see Sharman, J.C., *The Despot's Guide to Wealth Management: On the International Campaign against Grand Corruption* (Cornell University Press, 2017).

14 *Ibid*, 51.

15 Alagbe, J., 'More questions than answers over $322m Abacha loot sharing' (<https://punchng.com/more-questions-than-answers-over-322m-abacha-loot-sharing/>, 7 July 2018).

16 See BBC News, 'Nigeria ex-oil minister arrested in London' (<http://www.bbc.com/news/world-africa-34430597>, 2 October 2015).

17 Ribadu, N. (Press release by the first chairman of the Economic and Financial Crimes Commission) 'Bankers aid money laundering in Nigeria' (<http://www.premiumtimesng.com/news/more-news/252281-bankers-aid-money-laundering-nigeria-nuhu-ribadu.html>, 12 December 2017).

18 MLPA, s.2(1).

(the Ministry) or other authorities may designate.[19] Thus, section 5(1) of the MLPA provides that a DNFI whose business involves a cash transaction exceeding US$1,000 or its equivalent shall identify the customer by filling out a standard data form and presenting an approved identity document.[20] A DNFI that fails to comply is liable to a fine of ₦ 250,000 for each day during which the offence continues and suspension, revocation, or withdrawal of any licence to operate.[21]

The concept that lawyers are amongst the gatekeepers has generated considerable controversy. In Nigeria, sections 5 and 25 of the MLPA and the CBN's circular made thereunder[22] came under judicial scrutiny in *Nigerian Bar Association v Attorney General of the Federation*[23] (the *NBA* case). It was contended that classifying legal practitioners as a DNFI contravened section 37 of the Nigerian Constitution,[24] section 192 of the Evidence Act 2011, and the Legal Practitioner's Act 2004.[25] The Nigerian Bar Association sought an order of court deleting legal practitioners from the definition of DNFIs, similar to the Canadian case of *Attorney General of Canada v Federation of Law Societies of Canada*.[26] The Federal High Court struck down the provisions of sections 5 and 25 of the MLPA for classifying legal practitioners as 'traders' and held that legal practitioners are not 'traders' and do not have 'customers.' The Court further held that the legal profession is already well regulated by the provisions of the Legal Practitioners Act, the Rules of Professional Conduct for Legal Practitioners 2007,[27] and the Evidence Act.[28]

The decision of the court in the *NBA* case is inconsistent with the international AML/CFT standards developed and promoted by FATF.[29] The argument of the NBA that the legal profession is sufficiently regulated is unconvincing given the fact that extant laws and rules do not provide clear guidance for dealing with issues of ML/TF.

Overall, the MLPA is a good piece of legislation which reflects global standards on AML. Fundamentally, the MLPA contains comprehensive provisions to prohibit the laundering of the proceeds of a crime or illegal act, provide appropriate penalties, and expand the interpretation of financial institutions and scope

19 MLPA, s.25.
20 MLPA, s.5(1)(c) directs all DNFIs to record all transactions.
21 MLPA, s.5(6).
22 See Central Bank of Nigeria Circular Reference FPR/CIR/GEN/VOL.1/028 (<http://www.cbn.gov.ng/OUT/2012/CIRCULARS/FPR/ADDITIONAL%20KYC%20REQUIREMENT.PDF>, 2 August 2012).
23 Unreported decision of the Federal High Court of Nigeria in Suit No FHC/ABJ/CS/173/2013, December 17, 2014.
24 Constitution of the Federal Republic of Nigeria, 1999 (as amended).
25 Legal Practitioners Act, Cap L11, Laws of the Federation of Nigeria (LFN), 2004.
26 [2015] 1 S.C.R. 401.
27 See Rule 19(1) of the Rules of Professional Conduct for Legal Practitioners.
28 See the Evidence Act 2011, s.170, which grants privilege to lawyer/client communication but excludes communication made in furtherance of illegal purpose or information obtained by a legal practitioner evidencing that a crime or fraud has been committed during the course of his engagement by the client.
29 Recommendations 22 & 23 of the FATF (fn1).

of supervision of regulatory authorities on money laundering activities, amongst other things. The evident shortcomings are in enforcement rather than enactment.

The Economic and Financial Crimes Commission Act 2004

The EFCC (Establishment) Act, No.1 of 2004[30] directly responded to pressure from the FATF, which in 2001 (until 2005) named Nigeria as one of non-cooperative countries in the global fight against money laundering.[31] The EFCC Act established the Economic and Financial Crimes Commission (EFCC), which is charged with the responsibility of enforcing all economic and financial crimes laws.[32] The EFCC was also designated as the Nigerian Financial Intelligence Unit[33] (NFIU), which has the responsibility of coordinating the various institutions involved in the fight against ML/TF.[34] The designation of EFCC as the NFIU triggered the eventual suspension of Nigeria from the Egmont Group due to factors discussed later.[35]

Terrorism (Prevention) (Amendment) Act 2013

Following the September 2001 terrorist attacks, the United Nations Security Council (UNSC) passed Resolution 1373.[36] This resolution required all Member States to enforce sanctions against terrorism financing. Nigeria's initial responses were shown to be inadequate by the case of a young Nigerian, Umar Abdulmutallab, who on December 25, 2009, attempted to set off an explosive aboard Delta/North West Airlines Flight 253 to Detroit, which originated from Nigeria.[37] As a result of this event, the US Transportation Security Administration

30 The EFCC Act was initially enacted in 2002 but, subsequently, repealed and re-enacted by the EFCC Act 2004.

31 FATF, 'About the Non-Cooperative Countries and Territories (NCCT) Initiative' (<http://www.fatf-gafi.org/publications/high-riskandnon-cooperativejurisdictions/more/aboutthenon-cooperativecountriesandterritoriesncctinitiative.html>, 2019).

32 See the Explanatory Memorandum of the EFCC Act.

33 See EFCC Act, s.1(2)(c). The NFIU also functions as a national centre for receiving, analysing, and disseminating suspicious transaction reports (STR) and other information regarding potential money laundering or terrorist financing.

34 Section 7(2) provides that in addition to the powers conferred on the commission by this act, the commission shall be the coordinating agency for the enforcement of the provisions of (a) the Money Laundering Act, 2004 (now MLPA, 2011); (b) the Advance Fee Fraud and Other Related Offences Act, 2006; (c) the Failed Banks (Recovery of Debts) and Financial Malpractices in Banks Act, as amended; (d) the Banks and Other Financial Institutions Act 1991, as amended; (e) Miscellaneous Offences Act; and (f) any other law or regulation relating to economic and financial crimes, including the Criminal Code and Penal Code.

35 See the Egmont Group's Co-Chairs, 'Statement 24th Plenary of the Egmont Group of Financial Intelligence Units' (<https://egmontgroup.org/en/filedepot_download/1659/52>, 7 July 2017).

36 S/RES/1373 (2001).

37 Omolaye-Ajileye, A., 'Legal framework for the prevention of terrorism in Nigeria' (<http://www.academia.edu/12537054/Legal_Framework_for_the_Prevention_of_Terrorism_in_Nigeria?auto=download>, 21 May 2015).

(TSA) classified Nigeria as a 'Country of Interest' on the US Terror Watch List and so subjected passengers to enhanced security screening. One of the conditions to have Nigeria delisted from the US Terror Watch List was to enact further anti-terrorism legislation.[38] Beyond the international requirements to take action, Nigeria has been further motivated to pass laws because of the violent activities of Boko Haram after 2009.

There followed the Terrorism (Prevention) Act No. 10 of 2011. That Act fell short in a number of ways. It did not provide for the effective coordination of counter-terrorism efforts and intelligence, for extra-territorial application, or adequate punishment. It also failed to ensure due process and other safeguards for human right. Consequently, that Act was amended in 2013.[39]

The TPAA, No.6 of 2013, provides for a wide range of terrorism-related offences,[40] including the financing of terrorism. Thus section 13(1) prohibits making available funds, properties, or other services by any means, whether legitimate or otherwise, to terrorist organisations or individual terrorists with the knowledge or having reasonable grounds to believe that such funds or properties will be used to facilitate a terrorist act. The TPAA prescribes up to life imprisonment.[41] In addition, a convict may be required to forfeit any asset used to commit the offence or connected with it. In order to forestall delay in hearing terrorism cases, the Act empowers the Federal High Court[42] to adopt all legal measures necessary to avoid unnecessary delays and abuse.[43] The court can even refuse to entertain applications for stay of proceedings until judgement is delivered.[44] A noticeable gap in the TPAA is a failure to address the question of state-terrorism or state-sponsored terrorism.[45]

Certain provisions of the TPAA may threaten some fundamental rights guaranteed in Chapter 4 of the Constitution of the Federal Republic of Nigeria 1999 (as amended). For instance, section 27(1) of the TPAA, provides that

38 See Sampson, I.T. and Onuoha, F.C., 'Forcing the horse to drink or making it realise its thirst?' (2011) 5(3–4) *Perspectives on Terrorism* 33.

39 See also the EFCC Act 2004 ss.15, 46. For reviews, see Chukwuemerie, A.I., 'International legal war on the financing of terrorism: A comparison of Nigerian, UK, US and Canadian laws' (2006) 9 *Journal of Money Laundering Control* 71; Sampson, I.T., 'Nigeria: A critique of the EFCC Establishment Act' (2008) 4 *Nigeria Army Quarterly Journal* 314; Ejeh, E.U. et al., 'Nature of terrorism and anti-terrorism laws in Nigeria' (2019) 10 *Nnamdi Azikiwe University Journal of International Law and Jurisprudence* 186.

40 See generally ss. 3–24.

41 See s.13(2)(b), TPAA.

42 Section 32(1) also vests the Federal High Court of Nigeria with jurisdiction to try terrorist offences whether or not the offence was committed in Nigeria or completed outside of Nigeria.

43 Section 32(5).

44 Section 32(6).

45 Nwatu, S.I. and Ogbuabor, C.A., 'National security, terrorism, and development in Nigeria-Paper presented at the 45th Annual Conference of the Nigerian Association of Law Teachers held at the University of Lagos, 18–20 June 2012' (<http://www.unn.edu.ng/publications/files/NATIONAL%20SECURITY,%20TERRORISM%20AND%20DEVELOPMENT%20IN%20NIGERIA_%20S.%20I.%20NWATU%20&%20C.%20A.%20OGBUABOR.pdf>).

> the court may, pursuant to an ex-parte application, grant an order for the detention of a suspect under this Act for a period not exceeding 90 days subject to renewal for a similar period until the conclusion of the investigation and prosecution of the matter that led to the arrest and detention is dispensed with.

This provision is in direct contravention of section 35(4) of the Constitution.[46]

Similarly, section 28(4) provides that where a person arrested under the Act is granted bail by a court within the 90 days detention period stipulated by the Act, 'the person may, on the approval of the Head of the relevant law enforcement agency be placed under a house arrest and shall (a) be monitored by its officers; (b) have no access to phones or communication gadgets; and (c) speak only to his counsel until the conclusion of the investigation.' Arguably, placing a person under house arrest without a valid court order (as required by the Constitution (sections 6 and 36)) is illegal and susceptible to political abuse.

Subject to these criticisms, Nigeria's legal regime for dealing with terrorism is very detailed. However, until the perennial struggles against corruption, reinforced by worsening socio-economic conditions such as poverty, social injustice, and unemployment, are addressed and not exacerbated by counter-terrorism operations,[47] Nigeria will have to contend with terrorism for a long time to come.

Corrupt Practices and Other Related Offences Act 2000

The Corrupt Practices and Other Related Offences Act, No.5 of 2000 established the Independent Corrupt Practices Commission (ICPC), whose main goals are to investigate reports of corrupt practices, to eradicate corruption in public bodies, and to educate the public against corruption.[48] The ICPC also lists amongst its duties the prevention of corruption through studies of systems, practices, and procedure, as well as the mandate to tackle corruption in all forms both by investigation and education.

Despite these laudable provisions, Nigeria is ranked as one of the world's most corrupt countries.[49] In 2018, Nigeria ranked 144 out of 180 countries, having

46 Section 35(4) of the Constitution provides that 'any person who is arrested or detained in accordance with subsection (1)(c) of this section shall be brought before a court of law within a reasonable time, and if he is not tried within a period of- (a) two months from the date of his arrest or detention in the case of a person who is in custody or is not entitled to bail; or (b) three months from the date of his arrest or detention in the case of a person who has been released on bail he shall (without prejudice to any further proceedings that may be brought against him) be released either unconditionally or upon such conditions as are reasonably necessary to ensure that he appears for trial at a later date.'

47 Njoku, E.T., '"Laws for Sale:" The domestication of counterterrorism policies and its impact in Nigeria' in Romaniuk, S.N., Grice, F., Irrera, D., and Webb, S. (eds.), *Palgrave Handbook of Global Counterterrorism Policy* (Palgrave Macmillan, 2017).

48 See generally <https://icpc.gov.ng>.

49 Inter-governmental Action Group Against Money Laundering in West Africa (GIABA), *Mutual Evaluation Reports Anti-Money Laundering and Combating the Financing of Terrorism,*

scored just 27 point in the Transparency International Corruption Perception Index (CPI),[50] though it is recognised that the CPI has its limitations and distortions.[51] Nevertheless, the prevalence of financial crimes[52] in Nigeria tend to validate the CPI's ranking and raise concern about whether the elaborate legislative and regulatory frameworks in place are deliberately superficial so that the country may be seen as acting in compliance with global standards.

Nigeria's suspension from the Egmont Group and its implications

The NFIU, formally established in 2004 and domiciled within the EFCC, became fully operational in 2005. The establishment of the NFIU is based on the requirements of Recommendation 29 of the FATF Standards and Article 58 of the United Nations Convention against Corruption (UNCAC).[53] The NFIU was admitted into the Egmont Group of FIUs in 2007.[54] The NFIU has since then sought to develop standards and procedures for the receipt,[55] analysis, and dissemination of financial intelligence to law enforcement agencies; to perform onsite and off-site examination of financial institutions; and to enhance compliance with the legal and regulatory regime on AML/CFT in Nigeria as well as respond to global trends by collaborating with other FIUs globally. At least initially, the NFIU performed creditably, and so the Egmont Group approved the NFIU to mentor the FIUs of the Gambia, Liberia, and Sierra Leone and equally appointed the director of the NFIU as its regional representative for the West/Central African sub-region.[56]

Subsequently, however, the Egmont Group expressed reservations.[57] One concern was the leakage of confidential information[58] obtained from the Egmont

---

2007 (<https://www.giaba.org/media/f/310_GIABA__Mutual_Evaluation_Report_of__Senegal_Feb%200209%20(English)[1].pdf>, 2008).

50 Transparency International, *Corruption Perception Index 2018* <http://www.transparency.org/cpi2018>.

51 Saha, S., Gounder, R., and Su, J.-J., 'Is there a consensus towards transparency: International's Corruption Perceptions Index?' (2012) 20(1) *International Journal of Business Studies* 1.

52 See also Basel Institute of Governance, 'Basel AML Index 2018' (<http://www.baselgovernance.org/sites/default/files/2019-02/basel_aml_index_10_09_2018.pdf>, 2018). In the aforementioned report, Nigeria ranked 16 out of 129 countries surveyed with a risk score of 6.86.

53 UN General Assembly, UNCAC, A/RES/58/4, 2003.

54 The NFIU until recently drew its powers from the MLPA 2011 as amended and the EFCC Act 2004.

55 A comprehensive list of FIs and DNFIs that are required to submit reports to NFIU is contained in the MLPA 2011, s.25 as amended.

56 'NFIU Mentors FIU of Gambia, Liberia and Sierra Leone in the GIABA-EU Joint Project: Regional Peer-to-Peer Exchanges and Mentorship Programme' (<http://www.nfiu.gov.ng/index.php/2012-05-18-07-05-55/154-giabamentor>, 2019).

57 Egmont Group's Co-Chairs' Statement (fn 35).

58 The leaked information allegedly related to suspicious transaction reports and international exchanges: *ibid.* p. 1.

Group's secure web in flagrant violation of clause 7 of the interpretive note to FATF Recommendation 29, which requires that information received, processed, held, or disseminated by FIUs must be securely protected, exchanged, and used only in accordance with agreed regulations. The second concern pointed to Nigeria's non-compliance with clauses 8 and 10 of the interpretive note to Recommendation 29, which mandates that FIUs enjoy operational and financial autonomy. In effect, the NFIU is required to be an autonomous entity and not tied to the EFCC. The failure of the Nigerian government to promptly address these concerns led to the suspension of Nigeria from the Group on July 5, 2017.[59]

As a condition for re-admittance into the Egmont Group, Nigeria was required to devise a legal and regulatory framework that would ensure operational and financial autonomy of the NFIU by March 2018, failing which Nigeria risked being expelled from the group. The consequences of expulsion are grave. The suspension activated the denial to Nigeria of the Egmont secure web information exchange platform and stalled the process of Nigeria's application to join the FATF. Also, there was imminent threat that Nigerians would be unable to fund international transactions as expulsion would affect the usage of credit and debit cards issued by Nigerian banks. Implications of the expulsion for financial sector are also serious for the international ratings of Nigeria's financial institutions, resulting in their inability to engage in major transactions.

In order to address the suspension from the Egmont Group, the Nigerian National Assembly, on March 7, 2018, passed the Nigerian Financial Intelligence Unit Establishment Bill, which received presidential assent on July 11, 2018. The Act establishes an independent NFIU[60] as the central body in Nigeria responsible for requesting, receiving, and disseminating financial intelligence reports and other information to all law enforcement, security agencies, and other authorities.[61] The Act also establishes the office of the director of the NFIU, who shall be responsible for the administration and management of the NFIU, thus making it an autonomous body from the EFCC.[62] The Act also establishes a fund to which budgetary allocation approved by the National Assembly shall be paid to the unit.[63]

Another main feature of the Act is the establishment of the NFIU in the CBN for the purposes of institutional location and logistic support. Given that the core functions of the NFIU are different from that of the CBN, this location fully complies with Clause 9 of the interpretive note to Recommendation 29 of the FATF.[64]

59 Suberu, R.T., 'Strategies for advancing anticorruption reforms in Nigeria' (2018) 147(3) *Daedalus* 184.

60 Section 2(2).

61 See the Explanatory Note to the NFIU Act.

62 Section 5(1).

63 Section 11.

64 Clause 9 provides that a FIU may be established as part of an existing authority. When a FIU is located within the existing structure of another authority, the FIU's core functions should be distinct from those of the other authority.

Having addressed the prime concerns that led to the suspension of Nigeria's membership of the Egmont Group, the suspension was lifted in September 2018.[65] Undoubtedly, the lifting of the suspension will enhance and re-position Nigeria's drive to combat ML/TF through exchange of sensitive information and intelligence with other FIUs. Yet the episode illustrates once again that Nigeria tends to be reactive and reluctant in the fight against ML/TF, with reform usually implemented on the pain of international sanction or threat of it. As well as giving the wrong signal externally, this policy cycle results in legislation being passed on the basis of the pressure from the global standard setters without proper appreciation of the fitness of these standards to local circumstances and prevailing realities. As rightly pointed out by Amali,[66]

> Legal and regulatory reforms to International Anti-Money Laundering initiatives can only be achieved with a proper appreciation of the culture and unique peculiarities of the receptive jurisdiction where emphasis is placed on the local environment rather than a mere response to international requirement for the sake of it.

Hence, Nigeria's AML/CFT legal frameworks might be said to represent a form of 'cosmetic compliance' for the approval of the global standard setters. Ironically and hypocritically, the same developed countries setting the standards have been providing safe havens for illicit funds from developing countries like Nigeria.[67]

It is also pertinent to note that lack of inclusive participation to the formulation of global AML/CFT standards and imposition of economic sanctions by global standard setters, such as FATF on non-cooperative countries have been regarded as a breach of sovereignty norm[68] and even neo-colonialist.[69] More inclusive international cooperation would entail the following advantages. First, every country could bring forward perspectives about the peculiarities of their domestic challenges that could be factored into formulating the global AML/CFT standards. Second, inclusive participation would facilitate some sense of belonging and entitlement which would assist collaborative enforcement. Third, inclusive participation would engender transparency which has been lacking in the activities of the global regulatory bodies, such as FATF.[70] Lastly, participatory approaches could build consensus for AML/CFT drives and other associated reforms.

65 Egmont Group's Co-Chairs, 'Statement 25th Plenary of the Egmont Group of Financial Intelligence Unit' (<https://egmontgroup.org/en/filedepot_download/1659/58>, 5 October 2018).

66 Amali (fn 10) 21.

67 Organisation for Economic Co-operation and Development (OECD), Illicit Financial Flows from Developing Countries: Measuring OECD Responses (2014) (<http://www.oecd.org/corruption/Illicit_Financial_Flows_from_Developing_Countries.pdf>).

68 Hülsse, R., 'Even clubs can't do without legitimacy: Why the anti-money laundering blacklist was suspended' (2008) 2(4) *Regulation and Governance* 459.

69 Amali (fn 10) 136.

70 Alldridge, P., *What Went Wrong With Money Laundering Law?* (Palgrave Macmillan, 2016) 11.

The next part of this chapter will be devoted to examining why Nigeria's internationally certified AML/CFT legal frameworks have not been effective.

The systemic challenges to the implementation of AML/CFT standards in Nigeria

It is not in dispute that Nigeria has demonstrated a strong commitment to the fight against ML/TF, but the problem has been ineffective enforcement.[71] In fact, the country has been adjudged as having the most elaborate legal framework on AML/CFT within the West Africa region by the Inter-governmental Action Group against Money Laundering in West Africa (GIABA).[72] However, it is clear that a robust legal framework is simply not enough since effective implementation is of equal importance. The main obstacle to the effective implementation of the AML/CFT global standards in Nigeria has been its suitability to the social-cultural, political, and economic realities of Nigeria. A number of factors can explain why the imposed global AML/CFT standards have not been effective in Nigeria.

First, the interplay between corruption and money laundering has been one of the main obstacles to Nigeria's AML/CFT legal framework. Corruption is inextricably linked to money laundering and provides the enabling environment for money laundering to thrive in Nigeria.[73] The reporting entities are susceptible to bribes to collude in money laundering by refraining from reporting suspicious transactions or by tipping off clients about investigations.[74] Corruption also exists in the judicial sphere. The discovery of huge sums of money in raw cash[75] in the residential apartments of some of the serving justices of the superior courts during the sting operation conducted by the Department of State Services (DSS) in October 2016 exposed the alarming level of judicial corruption.[76] The rot in the judiciary reached its climax with the recent trial and conviction of the chief justice of Nigeria on April 18, 2019, by the Code of Conduct Tribunal on allegation of non-assets declaration (subject to appeal).[77]

71 See Amobi, C., 'Money laundering regulation in Nigeria: The problems with enforcement, the British connection and global efforts' (2010) 21(6) *European Business Law Review* 827.

72 GIABI, Anti-money Laundering and Combating the Financing of Terrorism Mutual Evaluation Report 2008 (<https://www.giaba.org/media/f/299_Mutual%20Evaluation%20Report%20of%20Nigeria.pdf>) 14.

73 See Mugarua, N., 'Uncoupling the relationship between corruption and money laundering crimes' (2016) 24(1) *Journal of Financial Regulation and Compliance* 74.

74 See Chaikin, D., 'Commercial corruption and money laundering: a preliminary analysis' (2008) 15(3) *Journal of Financial Crime* 269.

75 In the course of the operation, the DSS claimed it recovered $800,000 (£645,200); see BBC News, 'Nigeria seizes $800,000 in "anti-corruption raids" on judges' (<http://www.bbc.co.uk/news/world-africa-37603857>, 9 October 2016).

76 *Ibid.*

77 BBC News, 'Nigeria's top Judge Walter Onnoghen to Forfeit Bank Accounts' (<http://www.bbc.com/news/world-africa-47974690>, 18 April 2019).

Another major challenge militating against effective implementation of Nigeria's AML/CFT legal framework is the lack of political will to drive the process. As rightly pointed out by Brinkerhoff, successful anti-corruption efforts depend upon a strong political will.[78] In Nigeria, being connected to the ruling political class provides a safe haven to escape criminal prosecution.[79] A recent statement credited to the chairman of the current ruling party in Nigeria (the All Progressives Congress) tellingly stated, when welcoming new members to the party, that politicians' sins are forgiven when they join the ruling party.[80]

Closely associated with the lack of political will is the entrenched immunity clause in section 308 of the Nigerian Constitution.[81] The concept of immunity in section 308 of the 1999 Constitution was well elucidated by the Supreme Court in the case of *Bola Tinubu v IMB Securities Ltd*.[82] 'The immunity clause is meant to provide a shield for the person of the President, Vice President, Governor or Deputy Governor from frivolous or vexatious litigation in respect of personal or criminal proceedings that would distract him from the serious business of governance.' However, this purpose is manipulated by the chief executives to promote injustice and impunity. According to Asabor, the use of the protective shield of constitutional immunity as a legislative instrument in defence of corruption and money laundering by crooked public officials has attained an alarming scale and frequency.[83] Furthermore, when the corrupt officials leave public office and lose immunity, it is often too late to prosecute them as evidence is lost, and witnesses die or are otherwise unavailable. Given that the political elites are in the habit of abusing the constitutional immunity clause, it has negatively impacted on the fight against money laundering and needs to be reformed.[84]

Another recent and growing trend which has been seen as the mockery of the administration of criminal justice system in Nigeria is the concept of plea-bargaining as provided for under section 270 of the Administration of Criminal Justice Act, 2015.[85] The concept of plea bargain has been criticised for being used

78 Brinkerhoff, D.W. and Kulibaba, N.P., 'Perspectives on participation in economic policy reform in Africa' (1996) 31(3) *Studies in Comparative International Development* 123.

79 Soriwei, F., 'EFCC probes Buhari's ministers for corruption' (<https://punchng.com/efcc-probes-buharis-ministers-corruption/>, 16 October 2016).

80 Sunday, N., 'Once you join APC, your sins are forgiven; Oshiomole says as PDP lambasts him' (<http://www.vanguardngr.com/2019/01/once-you-join-apc-your-sins-are-forgiven-oshiomhole-says-as-pdp-lambasts-him/>, 18 January 2019).

81 Constitution of the Federal Republic of Nigeria 1999 (as amended).

82 [2000] 7 NWLR (Pt.767)581.

83 Asabor, I., 'Immunity in international law' *The Vanguard Newspaper* (2 October 2002).

84 GIABI (fn72) 14.

85 By s.270, 'Notwithstanding anything in this Act or in any other law, the prosecutor may receive and consider a plea bargain from a defendant charged with an offence either directly from the defendant or on his behalf; or offer a plea bargain to a defendant charged with an offence where the prosecutor is of the view that the offer or acceptance of a plea bargain is in the interest of justice, the public interest, public policy and the need to prevent abuse of legal process.'

to provide soft-landing for influential elitist law-breakers.[86] An illustration is the case of John Yusuf, a former assistant to director of the Police Pension Board.[87] Yusuf had been accused of embezzling ₦ 32.8 billion. He entered into a plea-bargaining agreement, consequent upon which he was sentenced to two years' imprisonment or an option of paying ₦ 750,000 as fine. As expected, he instantly paid the fine.[88] Another case is that of Lucky Igbinedion, the former governor of Edo State. Having been accused of looting approximately ₦ 4.4 billion, he entered into a plea-bargain and was fined the sum of ₦ 3.5 million whilst he forfeited three landed properties to the Federal Government of Nigeria.[89] In this way,[90]

> a common goat or yam thief goes to jail while the white or blue collar criminal is given a mere symbolic sentence, most of which is easier served in pleasurably surrounding or offered the opportunity of fines in lieu of incarceration.

The lack of synergy between investigative and law enforcement agencies has also been identified as one of the reasons why the AML/CFT legal frameworks have not been effective in Nigeria. The offence of money laundering is information driven, and the inability of the regulatory agencies to collaborate and harness meaningful information is detrimental to the effective implementation of the AML/CFT legal framework.[91]

Closely associated to lack of synergy is shoddy investigation and weak institutions leading to low conviction rates.[92] The typical practice in Nigeria is to arrest first and conduct trial on the pages of newspapers before looking for incriminating evidence against the accused, a practice which is usually counterproductive.

Lastly, the issue of poor standard of living is also a key factor militating against effective implementation of the AML/CFT legal frameworks in Nigeria. A poorly

86 On the other side of the spectrum, arguments have been advanced in support of plea bargaining in that it saves time and resources for the state and helps in decongesting the courts' criminal docket.

87 Nnanna, O., 'Beyond the thief and the judge' 4 February 2013 (<http://www.vanguardngr.com/2013/02/beyond-the-thief-and-the-judge/>, 4 February 2013).

88 The Court of Appeal Abuja Division increased the sentence; Yusuf will now serve a six-year prison sentence and pay a fine of ₦ 22.9 billion (<http://www.vanguardngr.com/2018/03/john-yusuf-pension-thief-refund-n22-9b-jailed-6-years/>, 22 April 2018). Another disturbing example is former inspector general of Nigeria's Police Tafa Balogun, who embezzled billions of Naira belonging to the Police Force and in 2005 was handed a six-month jail term for each of the eight counts as well as a fine of ₦ 500,000 for each count. The terms were, however, to run concurrently. See <http://www.socialistnigeria.org/paper/2005/nov-dec/2.html>, 2005.

89 *Federal Republic of Nigeria v Lucky Igbinedion* (2014) LPELR 22760.

90 Oyebode, A., 'Plea bargaining, public service rules and criminal justice in Nigeria' (<http://www.nigeriavillagesquare.com/articles/plea-bargaining-public-service-rules-and-criminal-justice-in-nigeria.html>, 13 December 2010).

91 Mugarura, N., *The Global Anti-Money Laundering Regulatory Landscape in Less Developed Countries* (Ashgate, 2012).

92 Adeniyi, N.M., Zul Kepli, M.Y., and Mohd Yasin, N., 'Money laundering: The paradox of deterrence mechanism' (2016) 11(3) *International Journal of Business, Economics and Law* 45.

paid civil servant has the tendency to compromise on integrity and consequently jeopardise the efforts to stamp out money laundering and other financial crimes.

Conclusion

This chapter has examined Nigeria's AML/CFT legal frameworks and its ineffective implementation on account of corruption, weak institutions, political interference, and lack of political will. The chapter also considered the suspension of Nigeria from the Egmont Group, its implication and the legislative response culminating in the NFIU Act. It is believed that, with the enactment of the NFIU Act and Nigeria regaining its membership in the Egmont Group, the NFIU will resume its autonomous status with full benefits of being a member of the Egmont Group. It might even be able to promote a better synergy between law enforcement agencies in the area of financial intelligence gathering in Nigeria.

More generally, Nigeria's AML/CFT legal frameworks have largely been influenced by the need to comply with global standards without due regard to its local peculiarities. Unless Nigeria tackles the myriad perennial struggles against corruption, which are reinforced by socio-economic conditions, the fight against ML/TF will be compromised. This chapter also advocates for inclusive participation and deliberation in the formulation of global standards and for the developed countries to shut their borders against illicit transfer of laundered funds from developing countries in order to make the global fight against ML/TF more effective.

17 The Qatar crisis, legitimacy, and the use of sanctions against terrorist financing

Ahmed Almutawa

Introduction

On June 5, 2017, a coalition consisting of Saudi Arabia, the United Arab Emirates (UAE), Bahrain, and Egypt instigated political and economic measures against Qatar, accusing the country of supporting and financing terrorist and extremist Islamist groups. These measures effected prohibitions on travel and residency, the provision of services, and the importation and exportation of goods.[1] They represented the culmination of an ongoing disagreement between the coalition countries and Qatar that had, in March 2014, seen Saudi Arabia, Bahrain, and the UAE withdraw their ambassadors from Qatar.

The diplomatic response in 2014 followed the failure of a secret agreement signed in Riyadh in November 2013[2] in which Qatar had agreed not to support the Muslim Brotherhood or any other groups or individuals 'that threaten the security and stability of the Council states.' A supplemental agreement of January 2014 emphasised, *inter alia*, the obligation not to provide such groups with a safe haven, financial or other support, or a media platform.[3] In November 2014, a new agreement affirmed Qatar's commitment to the first Riyadh Agreement aimed at preserving the unity of the Gulf Cooperation Council and the stability and security of its individual states.[4] This agreement, however, proved to be just a

1 Royal Embassy of Saudi Arabia, 'Kingdom of Saudi Arabia Cuts Off Diplomatic and Consular Relations with the State of Qatar' (<http://www.saudiembassy.net/news/kingdom-saudi-arabia-cuts-diplomatic-and-consular-relations-state-qatar>, 5 June 2017); World Trade Organization, *United Arab Emirates: Measures Relating to Trade in Goods and Services, and Trade-Related Aspects of Intellectual Property Rights: Request for the Establishment of a Panel By Qatar* (WT/DS526/2, 2017).

2 Hassan, I.K., 'GCC's 2014 crisis: Causes issues and solutions' in Abdullah, J. and Chabkoun, M. (eds.), *Gulf Cooperation Council's Challenges and Prospects* (Al Jazeera Center for Studies, 2015) 78, 80.

3 Sciutto, J. and Herb, J., 'Exclusive: The secret documents that help explain the Qatar crisis' *CNN Politics* (<https://edition.cnn.com/2017/07/10/politics/secret-documents-qatar-crisis-gulf-saudi/index.html>, 11 July 2017).

4 Katzman, K., 'Qatar: Governance, Security and US Policy' *Congressional Research Service Report* (R44533, 2017) 8.

temporary fix, and Qatar's alleged failure to abide by its terms eventually resulted in the sanctions.

The measures imposed by the coalition are most appropriately characterised as unilateral sanctions. They are an attempt by a single state, or group of states, to exert their power to coerce another state to change its policies without relying on the collective authority of an international body, such as the United Nations (UN).[5] Their use by the coalition is interesting because, at least in the context of support for terrorism, the trend since 9/11 has been to move away from unilateral sanctions aimed at a national government towards multilateral, smart, or targeted sanctions aimed at specific groups or individuals (with the proviso that state officials are often within the list).[6] Thus, whilst their use is not novel, the coalition's imposition of unilateral sanctions on Qatar runs counter to that trend and may be seen as a regressive response to the failure of the international community's use of targeted sanctions against terrorist financiers who have allegedly found a safe haven in Qatar.

The question addressed by this chapter is whether this use of sanctions is a legitimate response to Qatar's alleged failure to fulfil its international obligations on counter terrorism. The lack of publicly available, reliable information means it is not possible to reach a scholarly judgement regarding the allegations themselves. Other commentators have already carried out limited assessments,[7] from which it may be concluded that there is some substance to them but not sufficient to reach a definitive conclusion. As such, the starting point of this chapter is hypothetically to accept the veracity of the allegations and to focus on the legitimacy of the response. The chapter is divided into three parts. The first part explains the value of legitimacy and its importance to international relations. The second part considers the legality of the coalition's use of sanctions. The third part considers the wider aspects of the legitimacy of the sanctions.

The nature and value of legitimacy to international relations

Legitimacy is essentially a judgement on the rectitude of the use of power,[8] which relies on an evaluation of what is 'proper, or appropriate within some socially

5 Beaucillon, C., 'Practice makes perfect, eventually? Unilateral state sanctions and the extraterritorial effects of national legislation' in Ronzitti, N. (ed.), *Coercive Diplomacy, Sanctions and International Law* (Brill, 2016) 103, 104.

6 Happold, M., 'Economic sanctions and international law: An introduction' in Happold, M. and Eden, P. (eds.), *Economic Sanctions and International Law* (Hart, 2016) 28, 34.

7 Orton, K., *Qatar and the Gulf Crisis* (Henry Jackson Society, 2017) 30; Shideler, K., Froehlke, S., and Fischer, S., *The Role of Select Non-Governmental Organizations in Doha's Support for Terrorism* (<https://www.centerforsecuritypolicy.org/2017/09/26/center-catalogues-allegations-of-qatars-terrorism-support/>, 26 September 2017) 6; Naheem, M.A., 'The dramatic rift and crisis between Qatar and the Gulf Cooperation Council (GCC) of June 2017' (2017) 14 *International Journal of Disclosure and Governance* 265.

8 Coicaud, J.-M., *Legitimacy and Politics: A contribution to the Study of Political Right and Political Responsibility* (Cambridge University Press, 2002) 10.

constructed system of norms, values, beliefs and definitions.'[9] Determined by the interaction between the boundaries of legal, moral, and constitutional norms,[10] its evaluation is often a matter of degree between right and wrong.[11] For current purposes, it can be depicted as engaging with three aspects of a political measure: the implementing process, the authority for implementation, and the substance of the measure.[12]

The first of these requires that the measure is consistent with the rule of law,[13] being both legal and procedurally just. In the present context, which is concerned with the actions of one state towards another, the second element requires that there is some form of collective authority, reflecting accountability and collective approval. This may be achieved through international bodies, such as the UN,[14] or the Non-Aligned Movement (NAM).[15] UN conventions, for example, reflect a collective authority that bolsters the legitimacy of embodied norms.[16] Less formally, collective authority may be achieved pragmatically through the support of other states. The third element requires that the measure is substantively just, which means that it must protect 'at least the most basic human rights' of those affected by the measure.[17]

The importance of legitimacy lies in its power to encourage normative compliance,[18] particularly with those institutionalised norms that define the relationships and interactions between states as entities within the international community.[19] The pressure to comply comes both from the moral duty to do the right thing and from the consequences, which may be beneficial where the state's behaviour is legitimate but detrimental where the behaviour is illegitimate. For example, policies perceived as illegitimate may affect internal political stability

9 Suchman, M.C., 'Managing Legitimacy: Strategic and Institutional Approaches' (1995) 20 *Academy of Management Review* 571, 574.
10 Clark, I., *Legitimacy in International Society* (Oxford University Press, 2007) 19–20.
11 Franck, T.M., *The Power of Legitimacy among Nations* (Oxford University Press, 1990) 26.
12 Weber, M., *Economy and Society* (University of California Press, 1978) 215; Weber, M., 'Politics as a vocation',' in Owen, D. and Strong, T.B. (eds.), *The Vocation Lectures* (Hackett, 2004) 32, 34–38.
13 Beetham, D., 'Max Weber and the legitimacy of the modern state' (1991) 13 *Analyse & Kritik* 34, 43.
14 Mulligan, S.P., 'The uses of legitimacy in international relations' (2005) 34 *Millennium: Journal of International Studies* 349, 363–364.
15 Vieira, M.A., 'Understanding resilience in international relations: The non-aligned movement and ontological security' (2016) 18 *International Studies Review* 290, 291.
16 Shaw, M., 'Genocide and large-scale human rights violations' in Kaldor, M. and Rangelov, I. (eds.), *The Handbook of Global Security Policy* (Wiley Blackwell, 2014) 145, 146.
17 Buchanan, A., 'Political legitimacy and democracy' (2002) 112 *Ethics* 689, 703–704.
18 Hurd, I., 'Legitimacy and authority in international politics' (1999) 53 *International Organization* 379, 391.
19 Dingworth, K. and Pattberg, P., 'World politics and organizational fields: The case of transnational sustainability governance' (2009) 15 *European Journal of International Relations* 707, 720; Vetterlein, A. and Moschella, M., 'International organizations and organizational fields: Explaining policy change in the IMF' (2014) 6 *European Political Science Review* 143, 149.

and the support of citizens.[20] At the international level, the use of illegitimate measures may lose the support of other states[21] or even incur penalties, such as through the use of sanctions. In the present case, the coalition's sanctions may be similarly characterised as an attempt to secure Qatar's compliance with its obligations under the Riyadh Agreements and international law. However, to avoid condemnation by the international community, this use of sanctions must at least be lawful, a requirement which will be examined next.

The legality of the resort to sanctions against Qatar

Although the law on unilateral sanctions remains contested,[22] under the principle of sovereignty, it is 'well-established' that each state has the 'right . . . to determine . . . [its] own trading partners.'[23] Sovereignty, however, is constrained by various international legal obligations. One restraint is the General Agreement on Tariffs and Trade (GATT).[24] Of relevance is Article 21 ('Security Exceptions') by which

> nothing in this Agreement shall be construed . . . (b) to prevent any contracting party from taking any action which it considers necessary for the protection of its essential security interests . . . (iii) taken in time of war or other emergency in international relations.[25]

Article 21 was successfully relied on by the United States to defend its general embargo against Nicaragua from 1985 to 1990, which was intended to undermine the Sandinista government.[26] The Qatari dispute could be said to represent an 'emergency in international relations,' and the use of sanctions to secure Qatar's compliance with its international obligation to counter terrorism arguably falls under the exception allowed for measures 'necessary' to protect 'essential security interests.' Another relevant obligation arises from the ban on Qatar using coalition airspace, which might fall under the 'emergency conditions' of

20 Beetham, D., *The Legitimation of Power* (MacMillan, 1991) 33; Tyler, T.R., *Why People Cooperate: The Role of Social Motivations* (Princeton University Press, 2011) 3–4; Morris, C., 'State legitimacy and social order' in Kuhnelt, J. (ed.), *Political Legitimization without Morality* (Springer, 2008) 15, 16.

21 Scott, S.V. and Ambler, O., 'Does legality *really* matter? Accounting for the decline in US Foreign Policy legitimacy following the 2003 invasion of Iraq' (2007) 13 *European Journal of International Relations* 67, 68.

22 Happold (fn 6) 37.

23 Henderson, J.C., 'Legality of economic sanctions under international law: The case of Nicaragua' (1986) 43 *Washington and Lee Law Review* 167, 179.

24 GATT 1947, 55 UN Treaty Series 194, as incorporated in GATT 1994, 1867 UN Treaty Series 187.

25 WTO, 'Article XXI Security Exceptions' in *GATT Analytical Index* (WTO, 1998) 599 (<http://www.wto.org/english/res_e/booksp_e/gatt_ai_e/art21_e.pdf>).

26 Happold (fn 6) 33.

Article 89 of the Convention on Civil Aviation 1944.[27] However, rather than focusing on these specific obligations, this chapter addresses the general legality of the coalition's use of unilateral sanctions.

It has been suggested that the sanctions are an 'abusive or mala fide (bad faith) interference in Qatari affairs.'[28] Indeed, it has been claimed that the dispute is more about geo-politics, 'regime security,' Qatar's unilateral policies, or the regional hegemony of Saudi Arabia than about Qatar's support for terrorism *per se*.[29] More specifically the coalition's position on the Muslim Brotherhood may also be open to criticism. Although designated a terrorist organisation by Egypt and Saudi Arabia, it has not been designated by the UN or the United States. The United Kingdom also rejected the option of banning the Muslim Brotherhood, which is characterised as a political rather than terrorist organisation.[30] Likewise, the coalition's initial demand that Qatar shut down the Al-Jazeera news network may be characterised as an attempt to control foreign media contrary to the spirit of international law rather than a legitimate measure to counter extremism and terrorism.[31]

Rather than speculating further on the coalition's motives, this analysis focuses on the legitimacy of the coalition's sanctions as a lawful form of 'self-help' used 'for the limited purposes of securing the wrongdoing state's compliance with its primary and secondary obligations.'[32] Although the crisis appears to have been triggered by the payment of a ransom 'negotiated by Qatar and Iran' to Hay'at Tahrir al-Sham (an al Qa'ida ally) for the release of a hunting party,[33] the present dispute derives from the 2013/2014 Riyadh Agreements.[34] It should, however, be acknowledged again that the discussion that follows is constrained by the limited public information.[35]

27 Sreejith, S.G., 'Legality of the Gulf Ban on Qatari Flights: State Sovereignty at crossroads' (2018) 43 *Air & Space Law* 191.

28 Hofer, A. and Ferro, L., 'Sanction Qatar: Coercive interference in the state's domaine reserve' *European Journal of International Law Blog* (<http://www.ejiltalk.org/sanctioning-qatar-coercive-interference-in-the-states-domaine-reserve/>, 30 June 2017).

29 Fuller, G.E., Entekhabifard, C., Gorvett, J. and Schatz, J., 'Four views: Crisis in the gulf' (2017) 36.5 *Washington Report on Middle East Affairs* 20; Lynch, M., 'Three big lessons of the Qatar crisis' in Lynch, M. and Dahle, S. (eds.), *The Qatar Crisis* (POMEPS Briefings 31, 2017) 14, 15 (<https://pomeps.org/2017/10/12/the-qatar-crisis-pomeps-brief-31/>).

30 House of Commons Foreign Affairs Committee, *Political Islam,' and the Muslim Brotherhood Review* (2016–17, HC 118) paras. 33–50.

31 See UN Universal Declaration of Human Rights 1948, Article 19; International Telecommunication Union, International Telecommunication Convention (Nairobi, 1982) Article 35.

32 Trapp, K.N., *International Terrorism* (Oxford University Press, 2011) 183.

33 Orton, K., *Qatar and the Gulf Crisis* (Henry Jackson Society, 2017) 30. Those affected involved mainly Qatari citizens, including some members of the royal family.

34 CNN, Translated versions (<http://i2.cdn.turner.com/cnn/2017/images/07/10/translation.of.agreementsupdated.pdf>, 2017); see text at fn 2–4.

35 Compare *Military and Paramilitary Activities in and against Nicaragua (Nicaragua v United States)* (1986) ICJ Reports 14, [57].

Whilst the Riyadh Agreements allowed for 'GCC heads of states [to] take all the necessary measures against other non-abiding states,' they failed to provide for an explicit dispute resolution mechanism including sanctions. Given that all the states are members of the UN, any such measures would also need to be consistent with Articles 2(3) and 33 of the UN Charter. States are required 'first of all' to 'settle their international disputes by peaceful means' such as negotiation, mediation and arbitration. Article 33, however, also allows states to resolve disputes by 'peaceful means of their own choice.' The question, therefore, is whether sanctions are unlawful under the UN Charter as non-peaceful mechanisms.

Sanctions may normally be characterised as 'peaceful' when they do not involve military action. It has, however, been argued that because they are coercive and intended to cause harm, they should always be considered non-peaceful.[36] Unfortunately, the 'lack of definitional specificity' limits the value of the UN Charter for 'delineating boundaries' for the use of coercive sanctions.[37] Furthermore, even if sanctions are 'unquestionably incompatible with . . . article 2(3),' the UN Charter does not preclude their use as a form of self-help.[38] It is, therefore, necessary to look beyond Articles 2(3) and 33 and to consider whether the sanctions are consistent with the principle of non-intervention, which reflects the spirit of the UN Charter.[39]

The principle of non-intervention protects 'the right' of states to function 'without outside interference' by prohibiting other states from coercively intervening in matters that fall within the legitimate exercise of the affected state's sovereignty.[40] Whilst the use of coercive sanctions as 'cudgels for the attainment of foreign policy goals' is a *prima facie* breach of the principle,[41] this conclusion only applies where the intention is to interfere with, or subordinate, the legitimate sovereignty of the targeted country.[42] Where sanctions are used to constrain the behaviour of a foreign state that has exceeded its sovereign authority, and support for terrorism is almost certainly contrary to international law,[43] then the

36 Reisman, W.M., 'Sanctions and international law' (2009) 4 *Intercultural Human Rights Review* 9, 20.

37 Joyner, C.J., 'The transnational Boycott as economic coercion in international law: Policy, place and practice' (1984) 17 *Vanderbilt Journal of Transnational Law* 205, 242.

38 Blum, Y.Z., 'Economic Boycotts in international law' (1977) 12 *Texas International Law Journal* 5, 14, 15.

39 Kinacioglu, M., 'The principle of non-intervention at the United Nations: The charter framework and the legal debate' (Summer, 2005) *Perceptions* 15, 16.

40 *Military and Paramilitary Activities in and against Nicaragua* (*Nicaragua v United States*) (1986) ICJ Reports 14, [202–205].

41 Joyner (fn 37), 230.

42 UNGA, Resolution No. 66/186, *Unilateral economic measures as a means of political and economic coercion against developing countries* (2012).

43 UNGA Resolution No. 25/2625, *Declaration on Principles of International Law Concerning Friendly Relations and Cooperation Among States in Accordance with the Charter of the UN* (1970); UN GA Resolution No. 67/1, *Declaration of the High-Level Meeting of the General Assembly on the Rule of Law at the National and International Levels* (2012); UN SC Resolution No. 1373 *On threats to international peace and security caused by terrorist acts*

sanctions may be considered lawful as a form of self-help against the interfering state.[44] Indeed, such measures 'are a feature of a decentralised system by which injured States may seek to vindicate their rights and to restore the legal relations with the responsible State which has been ruptured by the internationally wrongful act.'[45] Whilst not prohibited by the UN Charter, they should, however, be necessary and proportionate to the circumstances of the situation.[46]

Bearing in mind the 'notoriously difficult task' of determining the intent of a state,[47] it is, nevertheless, important to note that the coalition justified its sanctions as a response to Qatar's alleged failures to meet its counter terrorism obligations under international law and the Riyadh Agreements. Since the impact of terrorism extends beyond the individual coalition states, the countermeasures might also benefit the region and the wider international community. Given that the only explicit mechanism provided for by the Riyadh Agreements was to allow the GCC heads of state to take necessary measures against non-abiding states, it is arguable that the sanctions are justified. However, it might also be argued that the coalition should have attempted to secure the authority of the UN for multilateral sanctions before implementing unilateral measures. This argument may be countered by the reasonable prediction that because it is unlikely that there would be support from the international community, the UN would not have authorised multilateral sanctions against Qatar. Pragmatically, this made unilateral sanctions the only realistic option for securing Qatar's compliance given the failure of the Riyadh Agreements and ongoing diplomacy. Although both Qatar and the coalition countries have presented their cases during the General Debates of the UN General Assembly's 72nd and 73rd sessions, the UN has neither condemned the use of sanctions against Qatar nor formally called for them to be lifted. The scope and impact of the sanctions, however, have raised 'concerns' for the UN special rapporteur on the negative impact of unilateral coercive measures on the enjoyment of human rights.[48]

In so far as the sanctions are a response to ongoing underlying support for terrorism (especially if ideological more than practical) rather than as protection against any 'grave and imminent peril,'[49] reliance on necessity as a justification appears to be ruled out. There are, however, two relevant forms of self-help permissible under international law.[50]

First, sanctions may be justified as an act of retorsion, but crucially, the applied '"unfriendly" conduct' must remain consistent with the state's international

(2001); UN International Convention for the Suppression of the Financing of Terrorism 1999 (UN Doc A/54/49).

44 Joyner (fn 37), 232.

45 UN, *Book 25: Materials on the Responsibility of States for Internationally Wrongful Acts* (2012) 304.

46 Blum (fn 38) 14.

47 *Ibid.*, 13.

48 *Report* (A/HRC/39/54, 2018) paras. 9–10.

49 ILC, Responsibility of States for Internationally Wrongful Acts 2001, Article 25.

50 Trapp (fn 32) 183–192.

obligations.[51] One of the criticisms of the coalition's sanctions is that they have significantly interfered with individual human rights. Since it is arguable that all states within the international community of the UN have an obligation not to breach the human rights of any individual that might be affected by the sanctions,[52] full justification of the coalition's sanctions as acts of retorsion may be difficult.

The second option is to justify sanctions as countermeasures.[53] As countermeasures, the sanctions should comply with provisions of the International Law Commission's (ILC) Code on the Responsibility of States for Internationally Wrongful Acts 2001.[54] This requires any such measures to be adopted in response to the target state's wrongdoing 'to induce that State to comply with its obligations.'[55] Consistent with the ruling in the *Air Services* case,[56] the measures must be proportionate, determined by the extent of any injury suffered and the 'gravity' of the target state's wrongful act.[57] It 'must take into account the importance of the positions of principle' and not simply the more measurable harm.[58] Furthermore, the power to take countermeasures does not affect the implementing states' obligation to protect fundamental human rights.[59] Finally, the countermeasures should be reversible[60] and should not be implemented without notification and the offer to negotiate with the target state.[61]

Turning to the proportionality of the sanctions, they were imposed with the aim of securing Qatar's commitment to its international obligations to respect the sovereignty of other states and to counter terrorism. Following the *Air Services* case, the importance of the principles of sovereignty, national security, and stability support the view that the sanctions are proportionate, particularly given the potential cost to human life caused by terrorism. Furthermore, since the sanctions involve a limited number of states, and given that the coalition has

51 *Ibid.*, 184; UN, *Draft articles on Responsibility of States for Internationally Wrongful Acts, with commentaries* (2008) 128.

52 Special Rapporteur, *Report on the negative impact of unilateral coercive measures on the enjoyment of human rights* (A/70/345, 2015) para. 13; Special Rapporteur, *Report on the negative impact of unilateral coercive measures on the enjoyment of human rights*, (A/HRC/36/44, 2017) para. 33.

53 *Air Service Agreement of 27 March 1946 (USA v France)* (1978) 18 Reports of International Arbitral Awards 417, [80].

54 Happold (fn 6) 29.

55 ILC, Responsibility of States for Internationally Wrongful Acts 2001, Article 49.

56 *Air Service Agreement of 27 March 1946 (USA v France)* (1978) 18 Reports of International Arbitral Awards 417.

57 ILC, Responsibility of States for Internationally Wrongful Acts 2001, Article 51.

58 *Air Service Agreement of 27 March 1946 (USA v France)* (1978) 18 Reports of International Arbitral Awards 417, [83].

59 ILC, Responsibility of States for Internationally Wrongful Acts 2001, Article 50.

60 *Case Concerning the Gabčíkovo – Nagymaros Project (Hungary v Slovakia)* (1997) ICJ Reports 7, [87].

61 United Nations, ILC, Responsibility of States for Internationally Wrongful Acts 2001, Article 52.

not implemented a blockade on trade between Qatar and third countries, the sanctions have a limited, albeit significant, impact on individual human rights. Furthermore, since they can be lifted, the sanctions satisfy the requirement of reversibility. Given the annual review under the Riyadh Agreements,[62] the likelihood that parties to the Agreements have made diplomatic attempts to persuade Qatar to amend its behaviour, and the public announcement of sanctions,[63] there was adequate notification.[64] Finally, the issuing of, and willingness to amend,[65] conditions for resolving the dispute,[66] and the coalition's willingness to engage with Kuwait's attempts to negotiate a resolution, all suggest that the coalition is acting in good faith to settle the dispute. It may, therefore, be concluded that there is an arguable case for endorsing the sanctions as lawful countermeasures. This conclusion is, however, contingent on the veracity and strength of the allegations of terrorism support made against Qatar, which have been hypothetically accepted for the purpose of this analysis, but which are fiercely disputed by Qatar and its allies. There are no official published data on terrorist attacks or activities linked to funding from Qatar-based financiers. The failure to publish such data weakens the coalition's position. It should, however, be noted that details of a Qatari connection have been published in connection with specific incidents, such as the Qatari businessman, Muhammad Sulaiman Haidar, who was linked to the 2015 terrorist bombing of Sitra, and allegedly financed terrorist activity in Bahrain between 2010–2015.[67] If alternative factual explanations for the coalition reaction are assumed to be more powerful factors, such as the attempt to protect Saudi hegemony, then the case for sanctions would be compromised.[68]

The legitimacy of the sanctions against Qatar

Although the sanctions may be characterised as lawful countermeasures based on assumed facts, two further factors must be considered. The first is the presence of collective authority. Legitimacy may be affected by the level of support within the international community for the use of sanctions to resolve disputes between states. The second factor is the impact of the sanctions on the innocent citizens of the targeted state, which will largely be determined by the impact on individual human rights and any measures implemented by the states imposing

62 As specified in the 2014 supplemental agreement: CNN, Translated versions (<http://i2.cdn.turner.com/cnn/2017/images/07/10/translation.of.agreementsupdated.pdf>, 5 March 2019).

63 See fn 1.

64 *Case Concerning the Gabčíkovo – Nagymaros Project* (fn 60), [84].

65 Gardner, F., 'Saudi-led bloc modifies demands to end Qatar crisis' *BBC News* (<www.bbc.com/news/world-middle-east-40654023>, 19 July 2017).

66 *Air Service Agreement of 27 March 1946 (USA v France)* (1978) 18 Reports of International Arbitral Awards 417, [91].

67 See, 'Qatar financed terrorism in Bahrain and support for the plot to overthrow the regime' (8 August 2017) *Gulf News* (<http://akhbar-alkhaleej.com/news/article/1084397>).

68 See fn 29.

the sanctions to mitigate that impact. These factors will now be applied to the coalition's sanctions.

The use of unilateral sanctions is controversial.[69] There is a long history of their use as a tool of foreign policy, and some nations, such as the United States, remain willing to employ them. However, whilst not making them illegal per se, the UN has for many years passed an annual resolution urging the United States to end its sanctions against Cuba.[70] The UN opposition to unilateral sanctions is supported by many individual nations and by the NAM, which includes all four coalition countries as members. At its 17th Summit, the NAM 'oppose[d] and condemn[ed]' the use of unilateral coercive sanctions and emphasised the legitimacy that comes from using UN processes and procedures.[71] Thus no endorsement of the coalition's sanctions against Qatar can be found from either the UN or the NAM.

The lack of support or general authority for the use of unilateral sanctions is exacerbated by the inherent lack of specific collective authority for their use. It would have been better for the coalition to implement unilateral sanctions only after exhausting the possibility of securing multilateral sanctions, such as through the collective authority of the UN,[72] or through submitting the dispute to the Permanent Court of Arbitration, or the International Court of Justice (ICJ).[73]

Turning now to the substantive impact, the sanctions were effectively untargeted since they failed to discriminate between ordinary citizens and the state. This is inconsistent with the historical trend towards targeted sanctions.[74] As such, the coalition sanctions are open to criticism. However, they were implemented, at least in part, because of the ineffectiveness of UN targeted sanctions against terrorists and terrorist financiers provided with a safe haven in Qatar. Where targeted sanctions fail because the UN Security Council has been unwilling or unable to secure Qatar's cooperation, this provides at least some justification for the coalition states to resort to more general sanctions that do not rely on that cooperation. Nevertheless, because they avoid the widespread and indiscriminate impact on human rights, targeted sanctions remain more overtly legitimate than general sanctions. It would, therefore, have been better had the coalition sanctions been more acutely targeted at the Qatari government and its officials.

69 Hofer, A., 'The developed/developing divide on unilateral coercive measures: Legitimate enforcement or illegitimate intervention?' (2017) 16 *Chinese Journal of International Law* 175.

70 UN GA Resolution No. 69/180 *Human Rights and unilateral coercive measures* (2014); UN GA *Resolution on the Necessity of ending the economic, commercial and financial embargo imposed by the United States of America against Cuba* (A/73/L.3, 2018).

71 *17th Summit of Heads of State and Government of the Non-Aligned Movement*, 17–18th September 2016, Margarita, Venezuela (NAM 2016/CoB/DOC.1.Corr.1) para. 24.

72 Joyner, C.J., 'Sanctions, compliance and international law: Reflections on the United Nations' experience against Iraq' (1991) 32 *Virginia Journal of International Law* 1, 32.

73 Trapp (fn 32) 188.

74 Happold (fn 6) 34.

Under Article 50 of the ILC Code, sanctions may only be used as countermeasures provided they do not affect the implementing states' obligations to protect fundamental human rights. This raises the questions of what rights are fundamental and whose rights should be respected. As explained next, the rights most heavily impacted by the sanctions are the rights to education, family life, property; and employment. Rather than being absolute rights, like the right not to be tortured, the obligation to respect these rights may be qualified by countervailing state interests, such as national security, which may allow an interference with the right to be justified as necessary and proportionate.[75] Regarding the question of whose rights must be respected by the coalition, it is arguable that the obligations apply not only to those individuals within the state's territory but also extend extraterritorially to citizens of the targeted state where the sanctions impact on those individuals' human rights.[76]

According to the Technical Mission from the UN Office of the High Commissioner for Human Rights (which concluded that the sanctions were 'arbitrary' and 'non-targeted'), there are four types of victim arising from the coalition sanctions: Qataris expelled from coalition states, coalition state nationals who have felt compelled to leave Qatar, migrant workers in Qatar who have lost their employment, and citizens of all countries whose freedom of movement has been affected.[77] Regarding freedom of movement, it should be noted, that Article 13 of the Universal Declaration of Human Rights protects free movement within a particular state rather than between states. Since the sanctions only affect movement between Qatar and the coalition states, Article 13 is not infringed. Furthermore, the coalition has tried to protect the right to freedom of religion under Article 18, by officially allowing pilgrimages to holy cities in Saudi Arabia regardless of the restriction on travel between Qatar and the coalition states for any other purpose.[78]

Perhaps the greatest impact has been on the rights to private and family life, education, employment, and private ownership. In its second Report on the crisis,[79] the Qatari National Human Rights Committee (NHRC) received 480 complaints about the impact of the sanctions on individual families. These included families where the husband and wife were of different nationalities and felt compelled to separate to comply with the sanctions. The NHRC also recorded

75 *Ibid.*

76 Special Rapporteur, *Report on the negative impact of unilateral coercive measures on the enjoyment of human rights* (A/70/345, 2015) para. 13. Special Rapporteur, *Report on the negative impact of unilateral coercive measures on the enjoyment of human rights* (A/HRC/36/44, 2017) para. 33.

77 OHCHR Technical Mission, *Report on the impact of the Gulf Crisis on human rights* (December 2017) 5, 14–15.

78 Agence France-Presse in Riyadh, 'Saudi Arabia to open borders with Qatar to let pilgrims attend hajj' *The Guardian* (<http://www.theguardian.com/world/2017/aug/17/saudi-arabia-open-border-qatar-pilgrims-attend-hajj>, 17 August 2017).

79 NHRC, *Second Report Regarding the Human Rights Violations as a Result of the Blockade on the State of Qatar* (1 July 2017).

139 cases where the education of Qatari nationals had been interrupted by the sanctions, such as by disrupting their university studies with some allegedly losing deposits. Furthermore, the NHRC reported 101 complaints regarding loss of employment and 651 complaints about the impact of the sanctions on the ability to access or dispose of property held in one of the coalition's states. Of course, even in these cases, the interference with those qualified rights may arguably be justified in the interests of national and regional security and stability. Even so, these complaints highlight the impact of the sanctions on individual citizens.

Given that the intent behind the sanctions was to pressure the Qatari government, and the coalition has maintained that it 'stand[s] by the Qatari people,'[80] the impact on individual rights has weakened the legitimacy of the sanctions. This might have been mitigated through the establishment of a mechanism for dealing with human rights complaints arising out of the sanctions, particularly since there is currently no regional human rights court. The establishment of such a mechanism is important for two reasons. First, it provides an independent forum for assessing the issues and any individual complaints. Second, it provides an opportunity to limit the impact of the sanctions. For example, a regional human rights court could recommend special dispensation for families of split nationality or in cases where an individual's education would be critically disrupted. Where mitigation is not feasible, then compensation could be provided.

An independent mechanism for dealing with human rights issues, perhaps administered by a more neutral GCC state, such as Kuwait, which has already been acting as a mediator during the crisis,[81] would help to reinforce the legitimacy of the coalition's approach. Such a mechanism would also address the UN Technical Mission's criticism that the sanctions were arbitrary because, *inter alia*, they were imposed without 'any legal recourse' for affected individuals.[82] It might also have pre-empted the preliminary decision of the ICJ that, in relation to the UAE's obligations under the International Convention on the Elimination of All Forms of Racial Discrimination 1965, the sanctions raised plausible human rights issues that warranted an order of provisional measures to re-unite split nationality families and allow Qataris to continue their education.[83] It should further be noted that the UN special rapporteur has suggested that there should be a UN-managed register of all 'unilateral coercive measures likely to have a human rights impact' and a compensation commission for individual victims of

80 Bahrain Minister for Foreign Affairs, Statement before the UN General Assembly, 72nd Session, New York City (<http://www.mofa.gov.bh/Default.aspx?tabid=7824&language=en-US&ItemId=7942>, 23 September 2017).

81 Staff authors, 'Gulf Dispute: Weighing Kuwait and US Mediation Efforts' *Gulf International Forum* (<https://gulfif.com/gulf-dispute-weighing-kuwait-and-u-s-mediation-efforts/>, 13 September 2018).

82 OHCHR Technical Mission, *Report on the Impact of the Gulf Crisis on Human Rights* (December 2017) 14.

83 *Application of the International Convention on the Elimination of All Forms of Racial Discrimination (Qatar v United Arab Emirates): Request for the Indication of Provisional Measures* (23 July 2018) ICJ General List No. 172.

unilateral coercive measures.[84] With no obvious end to the crisis, the coalition should ask Kuwait to establish an independent commission along those lines in order to deal with individual complaints. To support an independent commission, the coalition should also make a commitment to ensure that any property affected by the sanctions is preserved and returned to their owners once the sanctions have been lifted.

Conclusion

This chapter has examined the ongoing crisis between Qatar and the coalition led by Saudi Arabia. The focus was on the legitimacy of the measures imposed by the coalition, which, as a controversial response to Qatar's alleged failure to effectively implement *targeted* sanctions, have had only limited success in encouraging Qatar to amend its counter terrorism laws and establish a national list of designated terrorists.[85] Nor has Qatar been persuaded to shift its wider policy stances, though it did sign a Memorandum of Understanding with the United States on July 11, 2017, which set out a commitment for counter-terrorist financing.[86] For the coalition, that mere promise was insufficient because of lack of trust in Qatar. It is argued that unilateral sanctions may be justified as lawful countermeasures in international law provided certain (highly disputed) factual assumptions are made. It was, however, noted that the sanctions lack collective accountability and authority and have significantly affected individual human rights. Given that these factors weaken the legitimacy of the coalition's approach, the sanctions may be characterised as no more than arguably legitimate.

The coalition could further enhance the legitimacy of its position by establishing an independent mechanism for dealing with the effect of the sanctions on individual human rights. It should have the power to investigate and adjudicate in individual cases and to make recommendations for special dispensations to mitigate the impact of the sanctions. It should also have the power to award compensation from a fund established by the coalition countries. Such an approach would help to preserve the legitimacy of the sanctions and reassure the international community that the measures are aimed at the Qatari government rather than its citizens.

84 Special Rapporteur on the negative impact of unilateral coercive measures on the enjoyment of human rights, *Report* (A/HRC/36/44, 2017) paras. 4, 41–47.

85 By Qatar Decree No 4 of 2017 to amend Law No 11 of 2004 on combating terrorism provision is made, for the definition of terrorism, asset freezing powers and a national terrorist designation list, which is a significant change from Qatar's previous approach but 'was published without an annex of persons or entities to be designated': Levitt, M., *Assessing the US-Qatar Relationship* (26 July 2017) Testimony submitted to the [US] House Foreign Affairs Subcommittee on the Middle East and North Africa 2.

86 Daugirdas, K. and Mortenson, J.D. (eds), 'United States and Qatar Sign Memorandum of understanding regarding terrorism financing' (2017) 111 *American Journal of International Law* 1023.

18 Iran responds

International counter-terrorism financing framework

Zeynab Malakoutikhah

Introduction

Iran has a long track record with regard to terrorism, both as a victim and as a state sponsor. As a victim, Iran has been exposed to violent threats from three dimensions: dissident nationalists, foreign terrorists, and separatist terrorists.[1] Conversely, accusations of terrorism against Iran relate to financial and military support for non-state militant actors, such as Hizballah, Hamas, and the Palestinian Islamic Jihad, which are internationally designated as terrorist groups.[2] Iranian officials deny these allegations and claim that 'Iran is in the frontline of combating terrorism and religious extremism in the Middle East for humanitarian and strategic reasons, not for sectarian and political ones.'[3] The core problem, which has led to Iran being unable to integrate at the international level and to consequent economic sanctions being imposed,[4] comes down to the definition of 'terrorism.' The main explanation from Iran is that the non-state militant actors which it supports seek the right to self-determination and self-defence in the face of Israeli occupation. Consequently, they should be labelled 'National Liberation Movements' (NLMs), not terrorist groups.

1 Tabatabai, A., 'Other side of the Iranian coin: Iran's counterterrorism apparatus' (2018) 41(1&2) *Journal of Strategic Studies* 181; Malakoutikhah, Z., 'Iran: Sponsoring or combating terrorism?' (2018) *Studies in Conflict and Terrorism* (<https://doi.org/10.1080/1057610X.2018.1506560>).

2 Levitt, M., 'Hezbollah finances,' in Giraldo, J.K. and Trinkemas, H.A. (eds.), *Terrorism Financing and State Responses* (Stanford University Press, 2007); Byman, D., 'Iran, terrorism, and weapons of mass destruction' (2008) 31(3) *Studies in Conflict & Terrorism* 175; Hoffman, B., 'Recent trends and future prospects of Iranian sponsored international terrorism' in Alexander, Y. (ed.), *Middle East Terrorism: Current Threats and Future Prospects* (G.K. Hall, 1994); Levitt, M., *HAMAS: Politics, Charity, and Terrorism in the Service of Jihad* (Yale University Press, 2006). The United States determined Iran to be a state sponsor on January 19, 1984: Export Administration Act 1979 (P.L. 96–72), s.6 (j); Arms Export Control Act 1976 (P.L. 94–329), s.40; Foreign Assistance Act 1974 (P.L. 93–559), s.620A.

3 UNGA, 'Iran: Mr. Hassan Rouhani' (<https://gadebate.un.org/en/72/iran-islamic-republic>, 20 September 2017).

4 Katzman, K., 'Iran sanctions' (2015) 6(4) *Current Politics and Economics of the Middle East* 653; Happold, M. and Eden, P., (eds.), *Economic Sanctions and International Law* (Hart Publishing, 2016).

Within this context of confrontation, this chapter will examine Iran's response to the international counter-terrorism financing (CTF) framework. The international CTF framework can be revealed by three indicators: first, the United Nations (UN) 'consolidated list' of persons and entities subjected to the freezing of funds,[5] stemming from the United Nations Security Council Resolutions (UNSCR) 1267 and 1373; second, the International Convention for the Suppression of Financing Terrorism (1999) (hereinafter, the 'Financing Convention'), which has been adopted by 188 parties;[6] and, finally, attempts to foster and enforce national legislation inspired by UNSCR 1373 and other international organisations, such as the Financial Action Task Force (FATF).[7] Iran objects to these international CTF systems, which it perceives as supporting the interests of the most powerful Western countries.[8] Furthermore, the primary difficulty for Iran in terms of adjusting its domestic regulations in line with the international CTF framework is the exemption of NLMs which Iran grants in all laws and regulations related to terrorism.

One of the pillars of CTF is the requirement to prosecute those responsible for terrorist-related activities in order to deny a safe haven to the perpetrators of such crimes.[9] The main way to achieve this aim is through appropriate and sufficient laws and regulations, subject to their compatibility with human rights and the rule of law. Iran not only lacks an appropriate legal framework for CTF but also existing laws and regulations exempt NLMs from being labelled as terrorists, even if they carry out terrorist activities. Since Iran is not a party to the Financing Convention nor the UN Convention against Transnational Organised Crime (2000) (the 'Palermo Convention'), the country has been designated as a high-risk and non-cooperative jurisdiction by the FATF.[10] In 2007, the FATF urged its members to advise their financial institutions to take account of the risk arising from the deficiencies in Iran's AML/CTF regime by applying enhanced due diligence checks.[11] From 2009 to 2016, the FATF further called on its members

5 The 'consolidated list' covers 260 individuals and 82 entities as on 9 August 2018. See ISIL (Da'esh) and Al-Qaeda Sanctions Committee, 'Sanction Lists Materials' (<http://www.un.org/sc/suborg/en/sanctions/1267/aq_sanctions_list>).

6 UNTS 2178, p. 197, A/RES/54/109; <https://treaties.un.org/Pages/ViewDetails.aspx?src=IND&mtdsg_no=XVIII-11&chapter=18&lang=en>.

7 Walker, C., 'Counter-terrorism financing: An overview' in King, C., Walker, C., and Gurulé, J. (eds.), *The Palgrave Handbook of Criminal and Terrorism Financing Law* (Palgrave Macmillan, 2018) 738–739.

8 See Ehteshami, A. and Molavi, R. (eds.), *Iran and the International System* (Routledge, 2012).

9 UNODC, *Handbook on Criminal Justice Responses to Terrorism* (United Nations, 2009) 73.

10 Financial Action Task Force, 'High-risk and other monitored jurisdictions' (<http://www.fatf-gafi.org/countries/#high-risk>).

11 Financial Action Task Force, 'FATF statement-28 February 2008' (<http://www.fatf-gafi.org/countries/n-r/pakistan/documents/fatfstatement-28february2008.html>, 28 February 2008).

to apply effective countermeasures.[12] In June 2016, the FATF suspended countermeasures in order to monitor Iran's progress in terms of the implementation of an agreed Action Plan.[13] Although the details of the Action Plan are secret, it is understood to require, as a condition of removal from the FATF blacklist, that Iran should amend its Anti-Money Laundering Law (AML) and Law of Combating Financing of Terrorism (LCFT) and implement the Financing Convention and the Palermo Convention.

The aim of this chapter is to determine whether Iran, as a non-Western state, acting under very different normative beliefs and structures, can still comply with international expectations and whether these expectations can be viewed as normatively and politically universal. To this end, the chapter examines three time periods. First, it studies actions in the period from 2001 to 2008, when Iran relied on general pre-existing laws in the Islamic Penal Code (IPC) for CTF purposes. Second, it considers the period from 2008 to 2016, during which time Iran made an effort to remedy the absence of CTF regulations through AML Law (2008) and its executive 'by-law' (2009).[14] Third, from 2016 to the present day, Iran enacted specific laws and regulations to combat terrorism financing, including the LCFT (2016), a linked executive by-law (2017), the amendment of the LCFT (2018), and the amendment of AML Law (2019).

Reliance on general laws (2001–2008)

After the 9/11 attacks, the Supreme Leader Ayatollah Khamenei declared that 'mass killings of human beings are catastrophic acts which are condemned . . . wherever they may happen and whoever the perpetrators and the victims may be' and called the fight against terrorism a 'Holy War.'[15] Whilst the US-based 9/11 Commission stated, 'We have found no evidence that Iran or Hizballah was aware of the planning for what later became the 9/11 attacks,' allegations remain that Iran provided a safe haven for some Al-Qaeda members.[16] At the prompting of private litigants, US courts have since found Iran liable for the

12 Financial Action Task Force, 'FATF statement concerning Iran, Uzbekistan, Turkmenistan, Pakistan and São Tomé and Príncipe-26 February 2009' (<http://www.fatf-gafi.org/countries/n r/pakistan/documents/fatfstatementconcerningiranuzbekistanturkmenistanpakistanandsaotomeandprincipe-26february2009.html>, 26 June 2009).

13 *Ibid.*

14 Iran Constitution, art.138: 'These executive-bylaws are authorised by the Council of Ministers to frame procedures for the implementation of the laws. The ratification and the regulations of the government and the decisions of the commissions mentioned under this Article shall also be brought to the notice of the Speaker of the Parliament.'

15 Muir, J., 'Iran condemns attacks on US,' *BBC News* (<http://news.bbc.co.uk/2/hi/middle_east/1549573.stm>, 17 September 2001); Mottahedeh, R., 'Islam and the opposition to terrorism,' *New York Times* (30 September 2001).

16 9/11 Commission, *Final Report of the National Commission in Terrorist Attacks upon the United States* (US Government Printing Office, 2004), 239–241.

9/11 attacks, including under the controversial Justice Against Sponsors of Terrorism Act (JASTA),[17] and have required payment of $billions to the victims.[18] As for official responses to the post-9/11 international law requirements 'to prevent and suppress the financing of terrorism,'[19] Iran's initial report in December 2001 to the UN Security Council accepted that implementation of the UNSCR 1373 was a national responsibility but referred to the absence of a clear definition of terrorism, and the need to develop a common definition of terrorism with a focus on the inalienable rights of people under foreign occupation or colonial domination.[20] The report argued that existing Iranian laws were sufficient to facilitate the implementation of the UNSCR 1373,[21] although there is no criminal law definition of terrorism in Iranian law.

The Islamic Penal Code (IPC) became key in this regard. Since the IPC is extracted from *Shari'ah*, the penal system is affected by Islamic values and concepts.[22] As a result, under the IPC, terrorists are charged with the crimes, *mohare-beh* (Enmity against God)[23] and *fesad fel-arze* (Spreading corruption on the earth),[24] interchangeably.[25] Before the amendment of the IPC in 2013, these two criminal descriptors were placed under one criminal title which caused uncertainty.[26] However, since that amendment, they have been considered as two different crimes. *Moharebeh* is defined as 'drawing a weapon against the life, property

17 Pub.L. 114–222. See Johnson, L.A., 'JASTA: The practical and constitutional deficiencies of the justice against sponsors of terrorism act' (2018) 86(1) *George Washington Law Review* 231.

18 There are around 92 judgements in which $56bn has been awarded in damages: Kittrie, O., 'Iran still owes $53 billion in unpaid U.S. Court judgments to American victims of Iranian Terrorism' <http://www.fdd.org/analysis/2016/05/06/iran-still-owes-53-billion-in-unpaid-u-s-court-judgments-to-american-victims-of-iranian-terrorism/#_ftn1>, 6 May 2016). For example, *Greenbaum v Islamic Republic of Iran*, 451 F. Supp. 2d 90 (D.D.C. 2006); *Bennett v Islamic Republic of Iran*, 507 F. Supp. 2d 117 (D.D.C. 2007); *Acosta v Islamic Republic of Iran*, 574 F. Supp. 2d 15 (D.D.C. 2008); *Estate of Heiser v Islamic Republic of Iran*, 659 F. Supp. 2d 20 (D.D.C. 2009); *In re Islamic Republic of Iran Terrorism Litigation*, 659 F. Supp. 2d 31 (D.D.C. 2009); *Valore v. Islamic Republic of Iran*, 700 F. Supp. 2d 52 (D.D.C. 2010); *Rubin v Islamic Republic of Iran* 138 S. Ct. 816 (2018). See also *Certain Iranian Assets (Islamic Republic of Iran v. United States of America)*, ICJ 13 February 2019.

19 S/RES/1373 (2001), 28 September 2001.

20 UNSC, 'Report of Iran to the CTC Pursuant to paragraph 6 of the SCR 1373 (2001),' S/2001/1332, 31 December 2001, para 1.

21 *Ibid.*, para 4.

22 Qasemi, H.R., 'Iran and its policy against terrorism' (2016) 2(1) *Middle Eastern Review of Public Administration* 1, 13.

23 IPC (2013), art.279.

24 *Ibid.*, art.286.

25 The Qur'an, Verse 33 Meade: 'إِنَّما جَزاءُ الَّذينَ يُحارِبُونَ اللّهَ وَ رَسُولَهُ وَ يَسْعَوْنَ فِي الْأَرْضِ فَساداً أَنْ يُقَتَّلُوا أَوْ يُصَلَّبُوا أَوْ تُقَطَّعَ أَيْديهِمْ وَ أَرْجُلُهُمْ مِنْ خِلافٍ أَوْ يُنْفَوْا مِنَ الْأَرْضِ ذلِكَ لَهُمْ خِزْيٌ فِي الدُّنْيا وَ لَهُمْ فِي الْآخِرَةِ عَذابٌ عَظيمٌ' (trans: Indeed, the penalty for those who wage war against Allah and His Messenger and strive upon earth [to cause] corruption is none but that they be killed or crucified or that their hands and feet be cut off from opposite sides or that they be exiled from the land).

26 IPC Amendment (2013).

or honour [referring to female members of one's family] of people or threating them, in such manner that results in insecurity in the environment.'[27] The punishments for *moharebeh* include death (by hanging or crucifixion), amputation of right hand and left foot, or banishment,[28] at the discretion of the jurisdiction of the judge.[29] *Fesad fel-arze* refers to a person who

> widely commits crimes against physical integrity and crimes against internal or external security of the country, criminal libel, disorder in the state economic system, arson and anihilation, dissemination of toxic, microbial, and hazardous matters . . . that cause severe disorder in the public order of the country, create insecurity or conflict susbtantial damage upon the physical integrity or persons or public and private properties.[30]

The punishment for *fesad fel-arze* is solely the death penalty. Since the 2013 IPC Amendment, the scopes of these two crimes have been distinguished, but some concerns remain. For example, regarding *moharebeh*, the 2013 Amendment fails to clarify how an act must be carried out to cause insecurity; concerning *fesad-fel-arze*, it not only expanded its scope but also defined the offences of *fesad-fel-arze* in unclear and broad terms.[31] Numerous cases exist of individuals being sentenced to death and charged with *moharebeh* and *fesad-fel-arze* even though they had not participated in any violent acts.[32] The terrorism-related activities which have been engaged in by terrorist groups such as Mujahedin-e Khalq (MEK) and Jundallah are covered by the criminal concepts of *moharebeh* and *fesad-fel-arze* as their crimes are against national security.[33]

The definitions of the crimes of *moharebeh* and *fesad-fel-alrze* lack precision, which might lead to arbitrary interpretation and violation of the right to life under international human rights law.[34] Other criminals, such as robbers, thieves, or smugglers, who resort to weapons and who disrupt public security, can also be

27 IPC (2013), art.280.

28 *Ibid.*, art.282.

29 *Ibid.*, art.283.

30 *Ibid.*, art.287.

31 Amnesty International, 'Flawed reforms: Iran's new code of criminal procedure' (<http://www.amnestyusa.org/files/flawed_reforms_-_irans_new_code_of_criminal_procedure.pdf>, 11 February 2016).

32 Human Rights Watch, 'Codifying repression: An assessment of Iran's new penal code' (<http://www.hrw.org/sites/default/files/reports/iran0812webwcover.pdf>, 4 August 2012).

33 Habib zade, M. and Hakimiha, S., 'ضرورت جرم انگاری تروریسم در حقوق کیفری ایران (trans: The necessity for criminalisation of terrorism in the Iranian criminal law)' (2007) 2 *Faslname Modares Ulom Ensani* 47, 58; Matin-Asgari, A., 'Twentieth century Iran's political prisoners' (2006) 42(5) *Middle Eastern Studies* 689, 703.

34 Amnesty International, 'Broadcasting injustice boasting of mass killing' (<http://www.amnesty.org/download/Documents/MDE1350792016ENGLISH.pdf>, 1 November 2016).

charged with *moharebeh*.[35] The legislation does not require the offence to be of a particular scale or to take place in a public place. Moreover, due to its vagueness and breadth, *fesad-fel-arze* also infringes the right to freedom of expression, assembly and association. The punishment for all the aforementioned activities can be the death penalty, even though not all infractions are serious crimes.[36]

Since terrorism is not confined to activities involving weapons (as is covered by the criminal term, *moharebeh*), other terrorist activities, such as providing assistance, and financial support or intelligence, would have to be covered by *fesad-fel-arze*. The breadth and overlap of these crimes led legislators before 2008 not to criminalise terrorism any further.

No Article in the IPC refers to the offence of terrorism financing. It regards the aiding or abetting of an offence as a general issue: Article 126 states that 'every person who makes or procures instruments of offense or provides means for committing the offence and every person who facilitates preparation of an offence will be regarded as an aider and abettor.'[37] In June 2017, 5 members of ISIS attacked the Iranian Parliament and the mausoleum of Ayatollah Khomeini, killing 17 people and wounding 42.[38] Following the attacks, eight members of ISIS, who had a direct connection with the attackers, were arrested and convicted of the crime of abetting *fesad-fel-arze*. The main offences were membership of ISIS, weapon smuggling, and providing financial and military support for the attackers.[39]

In the light of international expectations, terrorism financing must be criminalised as a distinct offence with ancillary offences, not just as an ancillary offence to terrorism, so that the state will be able to cover the full range of forbidden activities. At present, aiding a terrorist act does not apply when no terrorist act has actually been carried out. Furthermore, if terrorism financing can only be considered as an ancillary offence, it is not possible to have ancillary offences to an ancillary offence.[40] So, in order to have effective CTF regulation, a stand-alone crime of terrorism financing is required together with ancillary offences. A stand-alone offence of terrorism financing would also bolster the CTF regulation system.[41] The terrorism financing ancillary offences would comprise attempts to commit the offence, participating as an accomplice in an offence, organising or directing others to commit, and contributing to the commission of the financing

35 Majidi, M., جرایم علیه امنیت *(trans: Crimes against Security)* (Mizan, 2007) 155.

36 Human Rights Watch (fn 32).

37 IPC (2013), art.126 (b) and (c).

38 Spencer, R., 'ISIS takes revenge on militias with strike against Iran,' *The Times* (8 June 2017) 36.

39 Mashregh News, 'هشت عضو گروه داعش به دار آویخته شدند (trans.: '8 Members of the ISIS were Hanged') (<http://www.mashreghnews.ir/news/872208/>, 22 June 2018).

40 Financial Action Task Force, 'Guidance on the Criminalisation of Terrorist Financing: Recommendation 5' (Financial Action Task Force, 2016).

41 Financial Action Task Force, 'Guidance: National Money Laundering and Terrorist Financing Risk Assessment' (2013).

offence.[42] Iran is expected to have a distinct offence of terrorism financing with ancillary offences in order to bolster the CTF system; solely relying on the IPC as a general criminal code is considered insufficient to prevent and suppress the offences of terrorism financing.

The anti-money laundering law (2008–2016)

Based on FATF Recommendation 3, money laundering should be criminalised to reflect the UN Convention against Illicit Traffic in Narcotic Drugs and Psychotropic Substances, 1988 (the Vienna Convention) and the Palermo Convention.[43] Iran ratified the Vienna Convention in December 1992 but is not a member of the Palermo Convention. However, based on the commitment to the FATF to implement the Action Plan of 2016,[44] the Iranian government prepared in 2018 a Bill to Join the Palermo Convention and declared that if Iran decides to join the convention, interpretive declaration or reservation will be made on Articles 15, 16, 18, and 35(2) of the Palermo Convention.[45] The delay in joining the Palermo Convention can be attributed to two issues. First, Iran believes that this convention might damage the legitimate right of nations or groups under foreign occupation to combat aggression and occupation and to apply their right to self-determination.[46] Joining the convention might make support of NLMs difficult for Iran. Second, there is disagreement about Article 7(1)(b) of the convention, which is related to cooperation and the exchange of information amongst administrative, regulatory, law enforcement, and other authorities.[47] This aspect will be discussed later.

Previously, Iran criminalised money laundering offences in 2008 through the AML Law (2008). The law included the criminalisation of money laundering, the establishment of the Anti-Money Laundering High Council, the establishment of the Financial Intelligence Unit (FIU), the identification and verification of customers' identity, and the introduction of suspicious transaction reports (STRs).[48] However, this 2008 law was not regarded by the FATF as sufficient, leading the FATF to call on all jurisdictions to apply countermeasures against Iran in 2009; these remained in place until 2016 when Iran committed to implement the Action Plan. By 2016, Iran was ranked as the highest risk country in terms

42 Financing Convention, art.2(4)-(5)(a)-(c).

43 Financial Action Task Force, 'International Standards on Combating Money Laundering and the Financing of Terrorism & Proliferation' (2012, updated in October 2018).

44 Financial Action Task Force, 'Public Statement-24 June 2016,' (<http://www.fatf-gafi.org/publications/high-riskandnon-cooperativejurisdictions/documents/public-statement-june-2016.html>, 24 June 2016).

45 Iran Parliament, *The Bill to Join the Palermo Convention* (May 2018) (<https://rc.majlis.ir/fa/legal_draft/show/982981>).

46 *Ibid.*

47 See Expediency Discernment Council, the Bill to Join the Palermo Convention (<https://rc.majlis.ir/fa/legal_draft/show/982981>, June 2018).

48 AML Law (2008), arts.2 to 4.

of money laundering by the Basel Institute on Governance because of its weak AML/CTF system, corruption, defective judicial system, poor financial sector standards, high political risks, and lack of public and financial transparency.[49]

The particular deficiencies to be examined further here are those associated with the need to differentiate between money laundering and terrorism financing, the design of the Iranian FIU, and the working of STRs. First, due to differences between money laundering and terrorism financing, relying solely on criminalising of money laundering cannot sufficiently prevent terrorism financing. The key differences are related to four factors.[50] The first difference is the vector of criminality: the sources of funds for financing terrorism might be from legitimate sources, including willing donors using legal fundraising, deceptive use of legal fundraising, and donated from legal income or illegitimate sources, such as raising money from criminal activities.[51] The second difference lies in the scale of operation: the ultimate end for a criminal enterprise is to raise as much as money as possible, but terrorist operations are much cheaper. For example, the Charlie Hebdo attack in Paris in 2015 cost $7,000,[52] the London attack in 2005 cost less than $8,000, and the Madrid bombing in 2004 cost $10,000.[53] The third difference relates to the variant response to identified risk: although the appropriate risk-based approach is constructed through customer due diligence, monitoring, reporting, record keeping, internal control, and risk assessments for both AML and CTF, with CTF, the risk approach is counterintuitive because the rarer risk is given undue attention.[54] The fourth difference is about the methods of illicit funding: when the funds are derived from an illegitimate origin, the perpetrators may use money laundering techniques to transfer their funds, but in general, for CTF, different techniques should be used, in particular with less reliance on suspicious transactions. In summary, although AML and CTF exploit the same vulnerabilities in financial systems,[55] criminalising money laundering cannot deliver effective CTF.

The second deficiency in the AML Law 2008 is related to the FIU. According to international expectations, 'The FIU is a central and national agency responsible for receiving, analysing and disseminating to the competent authorities, and

49 Basel Institute on Governance, 'Basel AML Index 2017, Report' (<https://index.baselgovernance.org/sites/index/documents/Basel_AML_Index_Report_2017.pdf>, August 2018).

50 King, C. and Walker, C., 'Counter-terrorism financing: A redundant fragmentation' (2015) 6(3) *New Journal of European Criminal Law* 372, 381.

51 Financial Action Task Force (fn 41).

52 Nesser, P. et al., 'Jihadi terrorism in Europe: The IS-effect' (2016) 10(6) *Perspectives on Terrorism* 3, 14.

53 Home Office, *Report of the Official Account of the Bombings in London on the 7th July 2005* (2005–06 HC 1087), paras 63 and 64; and Financial Action Task Force, 'Terrorist Financing' (29 February 2008).

54 King and Walker (fn 50) 383.

55 Hamin, Z. et al., 'Conceptualising terrorist financing in the age of uncertainty' (2016) 19(4) *Journal of Money Laundering Control* 397, 402.

disclosure of financial information.'[56] The FATF has declared a breach of the Action Plan 2016 because of the failure to secure the full independence of the FIU.[57] Iran's FIU is under the supervision of the Ministry of Economic Affairs and Finance and undertakes 'to collect and obtain information on suspicious transactions; to evaluate, scrutinise and analyse the information contained in the reports about suspicious transactions.'[58] One of the reasons that the FIU is not recognised as an independent body goes back to the main contention of this chapter, which is that Iran does not recognise some NLMs as terrorists. An independent FIU in FATF terms might exercise its power to stop or hinder financial support for some non-state militant actors. In fact, government departments are alleged to transfer funds to NLMs. For example, the US government has found that the Iranian Banks Saderat and Sepah are involved in transferring funds to groups, such as Hizballah and Hamas.[59] However, Iran denies it provides financial support for some groups, such as the Houthi in Yemen. Officials claimed that only humanitarian aid is sent to Yemen, not weapons or financial support.[60]

Another institutional defect of the Iranian FIU is the limited exchange of information with its foreign counterparts. Normally, FIUs are supposed to cooperate with each other: first, the request can be initiated by proactive analysis of STRs; second, the FIU can receive information from national law enforcement agencies which needs to follow money abroad; and third, the FIU channel can be used for diagonal cooperation (as a facilitator).[61] However, Iran is not a member of the Egmont Group (the international network of FIUs), and the official line is that it is not appropriate to exchange financial and economic information because other countries and their organisations will 'misuse' the received information to impose more effective sanctions against Iran.[62]

The third deficiency of the AML Law 2008 is that another specification in the FATF Action Plan requires the effective submission of STRs.[63] Suspicious transactions are described as 'transactions and operations which persons, having access to information and/or reasonable grounds, suspect that they are being

56 Egmont Group, *The Egmont Group: Annual Report 2007–2008* (2008).

57 Financial Action Task Force, 'FATF statement' (<http://www.fatf-gafi.org/publications/high-riskandnon cooperativejurisdictions/documents/public-statement-june-2018.html>, 29 June 2018).

58 AML by-law (2009), art.38.

59 Jacobson, M., 'An Iranian financial intelligence unit' (<http://www.washingtoninstitute.org/policy-analysis/view/an-iranian-financial-intelligence-unit-less-than-meets-the-eye> *The Washington Institute*, 2 April 2007). See European General Court, *Bank Saderal v. Council* (T-495/10), 20 March 2013; *Bank Mellat v. Council* (T-496/10), 29 January 2013; *Central Bank of Iran v. Council* (T-563/12), 25 March 2015.

60 Esfandiary, D., and Tabatabai, A., 'Yemen: An opportunity for Iran-Saudi dialogue?' (2016) 39(2) *The Washington Quarterly* 155, 164–166.

61 Amicelle, A. and Chaudieu, K., 'In search for transnational financial intelligence: Questioning cooperation between FIUs' in King, C., Walker, C., and Gurulé, J. (eds.), *The Palgrave Handbook of Criminal and Terrorism Financing Law* (Palgrave Macmillan, 2018) 651–652.

62 See Expediency Discernment Council (fn 47).

63 FATF (fn 57).

performed with the aim of money laundering or the financing of terrorism.'[64] Iran's Central Bank, other banks, financial and credit institutions, insurance companies, interest-free funds, charity organisations, municipalities, notaries, lawyers, accountants, auditors, authorised specialists of the Justice Ministry, and official inspectors are subjected by the 2008 AML Law to the duty of reporting of suspicious transactions.[65] The proof of effective suspicious transaction reporting practice is one of the requirements for removing Iran from the FATF blacklist, but Iran has been condemned for failure to comply. Although its AML regulations mention STRs,[66] the number of STRs that are related to terrorism financing has not yet been published, and all relevant departments, such as the FIU, the Anti-Money Laundering High Council, and banks consider the relevant information to be confidential.[67] Two main questions have not been answered: to what extent have the existing regulations concerning STRs been implemented in law and to what extent are they working effectively. For the first time in 2016, the cabinet ministers declared that the number of STRs in Iran for 2015–2016 was 2,927.[68] However, such statistics in Iran only cover the banks, companies, and institutions which operate under the supervision of the government or which are state owned.[69] For instance, it is estimated that about 20% of the transactions in Iran are outside the banking system, such as in cash or through the *Hawala* system,[70] sectors that are not supervised in practice.

The Law of Combating the Financing of Terrorism (2016–present day)

In 2001, UNSCR 1373 imposed a binding obligation on states to 'prevent and supress the financing of terrorist acts.' However, it was only relatively recently that Iran enacted the Law of Combating the Financing of Terrorism (LCFT) (2016). This law relates to the criminalisation of terrorism financing as a stand-alone offence; criminal liability for legal persons; identification, detection, and freezing or seizure of any funds used or allocated for the purpose of committing the offences; customer due diligence (CDD), record keeping, and STRs; and terrorist financing offences as predicate offences for money laundering. However, according to the FATF, this law still does not match the key international requirement of criminalising all terrorist financing because of the exemption for NLMs.[71] Consequently, an amended LCFT (2018) was drafted, which criminalises as offences the financing of terrorism as follows:

64 AML by-law (2009), art.1.
65 AML Law (2008), arts.5 and 6.
66 *Ibid.*, art.4; and AML by-law (2009), art.1(f).
67 Source: fieldwork conducted in Tehran, Iran in June/July 2018.
68 Shamshiri, M., '1394 معامله مشکوک به پولشویی در سال 2927 (2927 STRs in 2015–16)' *Taadol Newspaper* (20 March 2015) 4.
69 *Ibid.*
70 *Ibid.*
71 Financial Action Task Force (fn 57).

> Providing or collecting funds or assets, by any means, whether from a legitimate or illegitimate source and or using financial resources derived from . . . in full or in part, for carrying out any economic activity by oneself or another to carry out the following activities, or to provide them to terrorist individuals or terrorist organisations is considered financing of terrorism and is a crime.[72]

In this way, the amended law removes mental elements (wilfully and with intention or knowledge) from the offence of terrorism financing from the LCFT (2016). It is assumed that the legislator considered that the LCFT (2018) must be understood in light of the IPC, which means that removing the *mens rea* of the offences of terrorism financing in the amendment of the LCFT (2018) makes no difference[73] because the mental elements of a crime are explained in the IPC.[74] It also revised the material elements as follows; first, instead of ‘providing *and* collecting funds,’ it refers to ‘providing *or* collecting funds,’ and second, it provides the definition of a terrorist act, which is close to the catch-all definition of the Financing Convention,[75] and refers to two factors: committing or threatening to commit any violent act against a population or endangering their lives or freedom and influencing the policies, decisions, and measures Iran, other countries, and/or international organisations.[76] Regarding the international organisations, the LCFT (2016) only mentioned organisations which have offices in Iran,[77] such as the World Health Organisation, the United Nations International Children’s Emergency Fund, and the United Nations Office on Drug and Crime.[78] But this limitation was removed in the LCFT (2018). Finally, the amended LCFT (2018) criminalises the financing of terrorists and terrorist organisations without any direct link to committed terrorist acts.[79]

Another problem is related to the endorsement of NLMs. The LCFT (2016) refers to actions done by people, nations, groups, or liberation organisations to counter domination, foreign occupation, colonialism, and racism; such actions are not to be depicted as terrorist actions according to these regulations. It is the

72 LCFT (2018), art.1.

73 Hamid Shahcheragh, ‘بررسی مسوولیت مطلق کیفری در حقوق ایران (trans: Examining the Absolute Criminal Responsibility in the Iranian Law)’ (2012) *Majale Hoghoghi Dadgostari* 78, 78–114.

74 IPC (2013), arts.144 and 145.

75 Financing Convention, art.2(1)(b).

76 LCFT (2018), art.1(a).

77 LCFT (2016), art.1(a).

78 UN, ‘UN Offices in Iran’ (<http://www.un.org.ir/about-us-uniran/un-offices-in-iran>, 22 February 2019).

79 LCFT (2016), art.1. For more information see UNSC Res 2178, S/RES/2178 (2014), 24 September 2014; UNSC Res 2253, S/RES/2253 (2015), 17 December 2015; Sageman, M., *Leaderless Jihad: Terror Network in the Twenty-First Century* (University of Pennsylvania Press, 2008); and Financial Action Task Force, ‘Emerging Terrorist Financing Risks’ (<https://www.fatf-gafi.org/documents/documents/emerging-terrorist-financing-risks.html>, 2015).

duty of the Supreme National Security Council (SNSC)[80] to determine which groups or organisations are included.[81] Based on the overall policy of Iran which does not recognise some NLMs as terrorists even if they have engaged in violent activities and given that these activities are justified as self-defence or seeking the right to self-determination, the provision of finance to these groups will not be an offence under the LCFT (2016–2018). However, one of the key failures on the part of Iran in implementing the FATF Action Plan is deemed to be this very omission. As a result, the LCFT (2018) focuses on identifying terrorist groups rather than making exceptions.[82] It states that the

> determination of criteria for activities, individuals, terrorist organisations and groups subjected to this Law, by considering art 154 of the Constitution, and by emphasising the right of individuals, nations, NLMs with the aim of countering domination, foreign occupation, colonisation, and racism, is the duty of the SNSC.[83]

In practice, this amendment will likely not satisfy the FATF because only the word order has been changed, so that the financing of some NLMs will still not fall foul of the LCFT regime. The potential exemption remains underlined by Article 154 of the Iranian Constitution, which declares that 'it supports the struggles of the oppressed for their rights against the oppressors anywhere in the world.' This support remains one of the main pillars of Iranian foreign policy, which insists on supporting NLMs both financially and militarily.

The LCFT (2018) was intended to pave the way for Iran to join the Financing Convention and integrate with the international AML/CTF framework. In this regard, and based on the FATF's requirements, the government has prepared a Bill to Join the Financing Convention. The bill contains a declaration which makes two points. First, the legitimate struggles of people against colonial domination and foreign occupation in terms of seeking their right to self-determination are not included in Article 2(1)(a) of the Financing Convention.[84] Yet a special definition of terrorism has been included in the Financing Convention for the purpose of the offences of terrorism financing (Article 2(1)(a)), and it pointedly makes no exception for NLMs.

Second, the convention cannot be binding on Iran if there is a conflict with the Iranian Constitution.[85] Although the Bill does not determine the relevant Articles,

80 Iran Constitution, art.176: 'In order to protect national welfare, safeguard the Islamic Republic, and territorial integrity and national sovereignty, the SNSC is established under the leadership of the President.'

81 LCFT (2016), art.1, note 2.

82 Mahjourian, F., 'Iran's amendments to CFT law, a step in right direction' *Financial Tribune* (<https://financialtribune.com/articles/economy-business-and-markets/91774/iran-s-amendments-to-cft-law-a-step-in-right-direction>, 14 August 2018).

83 LCFT (2018), art.1, note 4.

84 The Government Cabinet, *The Bill to Join the Financing Convention* (23 October 2017).

85 *Ibid.*

the main conflicts with the Financing Conventions are Articles 152 and 154, which relate to the foreign policy of Iran in terms of defending the rights of all Muslim and supporting the NLMs. In addition, as Iran is an Islamic state, all laws and regulations must comply with Islamic criteria.[86] As an example, between 2012 and 2015, proposed bills on the LCFT were not endorsed on three occasions and were returned to Parliament to be modified because of perceived incompatibility with both *Shari'ah* and the Constitution.[87] Some officials in the Parliament and other organs, such as the Guardian Council, totally disagreed with the ratification of the Financing Convention for several reasons, the main one being the wish to give continued support to NLMs, including the avoidance of the extradition of members of NLMs and the continued operation of charities in Iran which collect money for the NLMs.[88] In Iran, it is believed that the Financing Convention and the FATF Recommendations are tools in the hands of imperialists to obtain financial intelligence with regard to Iran and its relations with the NLMs in order to impose more sanctions and put even more pressure on Iran.[89]

Conclusion

Iran is a non-Western state which maintains distinct normative beliefs and structures, which means that it cannot readily comply with international expectations about CTF. Equally, part of the problem is the international failure to articulate expectations in a way which can be viewed as normatively and politically universal. In particular, the absence of a definition of terrorism allows for Western powers in practice to enforce their vision of terrorism at the expense of all others. As it currently stands, the Iranian CTF regulations are condemned as incompatible with the international CTF framework. Since 2016, however, the government has attempted to integrate into the international community, even though Iran considers the international system to be illegitimate and unfair because it prioritises the interests and benefits of the most powerful countries. Consequently, the LCFT (2016) was enacted and terrorism financing was criminalised as a standalone offence. Furthermore, the government committed itself to implementing the FATF Action Plan. Although the Action Plan is secret, the four main requirements of the FATF comprise the amendments of the LCFT, amendments of the AML Law, and joining both the Financing Convention and the Palermo Convention. Iran's deadline is June 2019. However, only the LCFT (2018) and the AML Law (2019) have been amended. Other bills have not yet been enacted,

86 Iran Constitution, art.4: 'All civic, penal, financial, economic, administrative, cultural, military, political, and other laws and regulations must be based on Islamic criteria . . . .'

87 First Guardian Council comment (29 February 2012), Second Guardian Council Comment (21 August 2015), and Third Guardian Council Comment (25 December 2015).

88 Source: fieldwork conducted in Tehran, Iran in June/July 2018.

89 *Ibid.* and BBC Farsi, 'مخالفت رهبر ایران با تصویب لایحه مبارزه با تامین مالی تروریسم (trans: The Disagreement of the Supreme Leader with the enactment of the Bill of Counter-Terrorism Financing)' (<http://www.bbc.com/persian/iran-44547680>, 20 June 2018).

being returned to Parliament several times to be amended[90] since the Guardian Council considers them to be against the *Shari'ah* and the Iranian Constitution.[91] One of the main reasons for the incompatibility with international standards and also the lack of implementation of the Action Plan is the Iranian policy of supporting selected NLMs financially and militarily. This policy was adopted following the Islamic Revolution in 1979 and is reflected in the Iranian Constitution.[92] As a result, all Iranian regulations associated with terrorism and terrorist-related activities exempt some NLMs, and no obvious solution can be found to this impasse under the current international and national regimes.

90 Guardian Council, *The Rejection of the Amendment Bill to AML Law* (June and August 2018); *The Rejection of the Bill to Join the Palermo Convention* (March and June 2018).

91 Iran Constitution, art.4.

92 *Ibid.*, art.154.

Select bibliography

Alldridge, P., *Criminal Justice and Taxation* (Oxford University Press, 2017).

Al-Oumi, N., 'Illicit enrichment: Comparative analysis study to the Decree-Law No. 24 of 2012 setting up the Public Authority to Combat Corruption and the pertinent provision for financial disclosure' (2015) 39 *Kuwait Journal of Law* 65.

Al-Oumi, N., 'In pursuit of non-conviction based confiscation asset recovery: Comparative analysis study of the Kuwaiti criminal law' (2018) 42 *Kuwait Journal of Law* 89.

Amicelle, A. and Chaudieu, K., 'In search of transnational financial intelligence: Questioning cooperation between Financial Intelligence Units' in King, C., Walker, C., and Gurulé, J. (eds.), *The Palgrave Handbook of Criminal and Terrorism Financing Law* (Palgrave MacMillan, 2018).

Benson, K., 'Money laundering, anti-money laundering and the legal profession' in King, C., Walker, C., and Gurulé, J. (eds.), *The Palgrave Handbook of Criminal and Terrorism Financing Law* (Palgrave MacMillan, 2018).

Benson, K., *Lawyers and the Proceeds of Crime: The Facilitation of Money Laundering and Its Control* (Routledge, 2020).

Boles, J.R., 'Criminalizing the problem of unexplained wealth: Illicit enrichment offenses and human rights violations' (2014) 17 *New York University Journal of Legislation and Public Policy* 835.

Booz Allen Hamilton, *Comparative Evaluation of Unexplained Wealth Orders: Prepared for the US Department of Justice* (National Institute of Justice, 2011).

Braithwaite, J., 'Enforced self-regulation: A new strategy for corporate crime control' (1982) 80 *Michigan Law Review* 1466.

Braithwaite, J. and Fisse, B., 'Self regulation and the costs of corporate crime' in Shearing, C.D. and Stenning, P.C. (eds.), *Private Policing* (Sage Publications, 1987).

Bullock, K., 'Criminal benefit, the confiscation order and the post-conviction confiscation regime' (2014) 62 *Crime, Law and Social Change* 45.

Bullock, K. and Lister, S., 'Post-conviction confiscation of assets in England and Wales: Rhetoric and reality' in King, C. and Walker, C. (eds.), *Dirty Assets: Emerging Issues in the Regulation of Criminal and Terrorist Assets* (Ashgate, 2014).

Campbell, L., 'Corporate liability and the criminalisation of failure' (2018) 12(2) *Law and Financial Markets Review* 57.

Campbell, P.B., 'The illicit antiquities trade as a transnational criminal network: Characterizing and anticipating trafficking of cultural heritage' (2013) 20(2) *International Journal of Cultural Property* 113.

Campbell-Verduyn, M., 'Bitcoin, crypto-coins, and global anti-money laundering governance' (2018) 69(2) *Crime, Law and Social Change* 283.

Carr, I. and Goldby, M., 'Recovering the proceeds of corruption: UNCAC and anti-money laundering standards' (2011) 2 *Journal of Business Law* 170.

Cassella, S., 'The case for civil forfeiture: Why *in rem* proceedings are an essential tool for recovering the proceeds of crime' (2008) 11(1) *Journal of Money Laundering Control* 8.

Chappell, D. and Hufnagel, S. (eds.), *Contemporary Perspectives on the Detection, Investigation and Prosecution of Art Crime* (Ashgate Publishing, 2014).

Choo, K.-K.R., 'New payment methods: A review of 2010–2012 FATF Mutual Evaluation Reports' (2013) 36 *Computers & Security* 12.

Desmarais, F. (ed.), *Countering Illicit Traffic in Cultural Goods: The Global Challenge of Protecting the World's Heritage* (ICOM, 2015).

Dostov, V. and Shust, P., 'Cryptocurrencies: An unconventional challenge to the AML/CFT regulators?' (2014) 21(3) *Journal of Financial Crime* 249.

Ehteshami, A. and Molavi, R. (eds.), *Iran and the International System* (Routledge, 2012).

Enweremadu, D.U., 'Nigeria's quest to recover looted assets: The Abacha affair' (2019) 48 *Afrika Spectrum* 51.

European Commission, *On Improving Cooperation between EU Financial Intelligence Units* (SWD, 2017) 275.

European Union FIUs Platform, *Mapping Exercise and Gap Analysis on FIUs' Powers and Obstacles for Obtaining and Exchanging Information* (2016). Available at: http://ec.europa.eu/transparency/regexpert/index.cfm?do=groupDetail.groupDetailDoc&id=33583&no=2

Financial Action Task Force, *Money Laundering and Terrorist Financing Vulnerabilities of Legal Professionals* (Financial Action Task Force, 2013).

Fisher, J., 'The anti-money laundering disclosure regime and the collection of revenue in the United Kingdom' (2010) 3 *British Tax Review* 235.

Górka, J. (ed.), *Transforming Payment Systems in Europe* (Springer Heidelberg, 2016).

Gray, G.C., 'The regulation of corporate violations: Punishment, compliance, and the blurring of responsibility' (2006) 46(5) *British Journal of Criminology* 875.

Greenberg, T.S., Samuel, L.M., Grant, W., and Gray, L., *Stolen Asset Recovery: A Good Practices Guide for Non-Conviction Based Asset Forfeiture* (World Bank, 2009).

Gurung, J., Wijaya, M., and Rao, A., 'AML/CTF compliance and SMEs in Australia: A case study of the prepaid card industry' (2010) 13(3) *Journal of Money Laundering Control* 184.

Habibzade, M. and Hakimiha, S., 'ضرورت جرم انگاری تروریسم در حقوق کیفری ایران (trans: The necessity for criminalisation of terrorism in the Iranian criminal law)' (2007) 2(11) *Faslname Modares Ulom Ensani* 47.

Happold, M. and Eden, P. (eds.), *Economic Sanctions and International Law* (Hart, 2016).

Hardy, S.A., 'Is looting-to-order "just a myth"? Open-source analysis of theft-to-order of cultural property' (2015) 1 *Cogent Social Sciences*. http://dx.doi.org/10.1080/23311886.2015.1087110

Harvey, J. and Lau, S., 'Crime-money, reputation and reporting' (2009) 52(1) *Crime Law and Social Change* 57.

Hendry, J. and King, C., 'Expediency, legitimacy, and the rule of law: A systems perspective on civil/criminal procedural hybrids' (2017) 11(4) *Criminal Law and Philosophy* 733.

Herlin-Karnell, E. and Ryder, N., 'The robustness of EU financial crimes legislation: A critical review of the EU and UK anti-fraud and money laundering scheme' (2017) 27(4) *European Business Law Review* 427.

Hett, W., 'Digital currencies and the financing of terrorism' (2008) 15(2) *Richmond Journal of Law and Technology* 4.

HM Treasury and Home Office, *UK National Risk Assessment of Money Laundering and Terrorist Financing* (HM Treasury and Home Office, 2017).

Hofer, A., 'The developed/developing divide on unilateral coercive measures: Legitimate enforcement or illegitimate intervention?' (2017) 16 *Chinese Journal of International Law* 175.

Hurd, I., 'Legitimacy and authority in international politics' (1999) 53 *International Organization* 379.

Jusic, A., 'Kuwait's administrative risk-based model for the prevention of money laundering: Costs and benefits of compliance with the Financial Action Task Force (FATF) standards' (2017) 31 *Arab Law Quarterly* 101.

Keatinge, T., Moiseienko, A., Keen, F., Artingstall, D., and Wood, H., *No Rest for the Wicked: Driving Change in the UK's Post-FATF Evaluation AML Regime* (RUSI, 2019).

Kinacioglu, M., 'The principle of non-intervention at the United Nations: The Charter framework and the legal debate' (Summer, 2005) *Perceptions* 15.

King, C., 'Using civil process in pursuit of criminal law objectives: A case study of non-conviction-based asset forfeiture' (2012) 16 *International Journal of Evidence and Proof* 337.

King, C. and Walker, C. (eds.), *Dirty Assets: Emerging Issues in the Regulation of Criminal and Terrorist Assets* (Ashgate, 2014).

King, C., Walker, C., and Gurulé, J. (eds.), *The Palgrave Handbook of Criminal and Terrorism Financing Law* (Palgrave Macmillan, 2018).

Krueger, M., 'Mobile payments: The second wave' in Górka, J. (ed.), *Transforming Payment Systems in Europe* (Springer, 2016).

Law Commission, *Anti-Money Laundering: The SARs Regime Consultation Paper* (Law Commission No. 236, 2018).

Lawrence, I., 'Draconian and manifestly unjust: How the confiscation regime has developed' (2008) 76 *Amicus Curiae* 22.

Linn, C.J., 'Regulating the cross-border movement of prepaid cards' (2008) 11(2) *Journal of Money Laundering Control* 146.

Marshall, P., 'Does Shah v. HSBC Private Bank Ltd make the anti-money laundering consent regime unworkable?' (2010) 5 *Journal of International Banking and Financial Law* 287.

Middleton, D. and Levi, M., 'The role of solicitors in facilitating "organized crime": Situational crime opportunities and their regulation' (2004) 42(2/3) *Crime, Law and Social Change* 123.

Mitsilegas, V., 'New forms of transnational policing: The emergence of Financial Intelligence Units in the European Union and the challenges for human rights: Part 1' (1999) 3(2) *Journal of Money Laundering Control* 147.

Mitsilegas, V. and Vavoula. N., 'The evolving EU anti-money laundering regime: Challenges for fundamental rights and rule of law' (2016) 23 *Maastricht Journal of European and Comparative Law* 261.

Mugarura, N., *The Global Anti-Money Laundering Regulatory Landscape in Less Developed Countries* (Ashgate, 2012).

Narayanan, A., Bonneau, J., Felten, E., Miller, A., and Goldfeder, S., *Bitcoin and Cryptocurrency Technologies: A Comprehensive Introduction* (Princeton University Press, 2016).

National Crime Agency, *Suspicious Activity Reports (SARs) Annual Report 2018* (NCA, 2018).

Noseda, F., 'Common reporting standard and EU beneficial ownership registers: Inadequate protection of privacy and data protection' (2017) 23 *Trusts & Trustees* 404.

Oberson, X., *International Exchange of Information in Tax Matters: Towards Global Transparency* (Edward Elgar, 2015).

Okogbule, N.S., 'Official corruption and the dynamics of money laundering in Nigeria' (2007) 14(1) *Journal of Financial Crime* 49.

Osborne, D.E., 'The Financial Action Task Force and the legal profession' (2015) 60 *New York Law School Law Review* 421.

Paton, P.D., 'Cooperation, co-option or coercion? The FATF lawyer guidance and regulation of the legal profession' (2010) *Journal of the Professional Lawyer* 165.

Paul, K.A., 'Ancient Artifacts vs. Digital Artifacts: New tools for unmasking the sale of illicit antiquities on the dark web' (2018) 7(2) *Arts*. https://doi.org/10.3390/arts7020012

Reynolds, P., 'Tracking digital footprints: Anonymity within the bitcoin system' (2017) 20(2) *Journal of Money Laundering Control* 172.

Ryder, N., *Money Laundering: An Endless Cycle? A Comparative Analysis of the Anti-Money Laundering Policies in the United States of America, the United Kingdom, Australia and Canada* (Routledge, 2012).

Ryder, N., '"Too scared to prosecute and too scared to jail"? A critical and comparative analysis of enforcement of financial crime legislation against corporations in the USA and the UK' (2018) 82 *Journal of Criminal Law* 245.

Shepherd, K.L., 'The gatekeeper initiative and the risk-based approach to client due diligence: The imperative for voluntary good practices guidance for U.S. Lawyers' (2010) *Journal of the Professional Lawyer* 83.

Sinha, G., 'To suspect or not to suspect: Analysing the pressure on banks to be "policemen"' (2014) 15 *Journal of Banking Regulation* 75.

Suberu, R.T., 'Strategies for advancing anticorruption reforms in Nigeria' (2018) 147(3) *Journal of the American Academy of Arts and Sciences* 189.

Svedberg Helgesson, K. and Mörth, U., 'Involuntary public policy-making by for-profit professionals: European lawyers on anti-money laundering and terrorism financing' (2016) 54 *Journal of Common Market Studies* 1216.

Tabatabai, A., 'Other side of the Iranian coin: Iran's counterterrorism apparatus' (2018) 41(1&2) *Journal of Strategic Studies* 181.

Trapp, K.N., *State Responsibility for International Terrorism* (Oxford University Press, 2011).

UNODC, *Handbook on Criminal Justice Responses to Terrorism* (United Nations, 2009).

Weismann, M., 'The Foreign Corrupt Practices Act: The failure of the self-regulatory model of corporate governance in the global business environment' (2009) 88(4) *Journal of Business Ethics* 615.

Wells, C., *Corporations and Criminal Responsibility* (2nd ed., Oxford University Press, 2001).

Young, S.N.M. (ed.), *Civil Forfeiture of Criminal Property: Legal Measures for Targeting the Proceeds of Crime* (Edward Elgar, 2009).

Index

Note: numbers in bold indicate a table.

For Product Safety Concerns and Information please contact our EU
representative GPSR@taylorandfrancis.com
Taylor & Francis Verlag GmbH, Kaufingerstraße 24, 80331 München, Germany

www.ingramcontent.com/pod-product-compliance
Lightning Source LLC
LaVergne TN
LVHW011117300926
849160LV00008B/418

* 9 7 8 1 0 3 2 1 7 4 3 4 1 *